·THE BEST·
PUB
QUIZ
BOOK
OVER 7,500 QUESTIONS!
Ever! 4

THIS IS A CARLTON BOOK

1 84222 511 1

Questions set by The Puzzle House

Printed and bound in Great Britain

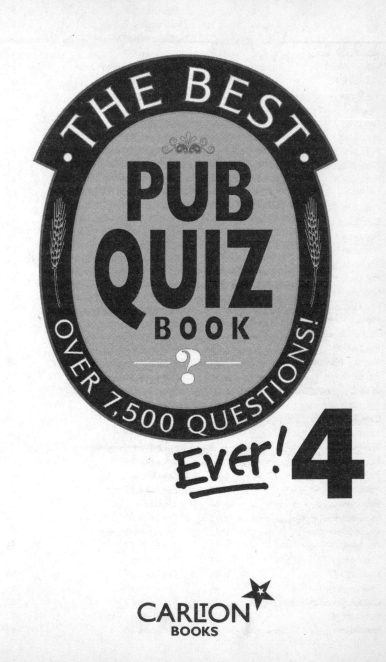

THE BEST

PUB QUIZ BOOK

?

OVER 7,500 QUESTIONS!

Ever! **4**

CARLTON
BOOKS

CONTENTS

MEDIUM 96

HARD ▶▶

HARD 184

INTRODUCTION

Cultural anthropologists are still debating the precise origins of popularity of the pub quiz, which regularly entertains teams of drinkers in every class of drinking establishment from the Flat Cap and Ferret to the King's Arms.

Though the truth is still shrouded in a bar-room haze, the pub quiz probably evolved in Britain and Ireland during the early days of television. Pubs, as we are all aware have always been places to drink, socialize and relax (among other things better left unmentioned). But in the 1940s, many pubs had an added draw: unlike the homes of yesteryear, the pubs had television. TV game shows in particular drew great attention from the imbibers. Pub regulars often called out answers to game show questions before the studio contestants did, prompting fellow pub goers to shout, "Why don't you go on that show?" to the most knowledgeable or loudest-mouthed bar "contestants".

Little has changed today … everyone wants to be a millionaire and no-one wants to be the weakest link. So, when you get bored of shouting the answers at your television and marvelling at the contestants' stupidity, pick up your coat and a copy of *The Best Pub Quiz Book Ever! 4* and head down to your local for a night of real entertainment.

Inside these hallowed pages, you'll find more than 7,500 questions covering a stunning range of topics, divided into laughably easy, reasonably medium, and brain-shreddingly hard. At the back, you'll also find a comprehensive set of guidelines on how to prepare for and run a successful quiz of your own, and a handy answer sheet template to photocopy and distribute.

On a more serious note, although every effort has been made to ensure that all of the answers are correct, in order to avoid heckling and dissent in the ranks, when setting your quiz make sure you note down all of the questions and the answers and if you are in any doubt about any, doublecheck them in advance.

So, there you go. Wade in, and have fun. After all, that's what it's all about.

THE EASY QUESTIONS

In this primary round the main objective is to keep breathing, these questions are so easy that even the most docile pub idiot could gurgle his way through them in the time it takes to down a pint.

The 'easy' questions are good for a warm-up round as they lull everyone into a false sense of security and make them feel intelligent before you move on to something a bit more taxing on their grey cells. If you are capable of recognising your own name, ordering a pint and navigating your way to the toilets, then the 'easy' questions should not prove too much of a challenge and you can breeze through them revelling in your huge brain capacity. Any inability to answer large numbers of these questions correctly can only be attributed to the failure to turn up your hearing aid sufficiently or the consumption of large quantities of alcohol.

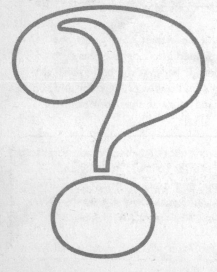

QUIZ 1 WHO'S WHO?

Answers - see Quiz 3, page 11

1 Which Paddy led the Liberal Democrats?
2 FW De Klerk was President of which country?
3 Which Hussein ruled Iraq during the Gulf War?
4 What were the initials of the US footballer Simpson accused of murdering his wife?
5 Which Gerry was a president of Sinn Fein in 2000?
6 Dr Spock made news in a book about looking after who or what?
7 Which UK party leader had a wife called Ffion?
8 Which name was shared by Steel and Owen of the Liberal/Social Democrat Alliance?
9 Which former Chancellor of the Exchequer is the father of TV cook Nigella Lawson?
10 Ferdinand and Imelda Marcos led which country beginning with P?
11 Who is Queen Elizabeth's II's only sister who suffered a series of strokes?
12 What is the first name of Zimbabwe's President Mugabe?
13 What was the name of Nelson Mandela's wife during the years he was in jail?
14 William Hague was a government minister in which country before leading his party?
15 Benazir Bhutto was Prime Minister of which Asian country?
16 Which Keenan was freed from Beirut after being held hostage for nearly four years?
17 Alex Salmond led which Nationalist Party?
18 In the period 1981–2001, which two US Presidents have had the same surname?
19 Who is Elisabeth Murdoch's media mogul father?
20 In the 1980s who became the USA's oldest President?
21 What was the surname of suffragettes Emmeline, Sylvia and Christabel?
22 Who was the youngest British Prime Minister of the 20th century?
23 Which Indian leader, the subject of an epic movie with Ben Kingsley, was *Time* magazine's Man of the Year in 1930?
24 Which Miss Lewinsky had the so called 'inappropriate relationship' with Bill Clinton?
25 Which Kray died in 2001 after being released from prison after suffering from cancer?
26 Which McGuinness became Northern Ireland's Education Minister after the Good Friday agreement?
27 David Trimble became First Minister in which country of the UK?
28 Which Joseph led the Communist party in the USSR for over 30 years?
29 Which Arthur led the 1980s miners' strike?
30 Deng Xiaoping was leader of which country?

TV SOAPS *See quiz 3, page 11*

ANSWERS

1 *Emmerdale.* 2 5. 3 *Coronation Street.* 4 Sharon. 5 Eve. 6 Manchester.
7 Police officer. 8 Dixon. 9 George. 10 Grant. 11 Linda. 12 Dingles. 13 Laura.
14 Butcher. 15 *Brookside.* 16 Roy. 17 Battersby. 18 Chester. 19 Alma.
20 Hancock. 21 *Coronation Street.* 22 Emma. 23 Hope. 24 Red. 25 Tiffany.
26 *Coronation Street.* 27 Peacock. 28 Nick. 29 *Crossroads.* 30 *Hollyoaks.*

QUIZ 2 POT LUCK I

Answers - see Quiz 4, page 12

1　Which of Durham, Kent and Suffolk is part of East Anglia?
2　What would a Venezuelan do with a Bolivar?
3　Who played Rachel in *Friends*?
4　What does the B stand for in LBW in cricket?
5　Which Spice Girl wore a dress with a Union Jack flag pattern?
6　Which word can be a worker's eating place or a cutlery set?
7　What was President George W Bush's father's first name?
8　Which caped hero flew his way round the city of Metropolis?
9　Which fruit goes in the pudding named after opera diva Nellie Melba?
10　What is a pomegranate?
11　Which was built first – the Eiffel Tower or the Empire State Building?
12　What comes after New South in the name of an Australian state?
13　Which has the most sides – a hexagon, a pentagon or a quadrilateral?
14　Capricorn, Libra, Phoenix – which of these is not a sign of the zodiac?
15　How many faces would a dozen dice have in total?
16　What shape is in the middle of the Japanese flag?
17　In e mail what does the e stand for?
18　What was the name of the bear that belonged to Christopher Robin?
19　In athletics, how many events have taken place when half a decathlon is completed?
20　What is coffee produced from?
21　Where did turkeys originally come from?
22　Who might display, on a British road, a sign worth fifty in Roman numerals?
23　What name is given to buying goods via the Internet?
24　Italy is the world's biggest producer of which drink?
25　Danny De Vito played which bird-like villain in *Batman Returns*?
26　Houston is in which US state?
27　On which continent is the Panama Canal?
28　Which brothers made the first controlled powered flight?
29　Did the pocket calculator become generally available in the 1940s, 1970s or 1990s?
30　In history the *Marie Celeste* was a type of what?

PEOPLE – STARS *See quiz 4, page 12*

ANSWERS

1 Dance. 2 Elton John. 3 Lennon. 4 Ireland. 5 Scotland. 6 Joely. 7 Gibb. 8 Laine.
9 Five. 10 Henshall. 11 Martine. 12 Snooker. 13 Sir Bobby. 14 Wade. 15 Red.
16 Iceland. 17 Jensen. 18 Lip. 19 Harry. 20 Honor. 21 Liverpool. 22 Slim.
23 Cruise. 24 Carol. 25 Charlie Dimmock. 26 Sarong. 27 Yorkshire. 28 Bean.
29 Terry. 30 Liverpool.

QUIZ 3 TV SOAPS

Answers - see Quiz 1, page 9

1 Which Channel 4 soap is a constant success in the ratings?
2 On which Channel did *Family Affairs* debut?
3 Which northern soap was the most successful of the 1990s?
4 Which former landlady of the Queen Vic returned to the Square in 2001 after 'living in America'?
5 In *Coronation Street* in September 2001 who did Fred marry?
6 Where did Bianca go when she left Albert Square?
7 In *Emmerdale* what responsible job does Angie Reynolds have?
8 Which Ron shot a suspected burglar in the summer of 2001?
9 Which *Straw Dogs* actress Susan joined the Albert Square cast as Terry's love interest?
10 Who was Phil Mitchell's brother as played by Ross Kemp?
11 Who did Mike Baldwin marry after he was divorced from Alma?
12 Which family did Lisa Riley belong to when she starred in *Emmerdale*?
13 Who did Ian Beale marry after his disastrous ceremony with Mel?
14 What is the profession of *Corrie*'s Fred?
15 In which soap did film actress Anna Friel make her name?
16 Who is Barry Evans' dad in *EastEnders*, sharing his name with an ex Liverpool FC boss?
17 Who were the *Coronation Street* 'family from hell', which included Toyah and Janice?
18 Where is *Hollyoaks* set?
19 Which *Coronation Street* character died of cancer in 2001?
20 Which actress Sheila came to Albert Square as Steve Owen's mum?
21 Which soap ran a campaign to free the Weatherfield One?
22 Who did Curly marry after Raquel left him?
23 Which Bob in *Emmerdale* shares his name with a US comedian?
24 What colour is Rita Sullivan's famous hair?
25 What was the name of the *EastEnders* character played by Martine McCutcheon?
26 Which soap introduced an extra Friday night instalment in 2001?
27 In *Coronation Street*, what is Ashley and Maxine's surname?
28 Who is the evil member of the *EastEnders* Cotton family?
29 Which Midlands soap returned to ITV in 2001?
30 Which teen soap features the Hunters and the Morgans?

QUIZ 4 PEOPLE – STARS

Answers - see Quiz 2, page 10

1 Michael Flatley was dubbed Lord of the what?
2 Which megastar sang his own song at Princess Diana's funeral?
3 After which Beatle did Liam Gallagher name his son with Patsy Kensit?
4 From where does ex *Ballykissangel* star Dervla Kirwan hail?
5 In which part of the UK did Madonna marry Guy Ritchie?
6 Which blonde actress Richardson split with Jamie Theakston in 2001?
7 What is the surname of music brother celebs Maurice, Robin and Barry?
8 Which Cleo is Mrs John Dankworth?
9 How many members of Hear'Say are there?
10 Which Ruthie starred in the musical *Peggy Sue Got Married*?
11 Which Ms McCutcheon played Eliza Doolittle on the London stage?
12 Ronnie O'Sullivan is a star in which sport?
13 Who is Jack Charlton's famous younger brother?
14 Which former tennis star Virginia had a father who was a clergyman?
15 When she was a Spice Girl, Geri Halliwell had what colour hair?
16 Bjork has an emblem from which country on her shoulder?
17 Which DJ David had the name 'Kid'?
18 What part of her body did Victoria Beckham seemingly pierce for a concert in August 2001?
19 Which singer Connick adds Junior to his name?
20 Which Ms Blackman, an ex Bond girl, has a brown belt in judo?
21 Sir Paul McCartney received the freedom of which city, his childhood home?
22 What does Fatboy Norman Cook add to his name for DJ purposes?
23 Which Tom split with wife Nicole Kidman in 2001?
24 Which first name is shared by TV stars Smillie and Vorderman?
25 Who is the female gardener on *Ground Force*?
26 David Beckham famously wore what normally female garment?
27 Opera star Lesley Garrett hails from which northern county?
28 Which zany Mr is Rowan Atkinson's most famous creation?
29 Who is broadcaster Alan Wogan's famous dad?
30 Which Merseyside football team does John Peel support?

QUIZ 5 POT LUCK 2

Answers - see Quiz 7, page 15

1 Which Dennis was the Footballer of The Year in England in 1998?
2 Which zodiac sign of Gemini, Pisces and Taurus represents a human shape?
3 Which Sharon starred in *Basic Instinct* and *Total Recall*?
4 How is a sound produced from a euphonium?
5 What colour is the magic linked with a wicked witch?
6 If you multiply the length of rectangle by the width what do you get?
7 A penny farthing was an early type of bike, but how many farthings made up the value of a penny farthing?
8 What is a nun's head dress called?
9 The Roman numeral M represents which number?
10 Manx, Marmalade and Tabby are all types of what?
11 In the saying, many what will make light work?
12 Following the gruesome nursery rhyme recipe, how many blackbirds would be baked in two pies?
13 Which fruit of grapes, pears and plums is bought by the bunch?
14 What form of transport is the French TGV?
15 Tortillas originally from which country?
16 Which garden-linked building gives its name to a climate effect?
17 What was the number of the first Apollo mission to land on the Moon?
18 The Dalai Lama is the spiritualist leader of which country?
19 Around which part of your body would you tie a cummerbund?
20 What did the Romans keep in a catacomb?
21 Which object appears on the Canadian flag?
22 What happens to the rows of letters when reading down an eye-test chart?
23 In Roman numerals what does XX stand for?
24 Which of Funny, Grumpy and Happy is not one of Snow White's seven dwarfs?
25 What did David Bowie call his first child?
26 If the first of a month is a Thursday, what day will the eighth be?
27 Cassata is a type of which food?
28 In *The Wombles*, which Great Uncle shares his name with a country?
29 Which side of a ship is starboard?
30 Which colour is usually used to show the sea on a map?

ANSWERS

POT LUCK 3 *See quiz 7, page 15*

1 New Zealand. 2 Vietnam. 3 English. 4 Sweetcorn. 5 Wales. 6 Aircraft. 7 Pistol. 8 East. 9 Pierce Brosnan. 10 Cricket. 11 Computer. 12 Madonna. 13 Europe. 14 Nests. 15 Invention. 16 (South) America. 17 Air. 18 Rake. 19 Flags. 20 1992. 21 Autobahn. 22 Needles. 23 Yellow. 24 Fluid ounces. 25 Apples. 26 180. 27 Egg. 28 Throat. 29 *Arthur*. 30 Easter.

QUIZ 6 MEMORABLE SPORTING MOMENTS

Answers - see Quiz 8, page 16

1 Which was the last birthday celebrated by Michael Owen before he scored against Romania in France 1998?
2 How many events did Denise Lewis compete in to win her heptathlon Olympic gold?
3 Against which country did England play the first ever test match in cricket?
4 Mike Powell beat Bob Beamon's long-standing record in which jumping event?
5 Allan Border made a record number of runs for which international cricketing side?
6 How long does Le Mans's most famous motor race last?
7 In which Greek city were the first Modern Olympics held?
8 In which decade did Roger Bannister run his first sub-four-minute mile?
9 Which Czech-born Martina won her ninth Wimbledon singles title in 1990?
10 Gymnast Nadia Comaneci was the first person ever to score what out of 10 at the Olympic Games?
11 In 1988 tennis was re-introduced at which four yearly sporting event?
12 What colour shirts were England wearing when they won the 1966 World Cup?
13 Eleven athletes from which country were killed at the Munich Olympics of 1972?
14 In which decade did Jesse Owens win four gold medals at the Berlin Olympics?
15 Charismatic gymnast Olga Korbut represented which country?
16 In which city were the 1980 Olympics, boycotted by the Americans?
17 Which cricketer Geoffrey made his hundredth 100 in a 1977 Test Match?
18 Which racehorse was taken from his box in an Irish stud in 1983 and was never seen again?
19 Which German Boris won Wimbledon in 1985?
20 Who, with Jayne Torvill, was awarded a full set of perfect Olympic sixes for ice dancing in 1984?
21 Which Steve was Sebastian Coe's main British rival in middle distance running in 1980?
22 What was the nickname of James Douglas who beat Mike Tyson in 1990?
23 Who hit six sixes in an over in 1968?
24 Which Manchester side won the European Cup in 1968?
25 In which Division were Sunderland when they beat Leeds for the FA Cup in 1973?
26 What is the nationality of Ballesteros who won the British Open in 1984?
27 How many times did Red Rum win the Grand National?
28 Which England footballer was as famous for his tears as for his talent in Italia 90?
29 Which Briton won gold in the triple jump in the 2001 World Championships?
30 Which English player was sent off against Argentina in the World Cup in France?

ANSWERS

NEW MILLENNIUM MOVIES See quiz 8, page 16
1 Diary. 2 Cage. 3 Travolta. 4 *Pearl Harbor.* 5 Ballet. 6 Egypt.
7 Cruz. 8 China. 9 Cruise. 10 Green. 11 Chocolate. 12 *Hannibal.*
13 Gibson. 14 *Bullwinkle.* 15 Caine. 16 Animation. 17 Desert Island.
18 Croft. 19 Finney. 20 III. 21 Kate Winslet. 22 X. 23 Satellite dish.
24 *Low Lifes.* 25 *Gladiator.* 26 St. Bernard dog. 27 Harry Enfield.
28 *Storm.* 29 *Toy Story 2.* 30 Ralph.

QUIZ 7 POT LUCK 3

Answers - see Quiz 5, page 13

1 Maoris were the first settlers in which country?
2 *The Deer Hunter* has which war as its subject matter?
3 What is the main language of North America's two main countries?
4 Which vegetable is produced from the plant maize?
5 In which part of the UK was Charlotte Church born?
6 Dennis Bergkamp refuses to use what type of transport?
7 Which weapon is used in Pete Sampras's nickname?
8 Mozambique is on which coast of Africa?
9 Who starred as 007 in *The World is Not Enough*?
10 Which sport is covered by the *Wisden Almanac*?
11 William Henry Gates III became seriously rich through which industry?
12 Which superstar did film producer Guy Ritchie marry in 2000?
13 Which continent is the most crowded and the smallest?
14 Which word describes homes for birds as well as sets of tables?
15 Frank Zappa was leader of the group The Mothers Of what – Convention, Intention or Invention?
16 In which continent is the Amazon rainforest?
17 A hovercraft moves along on a cushion of what?
18 Which one of the following tools is pronged, hoe, spade or rake?
19 What does a person hold in their hand when practising semaphore?
20 Which of the following was a leap year –1991, 1992, 1994?
21 What is the German word for a motorway?
22 What is applied to the body in acupuncture?
23 What colour does the skin become if someone suffers from jaundice?
24 What does the abbreviation 'fl oz' stand for?
25 Which fruit is mainly used when making a strudel?
26 How many degrees are there in a right-angled triangle?
27 What is the main ingredient of mayonnaise other than oil?
28 Laryngitis affects which part of your body?
29 In which movie did Dudley Moore first play a drunken millionaire with Sir John Gielgud in the role of his butler?
30 Lent comes before which Christian festival?

ANSWERS

POT LUCK 2 *See quiz 5, page 13*
1 Bergkamp. 2 Gemini. 3 Stone. 4 By blowing into it. 5 Black. 6 The area 7 Five
8 Wimple. 9 1000. 10 Cat. 11 Hands. 12 48. 13 Grapes. 14 Train. 15 Mexico.
16 Greenhouse. 17 11. 18 Tibet 19 The waist. 20 Dead bodies. 21 Maple leaf.
22 They get smaller. 23 20. 24 Funny. 25 Zowie. 26 Thursday. 27 Ice cream.
28 Bulgaria. 29 Right. 30 Blue.

QUIZ 8 NEW MILLENNIUM MOVIES

Answers - see Quiz 6, page 14

1   What did Bridget Jones write?
2   Which Nicolas starred in *Captain Corelli's Mandolin*?
3   Which John was the counter-terrorist in *Swordfish*?
4   Which 2001 movie was about a Japanese bombing 60 years before?
5   Billy Elliot trained to be what type of dancer?
6   Where is *The Mummy Returns* set?
7   Which Penelope played opposite Johnny Depp in *Blow*?
8   Where was *Crouching Tiger, Hidden Dragon* produced?
9   Which Tom teamed up – both on and off the screen – with Penelope Cruz in the movie *Vanilla Sky*?
10 What colour is Shrek?
11 What type of shop does Juliette Binoche open in *Chocolat*?
12 What was the sequel to *Silence of the Lambs* called?
13 Which Mel read Helen Hunt's thoughts in *What Women Want*?
14 What went with *Rocky* in the cartoon movie with Robert De Niro?
15 Which Michael co-starred with Sandra Bullock in *Miss Congeniality*?
16 What type of movie was *The Emperor's New Groove*?
17 Where is Tom Hanks trying to survive in *Castaway*?
18 Which Lara was a character in *Tomb Raider*?
19 Which Albert co-starred with Julia Roberts in *Erin Brokovich*?
20 Which *Jurassic Park* movie was released in 2001?
21 Which star of *Titanic* also starred in *Quills*?
22 In which TV *Files* did *Evolution*'s David Duchovny find fame?
23 What is *The Dish* in the title of the movie with Sam Neill?
24 What went with *High Heels* in the movie title?
25 Which Roman epic starred Russell Crowe?
26 Which animal is the hero of *Beethoven's 3rd*?
27 Which comedian invented the character and starred in the movie *Kevin & Perry Go Large*?
28 What was *Perfect* in the 2000 movie with George Clooney?
29 What was the sequel to *Toy Story* called?
30 Which Fiennes starred in *The End of the Affair*?

MEMORABLE SPORTING MOMENTS See quiz 6, page 14

ANSWERS

1 His 18th. 2 Seven. 3 Australia. 4 Long jump. 5 Australia. 6 24 hours. 7 Athens. 8 1950s. 9 Navratilova. 10 10. 11 Olympics. 12 Red. 13 Israel. 14 1930s. 15 USSR (Soviet Union). 16 Moscow. 17 Boycott. 18 Shergar. 19 Becker. 20 Christopher Dean. 21 Ovett. 22 Buster. 23 Gary (Garfield) Sobers. 24 United. 25 Second. 26 Spanish. 27 Three. 28 Paul Gascoigne. 29 Jonathan Edwards. 30 David Beckham.

QUIZ 9 POT LUCK 4

Answers - see Quiz 11, page 19

1 Duplo is a younger version of which favourite toy?
2 What is the name of Mrs Addams in *The Addams Family*?
3 What is a large gathering of Boy Scouts called?
4 What colour car does the Pink Panther drive in his cartoon show?
5 Which politically incorrect adjective is applied to Thomas The Tank Engine's Controller?
6 What's the difference between the highest single dart treble and the lowest single dart treble?
7 What shape is a tambourine?
8 In which month is the London Marathon usually held?
9 What is a Barbie's usual hair colour?
10 Which country hosted the last soccer World Cup played in the 20th century?
11 In computing what does O mean in OS?
12 In which Greek city is the Acropolis situated?
13 Chile is on which coast of South America?
14 The edelweiss is a native flower to which mountains?
15 The kiwi fruit also known as which gooseberry?
16 What did Jodhpur in India give its name to?
17 In which decade of the last century did the Channel Tunnel open to the public?
18 Lebanon is situated at the eastern end of which Sea?
19 A warning of which computer bug was given prior to the start of the year 2000?
20 Which US state is known as the Sunshine State?
21 What are the least number of points needed to win a single game in tennis?
22 Terracotta is made by baking what?
23 What is the abbreviation used for metre?
24 What type of *Sleep* was a classic Bacall and Bogart movie?
25 Which Frenchman gave his name to an item worn by ballet dancers?
26 Which McCartney is a well known dress designer?
27 Charlie Chaplin found fame in America but where was he born?
28 Which word means clever and can also be a stinging pain?
29 Which 19th-century American President was murdered in a theatre?
30 By which first name is athlete Frederick Carleton Lewis usually known?

POT LUCK 5 *See quiz 11, page 19*
1 Argentina. 2 CJ 3 Washington DC. 4 Children. 5 Long. 6 19th. 7 Morocco.
8 Plane. 9 Two. 10 Tail. 11 Water. 12 Gown. 13 Clint Eastwood. 14 Margaret.
15 Monsoon. 16 Raspberry. 17 West Ham. 18 Your family. 19 Polly. 20 1960s.
21 Top. 22 Cricket. 23 Ritual suicide. 24 Chicago. 25 Wine. 26 India.
27 Radioactivity. 28 Bamber Gascoigne. 29 Cribbage. 30 Tiger.

17

QUIZ 10 UK TOUR

Answers - see Quiz 12, page 20

1 Is Aberdeen to the north or south of Glasgow?
2 Prestwick and Gatwick are both what?
3 The Dales are mainly in which county?
4 On which Devon moor is there a famous prison?
5 Denbighshire is in the north of which country?
6 Who is London's Downing Street's most famous resident?
7 What is the capital of Scotland's Dumfries and Galloway region?
8 Which of Eastbourne, Esher and Eccles is on the coast?
9 In London, Richmond is on which river?
10 In which county is Rutland Water?
11 Where in the UK is Armagh?
12 Dorchester is the county town of which county?
13 Salford is part of which city?
14 Who has their HQ at Scotland Yard?
15 Sherwood Forest is associated with which historical hero?
16 Which food item is associated with London's Smithfield market?
17 Durham is in which part of England?
18 What is Eton's most famous institution?
19 Who has a home at Sandringham?
20 What is the highest mountain in Snowdonia National Park?
21 Which S in central London is an area associated with clubs and nightlife?
22 In which county is Stansted airport?
23 The resort of Aberystwyth is on which coast of Britain?
24 Dudley in the West Midlands is near which major city?
25 Ealing is an area of which city?
26 What is the Savoy in London as well as a theatre?
27 Prince William chose to go to St Andrews university in which part of the UK?
28 What is Salisbury's most famous building?
29 Who are trained at Sandhurst?
30 Which items of tableware is Sheffield famous for?

QUIZ 11 POT LUCK 5

Answers - see Quiz 9, page 17

1 The football team Boca Juniors play in which country?
2 Which initials did Pamela Anderson have in her Baywatch role?
3 In which city was Pete Sampras born?
4 UNICEF is an organisation caring for which people?
5 Which jump record was held by Bob Beamon for over 20 years?
6 In which century was explorer David Livingstone born?
7 Where did athlete Said Aouita come from?
8 In what type of transport did Charles Lindbergh make history?
9 How many people were on the poster for the 1990s movie *Titanic*?
10 Where does a scorpion have its sting?
11 What is most of the Earth's surface covered by?
12 Which word is a type of frock and also an academic robe?
13 Which star of spaghetti westerns appeared in Coogan's Bluff?
14 What was Mrs Victor Meldrew's first name?
15 What's the weather word linked to an Absolutely Fabulous character's surname?
16 Glen Cova and Malling Jewel are types of which fruit?
17 Which football team did TV terror Alf Garnett support?
18 Who do you favour if you are a nepotist?
19 What was the name of the hotel chambermaid in Fawlty Towers?
20 In which decade was Heartbeat first set?
21 Q is on which row on a British/US keyboard?
22 In which sport can there be a night watchman?
23 In Japan, what is Hara-Kiri?
24 *ER* is set in which city?
25 Oz Clarke is a TV expert on what?
26 In the 1980s there was a catastrophic chemical accident at Bhopal in which country?
27 What is detected by a Geiger counter?
28 Who was the first presenter of TV quiz show University Challenge?
29 In which card game do you peg for cards making 15?
30 Which of scarlet, swine and tiger, is not a type of fever?

ANSWERS

POT LUCK 4 *See quiz 9, page 17*

1 Lego. 2 Morticia. 3 Jamboree. 4 Pink. 5 Fat. 6 57. 7 Round. 8 April.
9 Blonde. 10 France. 11 Operating. 12 Athens. 13 West. 14 Alps. 15 Chinese.
16 Riding trousers (breeches/britches). 17 1990s. 18 Mediterranean
19 Millennium bug. 20 Florida. 21 Four. 22 Clay. 23 M (m). 24 Big. 25 Leotard.
26 Stella. 27 England. 28 Smart. 29 Abraham Lincoln. 30 Carl.

QUIZ 12 21ST CENTURY MUSIC

Answers - see Quiz 10, page 18

1 Which country does Ronan Keating come from?

2 What is Victoria Beckham's husband's first name?

3 What was the occupation of chart topper Bob?

4 Which number follows S Club in the band's title?

5 How many boys are there in Destiny's Child?

6 How are the Street Preachers described?

7 What is the surname of the two brothers in Oasis?

8 Which "Pie" did Madonna sing about?

9 What did Geri Halliwell say to do "If You Want to Run Faster"?

10 What was Billie's surname when she first topped the charts?

11 Which sporting event did Kylie Minogue close in 2000?

12 Which Craig had a hit with "Fill Me In"?

13 Which Mariah had a hit with Westlife in 2000?

14 Which Robbie was a "Rock DJ"?

15 What was Mel B called during her brief first marriage?

16 What type of music is LeAnn Rimes famous for?

17 How many girls are there in Destiny's Child?

18 Which teenage Charlotte wowed audiences on both side of the Atlantic?

19 What type of "Coffee" was a chart topper for All Saints?

20 "Never Had A Dream Come True" was the theme song to which children's TV charity?

21 Craig Phillips charted after winning on which Big TV show?

22 Who charted with The Bangles' "Eternal Flame"?

23 Who was "2 Faced" in 2000?

24 Whose third UK No 1 was "Oops I Did It Again"?

25 How many members of Westlife are there?

26 Which band named after a US state were "In Demand" in 2000?

27 Which Jones was a "Sex Bomb" with the Stereophonics in 2000?

28 Which band were formed from the *Popstars* TV show?

29 What is the surname of all the Corrs?

30 How is controversial rapper Marshall Mathers better known?

QUIZ 13　POT LUCK 6

Answers - see Quiz 15, page 23

1　In which sport can Canaries take on Owls?
2　How many colours are there on the German flag?
3　In a limerick which line does the third line rhyme with?
4　Which three initials was the 1960s' US President Johnson known by?
5　Which solo singer sang "Baby One More Time" in 1999?
6　What sort of creature is a shrike?
7　Edmund Hillary became the first man to climb which mountain?
8　Charles Holley became known as which entertainer Buddy?
9　Which word describes sailors as well as medicinal minerals?
10　What was Beijing called immediately before adopting the name Beijing?
11　In which US state is the resort of Orlando?
12　What was the occupation of the hero of the movie *Raging Bull*?
13　What covers most of the Antarctic?
14　Skater Kurt Browning comes from which country?
15　Pope John Paul II was born in which country?
16　T E Lawrence became known as Lawrence of where?
17　Carl Lewis found fame running and in which other athletics event?
18　What colour was Marilyn Monroe's hair in most of her movies?
19　Which country does Monaco border?
20　Which way do the stripes on the American flag run?
21　Which country was first to have ten kings all called Rameses?
22　A tsunami is another name for what?
23　Which Jim created *The Muppets*?
24　What do the British call what the Americans call the Fall?
25　Ellen MacArthur became known for her solo what?
26　What did a sundial used to tell?
27　Which of pink, purple or red is a primary colour?
28　The Wolf Cubs evolved as a junior branch of which organisation?
29　Yasser Arafat led which organisation known by its initials?
30　What was the horse made out of that was delivered to the ancient city of Troy?

TV STARS *See quiz 15, page 23*

1 Yorath. 2 Aspel. 3 Ainsley Harriott. 4 Rolf Harris. 5 *The Simpsons.*
6 Alistair McGowan. 7 Gloria Hunniford. 8 Chris Tarrant. 9 Sue Barker. 10 *Frost.*
11 Penguin. 12 Titchmarsh. 13 G. 14 McDonald. 15 Doctor/surgeon. 16 Kelly.
17 Vaughan. 18 Davidson. 19 Cilla Black. 20 Rantzen. 21 Lorraine Kelly.
22 Parrott. 23 Cook. 24 Graham Norton. 25 Parkinson. 26 Thaw. 27 David.
28 Smillie. 29 Jeremy. 30 Schofield.

ANSWERS

QUIZ 14 PLANTS & ANIMALS

Answers - see Quiz 16, page 24

1 What sort of creature is an aardvark?
2 What colour are a daisy's petals?
3 Which of the following dogs is the biggest: Pekinese, Labrador or St Bernard?
4 The dove is a member of which bird family?
5 What is the largest and most powerful land mammal?
6 What sort of feet do antelopes have?
7 A caribou is a type of what?
8 What is a rhododendron?
9 What is a Scots pine?
10 The lynx belongs to which family?
11 What do herbivores eat?
12 Where is a horse's muzzle?
13 How many nostrils does a dog have?
14 In the animal world what is an adder?
15 What colour are rhubarb stalks?
16 In the very early part of which season do snowdrops appear?
17 Which big cat has a mane?
18 What is an antirrhinum?
19 Mushrooms and puffballs are what types of living things?
20 Which of cacti, root vegetables or water lilies can survive in the desert?
21 In plants, pollination is the transfer of what?
22 Where do wetland plants grow?
23 What do carnivorous plants eat?
24 What colour are natural sponges?
25 How many tentacles does a starfish have?
26 Which animal can be field or harvest?
27 Where would an insect have its antenna?
28 In animals what is another name for the backbone?
29 Which is the heaviest of chimpanzee, gorilla or man?
30 Where are a deer's antlers?

POT LUCK 7 See quiz 16, page 24
1 Depp 2 Australia. 3 USA. 4 Spirits. 5 Jam. 6 Wales. 7 Square. 8 Canada.
9 Two. 10 Ear. 11 American Football 12 Toy Story. 13 India. 14 St Francis.
15 14. 16 Thinking Day. 17 Telescope. 18 Scarface. 19 Globe. 20 Abbey.
21 Lines of longitude. 22 Water. 23 Vacuum cleaner. 24 1950s. 25 His manager.
26 Photocopier. 27 Cake. 28 Harrison. 29 Latin. 30 Songs.

ANSWERS

QUIZ 15 TV STARS

Answers - see Quiz 13, page 21

1 How was sports commentator Gabby Logan known before her marriage?
2 Which Michael replaced Hugh Scully on the *Antiques Roadshow*?
3 Which chef replaced Fern Britton on *Ready Steady Cook*?
4 Which Australian presents *Animal Hospital*?
5 In which series are Marge and Homer the stars?
6 Who starred in his own show impersonating stars and made a *Big Impression*?
7 Which Irish presenter hosts *Open House* daily on Channel 5?
8 Who hosts the UK version of *Who Wants To Be A Millionaire*?
9 Who was the first female presenter of *A Question of Sport*?
10 David Jason starred in the detective series *A Touch of* what?
11 Which animal is the star of *Pingu*?
12 Which Alan succeeded Geoff Hamilton on *Gardener's World*?
13 Which Ali is the alter ego of Sacha Baron Cohen?
14 Which singer Jane found fame on *The Cruise*?
15 What was George Clooney's profession in *ER*?
16 Which Matthew hosts *Star In Their Eyes*?
17 Which Johnny moved from *The Big Breakfast* to the BBC in 2001?
18 Which Jim presented *The Generation Game*?
19 Which Liverpool singer presents *Moment of Truth*?
20 Who is the Esther of *That's Esther*?
21 Which Scottish presenter is the star of GMTV's *LK Today*?
22 Which snooker star John is a team captain on *A Question of Sport*?
23 What would you expect Antony Worrall Thompson to do on TV?
24 Who was the star of *So Graham Norton*?
25 Which Michael began his chat shows back in 1971?
26 Which John has played Morse and Kavanagh?
27 Which Attenborough presented *The Blue Planet* about life beneath the sea?
28 Which Carol presented *Changing Rooms*?
29 What is the first name of *Newsnight* interrogators Vine and Paxman?
30 Which Phillip, star of *Dr Doolittle*, presented *National Lottery Winning Lines*?

POT LUCK 6 *See quiz 13, page 21*
1 Soccer. 2 Three. 3 The fourth 4 LBJ. 5 Britney Spears. 6 Bird. 7 Mount Everest.
8 Holly. 9 Salts. 10 Peking. 11 Florida. 12 Boxer. 13 Ice. 14 Canada.
15 Poland. 16 Arabia. 17 Long jump. 18 Blonde. 19 France. 20 Horizontally.
21 Egypt. 22 Tidal wave 23 Henson. 24 Autumn. 25 Sailing. 26 Time. 27 Red.
28 Boy Scouts. 29 PLO. 30 Wood.

ANSWERS

23

QUIZ 16 POT LUCK 7

Answers - see Quiz 14, page 22

1 Which actor Johnny was in *Sleepy Hollow, Edward Scissorhands* and *Fear And Loathing In Las Vegas*?
2 Which of Australia, the UK and the USA does not have a large city called Birmingham?
3 The Sears Tower became the tallest skyscraper in which country?
4 Which word means ghosts and also means strong drinks?
5 Basketball's Michael Jordan featured in the movie *Space* what?
6 The Stereophonics come from which part of the UK?
7 Which shape name is given to the area in which Nelson's Column stands?
8 The Great Lakes border the USA along with which other country?
9 How many people usually play a game of chess?
10 Which part of the body can go before the words ache and muff?
11 Jerry Rice and Emmitt Smith are both connected with which sport?
12 In which *Story* was Woody a hero?
13 Mahatma Gandhi was a leader in which country?
14 Which Saint founded the Franciscan order of monks?
15 How many letters are there in the English alphabet between E and T?
16 What kind of Day do Scouts and Guides call the anniversary of their founder's birth?
17 Which instrument did Galileo invent as an aid to study the stars?
18 What was Al Capone's nickname, after he was injured in a knife fight?
19 What name is given to a world map presented in spherical form?
20 Queen Elizabeth II was crowned in what type of building?
21 Which type of lines on a map run north to south?
22 What does a coracle travel on?
23 William Hoover first marketed which household appliance?
24 In which decade did the Mini car first appear on British roads?
25 In the 1990s Macaulay Culkin sacked his dad from which job?
26 Invented as the xerox machine what is this device usually known as today?
27 French Queen Marie Antoinette famously said, "Let them eat" what?
28 Which Ford was *The Fugitive* on the big screen?
29 Which language was spoken by the ancient Romans?
30 Irving Berlin was famous for writing what?

QUIZ 17 SPORTING LEGENDS

Answers - see Quiz 19, page 27

1 Which sport did Joe Davis play in addition to billiards?
2 Jack Dempsey was a heavyweight what?
3 Which Ramsey took England to be World Cup champions?
4 Which Steve was knighted after the 2000 Olympics?
5 By which name was IVA Richards known?
6 Which country does tennis's Pete Sampras come from?
7 In which decade of the 20th century did Ayrton Senna meet his untimely death?
8 Which club has commemorative gate in memory of Bill Shankly?
9 In which position did soccer legend Lev Yashin play?
10 Mark Spitz won his seven gold medals in 1972 doing what?
11 Which motor racing star became Sir Jackie in the new millennium?
12 Brian Lara played international cricket for which country?
13 Athlete Frederick Carleton Lewis was better known by which first name?
14 Aussie cricketer Dennis Lillee was a specialist what?
15 Gary Lineker has which Churchillian middle name?
16 In addition to his sporting skill John McEnroe was also famous for what?
17 Diego Maradona led which side to World Cup victory in 1986?
18 Sir Stanley Matthews played for which famous seaside resort town?
19 Which Bobby captained England's World Cup soccer winning side?
20 Which Mr Moss was a successful motor racing legend of the 1950s?
21 Which boxer modestly announced "I am the greatest!", and went on to prove it?
22 Which 1990s football international is nicknamed Gazza?
23 Which US tennis star with 13 Grand Slams to his credit lost to Leighton Hewitt in the 2001 US Open?
24 Which Coe became an adviser to Tory Party leader William Hague?
25 In which gambling city did Evander Holyfield become world boxing champion in 1997?
26 In which decade was Arnold Palmer most successful in competition?
27 For which country did Jonah Lomu win his rugby caps?
28 Which British boxer did Mike Tyson beat to become champion in 1996?
29 Who did Denis Law play international football for?
30 Which childlike first name did baseball's George Herman Ruth have?

ANSWERS

MOVIES – HEROES & HEROINES See quiz 19, page 27

1 Hugh. 2 John. 3 *Madness*. 4 Grace. 5 Horror. 6 *Hamlet*. 7 Steel. 8 *Forrest*.
9 Dr Evil. 10 Cruise. 11 Sundance. 12 Pierce Brosnan. 13 Catwoman.
14 Robin Hood. 15 Doctor. 16 India. 17 Starling 18 The Mafia. 19 Soldier.
20 Pan. 21 Mel Gibson. 22 Kennedy. 23 Astronauts. 24 *Harry*. 25 Romeo.
26 *Schindler*. 27 Irons. 28 *Toy Story*. 29 Boxer. 30 Wayne.

QUIZ 18 POT LUCK 8

Answers - see Quiz 20, page 28

1 In which quiz show are individual contestants dismissed with Ms Robinson saying "Goodbye"?
2 Where would a spade, a club and a diamond be kept together?
3 King Hussein was ruler of which Middle East country?
4 In which country was John Lennon shot?
5 Which legendary king held court at Camelot?
6 How many letters are not vowels in the word queen?
7 Keith Floyd presents television programmes about what?
8 Which name links a Spice Girl and a queen of England?
9 Oxford bags were a type of which item of clothing?
10 What can be a musical sound or a short letter?
11 In place-names what can precede England, Hampshire and York?
12 What name is given to the part of a parachute jump before the parachute opens?
13 Shrove Tuesday – or Pancake Day – is celebrated in which month?
14 Caviar is a great food delicacy but what is it?
15 Northern Territory is a "state" in which country in the southern hemisphere?
16 A rhombus is a shape with how many sides?
17 Which word meaning talk is the name of a bird?
18 How many letters are there in the English alphabet before Y?
19 In Monopoly what do you pass, collecting £200, when you complete one circuit of the board and start another?
20 What is the name of the special mark on precious metals to denote their purity?
21 A kilogram is just over how many pounds in imperial weight?
22 Which country's cavalry is John Ford's film *Rio Grande* about?
23 How many minutes are there in half a day?
24 Dermatitis is the inflammation of what part of the body?
25 In communications, what does P stand for in the initials ISP?
26 Gibraltar is separated from which European country by the Neutral Zone?
27 What sort of transport is a clipper?
28 Which of dog, fish and rat is not a Chinese year?
29 The Vikings were historical people who came from where?
30 Is an area around a city designated not to be built on known as a green belt, a life belt or an urban belt?

ANSWERS

MUSIC CHARTS *See quiz 20, page 28*
1 The Builder. 2 Simpsons. 3 "Bohemian". 4 Billie. 5 Mariah Carey. 6 Green.
7 1950s. 8 "In a Bottle". 9 Rush. 10 Boyzone. 11 Rap. 12 "Stop". 13 Eminem.
14 Billie. 15 Ronan Keating. 16 911. 17 Ireland. 18 Prodigy. 19 Mel B.
20 1990s. 21 Kylie Minogue. 22 "Millennium Prayer." 23 "And the Beast". 24 R.
25 "Marmalade". 26 Diana Ross. 27 Billie. 28 Spice Girls. 29 1997.
30 Victoria Beckham.

QUIZ 19 MOVIES – HEROES AND HEROINES

Answers - see Quiz 17, page 25

1 Which Grant played the cad in *Bridget Jones's Diary*?
2 What was Jim Belushi's ill fated elder brother called?
3 What did King George suffer from in the Nigel Hawthorne and Helen Mirren movie?
4 Which Jones starred in *A View To A Kill* in 1985?
5 What type of movies made Boris Karloff famous?
6 Which Prince of Denmark is the hero of Shakespeare's most filmed play?
7 In which industry had the heroes of *The Full Monty*, based in Sheffield, worked?
8 Which *Gump* was the hero of a 1994 movie?
9 Which evil doctor was the enemy of Austin Powers?
10 Which Tom starred in *A Few Good Men*?
11 Which Kid was Butch Cassidy's sidekick?
12 Which James Bond actor got married in the summer of 2001?
13 What sort of woman did Michelle Pfeiffer play in *Batman Returns*?
14 Which heroic outlaw was *Prince of Thieves* on the big screen?
15 What was the title of Doolittle who could talk to the animals?
16 *Gandhi* was about a hero of which country?
17 What was the bird-related last name of the agent played by Jodie Foster in *The Silence of the Lambs*?
18 *The Godfather* was the head of which organisation?
19 What was the occupation of Private Ryan in Spielberg's movie?
20 Which Peter was the hero of *Hook* based on the children's story by JM Barrie?
21 Which actor starred in the *Lethal Weapon* movies and *Braveheart*?
22 What was the surname of the subject of *JFK*?
23 *Apollo 13* was about a group of what type of people?
24 Who was the hero who *Met Sally* in the movie with Billy Crystal and Meg Ryan?
25 Leonardo DiCaprio starred in a 1996 movie about which character *and Juliet*?
26 Which hero had a *List* in a Spielberg movie?
27 Which Jeremy starred in *Reversal of Fortune*?
28 In which *Story* was Woody a hero?
29 What was the occupation of the hero of *Raging Bull*?
30 Which John landed a best actor Oscar for *True Grit*?

SPORTING LEGENDS *See quiz 17, page 25*

ANSWERS

1 Snooker. 2 Boxer. 3 (Sir) Alf. 4 Redgrave. 5 Viv. 6 USA. 7 1990s.
8 Liverpool FC. 9 Goalkeeper. 10 Swimming. 11 Stewart. 12 West Indies.
13 Carl. 14 Fast bowler. 15 Winston. 16 His temper. 17 Argentina.
18 Blackpool. 19 Moore. 20 Stirling. 21 Cassius Clay/Muhammad Ali.
22 Paul Gascoigne. 23 Pete Sampras. 24 Sebastian. 25 Las Vegas.
26 1960s. 27 New Zealand. 28 Frank Bruno. 29 Scotland. 30 Babe.

QUIZ 20 MUSIC CHARTS

Answers - see Quiz 18, page 26

1 Which Bob went to No 1 with "Can We Fix It"?
2 Which family had a hit with "Do The Bartman"?
3 Which "Rhapsody" was a chart topper for Queen?
4 Which teenager had a 1998 hit with "Because We Want To"?
5 Which female singer went straight to No 1 in the US with "Fantasy"?
6 Which actor Robson had a string of hits in 1995 with Jerome Flynn?
7 In which age group was Cher when she hit No 1 with "Believe"?
8 Where was the "Genie" in the 1999 hit of Christine Aguilera?
9 Which Jennifer sang "The Power of Love" in 1985?
10 Which band's singles include "No Matter What" and "Words"?
11 What type of single was Puff Daddy's "I'll Be Missing You"?
12 Which Spice Girls hit put a stop to a run of No 1s?
13 Which controversial rapper's No 1s include "The Real Slim Shady" and "Stan"?
14 Which British teenager's second No 1 was "Girlfriend"?
15 Which Irish group member had a solo No 1 with "Life Is A Rollercoaster"?
16 Which US emergency phone number hit No 1 with "A Little Bit More"?
17 Westlife hit No 1 with their first seven singles and came from where?
18 Which band's singles include "Firestarter" and "Breathe"?
19 Which Spice Girl did Missy Misdemeanour Elliott record "I Want You Back" with?
20 In which decade did Wet Wet Wet have their huge No 1 hit "Love Is All Around"?
21 Which Australian singer/actress is the most successful ex-soap star in the British pop charts?
22 Which "Prayer" was a millennium chart topper for Cliff Richard?
23 What went with "Beauty" in the title of Celine Dion's first UK chart success?
24 Which Kelly charted with "I Believe I Can Fly"?
25 Which "Lady" was a 1998 chart hit for All Saints?
26 Which ex member of the Supremes has charted with Marvin Gaye and Lionel Richie?
27 Which future Mrs Evans charted with "Because We Want To?
28 Whose follow up to their first No 1 was "Say You'll Be There"?
29 In which year did Elton John have the best ever selling single?
30 Who was "Not Such an Innocent Girl" in 2001?

QUIZ 21 POT LUCK 9

Answers - see Quiz 23, page 31

1 Which shredded vegetable goes into sauerkraut?
2 What does the P stand for in the education initials PTA?
3 In 1997 Hong Kong was returned to the rule of which country?
4 Which sport did Basil D'Oliveira play?
5 Which US grunge band shares a name with the Buddhist state of bliss?
6 In film which Doctor could talk to the animals?
7 Which of these celebs has not guested on *Friends* – Duchess of York, George Clooney or Prince Charles?
8 Out of his six wives, how many did Henry VIII have beheaded?
9 Which tennis player's name was given to a 2001 computer virus?
10 Which Scotsman gave his name to a type of raincoat?
11 Which Mel voiced Rooster in *Chicken Run*?
12 Which word is a type of trousers and also means to breathe rapidly?
13 Who or what is a great bustard?
14 Who was the blonde in the movie *Some Like It Hot*?
15 Which planet is also the first name of a 2001 sporting champ?
16 What is the shape of a pie chart?
17 Which was the second country to send a man into space?
18 What colour is platinum?
19 The caribou is another name for what?
20 If a number is squared what is it multiplied by?
21 The collapse of a star leads to the formation of what type of a hole?
22 Which bone is the longest bone in the human body?
23 What does U stand for in VDU?
24 Which country do pop band OTT come from?
25 Hr is the abbreviation for what?
26 What type of creature is a mandrill?
27 If you possessed a Canaletto would you own a painting, a small barge or a tin of stuffed olives?
28 What is a fox's tail known as?
29 What did the Russians call their first spacemen?
30 In which decade did Steve Redgrave win his first Olympic gold?

POT LUCK 10 See quiz 23, page 31

ANSWERS

1 Bank. 2 *Philosopher's Stone*. 3 *Magic Johnson*. 4 Five. 5 Careers. 6 Linford Christie. 7 1980s. 8 Dylan. 9 Croatia. 10 Two. 11 *Kingfisher*. 12 Bird. 13 In water. 14 Stripes. 15 Bulb. 16 Private Frazer. 17 Ringo Starr. 18 Fish and chips. 19 Books. 20 Salmon. 21 *Fawlty Towers*. 22 West Ham United. 23 Gold. 24 West. 25 Yuppies. 26 France. 27 Tyres. 28 None. 29 Teaching. 30 March.

QUIZ 22 FAMOUS NAMES

Answers - see Quiz 24, page 32

1 What is Lucy Henman's tennis playing husband called?
2 What is the Prince of Wales's first name?
3 Which Chris did Billie Piper marry?
4 Who was the first British PM of the new millennium?
5 What is Chelsea Clinton's dad called?
6 What would you ask Anna Ryder Richardson to design?
7 Which Ms Boothroyd was the first lady Speaker of the House of Commons?
8 What is Christine Hamilton's ex MP husband called?
9 Which Gordon was Tony Blair's first Chancellor of the Exchequer?
10 Which of Paul McCartney's daughters is a dress designer?
11 Which 1960s model took over a morning TV show in September 2001?
12 Which Max acts as publicist to the famous?
13 What is the first name of ex athlete and William Hague adviser Lord Coe?
14 From which part of the UK does Eamonn Holmes come from?
15 Novelist Baroness James is known with which initials?
16 Which Jones, the hard man of football, has also carved out an acting career as a screen tough guy?
17 Under which female name is Paul O'Grady widely known?
18 What is the surname of TV brother celebs David and Jonathan?
19 What is the name of Dame Norma Major's husband?
20 What type of page does Claire Rayner write?
21 George Carey is Archbishop of where?
22 Which Miss MacArthur sailed around the world on her own?
23 Vidal Sassoon is famous in which beauty industry?
24 Which country is Ruby Wax from?
25 Who is Tessa Dahl's famous model daughter?
26 Who was Julian Lennon's famous dad?
27 What are the initials of Harry Potter creator Rowling?
28 What is the first name of MEP Glenys Kinnock's husband?
29 Martin Bell is famous for wearing what colour suit?
30 What is Leo Blair's mum called?

20TH CENTURY NEWS *See quiz 24, page 32*

QUIZ 23 POT LUCK 10

Answers - see Quiz 21, page 29

1 Robert Barclay founded what type of business?
2 Did a *Harry Potter* title feature The Philosopher's Hat, The Philosopher's Robe or The Philosopher's Stone?
3 What was Magic Johnson's autobiography called?
4 How many people were there in the original line up of Hear'Say?
5 Which word means vocations and also means moves wildly?
6 Which Briton is the oldest 100m Olympic winner of the 20th century?
7 In which decade of the 20th century was Britney Spears born?
8 What did Michael Douglas and Catherine Zeta Jones call their baby son?
9 Goran Ivanisevic plays tennis for which country?
10 How many kidneys do humans normally have?
11 What was the name of the boat in which Ellen MacArthur sailed around the world?
12 The now extinct dodo was what type of creature?
13 Where does a hippopotamus spend most of its life?
14 What type of pattern is on a raccoon's tail?
15 What does a hyacinth grow from?
16 In *Dad's Army* which character often declared, "We're doomed"?
17 Who was the first TV narrator of *Thomas the Tank Engine*?
18 What type of food is associated with Harry Ramsden's?
19 What do you fear if you have bibliophobia?
20 A smolt or smelt is a young of which creature?
21 Manuel the waiter appeared in which classic comedy series?
22 Which soccer club has a stand dedicated to the late Bobby Moore?
23 What were the 19th-century Forty Niners searching for?
24 Which is not the name of a sea – Black Sea, North Sea or West Sea?
25 In the 1980s, young upwardly mobile persons became known as what?
26 In which country would you watch Nantes play a home soccer match?
27 What was manufactured by the business set up by Harvey Firestone?
28 How many English kings known as Henry came after Henry VIII?
29 What was Ken Barlow's main career throughout his many years as a *Coronation Street* character?
30 Which month was named after Mars, the god of war?

POT LUCK 9 *See quiz 21, page 29*

1 Cabbage. 2 Parent. 3 China. 4 Cricket. 5 Nirvana. 6 *Dr Doolittle*.
7 Prince Charles. 8 Two. 9 Anna Kournikova. 10 Mackintosh. 11 Gibson.
12 Pants. 13 A bird. 14 Marilyn Monroe. 15 Venus. 16 A circle.
17 USA. 18 Greyish white. 19 Reindeer. 20 Itself. 21 Black hole.
22 Thigh (femur). 23 Unit. 24 Ireland. 25 Hour. 26 Monkey. 27 Painting.
28 Brush. 29 Cosmonauts. 30 1980s.

Answers - see Quiz 22, page 30

1 Who was Conservative party leader on 31 December 1999?
2 Fidel Castro took power on which island?
3 The tragedy of Aberfan took place in which part of the UK?
4 Charles de Gaulle was President of which European country?
5 Where did the Red Army come from?
6 Yves St Laurent found fame designing what?
7 Oskar Schindler, whose story was told in a Spielberg movie, was from which country?
8 Which former English king did Wallis Simpson marry?
9 Which S is an area of France where there was massive loss of life in WWI?
10 How was the USSR also known?
11 How many children did Tony Blair have when he became Prime Minister?
12 Lenin was a key figure in which revolution?
13 In which country did a Pan Am jumbo jet explode over Lockerbie in 1988?
14 Francois Mitterand was a Socialist head of state in which country?
15 The Battle of El Alamein was during which war?
16 The suffragettes campaigned for votes for whom?
17 Mao Tse Tung led the Long March in which country?
18 Which John succeeded Margaret Thatcher as Prime Minister?
19 In which decade of the 20th century did Nelson Mandela become South African president?
20 What was the first name of famous opera star Melba?
21 Which bandleader Miller disappeared over the English Channel during WWII?
22 In 1979 the Shah was deposed in which country?
23 Mussolini led which country in WWII?
24 After WWII, Germany was divided into West Germany and Communist what?
25 Where was the FA Cup Final held during the 1990s?
26 Particularly in the news in the 1980s, the NUM was the National Union of what?
27 Martin Bell beat which Hamilton to take the constituency of Tatton in the 1997 General Election?
28 How many UK Prime Ministers were there in the 1990s?
29 Arsenal soccer player Tony Adams was jailed for what offence?
30 In which seaside location did an IRA bomb explode at a Tory Party Conference in 1984?

QUIZ 25 POT LUCK 11

Answers - see Quiz 27, page 35

1 Which item is now the biggest cause of seabird death?
2 According to the Manic Street Preachers who were "The Masses Against"?
3 Who carries out their profession routinely wearing a tutu?
4 The UAE stands for which United Emirates?
5 Which word describes both a paragraph and a corridor?
6 What sort of *Hat* was the title of an elegant Fred Astaire movie?
7 A praying mantis is a type of what?
8 What is the name for a German from Hamburg?
9 The perambulator was an early type of what?
10 Which vegetable named character was created by Rowan Atkinson?
11 Which English queen's head was on the first postage stamp?
12 What is the currency of Luxembourg?
13 Which character did Joanna Lumley play in *The New Avengers*?
14 In the ancient world what type of Gardens were created at Babylon?
15 Which item can be carriage, grandmother, alarm or digital?
16 In which US state is Miami?
17 Who, in Holland, is known as Zinter Klaus?
18 Ferrari cars were originally manufactured in which country?
19 Which word for a dissolving substance also means financially in the black?
20 What animal goes before *Ballou* in the movie title?
21 What was the name of Lesley Joseph's character in *Birds of A Feather*?
22 Anna Edson Taylor became the first person to travel Niagara Falls in what?
23 What is the traditional colour of the headwear known as a fez?
24 Which fabric is made by worms?
25 What title does the vampire have in the story Dracula?
26 How many angles do 12 separate triangles contain in total?
27 On a compass, which direction is directly opposite to Northeast?
28 What does the middle letter stand for as used in HRH?
29 What sort of busters featured in a Sigourney Weaver movie – Blockbusters, Dambusters or Ghostbusters?
30 What did PM Tony Blair call his son, born in 2000?

POT LUCK 12 *See quiz 27, page 35*

ANSWERS

1 Watergate. 2 Wide. 3 11. 4 Japan. 5 New York. 6 Aeronautics. 7 Henry.
8 Fox. 9 Marathon. 10 Temperature. 11 Atlantic. 12 Rink. 13 Three. 14 Bridge.
15 Little John. 16 Scrooge. 17 Nine. 18 Diameter. 19 Nanny. 20 January.
21 New Orleans. 22 Three. 23 Spain. 24 Robinson. 25 Earl of Sandwich.
26 Wear it on the head. 27 USA. 28 Ash Wednesday. 29 First. 30 Green fingers.

QUIZ 26 TV COMEDY

Answers - see Quiz 28, page 36

1 In which country was *Father Ted* set?
2 How many *Friends* are there in the series of the same name?
3 Which Steve's alter ego is Alan Partridge?
4 Which Jennifer Saunders/Joanna Lumley show returned in 2001?
5 Which Caroline created Mrs Merton?
6 What sort of Minister is in *Yes Minister*?
7 Which Hancock hosted *They Think It's All Over*?
8 How many teams competed in *Have I Got News For You*?
9 Which animal follows *Drop The Dead* in the show about a newsroom?
10 What is the name of Harry Enfield's revolting teenager?
11 Mrs Bucket had which floral first name?
12 Where is the series *Chambers* set?
13 Which McBeal was a series with Calista Flockhart?
14 Where is Patrick Kielty from?
15 How many main characters were there in *Men Behaving Badly*?
16 What happened to Victor in the final episode of *One Foot in the Grave*?
17 Which US sitcom's cast included Michael Richards and Jerry Seinfeld?
18 Where did veteran comedian Dave Allen come from?
19 In which city was *The Liver Birds* set?
20 Which *Two* stars with the same first name began a long running comedy series in the 1970s?
21 Which June has starred in comedies from *Terry & June* to *Ab Fab*?
22 In *Are You Being Served?* which department along with ladies' fashions was shown?
23 In which series did the late Compo appear?
24 Which Frank was the star character in *Some Mothers Do 'Ave 'Em*?
25 Dawn French was the *Vicar* of where?
26 Which Irish presenter introduces programme of *Auntie's Bloomers*, featuring funny and embarrassing outtakes?
27 What was the name of Mrs Wayne Slob played by Kathy Burke?
28 *Two Point* how many children were in the popular sitcom?
29 Which *Ladies* were the subject of a series with Victoria Wood?
30 What colour is Lily Savage's hair?

QUIZ 27 POT LUCK 12

Answers - see Quiz 25, page 33

1 Which building was burgled by aides of President Nixon in 1972?
2 In Internet abbreviations, what does the middle w in www stand for?
3 What is the next prime number after 7?
4 Honda cars were originally manufactured in which country?
5 David Beckham's first son was named after an area of which city?
6 What does the first A stand for in NASA?
7 Which is the first name to have been used by eight kings of England?
8 What is Mulder's animal first name in the X Files?
9 Which name for a long race comes from a battle in the years BC?
10 What do Fahrenheit and Celsius measure?
11 The "Titanic" sank while travelling across which ocean?
12 What is the name for an ice hockey pitch?
13 How many colours appear on the Australian flag?
14 Cantilever, railway, suspension and toll can all go before which word?
15 Who was the tallest person in Robin Hood's gang of merry men?
16 What was the last name of the miser in *A Christmas Carol* by Charles Dickens?
17 In the English alphabet, how many letters are there before J?
18 What is the line across the middle of a circle called?
19 What was the day job that Mary Poppins did?
20 The Roman God Janus gives his name to which calendar month?
21 In the traditional song, is the "House Of The Rising Sun" in Newcastle, New Orleans or New York?
22 How many angles does an equilateral triangle contain?
23 Juan Carlos is king of which country?
24 Anne Bancroft was Mrs who in the movie *The Graduate*?
25 Was it the Earl of Burger, the Earl of Pancake or the Earl of Sandwich who gave his name to a popular type of food?
26 What would you do with a deerstalker?
27 Which of these three countries has got the biggest population – USA, Sweden or Greece?
28 What is the special day that follows Shrove Tuesday?
29 In which course is gazpacho usually served?
30 If you are good at growing plants you are said to have what?

POT LUCK 11 *See quiz 25, page 33*
1 Oil pollution. 2 "The Classes". 3 Ballet dancer. 4 Arab. 5 Passage. 6 Top.
7 Insect. 8 Hamburger. 9 Baby buggy. 10 *Mr Bean*. 11 Victoria. 12 Franc.
13 Purdey. 14 Hanging. 15 Clock. 16 Florida. 17 Santa Claus. 18 Italy.
19 Solvent. 20 Cat. 21 Dorien. 22 A barrel. 23 Red. 24 Silk. 25 Count.
26 36. 27 Southwest. 28 Royal. 29 *Ghostbusters*. 30 Leo.

ANSWERS

QUIZ 28 SOCCER

Answers - see Quiz 26, page 34

1 What does the second F stand for in FIFA?
2 Which Lancashire club received a record-breaking £15 million when Alan Shearer went to Newcastle?
3 Who is second only to Bobby Charlton as England's greatest goalscorer?
4 Pat Jennings won 119 full international caps for which British side?
5 Who scored a hat trick in England's 5–1 win over Germany in September 2001?
6 Which club did Glenn Hoddle leave when he rejoined Spurs in 2001?
7 Which manager George led Ipswich Town back to the Premiership in the year 2000?
8 Who was the first Frenchman to manage Liverpool?
9 Which entrepreneur was chairman of Fulham when they went into the Premiership?
10 Which credit card sponsored the Premiership from 2001?
11 Which side did Vialli take on after leaving Chelsea?
12 Which Joe left Manchester City immediately before Keegan took over?
13 Coventry City are nicknamed which shade of blue?
14 In which decade did the World Cup begin?
15 Who did Platini play international football for?
16 Which British football club is the richest in the world?
17 Which Peter is England's most capped goalkeeper?
18 Which major German side has Bayern before its name?
19 How was the UEFA Champions League formerly known?
20 Which quick sounding word precedes Vienna's name?
21 When was the previous World Cup before 1998?
22 Michael Owen was attached to which club when he scored for England in the World Cup in France 1998?
23 Which David then of Spurs was Footballer of the Year in 1999?
24 Dennis Bergkamp refuses to use which form of travel?
25 Which side plays at the Riverside Stadium?
26 AC and Inter are from which Italian city famous for its fashion?
27 The Jules Rimet trophy was the prize for which tournament?
28 Which company sponsored Divisions One to Three at the start of the 2001–2002 season?
29 Who captained England in their 2001 5–1 win over Germany?
30 Alphabetically which team is first in the Premiership?

TV COMEDY *See quiz 26, page 34*

ANSWERS

1 Ireland. 2 Six. 3 Coogan. 4 *Absolutely Fabulous.* 5 Aherne. 6 Government.
7 Nick. 8 Two. 9 *Donkey.* 10 Kevin. 11 Hyacinth. 12 Legal practice. 13 Ally.
14 Ireland. 15 Four. 16 Died. 17 *Seinfeld.* 18 Ireland. 19 Liverpool. 20 *Ronnies.*
21 Whitfield. 22 Menswear. 23 *Last of the Summer Wine.* 24 Spencer. 25 *Dibley.*
26 Terry Wogan. 27 Waynetta. 28 4. 29 *Dinner Ladies.* 30 Blonde.

QUIZ 29 POT LUCK 13

Answers - see Quiz 31, page 39

1 Which of these inventions was developed last – lightbulb, motor car or television?
2 How many sides do 13 rectangles have?
3 What sort of beans are used in the manufacture of chocolate?
4 *Heartbreak High* is set in which city?
5 Was the great plague of the 14th century known as The Black Death, The Cold Death or The Creeping Death?
6 What is John McEnroe's middle name?
7 What is the favourite food of Popeye?
8 What was spaceman Yuri Gagarin's home town renamed after his death?
9 How many letters are there in the English alphabet before M?
10 With which item of clothing is the name Levi Strauss linked?
11 Who set up a communications system that used dots and dashes?
12 The first atom bomb was dropped on the city Hiroshima, in which country?
13 Mark Spitz won seven gold medals at one Olympic Games doing what?
14 Which Susan of *Straw Dogs* fame starred in TV's EastEnders in 2001?
15 Which of Cantonese, German and Spanish is a major language that is spoken in South America?
16 What was the wife of a tsar called?
17 Where does a nun usually live?
18 What is the name of Fred Flintstone's pet?
19 If a number is not an odd number what is it?
20 Which comedian Jack's surname sounds like a letter of the alphabet?
21 How many women in total travelled to the Moon throughout the 20th century?
22 What is the name of the stick used in croquet to strike the ball?
23 What colour is Laa Laa of *The Teletubbies*?
24 Richard I of England was known as which Heart – Braveheart, Brokenheart or Lionheart?
25 Puri is a bread that originally came from which country?
26 What name is given to a bank of sand near the coastline?
27 A squirrel can be grey and which other colour?
28 What actually gets trapped in a Venus Fly Trap?
29 "Saving All My Love For You" was the first No 1 for which female singer?
30 What is a baked Alaska's outer layer made from?

POT LUCK 14 See quiz 31, page 39
1 California. 2 Maggie. 3 Ghost 4 Brazil. 5 Biography. 6 Around three hours.
7 Baker. 8 Gomez. 9 Musical instrument. 10 White. 11 Hawk. 12 Chelsea.
13 Boat. 14 White. 15 29th February. 16 Play. 17 Bolivia. 18 Walkman.
19 February/March. 20 Coral. 21 Rope. 22 Eight. 23 Belgium. 24 Alice.
25 Wood. 26 Johnny. 27 20th. 28 Moscow. 29 Desire. 30 Medical treatment.

QUIZ 30 MOVIES WHO'S WHO?

Answers - see Quiz 32, page 40

1 Which actress Grace had her face on Monaco's postage stamps?
2 Which Ford played Han Solo in the original *Star Wars* movie?
3 What is the surname of Susan, star of *Dead Man Walking*?
4 Who played Bridget in *Bridget Jones's Diary*?
5 Which Tom was the voice of Woody in the original *Toy Story*?
6 Which Woody had a son called Satchel Farrow?
7 Which star of *Mary Poppins* has written children's stories under the name Julie Edwards?
8 Which actress Kate announced a split from her husband Jim Threapleton in September 2001?
9 Which Kim married Alec Baldwin?
10 Annette Bening is the first wife of which Hollywood playboy actor director?
11 In which decade was Helena Bonham Carter born?
12 Which actor Richard was once married to supermodel Cindy Crawford?
13 Which Mel starred in *What Women Want*?
14 In which city of Northern Ireland was Kenneth Branagh born?
15 In film journalism, what sort of column did Hedda Hopper write?
16 Which Annette fell for Michael Douglas in *The American President*?
17 Which Tom married TV star Roseanne?
18 What is the first name of Spanish actor Banderas, husband of Melanie Griffith?
19 Which fantasy creature did Daryl Hannah play in *Splash*?
20 Which singer/actress played a music diva in *The Bodyguard*?
21 Which James Bond producer Cubby shares his name with a vegetable?
22 On which continent was Richard E Grant born?
23 Which Patsy who starred in The Great Gatsby was once Mrs Liam Gallagher?
24 Which family includes actors Davis, Patricia, Rosanna and Alexis?
25 What is the name of the actress daughter of John Drew Barrymore?
26 Which Kate is the daughter of Goldie Hawn?
27 *The Crying Game*'s director Neil Jordan hails from where?
28 What was silent star Joseph Keaton's nickname?
29 Which actor/director has a brother who is a famous wildlife expert?
30 Which Jeff did Geena Davis marry?

ANSWERS

EURO TOUR *See quiz 32, page 40*

1 Dublin. 2 Danish. 3 Dunkirk. 4 Dublin. 5 Greece. 6 Mediterranean.
7 Winter sports. 8 Rome. 9 Portugal. 10 Italy. 11 France. 12 Czechoslovakia.
13 Paris. 14 Switzerland. 15 Mountains. 16 West. 17 Spain. 18 Car.
19 Limerick. 20 Munich. 21 France. 22 Lisbon. 23 Brussels. 24 Berlin.
25 Spain. 26 France. 27 Hungary. 28 Ireland. 29 Arctic. 30 North.

QUIZ 31 POT LUCK 14

Answers - see Quiz 29, page 37

1 Los Angeles is in which US state?
2 Who is Bart Simpson's youngest sister?
3 A banshee is a type of what?
4 Which is the largest country in South America?
5 What category of book describes the life of another real person?
6 To the nearest hour, how many hours does it take Concorde to fly from New York to London?
7 In fiction, Sherlock Holmes lived in a street named after which type of worker?
8 Who is head of the family in the fiendishly funny *Addams Family*?
9 What is a clavichord?
10 What colour is the Taj Mahal?
11 Which bird is part of the name for a native American Indian's war axe?
12 Bill Clinton's daughter shares a name with which part of London?
13 In transport terms a smack is a small type of what?
14 What colour was Tin Tin's dog called Snowy?
15 When were you born if your birthdate occurs only once in four years?
16 In the saying, what will the mice do when the cat's away?
17 Which country along with Brazil in South America begins with a B?
18 What was the first personal stereo called?
19 The zodiac sign Pisces covers which two months?
20 What is the Great Barrier Reef made out of?
21 What is a lasso usually made from?
22 How many kings are there in two packs of playing cards?
23 In which country can you visit the Francorchamps race track?
24 Alice, Elizabeth, Mary and Victoria – which of these has never been the name of a queen of England?
25 What was a totem pole usually made from?
26 What is the name of presenter Zoe Ball's dad?
27 In which century was Coca Cola first produced?
28 Which city does a Muscovite come from?
29 What was the *Streetcar* named in the movie with Marlon Brando?
30 Is acupuncture a form of bicycle tyre repairing, medical treatment or recycling of waste material?

POT LUCK 13 *See quiz 29, page 37*

ANSWERS

1 Television. 2 52. 3 Cocoa beans. 4 Sydney. 5 The Black Death. 6 Patrick.
7 Spinach. 8 Gagarin. 9 12. 10 Jeans. 11 Morse. 12 Japan. 13 Swimming.
14 George. 15 Spanish. 16 Tsarina. 17 Convent. 18 Dino. 19 Even. 20 Dee.
21 None. 22 Mallet. 23 Yellow. 24 Lionheart. 25 India. 26 Dune. 27 Red.
28 Insects. 29 Whitney Houston. 30 Meringue.

QUIZ 32 EURO TOUR

Answers - see Quiz 30, page 38

1 In which Irish city is the Abbey Theatre?
2 What is the official language of Denmark?
3 What do the British call what the French call Dunkerque?
4 Dun Laoghaire is the port for which Irish city?
5 Rhodes is an island belonging to which country?
6 The Riviera is on the French/Italian coast on which sea?
7 St Moritz is famous for what type of sports?
8 St Peter's Basilica is in which Italian city?
9 Faro, or the Algarve, is in which country?
10 Rimini is a resort of the Adriatic in which country?
11 The Seine reaches the sea from which country?
12 Slovakia was formerly part of which country?
13 In which French city is the university called the Sorbonne?
14 Which European country is made up of cantons?
15 What are the Alps?
16 County Sligo is on which coast of Ireland?
17 Catalonia, Andalusia and Valencia are parts of which country?
18 The French town of Le Mans hosts what type of race?
19 Which Irish county has given its name to a comic rhyme?
20 Which German city is known locally as München?
21 In which country was the Academie Française founded?
22 Which city do the Portuguese call Lisboa?
23 Which city is also known locally as Bruxelles?
24 Which city replaced Bonn as Germany's capital?
25 Where would you spend pesetas?
26 In which country are baguettes and brioches traditional breads?
27 Which country beginning with H is to the east of Austria?
28 The Shannon is which country's chief river?
29 Lapland is nearest to which ocean?
30 In which part of Europe is the Baltic Sea?

QUIZ 33 POT LUCK 15

Answers - see Quiz 35, page 43

1 The *New York Herald* and the *Washington Post* are types of what?
2 Which letter along with H appears on pencils?
3 According to the legend, which weapon did William Tell use to shoot an apple off his son's head?
4 In a calendar year which is the first month to have exactly 30 days?
5 California is on which coast of the USA?
6 Which George played Dr Ross in *ER*?
7 Which West European country beginning with an S is landlocked?
8 Ford cars were originally made in which country?
9 Which word links a chess piece and an ancient soldier?
10 Pisa's famous leaning tower was built to house what?
11 C S Lewis wrote about *The Lion, The Witch and The* what?
12 Hermit and spider are types of what?
13 In which city was John Lennon murdered?
14 Who did France beat in the final of the 1998 FIFA World Cup?
15 How many pairs of ribs does a human have?
16 The game of boules comes from which country?
17 Which gas is believed to be encouraging global warming?
18 Which *Street* full of puppets is a children's TV show seen worldwide?
19 Which word names a conductor's stick and also a small French loaf?
20 The Disney animation about Moses was called *Prince of* where?
21 What is the second highest mountain in the world called?
22 Which John returned to prominence in the movie *Pulp Fiction*?
23 What does TV foodie Rick Stein specialise in?
24 What do people usually do with a Stradivarius?
25 Which TV show was responsible for the the catchphrase "Pass"?
26 What colour describes the extra time goal to decide certain football matches?
27 Which item of swimwear is named after an atoll in the Pacific?
28 In the human skeleton, is the fibula below or above the patella?
29 In which street would you have been wise to avoid the premises of a barber named Sweeney Todd?
30 In *Bewitched* which part of her body did Samantha move to cast a spell?

ANSWERS

POT LUCK 16 *See quiz 35, page 43*
1 Buffalo. 2 Pole vault. 3 Pacific. 4 Roald Dahl. 5 Never. 6 Ice. 7 Louis Pasteur.
8 Smith. 9 Mexico. 10 Cos. 11 French. 12 Beavis. 13 Moses. 14 Mozart.
15 Notting Hill. 16 Tsar. 17 52. 18 *Teletubbies*. 19 An earthquake. 20 Africa.
21 Motor town. 22 Nobel Prize. 23 Sun. 24 Knife. 25 "Beautiful". 26 A will.
27 Clubs. 28 None. 29 White. 30 Television.

QUIZ 34 MUSIC SUPERSTARS

Answers - see Quiz 36, page 44

1 Who was Simon's singing partner?
2 By which first name is Roderick David Stewart known?
3 Who has the surname Ciccone?
4 Freddie Mercury led which regal sounding band?
5 Which superstar member of the Jackson family was the first to appear in a Pepsi commercial?
6 Which Elton John song was reworked and dedicated to Princess Diana?
7 What was the Spice Girls' first album called?
8 How many members of TLC are there?
9 Which band's singles include "Country House" and "Beetlebum"?
10 Who made the album *Best of Bob Marley*?
11 Whose *Come On Over* album is a top selling country album in the US?
12 Which ex Take That member won a Brit Award for "She's The One" in 2000?
13 Whose hits include "Jesus To a Child" and "Outside"?
14 Which band has had the most gold albums of any band in the UK?
15 Which grandfather was a "Sex Bomb" in 2000?
16 In 2000 U2 received the keys to which city?
17 Which Beatle announced his engagement in 2001?
18 Which band's singles include "Common People" and "Disco 2000"?
19 Which band did Sting front?
20 Which late blue-eyed superstar had the first names Francis Albert?
21 Which *Jagged Little* album was a huge hit for Alanis Morissette?
22 Bjorn Again are a tribute band to which superstars?
23 Which Irish band made the album *By Request*?
24 Which Diana fronted The Supremes?
25 Eric Clapton had a transatlantic hit with "I Shot" who?
26 Which Presley married Michael Jackson?
27 Which George's early solo single was "Careless Whisper"?
28 Which band's singles include "Australia" and "A Design For Life"?
29 Who had hit albums *True Blue* and *Erotica*?
30 Who had huge hits with "Sacrifice" and "Rocket Man"?

TECHNOLOGY See quiz 36, page 44
1 Calculator. **2** *Toy Story.* **3** Cars. **4** Earthquakes. **5** Sky. **6** Sewing machine. **7** Sun.
8 1970s. **9** 1960s. **10** Two. **11** Water. **12** Read. **13** Fax. **14** Car. **15** Camera.
16 Apple Macintosh. **17** Personal. **18** Internet. **19** Stars. **20** Menu. **21** Bar code.
22 Temperature. **23** Camera. **24** Lap top. **25** Millennium bug. **26** Hearing.
27 Voice mail **28** 1980s. **29** IBM. **30** Hypertext.

ANSWERS

QUIZ 35 POT LUCK 16

Answers - see Quiz 33, page 41

1 What went before Bill in the Wild West's William Cody's name?
2 Sergey Bubka broke over 30 world records in which event?
3 What is the largest of the Earth's oceans?
4 Who wrote *The BFG* and *Revolting Rhymes*?
5 How many times did Queen Elizabeth I marry?
6 On which sporting surface did Wayne Gretzky find fame?
7 Which scientist pioneered the pasteurisation process to purify milk?
8 In the UK and the USA what is the most common surname for people?
9 The Aztecs came from which part of the world?
10 Which word names a Greek Island and a lettuce?
11 Other than English, which language is spoken in Canada?
12 Who went with Butthead in the TV series?
13 In the Bible which infant was hidden in bulrushes for his own safety?
14 Which famous composer had the first names Wolfgang Amadeus?
15 Which part of London, famous for its carnival, shares its name with a movie starring Hugh Grant?
16 What was the title of the Russian monarchs?
17 How many fortnights are there in two years?
18 Which characters had a vacuum cleaner called Noo Noo?
19 The Richter scale measures the strength of what?
20 On which continent is the world's largest desert?
21 Detroit's nickname is Motown – what does Motown stand for?
22 Masters Trophy, Nobel Prize and Oscar – which of these awards links with science?
23 Earth takes 365 days to travel round what?
24 What type of weapon is a kukri?
25 What kind of "Day" gave U2 a No 1 hit?
26 What does a testator make?
27 In whist, which trumps usually follow on after Hearts in descending order?
28 How many legs do a group of twelve seahorses have between them?
29 What colour are the stars on the American flag?
30 Paper, soap and television – which of these items could not have been found in a house in 1901?

POT LUCK 15 See quiz 33, page 41

ANSWERS

1 Newspaper. 2 B. 3 Crossbow. 4 April. 5 West. 6 Clooney. 7 Switzerland. 8 USA. 9 Knight. 10 Bells. 11 Wardrobe. 12 Crab. 13 New York. 14 Brazil. 15 Twelve. 16 France. 17 Carbon dioxide. 18 Sesame Street. 19 Baton. 20 Egypt. 21 K2. 22 Travolta. 23 Fish. 24 Play it. 25 Mastermind. 26 Golden goal. 27 Bikini. 28 Below it. 29 Fleet Street. 30 Her nose.

QUIZ 36 TECHNOLOGY

Answers - see Quiz 34, page 42

1   An abacus was an early type of what?
2   Which was the first full length feature film designed completely on computer?
3   What did engineer Louis Renault manufacture?
4   Charles Richter's scale measures what dangerous phenomenon?
5   Which of the following is a UK satellite TV company, Sky, Sun, Mars?
6   Which needlework machine did Isaac Singer invent?
7   What provides solar power?
8   In which decade did Apple computers first appear?
9   In which decade did man first land on the Moon?
10 A stereo music system has a minimum of how many speakers?
11 An aqueduct was constructed to carry what?
12 In CD-ROM what does the letter R stand for?
13 What is the more common name for a facsimile telegraphy machine?
14 The Ford Model T was an early model of what form of transport?
15 Which of these inventions was developed first – the camera, the modem or satellite television?
16 What make is a computer which has an apple symbol on it?
17 What does P refer to in PCs?
18 Which system of communication developed from ARPANET?
19 Astronomy is the study of what?
20 What's the name for the selection bar at the top of a computer monitor?
21 What kind of code is scanned at a supermarket?
22 What does a thermostat control?
23 Polaroid is a type of what?
24 What name is given to is a portable computer?
25 What computer problem was feared, seemingly unnecessarily, for 2000?
26 Audio refers to which of the senses?
27 Which mail is a type of telephone answering machine?
28 In which decade were PCs invented?
29 Which company manufactured the first generally available PC?
30 What does H stand for in HTTP?

MUSIC SUPERSTARS *See quiz 34, page 42*

1 Garfunkel. 2 Rod. 3 Madonna. 4 Queen. 5 Michael. 6 "Candle in the Wind". 7 *Spice*. 8 Three. 9 Blur. 10 Bob Marley. 11 Shania Twain. 12 Robbie Williams. 13 George Michael. 14 Queen. 15 Tom Jones. 16 Dublin. 17 Paul McCartney. 18 Pulp. 19 Police. 20 Sinatra. 21 *Pill*. 22 Abba. 23 Boyzone. 24 Ross. 25 "The Sheriff". 26 Lisa. 27 George Michael. 28 Manic Street Preachers. 29 Madonna. 30 Elton John.

QUIZ 37 POT LUCK 17

Answers - see Quiz 39, page 47

1 Which L is a country on the south-eastern frontier of Belgium?
2 Which was developed last – space flight, television or the telephone?
3 Born in Yugoslavia, Monica Seles eventually played for which country?
4 Which is the world's lowest sea?
5 Which sauce is eaten with turkey at Thanksgiving in the USA?
6 Which word names a mobile home and also a line of camels?
7 Which young blonde is a *Vampire Slayer* on TV?
8 How is Uluru also known?
9 Which sport is governed by FIFA?
10 What is the day job of the characters in *Baywatch*?
11 What was the first name of the Queen of Scots, beheaded in 1587?
12 What breed of dog was film and TV star Lassie?
13 How many continents is Russia in?
14 What main colour goes with white on the flag of Argentina?
15 Who can a contestant phone in *Who Wants To Be A Millionaire*?
16 Cleopatra's Needle now standing in London came from which country?
17 How many letters appear in the English alphabet before Q?
18 If Albert is the dad and Harold is the son what is the famous TV sitcom?
19 Brass was originally made from copper and which other metal?
20 The star sign Gemini is represented as what?
21 What is the French word meaning yellow?
22 How many straight lines are needed to make a plus sign?
23 Who won the first FA Cup Final played in Cardiff?
24 The coast of Belgium is on which Sea?
25 What is the colour of the cheapest property on a Monopoly board?
26 The most common pub name in the UK is The Red what – Giraffe, Lion or Elephant?
27 Which place name can go before Triangle and shorts?
28 Which initials are linked with genetic fingerprinting?
29 Diwali is an important feast in which religion?
30 How many individual squares are there on a chess board?

TV QUIZ & GAME SHOWS See quiz 39, page 47

ANSWERS

1 No limit. 2 Anne Robinson 3 Two. 4 Ulrika Jonsson. 5 *Celebrity Ready Steady Cook*.
6 *The Generation Game*. 7 Schofield. 8 John Parrott. 9 Channel Four. 10 Keith.
11 Tennis player. 12 Unlucky. 13 Mortimer. 14 *The Price Is Right*. 15 *Your Cards*.
16 Telephone. 17 Leather. 18 *Gladiators*. 19 Cilla's. 20 Trophy. 21 *Moment*.
22 Barrymore. 23 Smillie. 24 O'Connor. 25 Dustbin. 26 University Challenge.
27 Woman. 28 *They Think It's All Over*. 29 Glass. 30 £10,000.

QUIZ 38 SPORTING WHO'S WHO?

Answers - see Quiz 40, page 48

1   Mario Andretti found fame in which sport?
2   Which sisters fought out the US Open tennis final in 2001?
3   By which first name was cricketer Sir Garfield Sobers known?
4   What is the first name of the amateur golfer Rose who finished third in the 1999 Open Championship?
5   Decathlete Dean Macey competes in how many events?
6   How was athlete James Cleveland Owens better known?
7   Clive Lloyd captained which international cricket side?
8   Which young golfer was *Sports Illustrated*'s sportsman of the year in 1996?
9   Which sport did Michael Jordan play professionally for more than 12 years?
10 Which Marion is second only to Flo Jo as the fastest woman ever?
11 Who did the late Don Bradman play international cricket for?
12 Which country does racing driver Riccardo Patrese come from?
13 How did golfer Payne Stewart meet his tragic death in 1999?
14 What type of sporting competitor was Lammtarra?
15 Which Mr Fallon is a top money winning jockey?
16 Which national side did rugby's Rob Andrew play for?
17 Czech born Martina Hingis represents which country?
18 In which sport did Shaquille O'Neal make his name – and a fortune?
19 In which sport did Australian Dawn Fraser find fame?
20 World record holder Zola Budd originally came from which country?
21 What is the first name of South African rugby star Pienaar?
22 Novelist Dick Francis had a successful career as what type of sportsman?
23 Which Champion rode the Grand National winner Aldaniti in 1981?
24 Jockey Lester Piggott served a prison sentence for what evasion?
25 Will Carling captained which national rugby side?
26 Franz Klammer and Jean-Claude Killy are famous names in which winter sport?
27 What is the first name of Finnish F1 driver Hakkinen?
28 Graham Gooch is from which English county?
29 Which Caribbean island did Merlene Ottey compete for?
30 Maurice Greene sprints for which country?

POT LUCK 18 *See quiz 40, page 48*

QUIZ 39 QUIZ & GAME SHOWS

Answers - see Quiz 37, page 45

1 How long does the contestant have to answer the question in *Who Wants To Be A Millionaire?*?
2 Who asked the questions in the US version of *The Weakest Link*?
3 How many teams take part in one episode of *University Challenge*?
4 Which Swedish-born personality first presented *Dog Eat Dog*?
5 What is *Ready Steady Cook* with famous stars providing the ingredients called?
6 Lea Kristensen helped Jim Davidson on which Saturday night family show?
7 Which Phillip hosted *National Lottery: Winning Lines*?
8 Which snooker player led a team opposite Ally McCoist on *A Question of Sport*?
9 On which Channel was the afternoon show *Number One* shown?
10 Which actress Penelope presented a later series of *What's My Line?*?
11 Annabel Croft was what type of sportswoman before taking part in the 1980s *Treasure Hunt*?
12 In *Strike It Rich*, was a hotspot lucky or unlucky?
13 If Vic was Reeves who was Bob in *Shooting Stars*?
14 On which show did Leslie Crowther invite contestants to, "come on down."?
15 What did Bruce Forsyth invite contestants to *Play Right*?
16 Which means of communication replaced postal votes on *Opportunity Knocks*?
17 What was the chair covering made from on the original *Mastermind*?
18 Which show shared its name with Roman fighters?
19 Whose *Moment of Truth* is a family quiz show?
20 What was the prize in *The Krypton Factor*?
21 Mel B hosted the talent show, *This Is My* what?
22 Which Michael struck it *Lucky* then struck it *Rich*?
23 Which future TV star Carol was a hostess on *Wheel of Fortune*?
24 Which Des presented the 1990s *Take Your Pick*?
25 What receptacle was the booby prize on *3–2–1*?
26 Which student show has the phrase, "Your starter for 10"?
27 Was the first *Who Wants To Be A Millionaire?* millionaire a man or a woman?
28 Which sports quiz always ends with the end of the famous sporting quote, "It is now."?
29 What was the trophy usually made from on *Mastermind*?
30 How many thousand is the top prize on *Dog Eats Dog*?

POT LUCK 17 See quiz 37, page 45

ANSWERS

1 Luxembourg. 2 Space flight. 3 USA. 4 Dead Sea. 5 Cranberry. 6 Caravan.
7 *Buffy*. 8 Ayers Rock. 9 Football. 10 Lifeguards. 11 Mary. 12 Collie. 13 Two.
14 Light blue. 15 A friend. 16 Egypt. 17 16. 18 Steptoe & Son. 19 Zinc.
20 Twins. 21 Jaune. 22 Two. 23 Liverpool. 24 North. 25 Brown. 26 Lion.
27 Bermuda. 28 DNA. 29 Hindu. 30 64.

QUIZ 40 POT LUCK 18

Answers - see Quiz 38, page 46

1 For which movie with *Woman* in the title was Julia Roberts nominated for an Oscar?
2 What would a mural be painted on?
3 Which of these is not the name of a note in music – E, G or I?
4 Nero was the Emperor of which ancient empire when its main city was destroyed?
5 What was the first name of Boy Scouts founder Baden-Powell?
6 Lazlo Biro's most famous invention was used for what?
7 Mother Teresa was particularly noted for her work with the poor of which country?
8 Which studio made *The Lion King*?
9 What is another name for a cavy?
10 In the 1980s, over 250 died after a terrorist bomb exploded a plane over which town in Scotland?
11 Christopher Columbus became convinced that the Earth was what shape?
12 In Spanish, what is the number quatro?
13 What is the name of the largest species of penguin?
14 In heraldry, what is argent?
15 In which month is St David's Day?
16 Which of Madison, Maryland or Montana is not a state of the USA?
17 Who is Homer Simpson's boss?
18 Who had a hit single with "Independent Woman"?
19 The Angel, in Venezuela, is the world's highest what?
20 In digits, what time is quarter to five in the afternoon on a 24-hour clock?
21 What is the top colour on a rainbow?
22 What colour goes before land to name the world's largest island?
23 What is named after George Everest who was a Surveyor General of India?
24 Was Britney Spears' second album called *Best of Britney*, *Oops I Did It Again* or *True Brit*?
25 Nigeria is the largest country in which continent?
26 Who gave his name to a reading system designed for people who are visually impaired?
27 Which of the following is not a citrus fruit – lemon, lime or pear?
28 *The Blue Planet* was a TV documentary series about life where?
29 A pagoda is a type of what?
30 In which TV series did Lt Mitch Buchannon appear?

SPORTING WHO'S WHO? *See quiz 38, page 46*

ANSWERS

1 Motor racing. 2 Venus and Serena Williams. 3 Gary. 4 Justin. 5 Ten. 6 Jesse. 7 West Indies. 8 Tiger Woods. 9 Basketball. 10 Jones. 11 Australia. 12 Italy. 13 His Lear Jet suffered decompression, killing all on board, and later crashed. 14 Horse. 15 Kieren. 16 England. 17 Switzerland. 18 Basketball. 19 Swimming. 20 South Africa. 21 Francois. 22 Jockey. 23 Bob. 24 Tax. 25 England. 26 Skiing. 27 Mika. 28 Essex. 29 Jamaica. 30 USA.

QUIZ 41 HEADLINES

Answers - see Quiz 43, page 51

1 Tracey Emin caused a sensation with her work of art of a dirty and untidy what?
2 The Good Friday Agreement was drawn up to help solve problems in which part of the UK?
3 In which decade did Queen Elizabeth II come to the throne?
4 Rasputin hit the headlines for activities in which country?
5 Which island has a political party called Sinn Fein?
6 Which Princess did the future Lord Snowdon marry in 1960?
7 How was the trades union Solidarnosc known in English?
8 Which Maxwell disappeared off his yacht in 1991 before news about misappropriation of pension funds?
9 Marilyn Monroe is thought to have died due to an overdose of what?
10 Which Louis was killed by an IRA bomb in 1979?
11 BSE was also called mad what disease?
12 Which African country entertained only rebel cricket tours because its policy on apartheid meant no official tours could be made?
13 Ken Russell was a controversial name in which area of the arts?
14 Peter Mandelson was Secretary of State for which country before his controversial resignation?
15 Which tax, also called community charge, was the cause of riots in the 1990s?
16 1990's round the world yacht Maiden had a crew made up entirely of who or what?
17 Sir Ranulph Fiennes hit the headlines in what capacity?
18 In the 1970s the Americans withdrew troops from which V?
19 Which country has had most experience of spaceflight?
20 The campaign to ban which weapons was supported by Princess Diana?
21 Which O in Northern Ireland was the scene of an horrific bomb in 1998?
22 Which Royal ship ceased service at the end of the 1990s?
23 Apartheid was most well known in which African country?
24 Which television dolls virtually walked off the shelves in a 1990s Christmas buying frenzy?
25 Which sculpture of the North was erected near Gateshead?
26 Which meat did the government ban from being eaten on the bone during the crisis concerning BSE?
27 Princess Anne's daughter Zara hit the headlines with a pierced what?
28 In which decade did Edmund Hillary climb Everest?
29 Salman Rushdie hit the headlines with a controversial what?
30 How many goals did France score when they beat Brazil to win the World Cup?

GARDENING See quiz 43, page 51

ANSWERS

1 Yellow. 2 Wood. 3 Three. 4 Leaves. 5 Artichokes. 6 Over plants. 7 Bulbs.
8 Cut. 9 Cooking. 10 Lawnmower. 11 Compost. 12 Beans. 13 Hedge. 14 Holly.
15 Lavender. 16 Brownish/black. 17 One. 18 Small. 19 Roses. 20 Rockery.
21 Blue. 22 Sweet. 23 Cones. 24 Greenhouse. 25 Apples. 26 William.
27 Mowing. 28 Bulbs. 29 Blue. 30 Elderberries.

QUIZ 42   POT LUCK 19

Answers - see Quiz 44, page 52

1 Which actor links The Beach, Titanic and The Man In The Iron Mask?
2 How many people make up Westlife?
3 Who is in the title with The Owl in Edward Lear's poem?
4 What is FBI Agent Scully's first name in The X Files?
5 How many people are involved in a fencing match?
6 The movie Gandhi was about a hero of which country?
7 What are the sides of a stage called?
8 In music, the lines on which notes are written go in which direction?
9 Which people used C, D, L and M in their counting system?
10 John Glenn became the first person over 70 to do what?
11 What is the first name of Ms Hill who sang with the Fugees?
12 Which Texan gave his name to a tall hat – was it Homburg, Stetson or Tengallon?
13 A Bruxellois is a person coming from which city?
14 Which Kid was Butch Cassidy's sidekick?
15 Which of these three spoons is the largest – a coffeespoon, a dessertspoon or a tablespoon?
16 What is the piece of the mushroom above the stalk called?
17 What were the pyramids made out of?
18 In the past, Kampuchea was known by which of these names: Cambodia, Sri Lanka or Thailand?
19 Which common kitchen item can also be a type of drum?
20 Which girl band made a a movie called Honest?
21 Jonathan Edwards won an Olympic gold medal in which event?
22 What job did Peter and Andrew do before becoming disciples of Jesus?
23 Geometry is a branch of which subject?
24 Coal, diamonds, leather – which of these three items is not mined from underground?
25 What is the first of the three letters that invites you to turn over a piece of paper?
26 How many spaces are contained in a frame for noughts and crosses?
27 On a camera, what opens and closes to allow light in?
28 Is a kayak a type of currency, a hairy animal or a sailing craft?
29 Whose first No 1 hit was "Because We Want To"?
30 In the nursery rhyme Hey Diddle Diddle, who did a runner with the dish?

ANSWERS

1 Lou Reed. 2 Andrew Lloyd Webber. 3 Madonna. 4 Michael Jackson. 5 Ireland. 6 Suede. 7 Enrique. 8 U2. 9 Michael. 10 Robbie Williams. 11 Lopez. 12 Phil. 13 Noel. 14 Spice Girls. 15 Britney Spears. 16 Eternal. 17 Kylie Minogue. 18 Adams. 19 Take That. 20 Eva. 21 Three. 22 Barbie. 23 Canada. 24 Martin. 25 Sonny. 26 Kitten. 27 Five. 28 Simply Red. 29 Stephen. 30 Sinatra.

QUIZ 43 GARDENING

Answers - see Quiz 41, page 49

1 What is the most common colour for a daffodil?
2 What is decking usually made from?
3 How many people usually make up TV's Ground Force team?
4 What is a plant's foliage?
5 Which vegetables can be globe or Jerusalem?
6 Where does a cloche go?
7 What are tulips grown from?
8 What do secateurs do?
9 What are culinary herbs used for?
10 Which piece of garden equipment can be hover or rotary?
11 Which heap provides fertiliser for the garden?
12 Which vegetables can be French or broad?
13 If you grew a box in your garden what would it be?
14 Which prickly green shrub with red berries is a Christmas decoration?
15 Which purple aromatic plant takes its name from the Latin Lavo, meaning I wash?
16 What colour is peat?
17 How many wheels does a wheelbarrow usually have?
18 What is significant about bonsai plants?
19 Hybrid tea and floribunda are types of what?
20 Which part of the garden has decorative stones?
21 What is the most common colour of a cornflower?
22 Which Peas are decorative flowers?
23 What do conifers produce?
24 Which house is used for rearing delicate plants?
25 What sort of fruit do you grow if you grow Cox' s Orange Pippin and Bramley?
26 Which princely name follows Sweet in a cottage garden plant?
27 Which word describes cutting a lawn?
28 What do lilies grow from?
29 What is the most common colour for a delphinium?
30 Which fruits follow elderflowers?

HEADLINES *See quiz 41, page 49*

ANSWERS

1 Bed. 2 Northern Ireland. 3 1950s. 4 Russia. 5 Ireland. 6 Margaret. 7 Solidarity.
8 Robert. 9 Sleeping pills. 10 Mountbatten. 11 Cow. 12 South Africa. 13 Film.
14 Northern Ireland. 15 Poll Tax. 16 Women. 17 Explorer. 18 Vietnam.
19 Russia/USSR. 20 Landmines. 21 Omagh. 22 "Britannia". 23 South Africa.
24 Teletubbies. 25 Angel. 26 Beef. 27 Tongue. 28 1950s. 29 Book. 30 Three.

QUIZ 44 MUSIC WHO'S WHO?

Answers - see Quiz 42, page 50

1 How is Lewis Allan Reed better known?
2 Who is Timothy Miles Bindon Rice's most famous musical collaborator?
3 Who won the MTV Best Video for *Ray of Light*?
4 Who recorded the album *Thriller*?
5 Where do The Corrs come from?
6 Which band's singles include "Trash" and "Stay Together"?
7 Which Iglesias made the albums *Bailamos* and *Cosas El Amor*?
8 Which Irish band made the album *The Joshua Tree*?
9 Which Jackson has had the most platinum albums in the UK?
10 Which ex Take That member won a Brit Award for "Angel" in 1999?
11 Which Jennifer's name was linked to that of rapper Puff Daddy?
12 Which Collins, formerly of Genesis, won awards for his songs for the movie *Tarzan*?
13 Who is the oldest Gallagher brother?
14 Which band's singles include *2 Become 1* and *Too Much*?
15 Which teen queen charted with "Born To Make You Happy"?
16 Louise, aka Mrs Jamie Redknapp, belonged to which all girl band?
17 Which Aussie songstress got to No 1 on both sides of the Atlantic with "Spinning Around"?
18 What was Victoria Beckham's maiden name?
19 Which band's singles included "Relight My Fire" and "Back For Good"?
20 Which Cassidy had a posthumous hit with "Over The Rainbow"?
21 How many Bee Gees are there?
22 Which toy "Girl" was a hit for Aqua?
23 Which country does Celine Dion come from?
24 Which Ricky had the top selling album *Vuelve* in 1999?
25 Who was Cher's singing partner on her very first UK hit?
26 Which Atomic band had a hit with "Eternal Flame"?
27 How many members of Boyzone are there?
28 Which Mick Hucknall band has had the most platinum albums of any band in the UK?
29 What is the first name of songwriter Sondheim?
30 Which Frank was 70 when he had a single in the top ten?

POT LUCK 19 *See quiz 42, page 50*
1 Leonardo diCaprio. 2 Five. 3 *The Pussy Cat.* 4 Dana. 5 Two. 6 India. 7 Wings.
8 Horizontally. 9 Romans. 10 Travel in space. 11 Lauryn. 12 Stetson. 13 Brussels.
14 Sundance. 15 Tablespoon. 16 Cap. 17 Stone. 18 Cambodia. 19 Kettle.
20 All Saints. 21 Triple jump. 22 Fishermen. 23 Mathematics. 24 Leather. 25 P.
26 Nine. 27 Shutter. 28 Sailing craft. 29 Billie. 30 The spoon.

ANSWERS

QUIZ 45 POT LUCK 20

Answers - see Quiz 47, page 55

1 The Appleton girls were in which pop band?
2 What were the initials of foodmaker Mr Heinz?
3 Which Prince did Sophie Rhys Jones marry?
4 Orly airport is in which country?
5 VSO stands for what type of charitable service overseas?
6 In which country did Madonna marry in 2000?
7 What is the dog called in a Punch and Judy show?
8 In Enid Blyton's stories, what colour is Noddy's hat?
9 In which series did Rowf the dog play piano?
10 Queen Nefertiti ruled in which country?
11 In song, Nancy Sinatra had boots that were made for doing what?
12 In which country would you watch Real Sociedad play a home soccer match?
13 In which decade was Diana Spencer– later Princess Diana – born?
14 In military diplomacy SALT involves what kind of limitation talks – Secret Arms, Specialist Arms or Strategic Arms?
15 What did a spinet make?
16 What is the occupation of Phil, David and Tony Archer in the radio soap?
17 What type of map indicates areas of high and low ground?
18 What is the pattern on a bumblebee?
19 The port of Plymouth is in England and which other country?
20 Is Terry Wogan's radio show in the morning or the evening?
21 Which is the last month in a calendar year to have exactly 30 days?
22 In the signs of the zodiac, Pisces represents which creature?
23 What can be a sheet of paper or part of a plant?
24 How is the famous French lady Jeanne d'Arc known in English?
25 Which animal's 'eyes' did Percy Shaw invent to help motorists?
26 Thomas Barnardo set up homes for what type of people?
27 Which word completes the Shania Twain album title Come On ____?
28 What shaped puzzle did Mr Rubik invent?
29 Does the letter P in OPEC stand for – petroleum, plastic or price?
30 In which country is the musical Cabaret set?

ANSWERS

POT LUCK 21 *See quiz 47, page 55*
1 Saxophone. 2 None. 3 Bear. 4 Friendly. 5 Germany. 6 Leaves (vegetation).
7 Blood. 8 On land. 9 Nocturnal. 10 Change colour. 11 Vacuum cleaner.
12 The X Files. 13 Calorie. 14 Abacus. 15 Russia. 16 Yellow. 17 Japan.
18 Ballet. 19 Ginger. 20 Thomas. 21 Silver. 22 Drew Barrymore. 23 Little.
24 Fat. 25 USA. 26 China. 27 Second. 28 Kingdom. 29 Metals. 30 Steam.

QUIZ 46 MOVIES – GOLDEN OLDIES

Answers - see Quiz 48, page 56

1 Which bird's name goes between *Where* and *Dare* in the Richard Burton/Clint Eastwood film?
2 Which director Alfred's first Hollywood movie was *Rebecca*?
3 In which country is *The Sound of Music* set?
4 Which TV canine star was originally a male called Pal?
5 Where did Tarzan live?
6 On which night of the week was there *Night Fever*?
7 What went after "White" in the seasonal song from the movie *Holiday Inn*?
8 In which decade was *Gone With the Wind* made?
9 How many *Commandments* were in the title of the 1950s classic?
10 Which 1940s classic had the Ugly Sisters among its characters?
11 In how many days did David Niven travel *Around the World* in 1956?
12 Where was *An American* in the 1950s movie?
13 The action for *Bridge On The River Kwai* was set in which war?
14 Which musical movie was based on Dickens' *Oliver Twist*?
15 Which *High* time of day was an award winning movie with Gary Cooper?
16 Where was Gene Kelly *Singin'* in 1952?
17 Which Walt directed the first eight Oscar winning animation films?
18 What sort of animal was Bugs?
19 Who was the hero of *Goldfinger*?
20 What were the first movies with speech called?
21 What was the first name of movie star Ms Swanson?
22 *All Quiet* on which *Front* was a classic of the 1930s?
23 Which *Man* was a post-war thriller set in Vienna?
24 John Wayne was famous for playing what type of character?
25 Which future US President starred in *Stallion Road* in the 1940s?
26 Which convenient initials did the grumpy actor Fields have?
27 What type of *Encounter* did Celia Johnson and Trevor Howard have?
28 What was the name of the *Citizen* in the all time classic with Orson Welles?
29 What colour Brick Road was followed in *The Wizard of Oz*?
30 *Born Free* was about which African cats?

CELEBS See quiz 48, page 56

ANSWERS

1 Your house. 2 Andrew Lloyd Webber. 3 Sophie. 4 Red. 5 Frankie. 6 Feltz. 7 Richard. 8 Jules. 9 Madonna. 10 Nigella. 11 Cooking. 12 Wogan. 13 Wales. 14 Turner. 15 Butler. 16 Windsor. 17 Vet. 18 Jonathan. 19 Red. 20 Scotland. 21 David. 22 Swansea. 23 Harrison. 24 Cricketer. 25 Michael. 26 Hervey. 27 Clarissa. 28 Hurley. 29 Mansell. 30 Denise.

QUIZ 47 POT LUCK 21

Answers - see Quiz 45, page 53

1 Which instrument does Lisa play in *The Simpsons*?
2 How many teeth do most human babies have at birth?
3 What type of animal is Fozzie in *The Muppets*?
4 In comic books and movies what word describes Casper the ghost?
5 Supermodel Claudia Schiffer comes from which country?
6 A giraffe's diet consists mainly of what?
7 What contains red and white corpuscles?
8 Where did George Stephenson's Rocket travel – on land, on sea or in space?
9 A creature that is more active at night is said to be what?
10 What does a chameleon do to disguise itself?
11 What kind of machine did William Hoover develop?
12 Which TV series had the line "The truth is out there."?
13 Which of these terms is a measure of energy in food, calorie, fat, cholesterol?
14 Which ancient counting device uses beads and string?
15 Anna Kournikova is originally from which country?
16 What colour is Nintendo's Pikachu?
17 The first Disneyland in Asia was built in which country?
18 An entrechat and a glissade appear in what type of dancing?
19 Who made up the original Spice Girls along with Baby, Posh, Sporty and Scary?
20 The Rev Awdry wrote about which Tank Engine?
21 Which precious metal is associated with the Lone Ranger?
22 How is movie star Andrew Blyth Barrymore better known?
23 What did Stevie Wonder have before his name when he was a young performer?
24 What does a camel keep stored in its hump?
25 What is Britney Spears' home country?
26 Life size figures in terracotta of an army were found in which country?
27 Did World War I begin in the first, second or third decade of the 20th century?
28 A king rules a kingdom but what does a queen rule?
29 An alloy is a combination of two different what?
30 What powered James Watt's engine built in 1777?

ANSWERS

POT LUCK 20 *See quiz 45, page 53*
1 All Saints. 2 HJ. 3 Edward. 4 France. 5 Voluntary. 6 Scotland. 7 Toby. 8 Blue.
9 *The Muppets*. 10 Egypt. 11 Walking. 12 Spain. 13 1960s. 14 Strategic Arms.
15 Music. 16 Farmers. 17 Relief map. 18 Stripes. 19 America. 20 Morning.
21 November. 22 Fish. 23 Leaf. 24 Joan of Arc. 25 Cat's. 26 Children. 27 *Over*.
28 Cube. 29 Petroleum. 30 Germany.

QUIZ 48 CELEBS

Answers - see Quiz 46, page 54

1 What would you ask Laurence Llewellyn Bowen to design?
2 Sarah Brightman was married to which big theatre name?
3 Which Ms Dahl is famous in the modelling world?
4 What colour is Charlie Dimmock's hair?
5 How is Lanfranco Dettori better known?
6 Which Vanessa was in the celebrity *Big Brother* House?
7 Who left *This Morning* with Judy in 2001?
8 What is Jamie Oliver's wife called?
9 Guy Ritchie married which US megastar in 2000?
10 Which Lawson was dubbed 'a domestic goddess?
11 What were the *Two Fat Ladies* famous for on TV?
12 Which radio 2 star Terry's autobiography was called *Is It Me?*
13 From which part of the UK does Catherine Zeta Jones hail?
14 What is the surname of TV sister celebs Anthea and Wendy?
15 What was the position of the ex employee of Princess Diana who was arrested for theft of some of her property?
16 Which Barbara went from *Carry On* films to *EastEnders*?
17 Trude Mostue found TV fame in which profession?
18 Who is Paul Ross's famous younger brother?
19 Ex *EastEnder* Patsy Palmer aka Bianca has what colour hair?
20 The name of which country does Sean Connery have tattooed on his arm?
21 Which Mellor was dubbed the Minister of Fun?
22 Prince Charles received the freedom of which city, which has a link with his title?
23 Which Ford split with wife Melissa Mathison in 2001?
24 Jemima Khan married what type of sportsman in Imran Khan?
25 Which actor is ex beauty queen Shakira Caine married to?
26 What is the surname of tabloid celeb Lady Victoria?
27 What is the first name of Ms Dickson Wright, famous for her cooking and country pursuits?
28 Which Elizabeth ceased to be the main face of Estee Lauder in 2001?
29 Which ex racing driver Nigel has a black belt in judo?
30 What is the first name of TV blonde Ms Van Outen?

MOVIES – GOLDEN OLDIES See quiz 46, page 54

ANSWERS

1 *Eagles*. 2 Hitchcock. 3 Austria. 4 Lassie. 5 Jungle. 6 *Saturday*. 7 "Christmas".
8 1930s. 9 Ten. 10 *Cinderella*. 11 80. 12 Paris. 13 WWII. 14 *Oliver!* 15 Noon.
16 "In The Rain". 17 Disney. 18 Bunny. 19 James Bond. 20 Talkies. 21 Gloria.
22 *Western*. 23 *Third Man*. 24 Cowboy. 25 Ronald Reagan. 26 WC. 27 *Brief*.
28 *Kane*. 29 Yellow. 30 Lions.

QUIZ 49 POT LUCK 22

Answers - see Quiz 51, page 59

1 Which sprinter Michael won 200m and 400m gold at the Atlanta Olympics?
2 Which group included two girls with the same name but differentiated by letters of the alphabet?
3 Which W is a jacket that has no sleeves?
4 Which form of transport is Christopher Cockerell famous for developing?
5 What is the name for the place where coins manufactured?
6 Who was Gilbert's partner in writing comic operas?
7 What do you do if you dawdle – do you idle, do you run or do you rinse your mouth out?
8 In rhyme, what precedes "paddywack, give the dog a bone."?
9 Kissing the Blarney Stone is supposed to gift you the power to do what?
10 What is the usual colour of healthy parsley?
11 What were people looking for in the 1840s 'Rush' to California?
12 What sort of pit do athletes jump into during a triple jump?
13 Which Jennifer married Brad Pitt?
14 Which swimming stroke is named after an insect?
15 Which pop singer had a son called Prince Michael?
16 Which fabric is made from flax?
17 Korea is divided into how many countries?
18 Algeria is in which part of Africa?
19 Which classical composer had the names George Frederick?
20 According to the TV programme title *Sabrina is The Teenage* what – Doctor, Vampire or Witch?
21 At which Hill do *The Teletubbies* live?
22 In which Disney classic movie does Jiminy Cricket appear?
23 Which of these musical instruments does not use a reed when being played – clarinet, guitar or oboe?
24 How often is American football's Super Bowl contested?
25 In the wartime song what do you pack up in your old kit bag?
26 Which of black, purple and yellow is a primary colour?
27 In fiction, what did Oliver Twist ask for after he had eaten all his food in the workhouse?
28 Attila was a leader of which tribe of which group of people?
29 Which B is the second largest city in Spain?
30 In which country is the musical *Evita* set?

POT LUCK 23 *See quiz 51, page 59*

ANSWERS

QUIZ 50 TV CLASSICS

Answers - see Quiz 52, page 60

1 Who is Tracey's sister in *Birds of a Feather*?
2 Which series set in a prison shared its name with a breakfast food?
3 Who was Tom's wife in *The Good Life*?
4 What is British TV's longest running children's show?
5 Which BBC show ended its Saturday night run in 2001 when Premiership football moved to ITV?
6 On which night of the week is *Songs of Praise* usually shown?
7 Which *Team* included Mr T?
8 Which series with John Cleese was set in a hotel in Torquay?
9 Who was Inspector Morse's sidekick?
10 What was the occupation of Perry Mason?
11 Sergeant Wilson and Captain Mainwaring were in which *Army*?
12 In Morecambe & Wise, what was Morecambe's first name?
13 What was the nickname of Simon Templar, first played by Roger Moore?
14 Which *Challenge* was first presented by Bamber Gascoigne and later by Jeremy Paxman?
15 Which *Cars* were an early police drama?
16 Which *Doctor* first appeared in the 1960s in a phone box?
17 Which *Roundabout* became a children's classic?
18 What was the 90s revival of the classic *How* called?
19 *Jeux Sans Frontières* was also called *It's A* what?
20 Which Prime Minister's father in law was in *Till Death Us Do Part*?
21 Which weapon was used in the game show *The Golden Shot*?
22 Where did singer Val Doonican hail from?
23 Which puppet bear had friends called Sweep and Soo?
24 Which show was associated with a *Flying Circus*?
25 Who presented *The Generation Game* back in the 1970s?
26 Which Mike was famous for his impressions especially of politicians?
27 Barry Norman began the first of many review programmes on which subject in 1972?
28 John Craven pioneered a *Newsround* programme for whom?
29 What colour was the chair in *Mastermind*?
30 Which Mill hosted a lunchtime programme at one o'clock from the Midlands?

QUIZ 51   POT LUCK 23

Answers - see Quiz 49, page 57

1 In which country did Benazir Bhutto become the Prime Minister – Afghanistan, India or Pakistan?
2 What sort of engine was invented by Frank Whittle?
3 Which unofficial title is given to the wife of a US President?
4 What was the first name of scientist Newton?
5 Saddam Hussein first came to power in which country?
6 Which Winona links the movies *Little Women*, *The Crucible* and *Alien: Resurrection*?
7 Isis and Osiris were gods of which ancient people?
8 Which sewing items can also be a sharp pain?
9 A palais glide is a type of what?
10 On a Monopoly board, what colour is the most expensive property?
11 How many players are on court in a game of tennis singles?
12 What do the British call what the Americans call a diaper?
13 What was the main obstacle preventing King Edward VIII marrying Mrs Simpson?
14 Queen Boudicca led a revolt against which people?
15 What happens to water at 100 degrees centigrade?
16 What's the name for the instructions or programs used in computers?
17 Astronomer Edmond Halley gave his name to what?
18 What is the wife of an Earl called?
19 St Christopher is the patron saint of which group of people?
20 How many sides does a decagon have?
21 Which name can go before the words frost and knife?
22 Which part of the Earth was Jacques Cousteau famous for exploring?
23 What can be either a piece of thread or a long story?
24 Which device from the French Revolution is now used to trim paper?
25 What was the first leap year beginning with the numbers 20?
26 Which General made his 'last stand' at the Battle of The Little Big Horn?
27 Where on her body would a Muslim woman wear a yashmak?
28 Is a sorbet served hot, iced or warm?
29 What colour blood are you said to have if you have a noble family?
30 Which Peter had No 1s with "Flava" and "I Feel You"?

POT LUCK 22 *See quiz 49, page 57*
1 Johnson. 2 Spice Girls. 3 Waistcoat. 4 Hovercraft. 5 Mint. 6 Sullivan. 7 Idle.
8 Nick nack. 9 Talk. 10 Green. 11 Gold. 12 Sand pit. 13 Aniston. 14 Butterfly.
15 Michael Jackson. 16 Linen. 17 Two. 18 North. 19 Handel. 20 *Witch*.
21 Home Hill. 22 *Pinocchio*. 23 Guitar. 24 Every year. 25 Your troubles.
26 Yellow. 27 (Some) more. 28 The Huns. 29 Barcelona. 30 Argentina.

ANSWERS

Answers - see Quiz 50, page 58

1 Which part of the body is associated with Achilles?
2 Dairy farming is usually associated with the rearing of which animals?
3 A drone is a type of which insect?
4 What does the Kelvin scale measure?
5 In what sort of climate do rain forests appear?
6 What colour is amber?
7 What characteristic of reptiles is also a phrase used to describe a callous act?
8 What is the framework of ribs called?
9 What colour is a robin's breast?
10 Anorexia nervosa is what type of disorder?
11 Which continent grows the most rice?
12 Saliva is produced in which part of the body?
13 What sort of trail does a slug leave behind?
14 If you have laryngitis what may you lose?
15 Lumbago causes pain in which part of the body?
16 What is inserted in the body in acupuncture?
17 The Florida cougar is a member of which family?
18 Which eight-legged creature do many people have a phobia about?
19 On which continent are most elephants found?
20 What do arteries in the body carry?
21 Chimpanzee, gorilla and man – present company excepted – which is the most intelligent?
22 What is a black mamba?
23 Cats, dogs and sheep – which of these animals are sheared?
24 Which contains more lines a plus or a minus sign?
25 Mars is called what colour planet?
26 What colour are a flamingo's feathers?
27 Koalas are natives to which country?
28 If water freezes what does it become?
29 Which plant increases in popularity at Christmas when you kiss under it?
30 Which metal is used in thermometers?

QUIZ 53 THE OSCARS

Answers - see Quiz 55, page 63

1 Which Oscar-winner was a *Beauty*, with Annette Bening and Kevin Spacey?
2 In which country was Warren Beatty's political thriller *Reds* set?
3 Which Juliette won Best Supporting Actress for *The English Patient*?
4 Where was Nicolas Cage *Leaving* in his 1995 winner?
5 Which Julia won for *Erin Brokovich*?
6 Which Ben shared a screenplay Oscar with Matt Damon for *Good Will Hunting*?
7 Which Jennifer did Oscar-nominee Brad Pitt marry?
8 Which English Oscar winner Emma has a sister called Sophie?
9 In which US city was *The Godfather* set?
10 How old was Jessica Tandy when she won an Oscar for *Driving Miss Daisy*, in her 50, 60, 70s or 80s?
11 Which English Julie, a 1960s winner, was nominated for *Afterglow* in the 1990s?
12 In which film venue were the first Oscars presented?
13 Which fighter was the subject of the 2001 winner with Russell Crowe?
14 Which blonde American cried all the way through her acceptance speech for *Shakespeare in Love*?
15 What was the nationality of the main character in *Braveheart*?
16 Which Hilary won Best Supporting Actress for *Boys Don't Cry*?
17 Which language was *La vita e bella* in?
18 Which was the highest grossing Oscar-winner of the 1990s?
19 *Amadeus* was an Oscar winner about which composer?
20 *Dances With* which animals was the third-best Oscar-winning earner of the 1990s?
21 Which mythical creature follows *Crouching Tiger, Hidden* _____ in the movie title?
22 Which United studio had 13 winning films by the end of the millennium?
23 Which 1990s winner has *English* in the title?
24 In which decade was *Cabaret* a winner?
25 What sort of Games was *Chariots of Fire* about?
26 Which John won for *True Grit*?
27 Which Susan played a nun in *Dead Man Walking*?
28 How many Oscars had Julia Roberts won before *Erin Brokovich*?
29 Which Fonda won for *On Golden Pond*?
30 What type of *Foot* won for Daniel Day Lewis?

WORLD TOUR *See quiz 55, page 63*

ANSWERS

1 Virgin. 2 Switzerland. 3 Texas. 4 Salt. 5 South America. 6 New York. 7 Eskimo.
8 Rockies. 9 Africa. 10 Delhi. 11 Russian. 12 Amazon river. 13 Rhodesia. 14 Oil.
15 America. 16 Europe. 17 Africa. 18 South Africa. 19 New York. 20 Canal.
21 Canaries. 22 Long. 23 Cars. 24 Louisiana. 25 Australia. 26 Northwest.
27 Canada. 28 Cote d'Ivoire. 29 Sydney. 30 Africa.

QUIZ 54 POT LUCK 24

Answers - see Quiz 56, page 64

1 What type of specialist would look at your feet?
2 *Eyes Wide Shut* was the final movie made by which Stanley?
3 A skull and what else appeared on The Jolly Roger flag?
4 A bird's feather was used to make what type of old fashioned pen?
5 Which country in South American is also the name of a nut?
6 What are you said to tread if you act on stage?
7 In mythology, Neptune is the god of what?
8 What type of vegetable would a vampire not eat in a vegetarian restaurant?
9 How many days are there in April and May together?
10 Which part of the egg is used to make meringues?
11 What does a somnambulist do while asleep?
12 Is the *Today* programme on Radio 1, 2, 3 or 4?
13 Who or what were druids in Ancient Britain?
14 In song, who looked out on the Feast of Stephen?
15 What is needed for a game of whist?
16 If something is there to mislead it is said to be a red type of which fish?
17 Which country are Maoris indigenous to?
18 What was the nationality of the thinker Archimedes?
19 Which continent has the greatest number of people?
20 What does the first C stand for in CCTV?
21 What sort of fingers does a person have who is always dropping things called?
22 How many angles are contained in a pentagon?
23 Which of the following colours is not a type of rice – black, brown or white?
24 What is the maximum number of people who can sit in a rickshaw?
25 Ratatouille is made from what type of food?
26 What does a kilowatt measure?
27 Which Jack, who died in 2001, starred in *The Odd Couple*?
28 In which season is the festival of the Passover?
29 Which popular small car was invented by Alec Issigonis?
30 Who landed on the Moon along with Neil Armstrong?

QUIZ 55 WORLD TOUR

Answers - see Quiz 53, page 61

1　Which islands share their name with Richard Branson's airline?
2　Which country beginning with S borders the east of France?
3　Dallas is in which US oil state?
4　What does the Dead Sea taste of?
5　Ecuador is on which continent?
6　In which US city is the Empire State Building?
7　What is another name for Inuit?
8　What is the nickname for the Rocky Mountains?
9　Algeria is to the north of which continent?
10　Which city comprises Old Delhi and New Delhi?
11　What is the official language of Russia?
12　In Spanish it's Rio de las Amazonas, what is it in English?
13　What name did Zimbabwe have in the 1960s?
14　Saudi Arabia is famous for producing which fuel?
15　The Sioux are a native tribe of which continent?
16　Scandinavia is in which part of the world?
17　Which continent is the next largest after Asia?
18　Soweto is a suburb of Johannesburg in which country?
19　In which harbour is the Statue of Liberty?
20　What type of waterway is at Suez?
21　Gran Canaria is in which islands?
22　What describes the famous Beach resort in California where the Queen Mary was brought?
23　Los Angeles suffers from a severe smog problem due to a high percentage of which vehicles?
24　Which is the only US state to begin with L?
25　Aborigines are from which Commonwealth country?
26　In which part of the USA is Alaska?
27　Quebec is a French-speaking part of which country?
28　Which of the following used to be called the Ivory Coast, Cote d'Ivoire, Gold Coast or Rhodesia?
29　What is Australia's largest city?
30　On which continent is Swahili spoken?

ANSWERS

THE OSCARS See quiz 53, page 61

1 *American*. 2 Russia/Soviet Union. 3 Binoche. 4 *Las Vegas*. 5 Roberts. 6 Affleck.
7 Aniston. 8 Thompson. 9 New York. 10 80s. 11 Christie. 12 Hollywood.
13 *Gladiator*. 14 Gwyneth Paltrow. 15 Scottish. 16 Swank. 17 Italian. 18 *Titanic*.
19 Mozart. 20 *Wolves*. 21 *Dragon*. 22 Artists. 23 *The English Patient*. 24 1970s.
25 Olympics. 26 Wayne. 27 Sarandon. 28 None. 29 Henry. 30 *My Left Foot*.

QUIZ 56 POT LUCK 25

Answers - see Quiz 54, page 62

1 Who is the four-legged hero in the movie *The Wrong Trousers*?
2 What is at the end of a stick in lacrosse?
3 What does the letter M stand for in MTV?
4 Which youthful name was applied to baseball's George Herman Ruth?
5 What was the surname of the inventor of the saxophone?
6 What type of institution in America was named after John Harvard?
7 Which of these has least legs – bird, kangaroo or snake?
8 Where in the body is the smallest bone?
9 Which word names male rabbits and American money?
10 Which type of building did Louis XIV have built at Versailles?
11 Which sport did Hank Aaron play?
12 Nelson Mandela was born in which decade of the 20th century?
13 Which Wood is Winnie the Pooh's home?
14 Which TV series includes the characters Phoebe and Chandler?
15 What is the fastest team game in the world?
16 The Dreamcast video game console was developed by which computer company?
17 Which fishy sounding Captain is in the *Tintin* stories?
18 What does V stand for in VR?
19 Which country does Robert Pires play soccer for?
20 Which word names a metal container and also means is able to?
21 In which country was the first CD made?
22 What name was given to the English King Alfred –The Awful, The Great or The Lionheart?
23 How many beats to the bar are there in basic of rock music?
24 In movies, Dr Hammond was a character in which *Park*?
25 The Three Tenors first sang at which sporting event?
26 What are the US pop charts called – Billboard, Groundhog or Skateboard?
27 In *The Wizard of Oz* what sort of pet does Dorothy own?
28 In a knock-out competition how many games are left – excluding replays or third-place playoffs – after all the quarter finals are completed?
29 About how many countries are there altogether in Europe – 15, 50 or 100?
30 Which country was the first in the world to have a TV service?

POT LUCK 24 See quiz 54, page 62
1 A chiropodist/podiatrist. 2 Kubrick. 3 Cross bones. 4 Quill pen. 5 Brazil.
6 The boards. 7 Sea. 8 Garlic. 9 61. 10 White. 11 Walk. 12 Radio 4.
13 Priests. 14 Good King Wenceslas. 15 Pack of cards. 16 Herring.
17 New Zealand. 18 Greek. 19 Asia. 20 Closed. 21 Butterfingers. 22 Five.
23 Black. 24 Two. 25 Vegetables. 26 Electrical power. 27 Lemmon.
28 Spring. 29 Mini. 30 Buzz Aldrin.

ANSWERS

QUIZ 57 CLASSICAL MUSIC

Answers - see Quiz 59, page 67

1 Which is the title of an opera – The Crying Dutchman, The Flying Ditchman or The Flying Dutchman?
2 Which composer had the first names Johann Sebastian?
3 Edward Elgar was from which country?
4 What sort of music is *Tosca*?
5 How do you get a sound out of a saxophone?
6 What are the surnames of the Three Tenors?
7 Charlotte Church came from which part of the UK?
8 Which insect follows *Madame* in the title of an opera?
9 Which opera star Andrea had top selling albums *Romanza* and *Sogno*?
10 In which city is La Scala Opera House?
11 In which venue in London do The Proms take place?
12 What is a waltz?
13 Placido Domingo is particularly famous for which type of music?
14 How many performers are there in a string quartet?
15 In which country is the Sydney Opera House?
16 Which is the highest female voice?
17 What is the first name of conductor Rattle?
18 What was the name of opera singer Callas?
19 What was the nationality of Tchaikovsky?
20 What do you do to a tambourine to get a noise out of it?
21 Where do you hold a flute to play it?
22 Which is the largest of these instruments, violin, viola or double bass?
23 Which musical instrument did Sax invent?
24 Which musical instrument did Yehudi Menuhin play?
25 In which Garden is London's Royal Opera House?
26 Which overture with cannon and bell effects has a date for its title?
27 What night of the week is the Last Night of the Proms?
28 Which country does Kiri Te Kanawa come from?
29 Which is the lowest male voice?
30 *Riverdance* was based on classic, traditional dance from which country?

ANSWERS

21ST CENTURY NEWS See quiz 59, page 67

1 September. 2 50. 3 Labour. 4 London. 5 Conservative. 6 Hussein.
7 Marks & Spencer. 8 Gordon Brown. 9 Rail. 10 Foot & mouth. 11 Swedish.
12 Internet. 13 Rhys Jones. 14 Ships. 15 Alistair. 16 Three. 17 Concorde.
18 Sydney. 19 Asylum. 20 Straw. 21 Venus Williams. 22 Doctor/GP. 23 June.
24 Russia. 25 French. 26 *Bridget Jones*. 27 Florida. 28 Ann. 29 *Potter*. 30 Music.

QUIZ 58 POT LUCK 26

Answers - see Quiz 60, page 68

1 In movies, what career did young Billy Elliot want to follow?
2 From which country does goulash originate?
3 What can be odd, even or whole?
4 Apart from being a TV programme, what is a Blue Peter?
5 Which Shirley is nicknamed the Tigress of Tiger Bay?
6 In which US state is Walt Disney World?
7 "Just do it" was featured in ads for which company products?
8 Charles de Gaulle airport is in which city?
9 What is a flexible diving board called?
10 The movie and stage show *Grease* is set in which decade?
11 Both World War I and World War II began in which continent?
12 What is French for ten?
13 A clutch is a collection of what?
14 The Beaufort scale identifies different speeds of what?
15 Is *Woman's Hour* on Radio 1, 2, 3 or 4?
16 In the movie title who is described as *International Man of Mystery*?
17 What are the minimum number of notes needed to produce a chord?
18 Which part of a car did John Dunlop invent?
19 In its nickname Chicago is known as what type of city?
20 What type of animal was the first to travel in space?
21 In which country was the first Marathon race run?
22 Josiah Wedgwood found fame making what?
23 What was the first name of the character Dr Lecter in *The Silence of the Lambs*?
24 The emu comes from which country?
25 Tibia and fibula are names of of what?
26 Which English county is part of Superman's secret alias?
27 What is the playing area called in a basketball match?
28 What is Bart Simpson's full first name – is it Bartram, Bartholomew or Stobart?
29 What does Costa Blanca actually mean?
30 In a pack of cards what is the Queen of Spades often known as?

POT LUCK 27 *See quiz 60, page 68*

ANSWERS
1 Laurent Blanc. 2 1950s. 3 61. 4 Bloody. 5 19th March. 6 Two. 7 Sing.
8 A boot. 9 Maize. 10 90. 11 Sloth. 12 *Star Wars*. 13 Bicycle.
14 Between its shoulders. 15 China's. 16 Zebra. 17 Laura. 18 Peter.
19 Exploring. 20 Tintin. 21 Grimm. 22 Tyres. 23 Bear. 24 Virgin.
25 Spots. 26 60. 27 Oz. 28 "Hind". 29 Body Shop. 30 Dinosaur.

QUIZ 59 21ST CENTURY NEWS

Answers - see Quiz 57, page 65

1 In which month in 2001 was the World Trade Center in New York destroyed by a terrorist attack?
2 In 2002 how many years will Elizabeth II have been on the throne?
3 David Blunkett became Home Secretary for which party?
4 In which city did the ill-fated Millennium Dome open?
5 Jailed peer Lord Archer was Deputy Chairman of which political party?
6 Which Saddam led Iraq into the 21st century?
7 Which British store announced it was closing all its French outlets?
8 Which Chancellor gave the first Budget of the new millennium?
9 What sort of crash at Hatfield caused travel problems for many months?
10 Tony Blair postponed the 2001 General Election because of which farming disaster?
11 What nationality was the full-time England soccer manager who succeeded Kevin Keegan?
12 How did the Kilshaws adopt baby twin girls?
13 Who was the Sophie involved in Sophiegate?
14 Cammell Laird, which called in the receivers in 2001, manufactured what?
15 Which Campbell was Tony Blair's press secretary?
16 How many children did Madonna have when she married Guy Ritchie?
17 Which supersonic aircraft was grounded in 2000 after crashing outside Paris?
18 Where were the 2000 Olympic Games held?
19 Which seekers were apprehended in the Channel Tunnel?
20 Which Jack replaced Robin Cook as Foreign Secretary?
21 Which sister of Serena, won the first two Ladies Singles Championships of the 21st century at Wimbledon?
22 What was the profession of convicted mass murderer Harold Shipman?
23 In which month did the 2001 UK General Election take place?
24 Vladimir Putin became head of state of which country?
25 In September 2001 what was the nationality of the football managers of Liverpool and Arsenal?
26 Whose film *Diary* broke all box office records when it opened in 2001?
27 Results in which sunshine state held the result of the US Presidential election?
28 Which Shadow Home Secretary Widdecombe published a novel?
29 Which *Harry* was made into a movie?
30 Eminem hit the headlines in which field?

QUIZ 60 POT LUCK 27

Answers - see Quiz 58, page 66

1 Which retired French international player replaced Jaap Stam at Manchester Utd?
2 John F Kennedy became President of the USA in which decade?
3 How many days are there in June and July together?
4 What gruesome adjective was given to Mary I?
5 What is the date that it is two days after Saint Patrick's day?
6 How many sons did Princess Diana have?
7 If a lady is a soprano what does she do?
8 What is named after the Duke of Wellington – a type of boot, a metal helmet or a breed of dog?
9 What is popcorn made from?
10 A right-angled triangle contains one angle that must be how many degrees?
11 Which creature has a name that means idle and lazy?
12 Which sci fi movie was Harrison Ford's first film?
13 In 1995 Miguel Indurain was a record-breaker on what sort of vehicle?
14 Where on a horse are its withers?
15 In 1989 which country's students protested in Tianenmen Square?
16 Which of these is not a member of the cat family – panther, tiger or zebra?
17 What is the first name of President George W Bush's wife?
18 What was the name of the Russian Tsar who founded St Petersburg?
19 Captain James Cook became famous for doing what – cooking, exploring or swimming underwater?
20 Which cartoon young hero did Belgian Hergé create?
21 What was the last name of the fairy tale collecting brothers Jacob and Wilhelm?
22 Charles Goodyear developed what important item for cars?
23 Which animal is included in the nickname of Jack Nicklaus?
24 Which record company was founded by Richard Branson?
25 What type of markings does a cheetah have?
26 How many months are there in five years?
27 Which land contained a Yellow Brick Road?
28 Explorer Francis Drake had a ship called "The Golden" what?
29 Which environmentally friendly shop did Anita Roddick found?
30 A diplodocus was a type of what – a counting frame, a dinosaur or a steam bath from Roman times?

QUIZ 61   RICH AND FAMOUS

Answers - see Quiz 63, page 71

1   Judith Keppel was the first million-pound winner of what?
2   What is the Duke of Edinburgh's first name?
3   Which Al Fayed bought Harrods?
4   What is the first name of Lady Archer, wife of the disgraced peer?
5   Which blonde Ball had a baby called Woody?
6   Which Robbie's name was linked with Geri Halliwell?
7   Raymond Blanc is a rich and famous what?
8   Which train service is Richard Branson most associated with?
9   Which Ms Campbell was a supermodel in the 1990s and 2000s?
10 Which Ms Mills did Paul McCartney become engaged to in 2001?
11 What is the Countess of Wessex's first name?
12 What is Prince Michael of Kent's wife called?
13 Which Ms Kidd was one of the faces of the Nineties?
14 What is the nickname of Ms Legge Bourke, former 'nanny' to Princes William and Harry?
15 Which Peter had to resign from the Cabinet because of the purchase of a house in Notting Hill?
16 Which TV cook Smith has her own on-line service?
17 Which Palmer-Tomkinson has been dubbed the It Girl?
18 What is the first name of Princess Beatrice's mother?
19 Which Catherine did Michael Douglas marry?
20 Which TV interviewer is Lady Carina Frost's husband?
21 In which country were Victoria and David Beckham married?
22 Ex King Constantine was King of which European country?
23 Which William led the Conservative Party to defeat in the 2001 election?
24 Who is Prince William's younger brother?
25 Which 007 Roger had a father who was a policeman?
26 Cake-maker and actress Jane Asher has what colour hair?
27 Which Irish emblem does Patsy Kensit have tattooed on her ankle?
28 Which was the first of the Williams sisters to win the Wimbledon singles title?
29 Who is Jermaine Jackson's more famous younger brother?
30 What is Lady Thatcher's husband called?

ANSWERS

TV GREATS See quiz 63, page 71

1 Attenborough. 2 Thaw. 3 Monk. 4 *Keeping Up Appearances*. 5 Coltrane.
6 Yorkshire. 7 Square. 8 *The Good Life*. 9 Three. 10 David Frost. 11 *Friends*.
12 Dog. 13 French. 14 Flowerpot men. 15 Sybil. 16 *ER*. 17 Afternoon.
18 *Porridge*. 19 Doctor. 20 Red. 21 Tell a story. 22 Children. 23 Police.
24 New York. 25 Two. 26 Barker. 27 Perrin. 28 Dibley. 29 Charles.
30 Barrister (lawyer).

QUIZ 62 POT LUCK 28

Answers - see Quiz 64, page 72

1 Which Boys had a No 1 with "We're Going To Ibiza"?
2 How many kings are there on a chessboard at the start of a game?
3 How many do you score in darts with all three arrows in double top?
4 Which Pole was explorer Amundsen the first to reach?
5 What is the name for plant and animal remains preserved in rock?
6 Which of the Barrymore clan starred in the movie Charlie's Angels?
7 Would you expect an animator to collect beer mats, make cartoon movies or search for jewels?
8 What is the nationality of most Popes?
9 Sally Ride was the first American woman to travel where?
10 What was the surname of Wild West outlaw brothers Frank and Jesse?
11 What was the name of Pierre Curie's scientist wife?
12 Terrell Davis is famous for which sport?
13 How many different vowels are there in the word relieved?
14 How does twenty past six pm appear on a 24 hour clock?
15 What is the Paris's underground railway system called?
16 Which imaginary line goes across the middle of Africa?
17 Which term is used to describe developing countries?
18 What is the sparsely populated region of Australia called?
19 What do you collect if you are a philatelist?
20 In which country is the Ganges a sacred river?
21 Papyrus was an early form of what everyday item?
22 In Peter Pan, how many hands does Captain Hook have?
23 WHO is the world what organisation?
24 What do you do if you take part in a mazurka?
25 Actors and actresses join which trade union?
26 Which former England soccer boss has also managed Ipswich, Porto, Barcelona and Newcastle?
27 What are dried to make prunes?
28 In the 1960s, 'The Shrimp' was the nickname given to a famous what?
29 The Giro D'Italia – Tour of Italy – takes place in which sport?
30 How many rings are linked in the symbol for the Olympic Games?

POT LUCK 29 See quiz 64, page 72

ANSWERS

1 Pie. 2 (South) Yorkshire. 3 Arctic. 4 Walk. 5 Andrew. 6 Green. 7 Poles.
8 Eating in binges. 9 Panther. 10 East. 11 Giraffe. 12 Herd. 13 Wane.
14 Forrest. 15 Home page. 16 Two. 17 Japan. 18 Monkey. 19 Atlantic.
20 Star Wars. 21 Coach. 22 Pasta. 23 A pole. 24 Earthquakes. 25 Kentucky.
26 Whales. 27 Freestyle (normally front crawl). 28 Pacific. 29 Green. 30 Lopez.

QUIZ 63 TV GREATS

Answers - see Quiz 61, page 69

1 Which David with a famous brother investigated *The Private Life of Plants*?
2 Which John played Kavanagh QC?
3 What was the profession of Cadfael?
4 In which series might Hyacinth have tried to impress Emmet?
5 Which Robbie found fame as Cracker?
6 The classic *All Creatures Great and Small* was set in which county?
7 What shape was the medallion on a *Jim'll Fix It* badge?
8 Which 1970s sitcom was set in The Avenue, Surbiton?
9 How many Goodies were there?
10 Who fronted *The Frost Report*?
11 Which Channel 4 modern classic featured six New York chums?
12 What was the most famous pet in *Frasier*?
13 Who is the brunette in *French & Saunders*?
14 What type of Men were Bill and Ben?
15 What was the name of Mrs Basil Fawlty?
16 How is the drama set in a US Emergency Room better known?
17 At what time of day was *Emmerdale Farm* first screened?
18 *Going Straight* was the sequel to which hugely popular Ronnie Barker sitcom?
19 In the original *Heartbeat* what was the profession of Nick's wife?
20 What colour was Inspector Morse's Jaguar?
21 What did stars do on *Jackanory*?
22 John Craven established a news programme especially for whom?
23 *Juliet Bravo* was a popular series about someone in which profession?
24 In which city did Kojak work?
25 How many males shared a flat in *Men Behaving Badly*?
26 Which Ronnie played Arkwright in *Open All Hours*?
27 Which Reginald was played by the late Leonard Rossiter?
28 Alice was married by a female Vicar in which village?
29 Which Prince was interviewed by Jonathan Dimbleby in *The Private Man, The Public Role*?
30 What was the profession of TV great Horace Rumpole?

RICH AND FAMOUS See quiz 61, page 69
1 *Who Wants to be A Millionaire?*. 2 Philip. 3 Mohammed. 4 Mary. 5 Zoe. 6 Williams.
7 Chef. 8 Virgin. 9 Naomi. 10 Heather. 11 Sophie. 12 Princess Michael.
13 Jodie. 14 Tiggy. 15 Mandelson. 16 Delia. 17 Tara. 18 Sarah. 19 Zeta Jones.
20 David. 21 Ireland. 22 Greece. 23 Hague. 24 Harry. 25 Moore. 26 Red.
27 Shamrock. 28 Venus. 29 Michael. 30 Denis.

ANSWERS

QUIZ 64 POT LUCK 29

Answers - see Quiz 62, page 70

1 What sort of chart presents data seen as slices of a circle – a cake chart, a flow chart or a pie chart?
2 In which county was *The Full Monty* set?
3 The Inuit live around which ocean?
4 Aleksey Leonov was the first man to do what in space?
5 What is the first name of composer Lord Lloyd Webber?
6 What colour is a banana before it is ripe to eat?
7 What are the ends of a magnet called?
8 A bulimia sufferer has an urge to do what?
9 What name is given to a leopard that is coloured black?
10 Lake Tanganyika is in which part of Africa – east, north or south?
11 Which of these creatures has its head furthest from the ground – giraffe, gorilla or rhinoceros?
12 What is the term for a group of elephants?
13 The Moon is said to wax and what else?
14 Which *Gump* was the hero of a 1994 movie?
15 What is the introductory page of a web site known as?
16 Excluding borders, how many different colours appear on a chess board playing area?
17 In which country were the Winter Olympics held when they were staged in Nagano?
18 A howler is what type of creature?
19 At the beginning of the last century, Marconi sent radio signals across which ocean?
20 Which *Star* movie was the biggest box office success of the 1970s?
21 In the pantomime *Cinderella*, what is the pumpkin turned into?
22 Are Conchiglie and Rigatoni types of cheese, types of pasta or famous soccer strikers once of Juventus?
23 What is used to propel a punt?
24 What does a seismologist study?
25 In which state is the Derby, which is part of the USA's thoroughbred Triple Crown, run?
26 Which mammals will expire when stranded on dry land?
27 In swimming, what is the fastest competition stroke?
28 In which ocean is the US state of Hawaii?
29 In board games, what colour is the Reverend in Cluedo?
30 Which Jennifer did a voice over in *Antz*?

POT LUCK 28 *See quiz 62, page 70*

ANSWERS

1 Vengaboys. 2 Two. 3 120. 4 North Pole. 5 Fossils. 6 Drew. 7 Make cartoons.
8 Italian. 9 Space. 10 James. 11 Marie. 12 American Football. 13 Two.
14 18.20. 15 Metro. 16 Equator. 17 Third World. 18 Outback. 19 Stamps.
20 India. 21 Paper. 22 One. 23 World Health. 24 Dance. 25 Equity.
26 Bobby Robson. 27 Plums. 28 Model. 29 Cycling. 30 Five.

QUIZ 65 SPORTING ACTION REPLAY

Answers - see Quiz 67, page 75

1 Which Denise won Heptathlon gold in Sydney?
2 How was record breaking baseball star Henry Louis Aaron better known?
3 Who scored the goal which took England into the 2002 World Cup Finals?
4 Which Jack was the first golfer to win six US Masters titles?
5 Peter Shilton played a record number of soccer matches in which position?
6 At the end of the millennium, which Canadian born Briton was tennis's fastest server?
7 Maurice Greene was part of the gold medal winning 4x100m relay team in Sydney for which nation?
8 The Chicago Cubs and Chicago White Sox are cross city rivals in which sport?
9 In which country was England's 5–1 win over Germany in 2001?
10 What type of golfers compete for the Solheim Cup?
11 Which South American country has won soccer's World Cup more than any other?
12 Which American has won the Men's Singles at Wimbledon more than any other man?
13 Merlene Ottey has won 14 World Championship medals in what type of arena?
14 How is Eldrick Woods better known?
15 Which soccer side won the FA Cup, the Premier League and the European Champions League in 1999?
16 Which Martina is Wimbledon's most successful Ladies Champion?
17 What did Ed Moses jump over to win world records between 1977 and 1987?
18 How many were in the boat in which Steve Redgrave won his 5th Olympic gold?
19 What colour is Michael Schumacher's Ferrari driver's suit?
20 Joe Montana and Dan Marino were high-profile stars of which sport in the 1980s and 1990s?
21 Which Chris won the French Open tennis title seven times?
22 Which driver Alain was dubbed 'The Professor of the Track'?
23 Was Krisztina Egerszegi cold or wet when she won her five Olympic gold medals?
24 In which decade was the first Rugby League World Cup held?
25 In what colour shirts do India play floodlit cricket matches?
26 Where did the US women's basketball team win Olympic gold immediately after Atlanta?
27 In June 2000, which young American won golf's US Open by 15 strokes?
28 In what colour shirt did Geoff Hurst score the winning goal in the 1966 World Cup?
29 Dawn Fraser won four Olympic gold medals for which Olympic hosting nation?
30 At which stadium was was the final match of England's World Cup qualifying campaign, the 2–2 draw with Greece?

MOVIE MEMORIES See quiz 67, page 75

ANSWERS

1 *Arthur.* 2 Eastwood. 3 *Sleep.* 4 *Deer.* 5 Marilyn Monroe. 6 Grace Kelly. 7 US.
8 Henry VIII. 9 Harrison. 10 Notting Hill. 11 Mrs Robinson. 12 Rosanna. 13 *Cat.*
14 Ballet. 15 *Streetcar.* 16 *Ghostbusters.* 17 *Psycho.* 18 Disney. 19 Newman.
20 Purple. 21 *Shut.* 22 Lemmon. 23 Andrews. 24 Ewan. 25 *Notting Hill.* 26 Paris.
27 Powers. 28 Hairdresser. 29 Natalie Wood. 30 *Star Wars.*

QUIZ 66 POT LUCK 30

Answers - see Quiz 68, page 76

1 Which country's capital is on the Potomac river?
2 In Italy what is mascarpone?
3 How many points are awarded as a starter on *University Challenge*?
4 Where would you go to visit the Sea of Tranquillity?
5 To get past a portcullis would you go over it, through it or under it?
6 What was the first name of brilliant inventor Einstein?
7 In which of these countries is there not a place called Halifax – Canada, Austria or England?
8 Which creature may be Golden or Bald?
9 What sort of *Detective* was Ace Ventura?
10 Which colour can be linked with admiral, card and flag?
11 Which spirit was mixed with water to make grog?
12 In which industry had the heroes of *The Full Monty* worked?
13 Which English city has given its name to a bun and a wheelchair?
14 Are the pepper symbols held up by the audience in *Ready Steady Cook* coloured green or red?
15 Cape Horn is at the southern tip of which continent?
16 Mandarin is a form of which world language?
17 What was the first No 1 hit on both sides of the Atlantic for the Spice Girls?
18 The English king Alfred was said to have burnt what?
19 What is the most eaten food in Asia?
20 Michael Flatley became known as Lord of the what?
21 Which soccer star advertised Brylcreem then had his head shaved?
22 How many years are involved if a silver celebration is two years away?
23 Which part of his own body did painter Van Gogh cut off?
24 Gottlieb Daimler gave his name to what type of transport?
25 Who wrote the children's story *Matilda*?
26 Which team did Michael Schumacher drive for at the end of the 1990s?
27 Bill Gates was head of which computer company?
28 What kind of creatures inhabited the *Lake* in Tchaikovsky's ballet music?
29 Which 1990s champion was named after tennis great Martina Navratilova?
30 Leonardo DiCaprio starred in *The Man in the Iron* what?

POT LUCK 31 *See quiz 68, page 76*

ANSWERS

1 Venice. 2 Blow it. 3 X. 4 Spain. 5 Moss. 6 Emergency. 7 Red. 8 Monte Carlo. 9 521. 10 Australia. 11 Shark. 12 Space. 13 Culkin. 14 Skiing. 15 Round. 16 Music. 17 Dried fruit. 18 Horse. 19 Cathy Freeman. 20 The letter M. 21 New Zealand. 22 Who's there?. 23 Hay Fever. 24 Mad. 25 Playing cards. 26 Running. 27 Furniture. 28 Louise. 29 Heart. 30 Washington.

QUIZ 67 MOVIE MEMORIES

Answers - see Quiz 65, page 73

1 *Arthur 2: On the Rocks* was the sequel to what?
2 Which Clint appeared in *Coogan's Bluff*?
3 *The Big* what was a classic with Lauren Bacall and Humphrey Bogart?
4 Which *Hunter* had the Vietnam war as its subject matter?
5 Who was the famous blonde in *Bus Stop*?
6 Which future movie princess starred in *High Noon*?
7 Which country's Cavalry is John Ford's *Rio Grande* about?
8 *Carry On Henry* was a Carry On spoof about which English King?
9 Which Ford was *The Fugitive* on the big screen?
10 Which part of London, famous for its carnival, shares its name with a Hugh Grant movie?
11 How does Dustin Hoffman always address Mrs Robinson in *The Graduate*?
12 Which Arquette starred in *Pulp Fiction*?
13 What animal goes before *Ballou* in the movie title?
14 What type of shoes were the *Red Shoes*?
15 What was named *Desire* in the movie with Marlon Brando?
16 What sort of busters were the subject of a movie with Dan Aykroyd?
17 In which movie did Janet Leigh play Marion Crane?
18 Which studio made *The Lion King*?
19 Which Paul starred opposite real wife Joanne Woodward in *Mr & Mrs Bridge*?
20 *The Color* was what in the 1985 Steven Spielberg movie?
21 How were *Eyes Wide* in Stanley Kubrick's final movie?
22 Which Jack, who died in 2001, starred in *Missing*?
23 Which Julie starred in two of the top five box office musical successes of the 1960s?
24 Which McGregor played the young Obi-Wan Kenobi in *The Phantom Menace*?
25 Which Hill was trailed as 'an equal not a sequel' to *Four Weddings & A Funeral*?
26 Where was Marlon Brando's *Last Tango* in the 1970s?
27 Which Austin was played by Mike Myers?
28 What was Warren Beatty's job in *Shampoo*?
29 Which actress was on the poster for *West Side Story*?
30 Which sci fi movie was the biggest box office success of the 1970s?

SPORTING ACTION REPLAY See quiz 65, page 73

ANSWERS

1 Lewis. 2 Hank. 3 David Beckham. 4 Nicklaus. 5 Goalkeeper. 6 Greg Ruzedski. 7 USA. 8 Baseball. 9 Germany. 10 Professional ladies. 11 Brazil. 12 Pete Sampras. 13 Athletics track. 14 Tiger Woods. 15 Manchester United. 16 Navratilova. 17 Hurdles. 18 Four. 19 Red. 20 American football. 21 Evert. 22 Prost. 23 Wet (she is a swimmer). 24 1950s. 25 Blue. 26 Sydney. 27 Tiger Woods. 28 Red. 29 Australia. 30 Old Trafford.

QUIZ 68 POT LUCK 31

Answers - see Quiz 66, page 74

1 In which watery city is the Bridge of Sighs?
2 How would you get a note out of a bassoon?
3 Which letter is a Roman numerals and used in grading movies for viewing suitability?
4 The island of Majorca belongs to which country?
5 Which model Kate became the face of L'Oreal in 1998?
6 In a hospital what does E stand for in *ER*?
7 In the movies what colour is Superman's cape?
8 Which part of Monaco is famous for its car rally?
9 How many weeks are there in ten years?
10 The Murray is the main river of which country?
11 What sort of creature was the villain in the blockbuster movie *Jaws*?
12 Helen Sharman was the first female from the UK to go where?
13 What name is shared by acting brothers Kieran and Macaulay?
14 Franz Klammer found fame in which sport?
15 What shape is a bagel?
16 In which branch of the creative arts did Stravinsky find fame?
17 What is mincemeat made from?
18 A mustang is a wild what?
19 Which famous Australian lit the Olympic torch in Sydney?
20 In Bond movies Dame Judi Dench played a character whose name was identified by what?
21 Which of these countries is the furthest south – India, Japan or New Zealand?
22 What is always the second line of a "Knock knock" joke?
23 People suffer when the pollen count is high if they have which fever?
24 In *Alice In Wonderland* which word is used to describe The Hatter?
25 What is needed for a game of canasta?
26 How did Maurice Greene win gold at Sydney 2000?
27 Thomas Chippendale was famous for making what?
28 What is Madonna's second name?
29 In 1967 Christiaan Barnard performed the first transplant of what?
30 Which American city was named after the country's first President?

QUIZ 69 FOOD AND DRINK

Answers - see Quiz 71, page 79

1 What is an anchovy?
2 What would you find in the middle of a damson?
3 Darjeeling is a type of what?
4 Guinness was first made in which Irish city?
5 What is endive?
6 What would you do with a claret?
7 Saffron tinges food what colour?
8 Which vegetable shares its name with a fruit drink?
9 Which village in Leicestershire gives its name to a classic British blue cheese?
10 All citrus fruits are rich in which vitamin?
11 The island of Madeira shares its name with a cake and also what?
12 What colour is root ginger?
13 What are the tops of asparagus called?
14 Which of the following are not types of tomatoes, plum, orange, cherry?
15 What is rocket?
16 What is the most common fuel for a barbecue?
17 Sirloin is which meat?
18 What ingredient is balsamic?
19 What is the most common colour of an aubergine's skin?
20 Which food item is sold at London's Billingsgate market?
21 How is white wine usually served?
22 Mangetout and sugar snaps are types of what?
23 What is feta?
24 If coffee is drunk without milk or cream how is it described?
25 Which Earl gave his name to a type of mild tea?
26 Ciabatta bread originated in which country?
27 What sort of wine is chardonnay?
28 A shallot is a type of what?
29 What shape is the pasta used to make lasagne?
30 Seville is famous for which fruit used to make marmalade?

SEA LIFE See quiz 71, page 79
1 Fish. 2 Skate. 3 Blue whale. 4 Shell. 5 Calf. 6 Sharks. 7 Scorpion.
8 Portuguese. 9 Eight. 10 In the sea. 11 None. 12 Osprey. 13 Gills.
14 Herring. 15 10. 16 In the sea. 17 Whale. 18 Milk. 19 97%.
20 Poor. 21 Blubber. 22 Oxygen. 23 Cod. 24 White. 25 12%.
26 Sturgeon. 27 Shark. 28 Gold. 29 Blowhole. 30 Lobster.

ANSWERS

QUIZ 70 POT LUCK 32

Answers - see Quiz 72, page 80

1 Which group of people first developed central heating?
2 Which all girl pop band were the first to talk about "Girl power"?
3 Which country does supermodel Kate Moss come from?
4 In the movie *Beethoven* what sort of animal saves the day?
5 If the first of a month is a Tuesday what day will the tenth be?
6 In a building what can be made from thatch, slates or tiles?
7 Which country in the world has the most computers?
8 How did Marion Jones first win gold at Sydney 2000?
9 In the theatre who stands in for an actor or actress?
10 Which branch of science was Einstein famous for?
11 What colour was Queen Elizabeth I's hair?
12 Which James Bond actor was born on the same day as first man on the moon Neil Armstrong?
13 How many pieces of bread are used to make a club sandwich?
14 What name is given to an extra file sent with an e mail?
15 What were the first films with audible speech called?
16 In grammar what sort of word describes another word?
17 What does Giorgio Armani design?
18 Roger Bannister was the first man to run a mile in less than how many minutes?
19 Which bird can go before the words holed and toed?
20 What is Leonardo DiCaprio's real surname?
21 In which month of the year is Father's Day in the UK?
22 The novel *Watership Down* is about a colony of what?
23 What is the lead ballerina in a company called?
24 How many people play in a game of backgammon?
25 What is fi short for in hi-fi?
26 Where are the highest notes on a piano keyboard – to the far left, the far right, or in the middle?
27 What is the the name of the toy dinosaur in *Toy Story*?
28 Mark Antony was in love with which famous queen?
29 What is the currency of Belgium?
30 What was the name of the medic who was *Medicine Woman* in the TV series?

ANSWERS

POT LUCK 33 *See quiz 72, page 80*
1 Drum. 2 *Jurassic II*. 3 Hospital. 4 3. 5 Jan/Feb. 6 Polo. 7 Soup/Vegetables. 8 E.
9 Gym. 10 Ursula. 11 Weight. 12 A drop of golden sun. 13 Squares/checks.
14 Boy. 15 100. 16 Paris. 17 Lyrics for operas. 18 Dogs. 19 Face. 20 Ararat.
21 None. 22 White. 23 At. 24 Beetle. 25 Orbit. 26 Press ganging. 27 *Taxi*.
28 Gaggle. 29 Aubergine. 30 Morrissey.

QUIZ 71 SEA LIFE

Answers - see Quiz 69, page 77

1 The whale shark is the largest what?
2 Which fish shares its name with a sports boot?
3 What is the name of the heaviest mammal which lives in the sea?
4 A mollusc's body is covered in what?
5 What is a baby whale called?
6 Great white and hammerhead are types of what?
7 Which one of these creature has pincers – dolphin, lobster or seal?
8 Which nationality Man o' War is a sea creature?
9 The word octo means an octopus has how many tentacles?
10 Where would you find plankton?
11 How many legs does a seahorse have?
12 Which of these is not a fish – cod, osprey or perch?
13 A fish breathes through what?
14 A sardine is a young what?
15 How many tentacles does a squid have?
16 Where does a marine creature live?
17 Blue, fin and humpback are all types of what?
18 What do marine mammals feed their babies on?
19 Approximately how much of the Earth's water is in the oceans – 67%, 87% or 97%?
20 Which term best describes the eyesight of a whale – excellent, outstanding or poor?
21 What is the name for a whale's layer of fat?
22 What do fish absorb through their gills?
23 Which fish was at the centre of the so called fishing Wars involving Great Britain and Iceland?
24 What colour fur does a baby grey seal have?
25 How much of an iceberg is visible on or above the surface of the sea – 12% 50% or 90%?
26 Caviar is the name given to which fish's eggs, seen by many as a great delicacy?
27 Nurse and tiger are both types of what?
28 Which of the following is not a type of whale – Blue, Gold or White?
29 Which hole helps a dolphin to breathe?
30 Which of the following is the crayfish related to – lobster, sardine or whale?

FOOD AND DRINK See quiz 69, page 77

ANSWERS

1 Fish. 2 Stone. 3 Tea. 4 Dublin. 5 Salad plant. 6 Drink it. 7 Yellow.
8 Squash. 9 Stilton. 10 C. 11 A wine. 12 Brown. 13 Spears.
14 Orange. 15 Salad leaf. 16 Charcoal. 17 Beef. 18 Vinegar.
19 Purple. 20 Fish. 21 Chilled. 22 Peas. 23 Cheese. 24 Black.
25 Grey. 26 Italy. 27 White. 28 Onion. 29 Rectangular. 30 Oranges.

QUIZ 72 POT LUCK 33

Answers - see Quiz 70, page 78

1 On which instrument might a roll be played?
2 What was the second *Jurassic Park* movie called?
3 Where is the TV series *ER* set?
4 Which number on a dartboard is furthest from the ceiling?
5 The zodiac sign of Aquarius covers which two months?
6 Which sport is also a type of shirt collar?
7 What is usually served from a tureen?
8 On a keyboard which letter is directly below 3 and 4?
9 Where would you be if you were on a pommel horse?
10 What was the first name of Bond girl actress Andress?
11 A kilogram is a measure of what?
12 According to the song "Do-Ray-Mi", ray is a drop of what?
13 What is the pattern on gingham material?
14 Which word went before George in the name of the Culture Club lead singer?
15 Cent before a word relates to which number?
16 Near which city did Concorde crash on takeoff in 2000?
17 What does a librettist write?
18 What would you be displaying if you took part in Crufts?
19 In a suit of armour which parts of the body did the visor protect?
20 Noah's Ark was believed to have struck land at which Mount?
21 How many months of the year begin with a letter T?
22 What colour is the inside of a coconut?
23 How is @ pronounced in an e mail address?
24 A scarab, an Egyptian good luck charm, was shaped like which creature?
25 What is the term for a satellite's path round the Earth?
26 What name was given to the practice of kidnapping people to join the navy?
27 What sort of *Driver* was the evil Robert De Niro in the 1970s movie?
28 What is a group of geese called?
29 Eggplant is another name for what?
30 Which Neil is the voice of Bob The Builder?

POT LUCK 32 See quiz 70, page 78

ANSWERS

1 Romans. 2 Spice Girls. 3 England. 4 St Bernard dog. 5 Thursday. 6 Roof. 7 USA.
8 Running. 9 Understudy. 10 Physics. 11 Red. 12 Sean Connery. 13 Three.
14 Attachment. 15 Talkies. 16 Adjective. 17 Clothes. 18 Four. 19 Pigeon.
20 DiCaprio. 21 June. 22 Rabbits. 23 Prima ballerina. 24 Two. 25 Fidelity.
26 Far right. 27 Rex. 28 Cleopatra. 29 Franc. 30 Dr Quinn.

QUIZ 73 SOUNDS OF THE SIXTIES

Answers - see Quiz 75, page 83

1 Which group gazed at "Waterloo Sunset"?
2 Which Elvis hit was about a letter without a reply?
3 The Dakotas were not from Dakota; which UK city did they hail from?
4 Elvis's "Wooden Heart" was based on a folk song from which country?
5 Which Gerry & The Pacemakers No 1 became a football anthem?
6 What went with "Needles" in the title of a Searchers hit?
7 How many Beatles were there when they had their very first No 1?
8 Which word followed "Do Wah Diddy" in the title of a "Manfred Mann" hit?
9 What type of alpine singing featured on Frank Ifield's I Remember You?
10 Was Peter Noone 16, 26 or 36 when fronted Herman's Hermits?
11 Who could get "No Satisfaction" in 1965?
12 Which musical instrument was played by most of The Shadows?
13 How many people were there in Dave Clark's band?
14 Which famous daughter sang "These Boots Are Made For Walkin' "?
15 Which US west coast city was the subject of several hippy songs of the mid 1960s?
16 Who wrote Roy Orbison's recording of "Only The Lonely"?
17 What did the Beatles sing "Want to Hold" in the title of 1964 No 1 single?
18 Which Boys had "Good Vibrations" in 1966?
19 Which Cliff Richard hit became a standard song for celebratory occasions?
20 How many Everly Brothers were there?
21 What sort of "Children" did Billy J Kramer sing about?
22 Which Beatles song about a certain type of writer was released shortly after their last live concert?
23 How many Tops were there?
24 According to Eddie Cochran, how many "Steps to Heaven" were there?
25 What was "My Old Man" according to Lonnie Donegan in 1960?
26 On which fruity label was The Beatles' "Hey Jude" released?
27 Which 'bandits' backed Johnny Kidd?
28 Who went to No. 1 with "I Heard It Through the Grapevine" in 1969?
29 Which Liverpool lady went to No 1 with "Anyone Who Had a Heart"?
30 What sort of "Women" gave the Rolling Stones their 8th No 1?

LATE GREATS See quiz 75, page 83

ANSWERS
1 Barbara. 2 Yates. 3 Esther Rantzen. 4 Sammy. 5 London. 6 Wilde. 7 Sport.
8 Motor cycle. 9 London. 10 Spy. 11 Blyton. 12 Victoria. 13 Hailsham.
14 Shaving accessories. 15 Adam. 16 Charles. 17 Film. 18 Germany. 19 Jane.
20 France. 21 Richard. 22 *The Galaxy*. 23 Linda. 24 Albert. 25 Children.
26 Clothes. 27 Cello. 28 Paul. 29 Fables. 30 John F Kennedy.

QUIZ 74 POT LUCK 34

Answers - see Quiz 76, page 84

1 "Setting Sun" and "Block Rockin' Beats" were No 1s for which Brothers?
2 In Australia what is a jumbuck?
3 In *The Magic Roundabout* what kind of creature was Dougal?
4 What colour are triple-word squares in Scrabble?
5 What person would be a member of RIBA?
6 Which day of the year is described as Ash?
7 In *Oliver!* which character sings "As Long As He Needs Me"?
8 In which country was Elton John born?
9 What used to be sold by an apothecary?
10 Early Giant, Figaro and Nantes are types of which vegetable?
11 How many black cards are there in a standard pack of playing cards?
12 In printing, what are uppercase letters?
13 In which country is Zurich?
14 In the Bible which book follows directly after *Genesis*?
15 What is mulligatawny – an Irish port, a small owl or a type of soup?
16 What do you withdraw from an ATM?
17 Which French royal family share their name with a biscuit?
18 In the past in a hospital what was ether used for?
19 Is a kumquat a fruit or a vegetable?
20 Aloha means hello and goodbye on which island?
21 Which number upside down looks like an E on a calculator's LCD?
22 What is the term for an empty space from which air is removed?
23 Which word links a seaside confection and stone?
24 Were Luddites machine wreckers or prison reformers?
25 What is a large group of insects called?
26 What do the numbers on one standard die/dice total?
27 In medicine what is the term for the exchange of blood?
28 The feet of zebras take what form?
29 If Christmas Day was a Wednesday on what day would the following New Year's Day fall?
30 What does the word fauna describe?

POT LUCK 35 *See quiz 76, page 84*

ANSWERS

1 7. 2 John McEnroe. 3 Park Lane. 4 Before. 5 Hoops. 6 *Vanilla*. 7 Game.
8 Horse. 9 Top row. 10 Black. 11 Skull. 12 Three. 13 Gerard Houllier.
14 Magnus Magnusson. 15 Bees. 16 "Eleanor Rigby". 17 Turkey. 18 U.
19 "Edelweiss". 20 December. 21 New York. 22 Snail mail. 23 1960s. 24 Lion.
25 Diamonds. 26 Hugh. 27 Bernie Taupin. 28 South Africa. 29 Vatican City.
30 Its young are born and suckled in the mother's pouch.

QUIZ 75 LATE GREATS

Answers - see Quiz 73, page 81

1 What was the first name of prolific novelist Ms Cartland?
2 Who was the ex Mrs Geldof Paula?
3 Desmond Wilcox was the husband of which chat show hostess and TV presenter?
4 Which entertainer Davis added Junior to his name?
5 In which British capital city did Lord Olivier have a theatre named after him?
6 Which playwright Oscar is on the cover of The Beatles' *Sergeant Pepper* album?
7 Which type of TV show did Helen Rollason present?
8 What type of transport did Jennifer Paterson use in her TV cookery series?
9 In which city was Jill Dando murdered?
10 Kim Philby found notoriety as a what?
11 Which Enid wrote the *Noddy* books?
12 Which Queen said, "We are not amused"?
13 Which Lord sat in Parliament as Quintin Hogg?
14 King Camp Gillette pioneered which grooming aid?
15 According to Jewish and Christian teaching, who was the very first person?
16 Which Darwin set out his theory of evolution?
17 For which branch of the arts was James Dean famous?
18 In which country was actress Marlene Dietrich born?
19 What was the first name of novelist Miss Austen?
20 In which country did Princess Diana tragically die?
21 What was the first name of the late broadcaster Dimbleby, father of David and Jonathan?
22 The late Douglas Adams wrote about *The Hitch Hiker's Guide to* where?
23 What was the name Lady McCartney, wife of Sir Paul, who died from breast cancer?
24 Who was Queen Victoria's consort?
25 Roald Dahl mainly wrote stories for whom?
26 Christian Dior was famous for designing what?
27 Jacqueline Du Pré, whose story was told in the movie *Hilary & Jackie*, played which musical instrument?
28 Which actor Eddington found fame in *The Good Life* and *Yes Minister*?
29 What did Aesop write?
30 Which assassinated leader of the USA was the first Catholic to be elected as President?

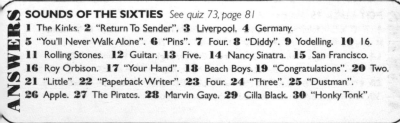

SOUNDS OF THE SIXTIES *See quiz 73, page 81*
1 The Kinks. 2 "Return To Sender". 3 Liverpool. 4 Germany.
5 "You'll Never Walk Alone". 6 "Pins". 7 Four. 8 "Diddy". 9 Yodelling. 10 16.
11 Rolling Stones. 12 Guitar. 13 Five. 14 Nancy Sinatra. 15 San Francisco.
16 Roy Orbison. 17 "Your Hand". 18 Beach Boys. 19 "Congratulations". 20 Two.
21 "Little". 22 "Paperback Writer". 23 Four. 24 "Three". 25 "Dustman".
26 Apple. 27 The Pirates. 28 Marvin Gaye. 29 Cilla Black. 30 "Honky Tonk".

QUIZ 76 POT LUCK 35

Answers - see Quiz 74, page 82

1 How many Days were in the title of Craig David's 2000 No 1?
2 Which sportsman said quite seriously, "You cannot be serious"?
3 In Monopoly what makes a set with Mayfair?
4 What does pre mean when it goes before a word?
5 What is the ball hit through in croquet?
6 What type of *Sky* was the movie with Tom Cruise and Penelope Cruz?
7 Which word can refer to a sporting fixture or a type of meat?
8 Which of these creatures is not in the same family as humans – chimpanzee, gorilla or horse?
9 Where do numbers most usually appear on a computer keyboard?
10 What colour is the nose of a polar bear?
11 Which is the furthest from the ground in the human body – the fibula, the patella or the skull?
12 How many leaves does a clover plant usually have?
13 Which Liverpool manager collapsed at a soccer match in October 2001?
14 Who on TV said, "I've started so I'll finish"?
15 Which creatures are kept in an apiary?
16 Which song by the Beatles mentions Father Mackenzie?
17 In which country would you watch Galatasaray play a home soccer match?
18 Horse shoes resemble which letter of the alphabet?
19 Which *Sound Of Music* flower was a hit?
20 In which month is the Jewish feast of Hannukah?
21 The Lincoln Center is in which US city?
22 What do Internet users derisively call postal mail?
23 Bob Dylan's music is particularly associated with which decade of last century?
24 What type of body does the ancient monument the Sphinx have?
25 Johannesburg is noted for the cutting of which gems?
26 Which Grant played the cad in *Bridget Jones's Diary*?
27 Who wrote the lyrics for "Candle In The Wind"?
28 Which of these countries does not spend dollars – Australia, New Zealand or South Africa?
29 Which city-state within Rome is the centre of the Roman Catholic Church?
30 What is the special feature of a marsupial?

POT LUCK 34 See quiz 74, page 82

ANSWERS

1 Chemical Brothers. **2** A sheep. **3** Dog. **4** Red. **5** Architect. **6** Wednesday.
7 Nancy. **8** England. **9** Medicine. **10** Carrot. **11** 26. **12** Capitals.
13 Switzerland. **14** *Exodus*. **15** Soup. **16** Money. **17** Bourbon. **18** Anaesthetic.
19 Fruit. **20** Hawaii. **21** 3. **22** Vacuum. **23** Rock. **24** Machine wreckers.
25 Swarm. **26** 21. **27** Transfusion. **28** Hooves. **29** Wednesday. **30** Animals.

QUIZ 77 TV TRIVIA

Answers - see Quiz 79, page 87

1 Which Spice Girl presented *This Is My Moment*?
2 Which group were formed after *Popstars*?
3 What sort of events take place according to the title of the series set in Midsomer Parva?
4 Who is Roy's other half in *Coronation Street*?
5 Formula 1 racing switched to which terrestrial TV channel for the 1999 series?
6 What is the first name of the builder on *Ground Force*?
7 How often is the drama series *Doctors* shown?
8 Which chef replaced Loyd Grossman on *Masterchef*?
9 Which Anne presents *The Weakest Link*?
10 Who hosts a *Supermarket Sweep* on daytime TV?
11 Which soap ran a publicity campaign where 'everyone's talking about it'?
12 At what time of day is GMTV broadcast?
13 What type of show does Trisha host on ITV1?
14 How many people compete against each other in *Countdown*?
15 Which phone number is the title of a show with Michael Buerk?
16 What type of *Rescue* does Wendy Turner Webster host?
17 How is *Breakfast* described on Channel 4?
18 Who or what is CBBC aimed at?
19 *TOTP 2* is a rerun of which TV show?
20 What type of *Feet* were in the title of the series with James Nesbitt and Helen Baxendale?
21 *This is 5* was the first programme shown on which channel?
22 *London's Burning* is about life in which emergency service?
23 On which day of the week was the children's morning show *Live & Kicking* shown?
24 What was ITV1's Saturday night show about the premiership called?
25 In which show might tubby toast appear?
26 If Alistair McGowan impersonated David Beckham who did Ronni Ancona 'do'?
27 Who can you 'ask' on *Who Wants To Be A Millionaire?*?
28 At what time of day is *Countdown* usually shown?
29 What does A stand for in the hospital drama *A & E*?
30 What is the first name of the older psychiatrist Dr Crane?

QUIZ 78 POT LUCK 36

Answers - see Quiz 80, page 88

1 What is a sudden rush of snow down a mountain known as?
2 In which part of London was the Millennium Dome built?
3 On a plane or a boat a galley is a type of what?
4 What was Jim Belushi's ill fated elder brother called?
5 What sort of weather occurs in a monsoon?
6 Which groups are linked together through Interpol?
7 Myanmar is a modern name for which country
8 What is pulped to make paper?
9 What does I stand for in the communications initials ISP?
10 Who played Mr Bumble in the movie *Oliver!*?
11 The society for magicians is called the Magic what?
12 How many miles are there in a marathon to the nearest mile?
13 The Suez Canal joins which continent to Asia?
14 Who created *Harry Potter*?
15 How was the ancient king Alexander described?
16 In which city did Princess Diana die?
17 If food is cooked au gratin what ingredient does it contain?
18 What colour is pure gold?
19 If a five shows on the top of a die/dice, what number is on the bottom?
20 Glenn Close acted in a movie about *101* dogs of which breed?
21 Which Jackson made the album *Thriller*?
22 Which material is used to make things in origami?
23 Who is Venus Williams' tennis player sister?
24 What is a person from Tangier called?
25 Who was the US President on 31 December 1999?
26 What did Madonna call her second child?
27 What is the currency of Canada?
28 What was the name of the explosive invented by Alfred Nobel?
29 Chris Boardman is involved in which type of racing?
30 Which of the following is not the name of a real Sea – Blue Sea, Red Sea or Yellow Sea?

ANSWERS

POT LUCK 37 *See quiz 80, page 88*
1 Cornflakes. 2 Pacific. 3 Dish. 4 Cricket. 5 France. 6 Great Lakes.
7 Scotland. 8 Heptathlon. 9 Finland. 10 Pavement. 11 Violin. 12 660.
13 Water. 14 Chess. 15 America. 16 Cartoons. 17 Happy. 18 Famine.
19 Two. 20 Police officers. 21 Estonia. 22 Fencing. 23 10. 24 Brass.
25 Thames. 26 50s. 27 Nine. 28 Winslet. 29 Eye. 30 Whirlpool bath.

QUIZ 79 SPORTS MIXED BAG

Answers - see Quiz 77, page 85

1 Which event on ice is the fastest team sport in the world?
2 What shape is a dartboard?
3 In which sport do players compete for the Davis Cup?
4 How often is the Epsom Derby held?
5 Which sportsmen compete for the Ryder Cup?
6 Formula I usually refers to which sport?
7 The Seoul Olympics were in which country?
8 Sumo is a type of what?
9 Which sport is played at Lord's?
10 Which season other than summer has an Olympic Games?
11 Which country has won most Olympic gold medals for judo?
12 The Prix de L'Arc de Triomphe is one of Europe's biggest events in which sport?
13 Which birds of prey did Sheffield's Rugby League club add to its name?
14 Who do Oxford compete against in the university boat race?
15 What do you travel in if you compete in a two man bob event?
16 What type of racing takes place at Ascot?
17 Boules is similar to bowls and originated in which country?
18 How many pins are there in bowling in a bowling alley?
19 Which B is one under par in golf?
20 What shape is a hockey stick?
21 In which decade was Tiger Woods born?
22 What is a table tennis ball made from?
23 What do you use to hit the shuttlecock in badminton?
24 In tennis how many events make up the Grand Slam?
25 If you throw the discus, competitively, what shape is the area you throw it from?
26 If you 'put' a shot what do you actually do with it?
27 How many legs or sections are there in an Olympic relay race?
28 How frequently are the Paralympics held?
29 The racecourse at Aintree is near which northern city?
30 Which of the following is not a major horse race in Britain, 1,000 Guineas, 2,000 Guineas, 10,000 Guineas?

TV TRIVIA *See quiz 77, page 85*
1 Mel B. 2 Hear'Say. 3 Murders 4 Hayley. 5 ITV1. 6 Tommy. 7 Daily.
8 Gary Rhodes. 9 Robinson. 10 Dale Winton. 11 *EastEnders.* 12 Morning.
13 Chat. 14 Two. 15 *999.* 16 *Pet.* 17 *Big.* 18 Children. 19 *Top of the Pops.*
20 *Cold.* 21 Channel 5. 22 Fire brigade. 23 Saturday. 24 *The Premiership.*
25 *Teletubbies.* 26 Victoria Beckham. 27 The audience. 28 Late afternoon.
29 Accident. 30 Frasier.

ANSWERS

QUIZ 80 POT LUCK 37

Answers - see Quiz 78, page 86

1 WK Kellogg created which present day breakfast favourite in the 19th century?
2 The name of which ocean means peace?
3 Which kitchen item is linked to receiving satellite television?
4 Which sport has wooden uprights that are 22 yards apart?
5 Which country did Renault cars originally come from?
6 Lakes Michigan, Erie, Ontario, Huron and Superior are known as what?
7 In *Mrs Doubtfire*, Robin Williams dressed up as a nanny from which country?
8 Denise Lewis won gold at the 2000 Olympics in which event?
9 Which country has the Finnmark as its currency?
10 What do the British call what the Americans call a sidewalk?
11 Which musical instrument is associated with Vanessa Mae?
12 How many minutes are there in exactly 11 hours?
13 What does a cactus store up inside it?
14 Gary Kasparov was famous for playing which game?
15 The explorer Amerigo Vespucci gave his name to which continent?
16 What did Barbera work with Hanna to create?
17 Which of Snow White's Seven Dwarfs begins with a H?
18 The charity Oxfam was founded to help relieve which world problem?
19 How many members of Oasis were brothers?
20 Which group of law enforcers was set up by Robert Peel?
21 Which of these countries is not included in Scandinavia – Denmark, Estonia or Norway?
22 In which sport is there a foil discipline?
23 How many letters remain in the English alphabet after P?
24 Trumpets and cornets belong to which section of instruments?
25 Vauxhall Bridge, Tower Bridge and Waterloo Bridge all cross which river?
26 Blondie's Debbie Harry was in which decade of her life when "Maria" topped the UK charts?
27 In sayings, how many lives is a cat meant to have?
28 Which Kate starred in the blockbuster movie *Titanic*?
29 Which part of the body refers to the centre of a storm?
30 What water feature did Roy Jacuzzi invent?

POT LUCK 36 *See quiz 78, page 86*

QUIZ 81 THE UNIVERSE

Answers - see Quiz 83, page 91

1 How many planets are there in our Solar System?
2 In space, what is Mir?
3 What's the name of the explosion that began Universe?
4 A constellation is a group of what?
5 To make a rainbow what weather conditions are needed?
6 In a storm what can be forked or sheet?
7 If the Moon looks like an illuminated circle what is it called?
8 What is a moving sheet of ice called?
9 In which country is the tropical rain forest of Amazonia?
10 Which layer above Antarctica has a hole in it?
11 Which of these is a danger to the environment, heavy rain, acid rain, drizzly rain?
12 The term fauna refers to what?
13 Which ocean is the deepest?
14 Which M is the largest lake in the USA?
15 What type of natural phenomenon is K2?
16 Which is the most valuable metal – gold, platinum or silver?
17 A monsoon is a wind which brings what along with it?
18 Which river is the longest – Amazon, Mississippi or Nile?
19 What is a meteorite made from?
20 In which southern hemisphere country is Ayers Rock?
21 Which Sea is the lowest point on Earth?
22 Reservoirs are man made to hold what?
23 Europe's longest river the Volga flows in which country?
24 Which of these regions has the most glaciers – Antarctica, Asia or Europe?
25 The water in rivers is provided by either melting snow or what?
26 Cumulus and Nimbostratus are types of what?
27 Which is the world's largest desert?
28 Which 'effect' is associated with global warming?
29 What colour is linked to caring for nature and the environment?
30 The Yangtze, Congo and Mekong are all types of what?

NEWSWORTHY *See quiz 83, page 91*
ANSWERS
1 European. 2 USA. 3 Republican 4 Edinburgh. 5 DH. 6 John Major. 7 BSE.
8 1940s. 9 Wall. 10 1980s. 11 National Lottery. 12 Prescott. 13 White.
14 Scottish. 15 Italian. 16 Eton College. 17 Cool. 18 Foot and mouth.
19 Portillo. 20 Livingstone. 21 Nanny. 22 £2. 23 Michael. 24 10 o'clock.
25 Channel 4. 26 Heath. 27 Ireland. 28 Clinton. 29 Peace. 30 Her children.

QUIZ 82 POT LUCK 38

Answers - see Quiz 84, page 92

1 In which country was Martina Hingis born?
2 Scotsman Mr Macintosh invented what type of fabric – easy clean, see through or waterproof?
3 Which ocean surrounds the North Pole – the Arctic Ocean, the Atlantic Ocean or the Indian Ocean?
4 Where can you purchase two items and still have bought lots?
5 In the carol, which Good King looked out on the feast of Stephen?
6 Which invention was developed last – CD, fax or photocopier?
7 Geronimo was a warrior involved in the fight against which government?
8 Which missile did David use to slay Goliath?
9 Which actor John famously danced with Princess Diana at the White House?
10 Is a valise a type of dance, a holdall or a sunken plain?
11 What is the name of the little girl in The Wizard of Oz?
12 Which ball is heaviest among these sports, table tennis, tennis, volleyball?
13 In which card game do you shout out if two cards match?
14 Who played Maximus in Gladiator?
15 Which doll is Ken's girlfriend?
16 How many Spice Girls were in the band at the time of their first No 1?
17 Simba's Pride was a sequel to which movie?
18 Daniel Fahrenheit created a device to measure what?
19 Which company launched the Playstation?
20 What colour is a female pheasant?
21 Which of these will not dissolve in water – salt, sand or sugar
22 How was Louis XIV of France known?
23 What did a troubadour do?
24 What number appears top left on a standard pocket calculator?
25 A fritillary is a type of what?
26 Aromatherapy treats people using what?
27 In Italy ciabatta is a type of what?
28 Which American hero died at the Alamo?
29 In 2001 which manager in the Premiership could claim to have 21 full internationals at his club?
30 Who definitely said, "I never said 'You dirty rat'."?

POT LUCK 39 See quiz 84, page 92

ANSWERS

1 5. 2 Piano. 3 Geri Halliwell. 4 Networking. 5 Celtic. 6 Down. 7 Ike. 8 17. 9 Red. 10 December. 11 White. 12 Carnivore. 13 Bat. 14 Chimpanzees. 15 Furniture polish. 16 Space Shuttle. 17 Pink. 18 Murder. 19 Mick Jagger. 20 Secrets. 21 Double bass. 22 "Rainbow". 23 Mercury. 24 Hover. 25 Eye. 26 Three. 27 Julia Roberts. 28 American Football. 29 Asia. 30 Rollercoaster.

QUIZ 83 NEWSWORTHY

Answers - see Quiz 81, page 89

1 What does the first E stand for in EEC?

2 Dwight D Eisenhower was President of which country?

3 Which of the following is a major US political party: Christian Democrat, Republican, Socialist?

4 Where is the HQ of the Scottish parliament?

5 What were the initials of controversial novelist Lawrence?

6 Which former British Prime Minister became a guardian to Princes William and Harry after their mother's death?

7 CJD was the human form of which disease?

8 In which decade was the first atomic bomb dropped on Hiroshima?

9 What was built across Berlin to stop East Germans escaping to the west?

10 In which decade was the disease AIDS identified?

11 Which money making draw did Camelot control – Football Pools, National Lottery or Premium Bonds?

12 Which John was Tony Blair's first Deputy Prime Minister?

13 What colour is the background of the flag of the Red Cross?

14 What does the S stand for in the British political party the SNP?

15 What nationality were all the Popes between 1522 and 1978?

16 Which school near Windsor did Princes William and Harry attend?

17 How was trendy Britain – Britannia – dubbed in the media in the 1990s?

18 Which animal disease closed down vast rural areas of the UK in 2001?

19 Which Michael was William Hague's last shadow Chancellor of the Exchequer?

20 Which Ken became the first popularly-elected London Mayor?

21 In what capacity was Louise Woodward employed when a baby died in her care?

22 Which value coin was introduced in Britain 1998?

23 Who is Ralf Schumacher's more successful brother?

24 The BBC *Nine O'Clock News* was moved to what time in the new millennium?

25 Which TV Channel won the right to broadcast Test cricket after the BBC lost out in the bidding battle?

26 Which former Prime Minister Edward left Parliament in 2001?

27 Bertie Ahern and Albert Reynolds were Prime Ministers of where?

28 Which 1990s US President had the first names William Jefferson?

29 Which Nobel Prize did Nelson Mandela win?

30 Who did Princess Diana leave most of her money to?

ANSWERS

THE UNIVERSE *See quiz 81, page 89*

1 Nine. 2 Space station. 3 Big Bang. 4 Stars. 5 Sun & rain. 6 Lightning. 7 Full moon. 8 Glacier. 9 Brazil. 10 Ozone layer. 11 Acid rain. 12 Animals. 13 Pacific. 14 Michigan. 15 Mountain. 16 Gold. 17 Rain. 18 Nile. 19 Rock. 20 Australia. 21 Dead Sea. 22 Water. 23 Russia. 24 Antarctica. 25 Rain. 26 Cloud. 27 Sahara. 28 Greenhouse. 29 Green. 30 River.

QUIZ 84 POT LUCK 39

Answers - see Quiz 82, page 90

1 On a calculator's LCD display which number resembles letter S?
2 Which instrument can be upright or a baby grand?
3 Who had her first solo top ten hit in 1999 with "Look At Me"?
4 Which word describes linking computers together?
5 Which was the first Scottish club that Chris Sutton played for?
6 Which direction do you travel when abseiling?
7 What was the nickname of US President Dwight Eisenhower?
8 If you have displayed 35 cards in a game of patience, how many are left to play?
9 What was the colour in the nickname of flying ace Manfred von Richthofen?
10 In the southern hemisphere, Christmas is in which month?
11 What is the main colour of the White House in Washington?
12 Someone whose diet consists exclusively of meat is known as a what?
13 What is the only mammal that can fly?
14 Who are the most intelligent creatures after humans – chimpanzees, elephants or horses?
15 What is beeswax chiefly used for?
16 What was the name of the first reusable spacecraft?
17 What colour is cooked salmon?
18 What sort of crime has been committed in the game Cluedo?
19 Who did Bianca de Macias marry in 1971?
20 What completes the book title, *Harry Potter And The Chamber Of ____*?
21 Which is the largest member of the violin family – the cello, the double bass, or the violin?
22 Which word completes the song title, "Somewhere Over The_____"?
23 Which planet is nearest to the Sun?
24 What does a kestrel do while looking for its prey?
25 Where on the body might a cataract appear?
26 How many pairs of legs does an insect have?
27 Which actress links the movies *Erin Brokovich*, *Runaway Bride* and *My Best Friend's Wedding*?
28 The Dallas Cowboys and Washington Redskins play which sport?
29 The giant panda is native to which continent?
30 In his No 1 hit, Ronan Keating thought "Life" was like which fairground ride?

ANSWERS

POT LUCK 38 *See quiz 82, page 90*
1 Czechoslovakia. 2 Waterproof. 3 Arctic. 4 Auction. 5 King Wenceslas. 6 CD
7 American. 8 Stone (rock/pebble). 9 Travolta. 10 Holdall. 11 Dorothy.
12 Volleyball. 13 Snap. 14 Russell Crowe. 15 Barbie. 16 Five. 17 *The Lion King*.
18 Temperature. 19 Sony. 20 Brown. 21 Sand. 22 The Sun King. 23 Sing. 24 7.
25 Butterfly. 26 Perfumed oil. 27 Bread. 28 Davy Crockett. 29 Sir Alex Ferguson.
30 James Cagney.

QUIZ 85 BIG SCREEN GREATS

Answers - see Quiz 86, page 94

1 Who is the father of Fraser Heston who played baby Moses in his dad's famous movie?
2 In most of her films what colour was Rita Hayworth's hair?
3 Which Sean played Harrison Ford's father in *Indiana Jones & The Last Crusade*?
4 Which Roy had a horse called Trigger?
5 In which country was Brigitte Bardot born?
6 What is the first name of Bridget Fonda's famous aunt?
7 Which Moore starred in *Indecent Proposal*?
8 How was Roscoe Arbuckle better known?
9 What type of movies was Lucille Ball famous for?
10 Where was Ingrid Bergman born?
11 Which comedy star Charlie did Paulette Goddard marry?
12 Who was famous for Goldwynisms such as,"A verbal contract isn't worth the paper it's written on."'?
13 Which Alec played Obi-wan Kenobi in the original *Star Wars*?
14 Which Hepburn starred in *My Fair Lady*?
15 Which Fred's autobiography was called *Steps In Time*?
16 Which actor Tom turned to directing with *That Thing You Do*?
17 Rex Harrison was Oscar-nominated for which ruling part in *Cleopatra*?
18 What condition led directly to Rock Hudson's death?
19 What did Yul Brynner notably shave to play the King in *The King and I*?
20 Which series of comedy films was Bob Hope famous for?
21 Which part of the UK is Anthony Hopkins from?
22 Which actor had the first names Humphrey DeForest?
23 How was Greta Louisa Gustaffson better known?
24 Who sang "Somewhere Over the Rainbow" in film *The Wizard of Oz*?
25 Who did Richard Burton marry after the release of *Cleopatra*?
26 What is Samuel Jackson's middle initial?
27 Who married Carole Lombard while making *Gone With the Wind*?
28 Which 'blue eyed' singer did Ava Gardner marry?
29 What is the surname of actors and directors Walter, John and Anjelica?
30 Who wrote *Lauren Bacall By Myself*?

POT LUCK 40 See quiz 86, page 94
ANSWERS
1 Corrs. 2 Arsenal. 3 Indian. 4 Backbone. 5 American. 6 Extinct. 7 Card game.
8 Earth. 9 Tango. 10 Yellow. 11 Boxing. 12 Mosquito. 13 1980s. 14 Elephant.
15 Away. 16 Hurricane. 17 Portugal. 18 Dog. 19 Vote. 20 Birds. 21 Furbies.
22 Nightingale. 23 TB. 24 E. 25 Brown. 26 Boxing. 27 Six. 28 Poisoning.
29 Y. 30 Respiratory system.

QUIZ 86 POT LUCK 40

Answers - see Quiz 85, page 93

1 Which Irish group were "Breathless" at making No 1 in the year 2000?
2 England keepers David Seaman and Richard Wright were together at which club in September 2001?
3 Which ocean is to the east of South Africa?
4 What does an invertebrate not have in its body?
5 Under which nationality did Navratilova play her final Wimbledon?
6 If an animal has not been sighted for 50 years it is described as what?
7 What kind of game is bridge?
8 Which was the first planet to be discovered that had water and oxygen?
9 Which dance was connected with Marlon Brando and Paris?
10 A natural sponge is what colour?
11 What is the sport of Riddick Bowe and Buster Douglas?
12 Which insect carries the disease malaria?
13 In which decade did Wet Wet Wet have their first hit?
14 Which African creature is the world's biggest land mammal?
15 What is the first word sung in the popular carol "Away In A Manger"?
16 Which is the fastest speed – a gale, a hurricane or a storm?
17 Which country is directly west of southern Spain?
18 What is a chihuahua?
19 Suffragettes campaigned so that women had the right to do what?
20 Ornithophobia is a fear of what?
21 Which toys speak Furbish?
22 Which bird shares its name with a famous nurse?
23 The disease tuberculosis is often abbreviated to which initials?
24 Which letter is the symbol of the euro currency?
25 What colour is a female blackbird?
26 The Marquis of Queensberry established rules relating to what?
27 How many noughts appear when one million is written in figures?
28 How does a venomous snake kill things?
29 A wishbone resembles letter of the alphabet?
30 What is the name of the system that enables humans to breathe?

THE MEDIUM QUESTIONS

On your toes folks, things are getting a little bit more tricky! Even the reigning pub quiz champions will be getting a bit hot under the collar ... although you are bound to get the odd smug bar steward who fancies his chances!

Once you have dipped your toes into the amazingly simple 'easy' questions you can ease yourself into something a little more challenging in the form of the 'medium' questions – which as the name cunningly suggests are of a medium level of difficulty. These will probably form the majority of the questions (unless you happen to be in the bar at a MENSA convention) as they are difficult enough to get your teams huddling round, whispering and dredging their brains for that answer that is lurking on the tips of their tongues!

QUIZ 1   WHO'S WHO?

Answers - see Quiz 3, page 99

1   In the 1990s religious education teacher Robert Fraser resigned after revelations he worked part time as a what?
2   Which position did Tony Blair have in the Shadow Cabinet before he became leader of the Labour Party?
3   Barbara Castle became Baroness Castle of which town which was her constituency?
4   Nicolae Ceausescu led which country until 1989?
5   What did Gandhi's title Mahatma mean?
6   Who was George W Bush's first Attorney General?
7   What is the first name of Mrs Al Gore, wife of the former Vice President?
8   Who was Iain Duncan Smith's first Shadow Chancellor?
9   Roy Jenkins became Baron Jenkins of where?
10 How old was Steven Jobs when he developed the first Apple computer?
11 Who was the youngest Kennedy brother, son of ex Ambassador Joseph Kennedy?
12 Who was the 1st Earl of Stockton?
13 Who left for the Soviet Union with Guy Burgess and Donald Maclean?
14 Richard Beeching is best remembered for his closure of what?
15 Which leader of a Northern Ireland-based party has the first names Ian Richard Kyle?
16 What was John Prescott train to be immediately after leaving school?
17 Which Simon suffered horrendous injuries in the Falklands War?
18 Gitta Sereny caused controversy over her book about which child murderer?
19 Jane Couch became the first woman in Britain to be given a licence to do what?
20 The new British Library was opened near which station?
21 Which Diane won a court case to have the child of her deceased husband using his frozen sperm?
22 Who was in *The Sun's* 1998 photo headed 'Is this the most dangerous man in Britain?'
23 How was Aneurin Bevan familarly known?
24 Which Eileen was Glenn Hoddle's faith healer during France 98?
25 What was the name of Bernadette McAliskey's daughter who was wanted in Germany on terrorist charges?
26 Which Paymaster General had problems with offshore tax havens and loans to an MP?
27 Which Welsh Secretary Ron had a 'moment of madness' on Clapham Common?
28 Which world leader has twin daughters called Barbara and Jenna?
29 Against which newspaper did Lord Archer bring his 1980s lawsuit which saw him back in the dock in 2001?
30 George W Bush was Governor of which state before he became President?

ANSWERS

TV FAMOUS FACES See quiz 3, page 99
1 Interiors. 2 Adams. 3 Ainsley Harriott. 4 Nick. 5 Chris 6 Francesca Annis.
7 Leslie Ash. 8 Oxo. 9 Sam Ryan. 10 The weather. 11 Samantha Janus.
12 Sue Johnston. 13 Mariette. 14 *Wheel of Fortune.* 15 Kathy Staff.
16 Royals. 17 Glenda Jackson. 18 Ainsley Harriott. 19 Daniela Nardini.
20 Ronni Ancona. 21 Nesbitt. 22 John Parrott. 23 Problems.
24 Christopher Timothy. 25 Andrew Castle. 26 Steve Coogan.
27 Robson Green. 28 Nicholson. 29 Melvyn Bragg. 30 Baxendale.

QUIZ 2 POT LUCK I

Answers - see Quiz 4, page 100

1 What was the Black day of the week when the stockmarket crashed in 1987?
2 What was the name of the family in the Beverly Hillbillies?
3 Where in London was the first Virgin record shop?
4 Which E is the driest inhabited country in the world?
5 What is a pachyderm – a briefcase, a thick skinned animal or a tree?
6 How many teeth does an anteater have?
7 Which is the smallest of our Solar System's planets?
8 Which Pope travelled to more countries than any other?
9 The game of mahjong originated in which country?
10 Phil Neal and Bruce Rioch have both managed which soccer club?
11 Which first name comes from a Latin word that means small?
12 In 1998 who replaced Judith Chalmers as presenter of TV's Wish You Were Here?
13 The city of Salonika is in which country?
14 Tom Rowlands and Ed Simons became which Brothers?
15 In which fictional village was TV drama *Heartbeat* set?
16 A manifest is a detailed list of a ship's what?
17 In which country was the organisation Greenpeace founded?
18 Which zodiac sign links August and September?
19 What was Billie's follow up to "Because We Want To"?
20 The Oxford vs Cambridge Boat Race is staged between Putney and where?
21 What does C stand for in the award CBE?
22 Elk, Fox and Wolf can all have which other animal added to their names?
23 Who had his statue removed from Russia's Red Square in 1991?
24 In which Essex suburb is Birds of A Feather set?
25 What do frogs and toads not have which other amphibians have?
26 Who is inaugurated on Inauguration Day, 20th January?
27 Bonny Lad, Express and White Windsor are varieties of which vegetable?
28 Which TV detective was based at Denton police station?
29 Which famous clown shares his name with the Royal Family of Monaco?
30 Which co star also became Brad Pitt's off screen partner while making the movie Se7en?

QUIZ 3 TV FAMOUS FACES

Answers - see Quiz 1, page 97

1 What would Linda Barker design on TV?
2 Which Helen become a famous face on *Big Brother*?
3 Who replaced Fern Britton as presenter of *Ready Steady Cook*?
4 Who is Dot's villainous son in *EastEnders*?
5 Which Tate has Peter Amory played in *Emmerdale* since 1989?
6 Which actress has played opposite Trevor Eve and Robson Green on TV and Ralph Fiennes in real life?
7 Who left *Men Behaving Badly* and moved on to *Where The Heart Is*?
8 Lynda Bellingham is famous for which ad?
9 What was the name of Amanda Burton's character in *Silent Witness*?
10 What would Martyn Davies talk about on TV?
11 Which former *Eurovision Song Contest* entrant starred in the series *Liverpool One*?
12 Which actress has had major roles in *Brookside* and *The Royle Family*?
13 Which role did the second Mrs Michael Douglas play in *The Darling Buds of May*?
14 Which TV quiz show did Carol Smillie appear on in the early part of her TV career?
15 Who left *Last of the Summer Wine* to rejoin the new look *Crossroads*?
16 Jennie Bond presents items on which area of news for the BBC?
17 Which future MP famously appeared on *The Morecambe & Wise Show*?
18 Which chef presented a series of *Gourmet Express* programmes?
19 Which actress starred in *This Life* and *Undercover Cop*?
20 Who starred with Alistair McGowan and is famed for her impression of Victoria Beckham?
21 Which James played Adam in *Cold Feet*?
22 In *A Question of Sport*, who is team captain opposite Ally McCoist?
23 What does Denise Robertson deal with on *This Morning*?
24 Which former TV vet plays Dr Mac McGuire in *Doctors*?
25 Which former tennis player is part of the GMTV team?
26 Who created the character Pauline Calf?
27 Who starred in *Reckless*, *Grafters* and *Touching Evil*?
28 Which Michael is TV's longest serving foreign correspondent?
29 Who presents *The South Bank Show*?
30 Which Helen starred in *Cold Feet*?

QUIZ 4 FAMOUS NAMES

Answers - see Quiz 2, page 98

1 Which Irish born Thomas founded his East End Mission for destitute children in 1867?
2 Who was the first couturier to design for men as well as women?
3 Dame Elisabeth Frink found fame in which field?
4 Where was Margaret Thatcher born?
5 Mikael Baryshnikov defected to the USA while with which ballet company?
6 Who became Archbishop of Canterbury in 1991?
7 Lew Grade became Baron of which venue associated with the film industry?
8 Who founded the Royal Shakespeare Company?
9 What was the trade of George Harrod who founded the famous London store?
10 Who designed Queen Elizabeth II's coronation gown?
11 What did Gertrude Jekyll design?
12 Which Poet Laureate preceded Andrew Motion?
13 Cecil Beaton was famous for working on *Vogue* magazine in what capacity?
14 How has Chris Bonington found fame?
15 Which Wimbledon champion was called up for military service in 2001?
16 In which decade did Bruce Oldfield display his first collection?
17 What name was Pocahontas given when she was brought to Britain?
18 George Balanchine is a famous name in which branch of the arts?
19 Toni & Guy is what type of famous business?
20 Which famous name in the food world opened in Russia in 1990?
21 Which band leader won the first gold disc?
22 Clarence Darrow modified a board game called The Landlord's Game and renamed it what?
23 Barnum and Bailey together founded what type of entertainment?
24 Who was the first cartoon character to have a statue erected in his honour in the US?
25 Which Sally was the first US woman in space?
26 Who wrote the *Talking Heads* series of monologues?
27 Ellery Queen is a name associated with what type of fiction?
28 Which musical instrument did Art Tatum play?
29 What name did Shirley Temple use when she was a US Ambassador?
30 What is the first name of opera singer – now a Dame – Baker?

QUIZ 5 POT LUCK 2

Answers - see Quiz 7, page 103

1 Dermatology is concerned with the study of human what?
2 Alistair Cooke became famous for broadcasting his 'Letter from' which country?
3 John Ravenscroft has been broadcasting over 30 years under which name?
4 Disney's feature length cartoon *Pinocchio* was released in which decade?
5 Whose debut album was *Northern Soul* in 1992?
6 Which game was Abner Doubleday credited with inventing?
7 Which of the Kennedy family was involved in the Chappaquiddick incident in the 1960s?
8 Which name was shared by Charlie Chaplin and Diana Princess of Wales?
9 In Hollywood, which Jean was dubbed the first 'Blonde Bombshell'?
10 Which describes Rubik's cube – two-dimensional, three-dimensional or four-dimensional?
11 Which stewed item goes into a compote?
12 In which TV series could a patient have been treated by Dr Jack Kerruish?
13 In which country are the Altamira cave paintings?
14 In batik what is painted on to fabric along with dye?
15 *Monty Python's Flying Circus* used which "Bell" as its theme music?
16 What is contained or held in a creel?
17 Dolores O'Riordan fronted which band in the 1990s?
18 Which Alexander discovered penicillin?
19 Who hosted the 1990s revival of TV's *Going For A Song*?
20 Which children's rhyme is linked to the Black Death?
21 What does tempus fugit mean?
22 What do the letters PB indicate by a sporting competitor's name?
23 A pipistrelle is what kind of creature?
24 What was the name of Phil and Kathy Mitchell's son in *EastEnders*?
25 In which country could you watch Alaves play a home soccer match?
26 Which Saint is commemorated at Lourdes?
27 What is the compass point name of the Colonel who was the centre of the US Irangate affair?
28 From which city was the first of TV's *Songs of Praise* broadcast?
29 Who did Caroline Quentin play in TV's *Jonathan Creek*?
30 The Manhattan Project was the codename for the development of what?

POT LUCK 3 *See quiz 7, page 103*

ANSWERS
1 Blackburn Rovers. 2 Mullet. 3 Samuel. 4 *Pride & Prejudice*. 5 Frisbee. 6 Electrician.
7 Paul Hogan. 8 William Hague. 9 Related. 10 India. 11 Boston. 12 Thelma.
13 Iraq. 14 Nicky Campbell. 15 H. 16 Mississippi. 17 Angola. 18 Jester.
19 1930s. 20 A capo. 21 Argentina. 22 Tammy Wynette. 23 Atonement. 24 Mule.
25 Lightning war. 26 *Bergerac*. 27 Jacob. 28 Scargill. 29 Take That. 30 1974.

QUIZ 6 THE UK

Answers - see Quiz 8, page 104

1 In London, which famous cathedral is near to the Barbican?
2 Where is the National Exhibition Centre?
3 Which Cross is at the west end of The Strand?
4 Cheddar is in which hills?
5 In which Essex town is Anglia University?
6 Which area of London is famous for its Dogs' Home?
7 The Bristol Channel is an extension of which river?
8 Where is the University of Kent's main campus?
9 In which season would you see Blackpool's famous illuminations?
10 What is the name of Chesterfield's church with the famous twisted spire?
11 The Cheviot Hills run into which countries?
12 Barrow-in-Furness is on which county's coast?
13 In which county is the Prime Minister's country home?
14 What was Cleveland's county town?
15 On which island is Fingal's Cave?
16 The National Motor Museum is near which stately home?
17 Clydebank is famous for which industry?
18 In which county is the Forest of Dean?
19 What is Antony Gormley's famous sculpture near Gateshead?
20 What is London's second airport?
21 Which racecourse exclusively for flat racing is near Chichester?
22 Which city of south west England was known to the Romans as Aqua Sulis?
23 In which part of London is the Natural History Museum?
24 Where did the Yvonne Arnaud theatre open in 1965?
25 In November 2001 many terminals did Heathrow Airport have?
26 What is Hull's full name?
27 Which town of north east Scotland is a terminus of the Caledonian Canal?
28 In which London borough is the National Maritime Museum?
29 What is the UK's electronic surveillance service at Cheltenham called?
30 In which London street are the offices of the Bank of England?

ANSWERS

SPORTING ACTION REPLAY See quiz 8, page 104
1 1900. 2 Shorts. 3 Mexico City. 4 Essex. 5 Durham. 6 35. 7 Mile.
8 Montreal. 9 French. 10 Smith. 11 Joe Davis. 12 Four. 13 Chris Evert.
14 Nick Faldo. 15 Jim Clark. 16 Graf. 17 Florence Griffith Joyner.
18 Gavin Hastings. 19 Evander Holyfield. 20 Dream Team. 21 Bobby Jones.
22 Peter Fleming. 23 US boycott. 24 12. 25 US. 26 Atlanta.
27 Shoemaker. 28 Seven. 29 Gareth Edwards. 30 Six.

QUIZ 7 POT LUCK 3

Answers - see Quiz 5, page 101

1 Ray Harford and Roy Hodgson have both managed which soccer club?
2 The name of which fish means a star in heraldry?
3 What was the first name of Mr Ryder of Ryder Cup fame?
4 Jennifer Ehle played Elizabeth Bennet in a 1990s TV adaptation of which classic novel?
5 The Pluto Platter had changed its name to what when it started to sell to the public?
6 What was the day job of Lech Walesa before he became a Polish leader?
7 Who created the character Mick 'Crocodile' Dundee?
8 "No ideas, no experience, no hope" was how Edward Heath spoke of which political person?
9 In finance, what does the letter R in SERPS stand for?
10 Rudyard Kipling was born in which country?
11 In the US, New York and which other north-eastern city stage major marathons?
12 In *The Likely Lads*, what was the name of Bob's wife?
13 Where were thousands of Kurds killed in the 1980s?
14 Who was the first UK presenter of TV's *Wheel of Fortune*?
15 In music, which of the following is not a note, F, G, H?
16 Which major river flows through New Orleans?
17 Which country was formerly known as Portuguese West Africa?
18 In the comic opera *The Yeoman Of The Guard*, what is the job that Jack Point carries out?
19 She's still going strong but in which decade was Tina Turner born?
20 What is used to raise the natural pitch of a guitar?
21 Aconcagua is the highest peak in which country?
22 Under which name did singer Virginia Pugh find fame?
23 The special Jewish day Yom Kippur is also known as the Day of what?
24 Which animal shares its name with Samuel Crompton's spinning machine?
25 What does Blitzkrieg mean, from which the word Blitz originated?
26 In which TV series did the character Charlie Hungerford appear?
27 Which J was George Gershwin's original first name?
28 Which Arthur was President of the National Union of Mineworkers in the 1980s?
29 Which pop band featured Gary Barlow and Jason Orange?
30 1966 saw Sir Alf Ramsey's finest hour as England manager, but in which year was he sacked?

POT LUCK 2 *See quiz 5, page 101*

1 Skin. 2 America. 3 John Peel. 4 1940s. 5 M People. 6 Baseball. 7 Edward.
8 Spencer. 9 Jean Harlow. 10 Three-dimensional. 11 Stewed Fruit. 12 *Peak Practice*.
13 Spain. 14 Wax. 15 The Liberty Bell. 16 Fish. 17 Cranberries. 18 Fleming.
19 Michael Parkinson. 20 Ring-a-ring-a-roses. 21 Time flies. 22 Personal best.
23 Bat. 24 Ben. 25 Spain. 26 Bernadette. 27 North. 28 Cardiff.
29 Maddy Magellan. 30 Atomic bomb.

QUIZ 8 SPORTING ACTION REPLAY

Answers - see Quiz 6, page 102

1 In which year were women first allowed to compete at the Olympics Games?
2 In 1934 what were women players allowed to wear at Wimbledon?
3 Where did Bob Beamon make his record-breaking long jump?
4 Allan Border played county cricket for Gloucestershire and which other county?
5 Ian Botham played cricket for Somerset, Worcestershire and which other county?
6 Sergei Bubka has broken in excess of how many world records 35, 65, 95?
7 In 1981 Sebastian Coe broke the world record in the 800m, 1500m and what?
8 Where in 1976 did Nadia Comaneci win her perfect 10 in Olympic gymnastics?
9 Which tennis Grand Slam did Jimmy Connors never win?
10 What was Margaret Court's name when she became the first Australian woman to win Wimbledon?
11 Who made the maximum snooker break of 147 in 1955, later acknowledged as a then world record?
12 How many Prix de L'Arc de Triomphe wins did Pat Eddery have in the 1980s?
13 Which American tennis player was undefeated on clay between 1973 and 1979 and had 18 Grand Slam titles?
14 Which Briton first played in the Ryder Cup in 1977 aged 20?
15 Which Scottish driver broke Juan Fangio's record 24 F1 Grand Prix wins?
16 Monica Seles was stabbed on a tennis court because of a supporter's fanatical devotion to which player?
17 Who won the Jesse Owens Award as the outstanding athlete of 1988, the year she broke world records in Seoul?
18 Who captained the British Lions tour of New Zealand in 1993?
19 Out of whose ear did Mike Tyson take a bite during a boxing match in 1997?
20 What was the 1992 US basketball team dubbed?
21 Which golfer born at the beginning of the 20th century in Atlanta was responsible for founding the US Masters in Augusta?
22 Who did John McEnroe win seven of his eight Grand Slam doubles titles with?
23 The 1976 and 1984 winner, what stopped Ed Moses getting Olympic gold in 1980?
24 How old was Lester Piggott when he had his first winner?
25 Which Open was Jack Nicklaus' first win?
26 Where did Steve Redgrave win the fourth of his five Olympic gold medals?
27 Which Willie was the first jockey to ride more than 8,000 winners?
28 When Mark Spitz won seven Olympic golds how many world records did he break?
29 Who became Wales's then youngest ever Rugby captain in 1968?
30 How many times was Steve Davis World Snooker Champion in the 1980s?

THE UK See quiz 6, page 102
1 St Paul's. 2 (near) Birmingham. 3 Charing Cross. 4 Mendips. 5 Chelmsford.
6 Battersea. 7 Severn. 8 Canterbury. 9 Autumn. 10 All Saints. 11 England/Scotland.
12 Cumbria. 13 Buckinghamshire. 14 Middlesbrough. 15 Staffa. 16 Beaulieu.
17 Shipping. 18 Gloucestershire. 19 Angel of the North. 20 Gatwick. 21 Goodwood.
22 Bath. 23 South Kensington. 24 Guildford. 25 Four. 26 Kingston Upon Hull.
27 Inverness. 28 Greenwich. 29 GCHQ. 30 Threadneedle Street.

ANSWERS

QUIZ 9 · POT LUCK 4

Answers - see Quiz 11, page 107

1 Ocean Colour Scene came from which city?
2 What was Lester Piggott jailed for in 1987?
3 Which TV series was based on the *Constable* novels by Nicholas Rea?
4 What does the term largo mean in music?
5 In cricket, how many bails are on the two sets of wickets?
6 The words of William Blake appear in which stirring song?
7 Who was the first person to have been soccer coach of England and Australia?
8 What did Ben Travers specialise in writing?
9 Joaquin Rodrigo wrote a concerto in the 1930s for which solo instrument?
10 Which movie sequel had the subtitle *Judgment Day*?
11 The composer Sibelius is associated with which country?
12 In Shakespeare's play which king does Macbeth murder?
13 Which P was a country that Paddington bear came from?
14 What did the J stand for in the name of rugby legend JPR Williams?
15 The Golan Heights are on the border of Israel and which other country?
16 Which subject was George Stubbs famous for painting?
17 Who was the female co presenter of TV's *Crimewatch* before Jill Dando?
18 Who goes with *Bess* in the title of George Gershwin's opera?
19 Which book includes extracts from Jonathan Harker's diary?
20 In which TV series did Samantha Janus star as Isobel de Pauli?
21 What was Count Basie's actual first name?
22 How many shots does each player get at the target in curling?
23 Susanna Hoffs fronted which band?
24 Where is the Sea of Showers?
25 In which decade did Jesse Owens set a long jump record that would remain unbroken for 25 years?
26 Which musical instrument is Vladimir Ashkenazy famous for playing?
27 The city of Alexandria is in which country?
28 Which Stephen wrote the song "Send In the Clowns"?
29 Ron Atkinson and Danny Wilson have both managed which soccer club?
30 Kayak, rotor and noon are all examples of what type of words?

POT LUCK 5 *See quiz 11, page 107*
1 Ridley. 2 Back to basics. 3 Iceland. 4 The Scarlet Pimpernel. 5 France.
6 *All About Eve.* 7 Fawlty Towers. 8 Die. 9 Kingsley. 10 Liverpool. 11 1940s.
12 Birmingham. 13 Martin Scorsese. 14 Ackroyd. 15 Southampton. 16 Conciliation.
17 Greek. 18 Rhapsody. 19 Doncaster. 20 Spinach. 21 Whooping cough.
22 Seinfeld. 23 Chile. 24 Jean Alexander. 25 Manchester. 26 Simon Le Bon.
27 Celtic. 28 *Parallel Lines.* 29 1930s. 30 Warriors.

QUIZ 10 MOVIES WHO'S WHO?

Answers - see Quiz 12, page 108

1 Which Norfolk born actor's movies include *My Best Friend's Wedding* and *The Madness of King George*?
2 Who, in October 2000, was Woody Allen's mother-in-law?
3 Who was Meg Ryan's husband in real life when she made *Sleepless in Seattle*?
4 How tall is Melanie Griffith – 5'2", 5'9" or 6'1"?
5 Which French actress made her debut in *And God Created Woman*?
6 What was the original nationality of director Milos Forman?
7 Which Oscar winning actress founded the production company Egg Pictures?
8 Who was Clark Gable's leading lady in his final movie?
9 Who is Kate Hudson's famous actress mother?
10 What are Nick Park's most famous movie characters made from?
11 Which movie shot Quentin Tarantino to prominence?
12 Who played Jack Ryan in *Patriot Games*?
13 Which English playwright scripted *The French Lieutenant's Woman*?
14 In which country was actress Neve Campbell born?
15 Which Steven directed *Sex, Lies and Videotape*?
16 Which star of *Dead Man Walking* was the voice of *Ivy* in *Cats and Dogs*?
17 Which star of *Batman Returns* and *A View to a Kill* danced on Fatboy Slim's *Weapon of Choice*?
18 Darryl Hannah passed on the role of Shelby in *Steel Magnolias* to whom?
19 Who played the title role in the movie about the US president who resigned in office?
20 What is Penelope Cruz's occupation in *Woman On Top*?
21 Who is the voice of the princess in *Shrek*?
22 Who played the title role in *Miss Congeniality*?
23 Who played Mrs Jack Stanton, wife of the Governor, in *Primary Colors*?
24 Who starred in the original *Thomas Crown Affair* and the 1999 remake?
25 Who played the fitness teacher in *Perfect*?
26 Who was Robin Williams' wife in *Mrs Doubtfire*?
27 In 1999 which Shakespeare play did Kenneth Branagh bring to the big screen in the style of an MGM musical?
28 Who won Best Supporting Actress Oscar for *LA Confidential*?
29 How did Christopher Reeve receive his tragic injuries causing almost total immobility?
30 Which late actor starred with Keanu Reeves in *My Own Private Idaho*?

MUSIC – BANDS *See quiz 12, page 108*
1 Bon Jovi. 2 TLC. 3 En Vogue. 4 Ace of Base. 5 Appleton. 6 Beatles.
7 "Bohemian Rhapsody". 8 "I Want To Hold Your Hand". 9 "Help!". 10 Two.
11 "Country House". 12 "Words". 13 "Tsunami". 14 Pulp. 15 Prodigy.
16 Def Leppard. 17 Guns N' Roses. 18 U2. 19 Chemical Brothers. 20 REM.
21 The Bangles. 22 Newcastle. 23 "Doctor Jones". 24 "Mulder & Scully".
25 Northern Ireland. 26 *The Great Escape*. 27 Creation. 28 Boyzone.
29 *Gold*. 30 Boyzone.

QUIZ 11 POT LUCK 5

Answers - see Quiz 9, page 105

1 In *Coronation Street* what goes with Newton to make the beer for the Rovers' Return?
2 Which John Major campaign urged a return to traditional values?
3 The Althing is the parliament of which country?
4 In fiction, Percy Blakeney was the alias of which hero?
5 In which country was cubism founded?
6 Before *Titanic* what was the last film to win 14 Oscar nominations?
7 Which TV comedy series featured Miss Tibbs and Miss Gatsby?
8 Lester Piggott's first Derby winner was called Never Say what?
9 Which Mr Amis wrote *Lucky Jim*?
10 Bob Paisley and Graeme Souness have both managed which soccer club?
11 Still looking Ab Fab, in which decade was Joanna Lumley born?
12 The M1 was originally constructed to link London to where?
13 Harvey Keitel is particularly known for his work with which movie director?
14 Agatha Christie wrote about *The Murder of Roger* who?
15 What was Alan Shearer's first league club?
16 What does the C stand for in ACAS?
17 What was the nationality of fable writer Aesop?
18 What did George Gershwin write "in Blue"?
19 In horse racing where is the Lincoln Handicap held?
20 What S is added to pasta to make it green?
21 The illness pertussis is more commonly known as what?
22 Which US sitcom ran to 180 episodes, before finishing in 1998?
23 The southernmost part of South America is owned by which country?
24 Which former soap star became Auntie Wainwright in *Last of the Summer Wine*?
25 The Halle Orchestra is based in which English city?
26 Which pop personality married Yasmin Parvaneh in 1986?
27 Which club did Jock Stein lead to European success?
28 "Sunday Girl" featured on which Blondie album?
29 In which decade was the movie *Gone With the Wind* made?
30 In rugby, what was added to Wigan's name in 1997?

POT LUCK 4 *See quiz 9, page 105*

ANSWERS

1 Birmingham 2 Tax evasion. 3 Heartbeat. 4 Slowly. 5 Four. 6 Jerusalem.
7 Terry Venables. 8 Theatrical farce. 9 Guitar. 10 *Terminator II*. 11 Finland.
12 Duncan. 13 Peru. 14 John. 15 Syria. 16 Horses. 17 Sue Cook.
18 Porgy. 19 *Dracula*. 20 *Liverpool One*. 21 William. 22 Two.
23 The Bangles. 24 The moon. 25 1930s. 26 Piano. 27 Egypt.
28 Sondheim. 29 Sheffield Wednesday. 30 Palindromes.

QUIZ 12 MUSIC – BANDS

Answers - see Quiz 10, page 106

1 Whose Best of 1990s album was *Cross Road*?
2 T Boz, Left Eye and Chilli make up which band?
3 Who had a hit with "Don't Let Go"?
4 *Happy Nation* was the debut album of which Scandinavian band?
5 What was the surname of the sisters in All Saints?
6 Which band had 18 consecutive UK Top Ten hits between July 1964 and March 1976?
7 What was Queen's best selling single?
8 Which Beatles single was their first No 1 in the US?
9 Which Beatles single was a charity release by Bananarama plus Dawn French and Jennifer Saunders?
10 How many albums did the Spice Girls release in the 20th century?
11 What was Blur's first UK No 1?
12 Which 1996 Boyzone hit was a previous hit by the Bee Gees?
13 Which 1999 Manic Street Preachers hit shares its name with a natural disaster?
14 Who had a hit with "This Is Hardcore"?
15 Whose album *Fat of the Land* debuted at No 1 on both sides of the Atlantic?
16 Joe Elliot was vocalist with which heavy metal band?
17 Who had an "Appetite for Destruction" in 1987?
18 Whose album had some *Rattle & Hum* in 1988?
19 Who had the award winning 1999 album *Surrender*?
20 Who were "Out of Time" in 1991?
21 Who had the original hit with Atomic Kitten's "Eternal Flame"?
22 Which city did the 1960s band The Animals come from?
23 What was Aqua's follow up to "Barbie Girl"?
24 Which Catatonia hit shared its name with a TV duo?
25 Which part of the UK did Ash come from?
26 Which Blur album shared its name with a Steve McQueen film?
27 On which label did Oasis have their first Top Ten Hit?
28 Shane Lynch was a member of which band?
29 What was Abba's Greatest Hits album called?
30 Which band had 16 consecutive UK Top Ten hits between December 1994 and December 1999?

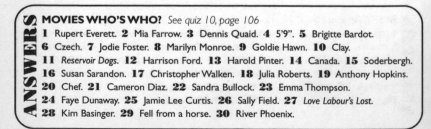

MOVIES WHO'S WHO? *See quiz 10, page 106*

1 Rupert Everett. 2 Mia Farrow. 3 Dennis Quaid. 4 5'9". 5 Brigitte Bardot.
6 Czech. 7 Jodie Foster. 8 Marilyn Monroe. 9 Goldie Hawn. 10 Clay.
11 *Reservoir Dogs*. 12 Harrison Ford. 13 Harold Pinter. 14 Canada. 15 Soderbergh.
16 Susan Sarandon. 17 Christopher Walken. 18 Julia Roberts. 19 Anthony Hopkins.
20 Chef. 21 Cameron Diaz. 22 Sandra Bullock. 23 Emma Thompson.
24 Faye Dunaway. 25 Jamie Lee Curtis. 26 Sally Field. 27 *Love Labour's Lost*.
28 Kim Basinger. 29 Fell from a horse. 30 River Phoenix.

ANSWERS

QUIZ 13 POT LUCK 6

Answers - see Quiz 15, page 111

1   In France all motorways begin with which letter of the alphabet?
2   What does the Blue Cross Charity provide aid to?
3   Where does a hydrophyte plant live?
4   In the song "Rule Britannia" what is Britannia told to rule?
5   Which soccer side won four championships in a row with Johan Cruyff as boss?
6   *All In the Family* was a US spin off from which UK sitcom?
7   In which western classic did John Wayne play The Ringo Kid?
8   What is the qualification to be Father of the House in the House of Commons?
9   In music, which note is written on the bottom line of the treble clef?
10 The Copacabana beach is in which South American city?
11 Whose first No 1 single used the title of a novel by one of the Bronte sisters?
12 In which TV series did you meet the characters Egg, Milly, Anna and Miles?
13 How many years before *Star Wars* is the action of *The Phantom Menace*, 22, 32 or 42?
14 Which band became the most successful 1990s Scandinavian act on the US singles chart?
15 If you were an LLD what subject would you have studied?
16 What was US President Lyndon Johnson's middle name?
17 Joe Royle and Mike Walker have both managed which soccer club?
18 In *Coronation Street* what type of pet was Mavis's Beauty?
19 Which Napoleonic battle gave its name to a famous chicken dish?
20 In which decade of last century were BBC TV programmes first broadcast?
21 The Beautiful South were formed after the break up of which group?
22 What was Hetty Wainthropp's young assistant sleuth called?
23 What was the first name of Eva Peron's husband?
24 Who used Marx Brothers film titles as album titles?
25 When was US hospital drama *St Elsewhere* first screened in the UK?
26 Giovanna Gassion sang under which name?
27 How many states were in the original union of the United States?
28 What would a palaeontologist study?
29 R.E.M. sang about "Shiny Happy" what?
30 What do the words post mortem actually mean?

QUIZ 14 PLANTS

Answers - see Quiz 16, page 112

1 What is the main characteristic of the wood of the balsa tree?
2 Plantain is a type of which fruit?
3 What is another name for the blackthorn?
4 Which industry's demands meant that rubber production increased in the last century?
5 What does a berry typically contain?
6 In a biennial plant, when do flower and seed production usually occur?
7 What name is given to small hardy plants ideal for rockeries, such as saxifraga?
8 The name tulip is derived from a Turkish word meaning what type of headgear?
9 What type of soil is vital for growing rhododendrons?
10 What is the most common colour of primula vulgaris or common primrose?
11 Clematis is a member of which family of wild flowers?
12 How many petals does an iris usually have?
13 What nationality was the botanist who gave his name to the dahlia?
14 How is the wild Rosa canina better known?
15 What colour is the rose of York?
16 Antirrhinums are also called what?
17 What is gypsophilia mainly grown for?
18 Which Busy plant has the name Impatiens?
19 Forget Me Nots are usually which colour?
20 Which TV cook Ms Lawson shares her name with the Love In A Mist flower?
21 How are the papery daisy-like flowers of helichrysum better known?
22 In which season do Michaelmas daisies flower?
23 Which best describes leaves of a hosta – scalloped, spiky or very large?
24 Which of the following flowers are not grown from bulbs – pansies, snowdrops and tulips?
25 What sort of bell is a campanula?
26 Muscari are what type of hyacinth?
27 What is used to make a mulch – chemicals, organic material or seeds?
28 What is always to be remembered about the seeds of the laburnum?
29 What colour are the ripe fruits of the mulberry tree?
30 What is the most common colour for alyssum, often used in borders and hanging baskets?

QUIZ 15 PAST TIMES 1900–1950

Answers - see Quiz 13, page 109

1 What was the code name of the project to develop the atom bomb?
2 Who was Prime Minister during the Abdication of Edward VIII?
3 In which city did Edith Cavell work in WWI?
4 Which Prime Minister declared war on Germany in 1939?
5 The Anschluss concerned Nazi Germany and which other state?
6 In which decade of the 20th century was the Boy Scout movement founded?
7 How was the Geheime Staatspolizei better known?
8 According to the wartime slogan, careless talk does what?
9 What was Tsar Nicholas II's wife called?
10 In which year was the Easter Rising in Dublin?
11 Lord Nuffield founded which car company which originally bore his name?
12 What type of clinic did Marie Stopes open?
13 Which Russian leader died in 1924?
14 In which decade did the Wall Street Crash take place?
15 In which German city was the Nazi party founded?
16 Which 'Queen' left on her maiden voyage across the Atlantic in 1946?
17 Which Duke and Duchess famously visited Hitler in Berlin in 1937?
18 Which French beaches were evacuated in 1940?
19 Which island received a medal for gallantry after WWII?
20 Which city called the German Florence was heavily bombed in 1945?
21 Which now annual arts Festival opened in for the first time in 1947?
22 What shape was the main part of the first AA badge which appeared in 1906?
23 What nationality was Robert Peary who reached the North Pole in 1909?
24 What was Dr Crippen's mistress's first name, with whom he tried to flee to Canada after murdering his wife?
25 Which East End street was the scene of siege by anarchists in 1911?
26 Taking the King's what meant that volunteers had signed up for the army?
27 Who succeeded Kitchener as War Secretary in 1916?
28 Who did the then Duke of York marry in 1923?
29 Which Bridge had the then longest span when it opened in 1932?
30 Which monarch made the first Christmas radio broadcast?

POT LUCK 6 See quiz 13, page 109

ANSWERS

1 A. 2 Animals. 3 In water. 4 The waves. 5 Barcelona. 6 *Till Death Us Do Part.*
7 *Stagecoach.* 8 Longest serving MP. 9 E. 10 Rio de Janeiro. 11 Kate Bush.
12 *This Life.* 13 32. 14 Roxette. 15 Law. 16 Baines. 17 Everton. 18 Budgie.
19 Marengo. 20 1930s. 21 The Housemartins. 22 Geoffrey. 23 Juan. 24 Queen.
25 1983. 26 Edith Piaf. 27 13. 28 Fossils. 29 People. 30 After death.

QUIZ 16 POT LUCK 7

Answers - see Quiz 14, page 110

1 What was Dorien's surname in *Birds of a Feather*?
2 What was Elvis Presley's middle name?
3 In the USA, where is the President's official country home?
4 The Sandanista guerrillas overthrew the government of which country in 1979?
5 Talking about Fred Astaire, Ginger Rogers said "I did what he did but I did it …" in which way?
6 Which board game features a racing car, a top hat and a dog?
7 What was the only hit of one hit wonders Doop?
8 Which President of the USA had Walter Mondale as Vice President?
9 Cerys Matthews became lead singer with which band in the mid 1990s?
10 The "General Belgrano" was sunk in which conflict?
11 Who won an Oscar for *The Sunshine Boys* at the age of 80?
12 Who took "Promise Me" into the charts in the early 1990s?
13 Which country were the aggressors in the Pearl Harbor attack of the 1940s?
14 Who played Lord Alfred Douglas in the movie *Wilde*?
15 Whose TV roles have included Arkwright and Fletcher?
16 What was the trade of Charles Lewis Tiffany?
17 In which part of the human skeleton are the metatarsels?
18 Whose last words were reputedly, "Thank God I have done my duty"?
19 Which Tony Di Bart No 1 hit from 1994 is the name of a group?
20 How many best actor Oscars did Sean Connery get for his portrayal of James Bond?
21 What was the name of John F Kennedy's brother who predeceased him?
22 IC sounds like it ought to be Iceland's international vehicle registration but isn't – but what is?
23 The Bass Strait lies between which two islands?
24 Which Pulp single title is also the name of a charity?
25 Who opened The Royal Albert Hall?
26 What is Tony Blair's eldest child named?
27 For which 1990s film with a prison theme did Johnny Cash contribute to the soundtrack?
28 A sea containing many islands is called what?
29 Who succeeded Queen Victoria?
30 Which gallery displays the *Mona Lisa*?

ANSWERS

PLANTS See quiz 14, page 110
1 Light. 2 Banana. 3 Sloe. 4 Automobile. 5 Seeds. 6 Second year. 7 Alpines.
8 Turban. 9 Lime free. 10 Yellow. 11 Buttercup. 12 Three. 13 Swedish.
14 Dog rose. 15 White. 16 Snapdragons. 17 Flower arranging. 18 Lizzie.
19 Blue. 20 Nigella. 21 Everlasting flowers. 22 Autumn. 23 Very large.
24 Pansies. 25 Canterbury bell. 26 Grape. 27 Organic material. 28 Poisonous.
29 Dark red. 30 White.

QUIZ 17 TV TRIVIA

Answers - see Quiz 19, page 115

1 What was the name of the 1999 BBC series about prehistoric creatures?
2 Where did Mavis leave for when she left *Coronation Street*?
3 Which Nick Berry series was set in the west country?
4 Which drink did Paul Daniels and Debbie McGee advertise singing off key around a piano?
5 What is Betty's culinary speciality in *Coronation Street*?
6 Who played writer Peter Mayle in the ill fated series *A Year In Provence*?
7 What is the prize to aim for in Cilla's *Moment of Truth*?
8 What sort of creature is the eponymous character in *Rex The Runt*?
9 In which comedy about relationships did Jack Davenport play Steve while Gina Bellman played Jane?
10 Singer Adam Rickitt found fame in which soap?
11 In *Countdown*, how many people occupy Dictionary Corner?
12 How long do the cooks have to cook their team member's ingredients in *Ready Steady Cook*?
13 Which ex *Coronation Street* actress played 1970s TV star Coral Atkins in *Seeing Red*?
14 In 2001 what momentous new purchase did Deirdre make in *Coronation Street*?
15 In *Bargain Hunt*, what sort of bargains are being hunted?
16 Which former TV vet narrates *Vets In Practice*?
17 What is the postcode of Albert Square, Walford?
18 On which show did Hear'Say shoot to stardom?
19 How many contestants started out in each edition of *The National Lottery: Winning lines*?
20 In which series would the Skelthwaite Arms feature?
21 Which Tony played the Sheriff in *Maid Marian and Her Merry Men*?
22 Which comedy show was famous for its 'Fork handles' sketch?
23 What was the name of Keith Harris's duck?
24 Which *Rainbow* character was pink?
25 Who hosted *A Question of TV*?
26 Who is the presenter of *Changing Rooms*?
27 Which comedy show was famous for its 'Dead Parrot' sketch?
28 How many contestants start out on the original, BBC2 version, of *The Weakest Link*?
29 In *Coronation Street* what is the occupation of Curly's second wife?
30 Who first presented the interactive travel series *Holiday: You Call the Shots*?

CELEBS See quiz 19, page 115
1 Priscilla. 2 Chicago. 3 Her dogs. 4 Miss Whiplash. 5 Bruce Forsyth 6 Eight. 7 Denise Van Outen. 8 Playboy. 9 Edward VIII. 10 Gabriela Sabatini. 11 Mary Quant. 12 Newspapers. 13 Prince Andrew. 14 Gilles. 15 Niece. 16 Cambridge. 17 Natasha. 18 Highgrove. 19 Catherine. 20 Devonshire. 21 Bernie Ecclestone. 22 Andrew Lloyd Webber. 23 Follett. 24 Norway. 25 Barbara. 26 Harrison Ford. 27 Kathleen Turner. 28 Bristol. 29 Nadine. 30 RJ-H.

QUIZ 18 POT LUCK 8

Answers - see Quiz 20, page 116

1   On which day are US elections for the Senate and Congress always held?
2   Which Harris had a huge hit with "Macarthur Park"?
3   In *Bewitched* what was the name of Samantha's mother?
4   On a Monopoly board what is the first station reached after Go?
5   Which franc is the official currency of Liechtenstein?
6   Howard Wilkinson and George Graham have both managed which soccer club?
7   The term alter ego originates from which language?
8   Which female singer performed with the Miami Sound Machine?
9   Which place was *Revisited* in the title of an Evelyn Waugh novel?
10 What can be cardinal, ordinal or prime?
11 Who quite literally took "Trash" into the charts in the mid 1990s?
12 In which war did the Battle of the Bulge take place?
13 In the past which creatures were used by doctors to drain blood?
14 Which Howard discovered Tutankhamun's tomb in the Valley of the Kings?
15 Who sang about "The Good Ship Lollipop"?
16 What was Southern Rhodesia renamed in the 1980s?
17 Whose debut album was *The Violin Player*?
18 Which US First Lady is credited as being the first to use the name?
19 What was the first movie to play John Wayne opposite Maureen O'Hara?
20 "Oh What A Beautiful Morning" comes from which musical?
21 Which river cuts through the Grand Canyon?
22 Who wrote "Nessun Dorma", now regarded as Pavarotti's theme tune?
23 "And I'll cry if I want to" is the second line of the chorus of which song?
24 Ralph McTell wrote and sang about the "Streets Of" where?
25 What sport is played at Roland Garros?
26 On which Sea is the Gaza Strip?
27 Roger Waters and Dave Gilmour were members of which long lasting group?
28 What has the Nursery End and the Pavilion End?
29 According to the play title, Sir Thomas More was *A Man For* what?
30 How many members of the Righteous Brothers were actual brothers?

QUIZ 19 CELEBS

Answers - see Quiz 17, page 113

1 What was the name of the wife Elvis Presley sued for divorce on his 38th birthday?
2 In which city did Hugh Hefner open his first Playboy Club?
3 In 1991 Queen Elizabeth II needed medical treatment after breaking up a fight between whom?
4 How did Lindi St Clair, who battled with the Inland Revenue over the nature of her earnings, style herself?
5 Which veteran TV entertainer and game show host has a South American wife called Wilnelia?
6 By the end of the 20th century how many times had Elizabeth Taylor been married?
7 Which blonde TV presenter did Jamiroquai's Jay Kay split with in the new millennium?
8 Which magazine did Hugh Hefner found?
9 Who was the first English king to travel in an aeroplane?
10 Which Argentine tennis player shares her birthdate – 15 years later – with Olga Korbut?
11 Which designer is most associated with the Sixties and the mini skirt?
12 Lord Beaverbrook is a famous name in which field?
13 Who was the first Royal to visit New York after September 11th 2001?
14 Who is Jacques Villeneuve's famous father?
15 What relation is Bridget Fonda to Jane Fonda?
16 At which university did Vanessa Feltz study?
17 What is the name of Sir Michael Caine's daughter?
18 What is the name of the Prince of Wales's Gloucestershire home?
19 What is Mrs Frankie Dettori called?
20 Chatsworth in Derbyshire is owned by the duke of where?
21 Who owned Formula 1 racing when its broadcasting rights were sold to ITV in 1996?
22 Whose theatre company did Prince Edward join when he left the Royal Marines?
23 What is the surname of Labour stalwart and author Ken and image consultant Barbara?
24 In which country was Mariella Frostrup born?
25 What is Frank Sinatra's widow's first name?
26 Which actor was married to screenwriter Melissa Mathison?
27 Who was the first US star to play The Graduate's Mrs Robinson on a London stage?
28 Which Marquess is the brother of It Girl Victoria Hervey?
29 What was the first name of Ms Milroy Sloan who in 2001 made allegations against the Hamiltons?
30 What was the Countess of Wessex's PR company called?

TV TRIVIA See quiz 17, page 113

ANSWERS

1 *Walking With Dinosaurs.* 2 Lake District. 3 *Harbour Lights.* 4 Lager.
5 Hot pot. 6 John Thaw. 7 £20,000. 8 Dog. 9 *Coupling.*
10 *Coronation Street.* 11 Two. 12 20 minutes. 13 Sarah Lancashire.
14 Glasses. 15 Antiques. 16 Christopher Timothy. 17 E20. 18 *Popstars.*
19 49. 20 *Where the Heart Is.* 21 Robinson. 22 *The Two Ronnies.*
23 Orville. 24 George. 25 Gaby Roslin. 26 Carol Smillie.
27 Monty Python. 28 Nine. 29 Police officer. 30 Jamie Theakston.

QUIZ 20 EURO TOUR

Answers - see Quiz 18, page 114

1 In which county is Bantry Bay in the south of Ireland?
2 What is Italy's Capodimonte famous for?
3 In which city is the Pompidou Centre?
4 Which island is called Kefallinia in Greek?
5 From which resort at the foot of Mont Blanc does the highest cable car in the world rise?
6 What do the British call what the French call Les Iles Normands?
7 Which province of the Irish Republic includes Galway and Sligo?
8 The Amalienborg Palace is the home of which Royal Family?
9 Which Scandinavian country is called Suomi in its own language?
10 The Baltic states are made up of Latvia, Lithuania and where?
11 What is Germany's Schwarzwald?
12 Which monument is at the opposite end of Paris's Champs Elysées from the Place de la Concorde?
13 Where was a refugee camp built for asylum-seekers near the Channel Tunnel?
14 Where is the park called the Bois de Boulogne?
15 What is the capital of the state of the Tyrol?
16 Ithaca is off the west coast of which country?
17 Which Scandinavian strait has a name which means cat's throat?
18 In which Sea are the Balearic Islands?
19 Which breed of dog comes from Kerry in south west Ireland?
20 In which city is the Prado art gallery?
21 Which town of Lombardy gave its name to a bright reddish mauve dye?
22 What is the Bourse in Paris?
23 On which Sea is Odessa?
24 Which country has the rivers Douro, Tagus and Guadiana?
25 What is the chief city of Catalonia, and Spain's second largest?
26 Which is the farthest north, Belaru, Ukraine or Estonia?
27 What was St Petersburg called for much of the 20th century?
28 Which Sea is to the west of Denmark?
29 Which is the most easterly city, Stuttgart, Munich or Hanover?
30 The Basque country surrounds which mountains?

POT LUCK 8 See quiz 18, page 114
1 Tuesday. 2 Richard. 3 Endora. 4 Kings Cross. 5 Swiss franc. 6 Leeds. 7 Latin.
8 Gloria Estefan. 9 *Brideshead*. 10 A number. 11 Suede. 12 World War II.
13 Leeches. 14 Carter. 15 Shirley Temple. 16 Zimbabwe. 17 Vanessa Mae.
18 Eleanor Roosevelt. 19 *Rio Grande*. 20 Oklahoma. 21 Colorado. 22 Puccini.
23 "It's My Party". 24 London. 25 Tennis. 26 Mediterranean. 27 Pink Floyd.
28 Lord's Cricket Ground. 29 *All Seasons*. 30 None.

QUIZ 21 POT LUCK 9

Answers - see Quiz 23, page 119

1 Gwen Stefani was lead singer with which band?
2 Who became the first Briton to hold a world javelin record?
3 Where in Germany is a passion play staged once every ten years?
4 Which sport can be played under Australian, Association or Gaelic rules?
5 Which country did the Bay City Rollers come from?
6 Which US president had the middle name Milhous?
7 Ellis Island is in which harbour?
8 What was the rank of Georges Simenon's Maigret?
9 Tommy Docherty quipped that he'd had more what than Jack Nicklaus?
10 Which instrument did Suzi Quatro play on stage?
11 In American Football which creatures are linked to the Chicago team?
12 Artists Manet and Monet both came from which city?
13 When England won soccer's World Cup what colour were the team's shirts?
14 Agatha Christie wrote romantic novels under the pseudonym of Mary who?
15 Which country became the first to legalise abortion?
16 Which early pop classic song begins, "I'm so young and you're so old"?
17 In American college football what can go after Cotton, Orange and Sugar?
18 In popular music, who was Bacharach's long time writing partner?
19 In which country is the oldest angling club in the world?
20 Which Jeff played a mathematician in the movie *Jurassic Park*?
21 What is the next white note on a keyboard below G?
22 Which actor became a human cartoon in the movie *The Mask*?
23 Which city do the Afrikaaners know as Kaapstad?
24 Which motorway links up with the M25 closest to Heathrow Airport?
25 Which Joplin was one of the originators of ragtime?
26 Which actress starred as Princess Leia in the *Star Wars* trilogy?
27 Who joined Rod Stewart and Sting on the 1994 hit "All For Love"?
28 What does Honolulu mean in Hawaiian?
29 What is the traditional colour of an Indian wedding sari?
30 Which pop group had the last word of the Lord's Prayer as the first word of its name?

POT LUCK 10 *See quiz 23, page 119*

1 Jason. 2 John Barnes. 3 The Rockies. 4 Spanish. 5 Baby. 6 *As Time Goes By.*
7 Smallpox. 8 Jude. 9 Bottom. 10 Cop. 11 *The Little Mermaid.*
12 Christopher Biggins. 13 Atlantic. 14 "I Believe". 15 Austria. 16 Hormones.
17 Clannad. 18 Latent. 19 Gabrielle. 20 22. 21 Horse. 22 Thumb.
23 "Boombastic". 24 Gianni Versace. 25 Tony Blair. 26 Colchester.
27 Monica Lewinsky. 28 Susan Hampshire. 29 Ealing Comedies. 30 Desert Storm.

117

QUIZ 22 SOCCER

Answers - see Quiz 24, page 120

1 Which Italian club did Paul Gascoigne play for?
2 Against which side did David Beckham score his first pro own goal in autumn 2001?
3 Who did Glen Hoddle play for just before he became England manager?
4 Which side inflicted Manchester United's first defeat of the 2000–01 season?
5 In which county was Bobby Charlton born?
6 Which overseas player led Naples to their first ever Italian championship?
7 How old was Stanley Matthews when he made his debut for England?
8 With which club side did Bobby Moore end his career?
9 Whose autobiography was called *My World*?
10 Jaap Stam signed for Manchester United from which club?
11 In the Germany vs England 2001 World Cup qualifier, what was the score at half time?
12 Which club did Chris Sutton first join immediately after he left Blackburn Rovers?
13 Who were the opposition in Gary Lineker's final international when he was taken off by Graham Taylor?
14 Which manager preceded Graeme Souness and Tony Parkes at Blackburn Rovers?
15 In which decade was the European Champions Cup inaugurated?
16 Who won the last FA Cup Final of the 20th century?
17 John Hartson left West Ham for which club in 1999?
18 Who managed Manchester City immediately before Kevin Keegan?
19 The leading goalscorer in the 1998 World Cup finals came from which country?
20 When Sunderland beat Leeds in the FA Cup final of 1973, how many goals did they score?
21 Who is the most southerly side to win the FA Premier League?
22 Who was the last side to win the old Division 1?
23 Which London side won the European Cup Winners Cup in 1998?
24 In France 98 who was England's top scorer along with Michael Owen?
25 Who beat Manchester United in their first FA Cup campaign of the 21st century?
26 Who did Scotland play the same day that England beat Germany 5–1?
27 Against which team in a 4–3 defeat was Manchester United's Roy Keane sent off in September 2001?
28 Which soccer club did Bobby Charlton manage before becoming a Manchester United director?
29 Who has presented the Footballer of the Year award since 1948?
30 Before Michael Owen in Germany, who was the last England player to score a hat trick in international football?

MOVIE DIRECTORS & PRODUCERS See quiz 24, page 120

ANSWERS

1 Joel. 2 Baz Luhrmann. 3 Steven Spielberg. 4 Director. 5 James Cameron.
6 Cecil B de Mille. 7 Gilbert & Sullivan (*Topsy Turvy*). 8 *Evita*. 9 Mel Brooks. 10 Jordan.
11 Rob Reiner. 12 Tokyo. 13 Nora Ephron. 14 Vincente Minnelli. 15 Mike Nichols.
16 Sylvester Stallone. 17 Tim Robbins. 18 Tchaikovsky. 19 *Raging Bull*.
20 Tony and Ridley Scott. 21 Nicole Kidman and Tom Cruise. 22 Penny. 23 *Nixon*.
24 Richard Attenborough. 25 Quentin Tarantino. 26 *Apollo 13*. 27 Brooklyn.
28 *Monty Python's Flying Circus*. 29 1970s. 30 Kevin Costner.

QUIZ 23 POT LUCK 10

Answers - see Quiz 21, page 117

1 What is the real first name of Jay Kay of Jamiroquai?
2 Who became the first person to wear white boots in an FA Cup Final?
3 In which mountain range is Mount Elbert the highest peak?
4 Which nationality goes with The Riding School in Austria?
5 Who or what was swimming on the cover of Nirvana's album _Nevermind_?
6 On TV, which show's theme song begins, "You must remember this."?
7 Variola is the medical name for which disease?
8 Which name appears in a Beatles song title and in a Thomas Hardy novel title?
9 In which British TV series did Richie and Eddie first appear?
10 What was the profession of Michael Douglas' character in the movie _Basic Instinct_?
11 Hans Christian Andersen's memorial statue in Copenhagen takes the form of which character?
12 Which actor played Lukewarm in _Porridge_?
13 Which is the saltiest of the major oceans of the world?
14 What was coupled with Robson and Jerome's _Up On The Roof_?
15 German leader Adolph Hitler was born in which country?
16 The pituitary gland controls the production of what in the body?
17 Which Irish band performed a 1991 TV concert as a tribute to Brian Keenan?
18 Which word describes hidden or concealed heat?
19 Which female vocalist featured on East 17's mid-1990s hit "If You Ever"?
20 At what age did Will Carling first captain England at rugby?
21 A Lippizaner is what type of animal?
22 A pollex is another name for which part of the body?
23 What was the second No 1 for Shaggy?
24 In 1997, whose funeral in Milan was attended by Elton John and Naomi Campbell?
25 Which famous person includes Anthony Charles Lynton in his name?
26 Blur formed in which East Anglian town?
27 Linda Tripp was the confidante of which person in the 1990s news?
28 Which well respected actress has been President of the Dyslexia Institute?
29 Which comedies was Michael Balcon responsible for?
30 In the 1990s, the operation to eject Iraqis from Kuwait was codenamed which Operation?

ANSWERS

POT LUCK 9 _See quiz 21, page 117_

1 No Doubt. 2 Fatima Whithread. 3 Oberammergau. 4 Football. 5 Scotland.
6 Nixon. 7 New York. 8 Inspector. 9 Clubs. 10 Bass guitar. 11 Bears. 12 Paris.
13 Red. 14 Westmacott. 15 Iceland. 16 "Diana". 17 Bowl. 18 Hal David.
19 Scotland. 20 Goldblum. 21 F. 22 Jim Carrey. 23 Cape Town. 24 M4. 25 Scott.
26 Carrie Fisher. 27 Bryan Adams. 28 Sheltered bay. 29 Scarlet. 30 Amen Corner.

QUIZ 24   MOVIES DIRECTORS & PRODUCERS

Answers - see Quiz 22, page 118

1 Who is Ethan Coen's director brother?

2 Who directed *Moulin Rouge*, starring Nicole Kidman and Ewan McGregor?

3 Which prolific – and wealthy – director produced and wrote *Poltergeist*?

4 What was George Lucas's role in the original *Star Wars*?

5 Who directed the movie about the most disastrous disaster at sea in peace time?

6 Who had the middle name Blount but only used his initial?

7 Which musical duo was the subject of a Mike Leigh movie with Jim Broadbent?

8 Which musical did Alan Parker direct before the drama *Angela's Ashes*?

9 How is Melvin Kaminski of *Young Frankenstein* better known?

10 Which Neil was Oscar nominated as director and also writer for *The Crying Game*?

11 Whof was the director of *When Harry Met Sally*?

12 In which city was Akira Kurosawa born?

13 Which lady was the director of the hit movies *Sleepless in Seattle* and *You Got M@il*?

14 Which father of a musical star directed *An American in Paris*?

15 How is the director of *Wolf* and *The Birdcage* born Michael Igor Peschkowsky better known?

16 Which actor directed *Rocky IV*?

17 Who was Oscar nominated for *Dead Man Walking*?

18 Ken Russell's *The Music Lovers* was about which Russian composer?

19 For which movie with Robert De Niro did Martin Scorsese receive his first Oscar nomination?

20 Which brothers bought Shepperton Studios in 1994?

21 Which then husband and wife were the stars of Kubrick's *Eyes Wild Shut*?

22 What is the name of Garry Marshall's fellow director sibling, formerly married to the director of *When Harry Met Sally*?

23 Which president was the subject of the 1995 movie written and directed by Oliver Stone?

24 Who was the director of *Gandhi*?

25 Who was the subject of the biography *King Pulp*?

26 Which movie about an Apollo moon mission had Ron Howard as director?

27 Where in New York was Woody Allen born?

28 Terry Gilliam was a member of which comedy team?

29 In which decade did Stanley Kubrick direct the controversial *A Clockwork Orange*?

30 Which Oscar winning actor directed *Dances With Wolves* and *The Bodyguard*?

ANSWERS

SOCCER *See quiz 22, page 118*

1 Lazio. 2 Blackburn Rovers. 3 Chelsea. 4 Newcastle. 5 Northumberland.
6 Diego Maradona. 7 20. 8 Fulham. 9 David Beckham. 10 PSV Eindhoven. 11 1–2.
12 Chelsea. 13 Sweden. 14 Brian Kidd. 15 1950s. 16 Manchester United.
17 Wimbledon. 18 Joe Royle. 19 Croatia. 20 One. 21 Arsenal. 22 Leeds.
23 Chelsea. 24 Alan Shearer. 25 West Ham. 26 Croatia. 27 Newcastle.
28 Presto North End. 29 Football Writers' Association. 30 Alan Shearer.

QUIZ 25 POT LUCK 11

Answers - see Quiz 27, page 123

1 Reba McEntire's best of album was called *Moments and* what else?
2 Scientist Rene Descartes said "I think therefore …" what?
3 What was Paul Nicholls' first major TV series after leaving the cast of *EastEnders*?
4 An ossicle is a small what?
5 In which decade did Einstein die?
6 Which species of trees and shrubs come from the genus Malus?
7 Approximately how many feet are there in a fathom?
8 Who had an album that saw her *Sittin' On the Top of the World*?
9 What was the name of the character played by Harry Enfield when he was in *Men Behaving Badly*?
10 Who said, "Honey I forgot to duck" after a failed assassination attempt?
11 In computing, how many bits are there in a byte?
12 What was the last name of chef Gareth in TV's *Chef!*?
13 A snapper is a type of what when it is red, yellowtail or gray?
14 How many seconds are there in a quarter of an hour?
15 In which country were the world's first known theatres built?
16 Which TV series was set at the Globelink News Office?
17 Terry Butcher and Lawrie McMenemy have both managed which soccer club?
18 Which popular sit com star actor used to worked in a hospital laboratory?
19 Phidippides was the first runner of which epic race?
20 Which novelist created the character George Smiley?
21 Where in the human body is the scapula?
22 Which university is the oldest in the USA?
23 The movies *Charlie's Angels* and *E.T.* both featured which actress?
24 Which Thomas introduced the blue and white pottery known as Willow pattern?
25 The Longmuir brothers were in which teen idol band?
26 The Beeching report led to vast cuts in which service?
27 At Royal Ascot which day is Ladies' Day?
28 In which country would you watch Lokeren play a home soccer match?
29 Which singer called his son Otis in tribute to Otis Redding?
30 In which country did the Sharpeville massacre take place?

POT LUCK 12 See quiz 27, page 123
ANSWERS
1 *Buffy the Vampire Slayer*. 2 Kinetic energy. 3 Los Angeles. 4 Peas. 5 The phoenix. 6 Twopence. 7 REM. 8 Horizontally. 9 The Elephant Man. 10 Sadat. 11 Henrietta 12 Fireball XL5. 13 Beirut. 14 Gymnast. 15 Anfield. 16 Spungeon. 17 Dutch. 18 Bouvier. 19 Jimi Hendrix. 20 Paul Gascoigne. 21 Woodward 22 Labour. 23 Skiing. 24 Chess. 25 Orenthal. 26 MP. 27 One. 28 Poisoned himself. 29 Dame Nellie Melba. 30 Los Angeles.

QUIZ 26 MUSIC CHARTS

Answers - see Quiz 28, page 124

1 What was Oasis's first release of the new millennium?
2 Which Aqua chart hit was the name of a toy?
3 Who sang "I'll be Missing You" with Puff Daddy?
4 Which Mariah Carey single was the first to debut at No 1 in the US, in 1995?
5 In the UK how many albums have to be sold for it to go platinum?
6 Who was the first male rapper to have two solo No 1's?
7 S Club 7's "Never Had a Dream Come True" raised money for which charity?
8 Which was the first band to have seven successive No 1s with their first seven releases?
9 Which British band had the first No 1 of the new millennium?
10 Which girl's name featured in a mega hit for Dexy's Midnight Runners?
11 Which was Wham!'s best-selling Christmas single?
12 Which 2000 Spiller song stopped Victoria Beckham from having her first solo No 1?
13 What was the English title of Sarah Brightman's "Con Te Partiro" which she sang with Andrea Bocelli?
14 Who first made the Top Twenty with "Linger"?
15 In 2000 Oxide & Neutrino charted with a reworking of the theme of which hospital series?
16 Who sang "How Do I Live" in 1998?
17 Whose "Killing Me Softly" was a top seller in 1996?
18 Which song from Bridget Jones's Diary did Geri Halliwell have a hit with in 2001?
19 What was Britney Spears' second UK No 1?
20 What was Elton John's first solo No 1 in the US?
21 "Three Lions" charted in which World Cup year?
22 Which family charted with "Mmmbop"?
23 Which Oasis member sang on The Chemical Brothers' "Setting Sun"?
24 What was Michael Jackson's last No 1 of the 20th century?
25 In which decade did Japan have their first Top Ten hit?
26 Who hit No 1 with "Deeper Underground" in 1999?
27 Chef's 1998 No 1 came from which cartoon series?
28 Who charted with "All Right Now" in the 1970s and with a1990s remix?
29 "Vision Of Love" was the first Top Ten hit for which singer?
30 In which decade did smooth soul group the Chi-Lites have most hits?

PAST TIMES – 1950 ON *See quiz 28, page 124*

ANSWERS

1 Kenneth Clarke. 2 Germany. 3 Malawi. 4 Cuba. 5 Palestine. 6 1940. 7 Chile.
8 Jacques Chirac. 9 Ronald Reagan. 10 1960s. 11 Barbara. 12 China.
13 Greenham Common. 14 Alexander Gromyko. 15 Salisbury. 16 Erich Honecker.
17 Westminster Abbey. 18 Karadzic. 19 Hampstead & Highgate. 20 Cambodia.
21 Alabama. 22 Charles Manson. 23 Warren. 24 Cricket. 25 Linda Tripp.
26 Humphrey. 27 Chris Evans. 28 Pigs. 29 Althorp. 30 Belfast.

QUIZ 27 POT LUCK 12

Answers - see Quiz 25, page 121

1 Which TV character lived in Sunnydale?
2 What name is given to the energy produced when something moves?
3 In movies, E.T. arrived in which city of California?
4 What can be Hurst Beagle or Kelvedon Wonder?
5 In legend which bird rose from its own ashes?
6 In *Mary Poppins* how much does it cost for a bag to Feed The Birds?
7 Which three initial letters stand for the speedy reactions of the organ of sight?
8 In a window a transom is a bar situated in which way?
9 What type of man was John Merrick known as?
10 Who became the first Egyptian leader to visit Israel?
11 What is the middle name of Joan Collins?
12 Which craft did Steve Zodiac command?
13 Keanu Reeves was born in which war torn city?
14 Nadia Comaneci became famous as a what?
15 At which ground did Bill Shankly suffer his fatal heart attack?
16 Which Nancy was linked with Sid Vicious?
17 What was the nationality of spy Mata Hari?
18 What was Jacqueline Kennedy's surname before her marriage to the future US President?
19 Which rock musician prophetically said, "Once you're dead you're made for life"?
20 Which controversial footballer briefly was the husband of Sheryl Failes?
21 Which journalist was Bernstein's partner in investigating Watergate?
22 TV chat man Robert Kilroy-Silk was an MP for which party?
23 Which activity was Sonny Bono involved in at the time of his accidental death?
24 Bobby Fischer was the first American world champion in which sport?
25 What does O stand for in OJ Simpson's name?
26 Diane Abbot became Britain's first black woman to serve as what?
27 How many of the Beatles were not known by their real names?
28 What final act did Hermann Goering do some hours before his execution?
29 How was Australian singer Helen Porter Mitchell better known?
30 Marilyn Monroe was born and died in which city?

POT LUCK 11 See quiz 25, page 121

1 *Memories.* 2 I Am. 3 *City Central.* 4 Bone. 5 1950s. 6 Apple. 7 Six.
8 LeAnn Rimes. 9 Dermot. 10 Ronald Reagan. 11 Eight. 12 Blackstock.
13 Fish. 14 900. 15 Greece. 16 *Drop The Dead Donkey.* 17 Sunderland.
18 Richard Wilson. 19 Marathon. 20 John Le Carre. 21 Shoulder blades.
22 Harvard. 23 Drew Barrymore. 24 Thomas Turner. 25 Bay City Rollers.
26 Railway. 27 Thursday (third day). 28 Belgium. 29 Bryan Ferry. 30 South Africa.

QUIZ 28 PAST TIMES – 1950 ON

Answers - see Quiz 26, page 122

1 Who was the other final contender for the Tory leadership contest in 1997 when William Hague won?
2 In which country were the Baader Meinhof gang based?
3 Hastings Banda became Prime Minister of which country in 1964?
4 The Bay of Pigs near which island was an area which triggered a missile crisis in 1961?
5 Black September were a terrorist group from which country?
6 In which year did the Battle of Britain begin?
7 Pinochet led a military coup in which country?
8 Who succeeded Mitterand as President of France?
9 Milton Friedman was policy adviser to which US President in the 1980s?
10 In which decade did Colonel Gaddafi seize power in Libya?
11 What was the name of the first First Lady called Bush?
12 Where was there the 'Great Leap Forward' in the 1950s?
13 Which site in Berkshire was the scene of anti nuclear protests, mainly by women, in the 1980s?
14 Who was Soviet Foreign Minister for almost 30 years in the latter half of the 20th C?
15 What was the former name of Harare?
16 Who was East German leader from 1976 to 1989?
17 In which building was Princess Diana's funeral service held?
18 Who became Bosnian president in 1992?
19 In 1992 Glenda Jackson became MP for which constituency?
20 Where did the Khmer Rouge operate?
21 In which state did Martin Luther King lead the famous bus boycott?
22 Who led the sect which killed actress Sharon Tate?
23 Which Commission was set up to investigate the assassination of John F Kennedy?
24 Kerry Packer set up a rebel sports tour in which sport in the 1970s?
25 Who was Monica Lewinsky's confidante?
26 What was the name of the cat 'evicted' from Downing Street as the Blairs moved in?
27 Who bought Virgin Radio from Richard Branson in 1997?
28 Who were the Tamworth Two?
29 Where was Princess Diana buried?
30 Where is the Maze prison?

MUSIC CHARTS *See quiz 26, page 122*

1 "Go Let It Out". 2 "Barbie Girl". 3 Faith Evans. 4 "Fantasy". 5 300,000.
6 Eminem. 7 Children in Need. 8 Westlife. 9 Manic Street Preachers. 10 "Eileen".
11 "Last Christmas". 12 "Groovejet". 13 "Time To Say Goodbye". 14 Cranberries.
15 *Casualty.* 16 LeAnn Rimes. 17 The Fugees. 18 "It's Raining Men".
19 "Born To Make You Happy". 20 "Crocodile Rock". 21 1998. 22 Hanson.
23 Noel Gallagher. 24 "Blood on the Dance Floor". 25 1980s. 26 Jamiroquai.
27 *South Park.* 28 Free. 29 Mariah Carey. 30 1970s.

ANSWERS

QUIZ 29 POT LUCK 13

Answers - see Quiz 31, page 127

1 The true life exploits of Harold Abrahams were told in which movie?
2 Who mysteriously vanished off the yacht Lady Ghislaine?
3 In which street did the infamous Rose and Frederick West live in Gloucester?
4 What is actor Michael Caine's real first name?
5 US President Andrew Jackson was nicknamed Old what?
6 In which country could you watch rugby at Ellis Park?
7 Which saint is on the Pope's signet ring?
8 What colour are the stars on the flag of the European Union?
9 Which country had a President with a spouse named Ladybird?
10 Japp Stam left Manchester United to go to which club?
11 What is Spike Milligan's real first name?
12 In which country was the scientist Gabriel Fahrenheit born?
13 What was the first name of the late Princess Diana's stepmother?
14 What do Harvard Rules govern?
15 In mathematics, the abbreviation HCF stands for what?
16 How many seconds are there in a single round of championship boxing?
17 Whose songs were featured in the movie *Toy Story*?
18 Which actress, famous as a TV detective, was christened Ilynea Lydia Mironoff?
19 Which was the last host nation to have the Olympic Games opened by the country's king?
20 Which aspect of the weather is brontophobia the fear of?
21 Which of these games has the largest playing area – polo, soccer or tennis?
22 How many ribs has the human body?
23 *Grace and Favour* was a sequel to which sitcom?
24 Which plants have a life cycle of more than one year but less than two?
25 What nationality was mathematician Sir Isaac Newton?
26 What type of creature is equally at home on land and in water?
27 How many oxygen atoms are contained in a molecule of water?
28 PCs Stamp and Quinnan worked at which police station on TV?
29 What is the study of fluids moving in pipes known as?
30 Which band asked, "What's the Frequency Kenneth?"?

POT LUCK 14 *See quiz 31, page 127*

1 Ag. 2 *Taggart*. 3 Human glands. 4 The sun. 5 "The Calypso", 6 Southampton.
7 Three. 8 *Good Morning Vietnam*. 9 Gerald Ford. 10 Nuremberg. 11 Pierce Brosnan.
12 France. 13 Tom Cruise. 14 Weightlifting. 15 Vikings. 16 *Gone With The Wind*.
17 Battles. 18 Boer War. 19 Leicester. 20 Donald Maclean. 21 Porter. 22 Archery.
23 M6. 24 A roof. 25 London Marathon. 26 Marion. 27 Piccadilly. 28 Napoleon.
29 Decathlon. 30 July.

QUIZ 30 TV PRESENTERS

Answers - see Quiz 32, page 128

1 Which *Points of View* presenter wrote an autobiography called *Is It Me??*
2 Which presenter appeared in the comedy *'Orrible*?
3 Who replaced Loyd Grossman as presenter of *Masterchef*?
4 Who presented *Before They Were Famous*?
5 Who preceded Michael Aspel on *The Antiques Road Show*?
6 Which David Attenborough series of 2001 was about life in and under the sea?
7 Who presented and co devised *Art Attack*?
8 Who moved from *Wheel of Fortune* to a daily show on Radio Five Live?
9 Who was the wine buff on *Food & Drink* when Antony Worrall Thompson and Emma Crowhurst became regular food experts?
10 What would Peter Cockcroft talk about on TV?
11 Who replaced Vanessa on ITV's morning chat show?
12 Which Irish presenter introduced *Animal Hospital* with Rolf Harris?
13 Which daytime show does Gloria Hunniford present regularly on Channel 5?
14 Who introduced the celebrity version of *Stars In Their Eyes*?
15 Who presented Saturday Show with Joe Mace?
16 Alvin Hall presents programmes about looking after your what?
17 Jeremy Bowen and Sophie Raworth present the news at what time of day?
18 Which ex Blue Peter presenter introduced *The Big Breakfast*?
19 Which actress introduced a *Watercolour Challenge* on daytime TV?
20 Which business programme is presented by Adrian Chiles?
21 Who hosts *Fifteen To One*?
22 Who first presented *The National Lottery: Winning Lines*?
23 Who introduces the *Bloomers* series about BBC TV outtakes?
24 Who replaced the late Jill Dando on *Crimewatch*?
25 Which sport does John McCririck present?
26 Which ex footballer tested the teams on *Friends Like These*?
27 In 2001 which Irish comic broadcast his show *Live from Belfast*?
28 Who tested contestants on the comedy game show *Oblivious*?
29 Who replaced Paul Daniels on *Wipeout*?
30 Rachel De Thame offers advice on what?

WORLD TOUR See quiz 32, page 128

ANSWERS
1 Greenland. 2 Indonesia. 3 Argentina. 4 California. 5 Gulf of Finland.
6 Casablanca. 7 Two. 8 Azerbaijan. 9 Bejing. 10 North Africa.
11 Cairo. 12 Manhattan. 13 Saigon. 14 Hawaii. 15 Tigris.
16 Brooklyn. 17 Andes. 18 Cape Horn. 19 Bass. 20 Click.
21 Indonesia. 22 Jodhpur. 23 Johannesburg. 24 Atlantic. 25 Bronx.
26 Chechenya. 27 Costa Rica. 28 China. 29 Indian. 30 Barbados.

QUIZ 31 POT LUCK 14

Answers - see Quiz 29, page 125

1 What is the chemical symbol for silver?
2 Which TV cop show featured DCI Michael Jardine?
3 What are the islets of Langerhans?
4 What does a heliologist study?
5 What was the name of the research ship used by Jacques Cousteau?
6 Dave Jones and Glenn Hoddle have both managed which soccer club?
7 How many pins are there in the front two rows in ten-pin bowling?
8 Which movie gave Robin Williams his first Oscar nomination?
9 Who became US President when Richard Nixon resigned?
10 In which city did trials of major Nazi leaders begin in 1945?
11 Which screen James Bond also starred in the movie *Dante's Peak*?
12 In which country is Satolas international airport?
13 In the movies, who played war veteran Ron Kovic?
14 What are you doing if you carry out a snatch lift and a jerk lift?
15 In American Football which warriors come from Minnesota?
16 In which movie classic was Olivia de Havilland cast as Melanie Wilkes?
17 What do The Sealed Knot Society re-enact?
18 The Siege of Ladysmith took place during which war?
19 Brian Little and Martin O'Neill have both managed which soccer club?
20 Who fled together with Guy Burgess to the USSR in 1951?
21 What was the surname of the family featured in *2Point4 Children*?
22 In which sport is there a gold coloured target area worth 10 points?
23 Which motorway takes you south from Carlisle?
24 What is a cupola?
25 Which annual event began in London in 1981?
26 What was John Wayne's less than tough sounding real first name?
27 Where in London was the first Fortnum & Mason opened?
28 In *Dad's Army*, air raid warden Hodges likens Captain Mainwaring to which leader?
29 In which event did Daley Thompson win Olympic gold?
30 In which month do the French celebrate Bastille Day?

POT LUCK 13 *See quiz 29, page 125*

ANSWERS

1 *Chariots of Fire*. 2 Robert Maxwell. 3 Cromwell Street. 4 Maurice. 5 Hickory.
6 South Africa. 7 St Peter. 8 Yellow. 9 USA. 10 Lazio. 11 Terence. 12 Germany.
13 Raine. 14 American football. 15 Highest common factor. 16 80.
17 Randy Newman. 18 Helen Mirren. 19 Spain. 20 Thunder. 21 Polo. 22 24.
23 *Are You Being Served?*. 24 Biennials. 25 English. 26 Amphibian. 27 One.
28 Sun Hill. 29 Hydraulics. 30 R.E.M.

QUIZ 32 WORLD TOUR

Answers - see Quiz 30, page 126

1 Baffin Island is between Baffin Bay and which island?
2 Bali is a mountainous island of which country?
3 The Falkland Islands are off which country?
4 Which US state is dubbed the Golden State?
5 Helsinki is on which Gulf?
6 Which city, also the name of a film, has the world's largest mosque?
7 How many islands make up Fiji?
8 Baku is the capital of which country on the Caspian Sea?
9 Where is the Forbidden City?
10 The Barbary Coast is the Mediterranean coast of where?
11 Which Egyptian city is Africa's largest city?
12 Greenwich Village is in which borough of New York City?
13 On which river is Ho Chi Minh City?
14 Where is Waikiki Beach?
15 Baghdad is on which river?
16 In which borough of New York City is Coney island?
17 In which mountains is the volcanic Cotopaxi?
18 Where are the Roaring Forties?
19 Which strait separates Australia from Tasmania?
20 What special sound is made in the language of the Hottentots of south west Africa?
21 Which country was formerly the Dutch East Indies?
22 Which city gave its name to a type of riding breeches?
23 What is South Africa's largest city?
24 In which ocean are the Bahamas?
25 Which part of New York was named after Jonas Bronck?
26 Which conflict torn country has Groznyy as its capital?
27 Which country is between Nicaragua and Panama?
28 K2 is on the border of Pakistan and which country?
29 In which ocean are the Comoros?
30 Which is the most easterly of the Windward Islands in the Caribbean?

ANSWERS **TV PRESENTERS** See quiz 30, page 126
1 Terry Wogan. 2 Johnny Vaughan. 3 Gary Rhodes. 4 Angus Deayton. 5 Hugh Scully.
6 *The Blue Planet.* 7 Neil Buchanan. 8 Nicky Campbell. 9 Oz Clarke. 10 Weather.
11 Trisha. 12 Shauna Lowry. 13 *Open House.* 14 Matthew Kelly. 15 Dani Behr.
16 Money. 17 Breakfast. 18 Richard Bacon. 19 Hannah Gordon. 20 *Working Lunch.*
21 William G Stewart. 22 Phillip Schofield. 23 Terry Wogan. 24 Fiona Bruce.
25 Horse racing. 26 Ian Wright. 27 Patrick Kielty. 28 Davina McCall.
29 Bob Monkhouse. 30 Gardening.

QUIZ 33 POT LUCK 15

Answers - see Quiz 35, page 131

1 Steffi Graf's dad was jailed for what?
2 Which country gave the Statue of Liberty to the USA?
3 In October 2001 which artist's work was thrown away by the cleaners as they thought it was rubbish?
4 What was Mel Gibson's first movie where he was actor, director and producer?
5 In motor racing, what colours are on the flag at the end of a race?
6 Which series with Prunella Scales had three years on radio before transferring to TV?
7 Which racecourse is famous for its Royal Enclosure?
8 Where in the UK is the National Motor Museum?
9 What is the maximum number of pieces that can appear on a chessboard?
10 In Gershwin's song, if it's "Summertime," the living is what?
11 Whereabouts in London did Laura Ashley open her first shop?
12 In credit terms, what does A stand for in an APR?
13 What is the world's biggest selling copyrighted game?
14 What do the Americans call hockey played outside?
15 In which country did karaoke singing originate?
16 What would be your hobby if you used slip?
17 Lennie Lawrence and Colin Todd have both managed which soccer club?
18 Which 1980s band included Cook, Heaton and Hemingway?
19 What was the first capital of the United States?
20 How are Patrick Fyffe and George Logan better known?
21 Which Christian name was shared by former British PMs Winston Churchill and James Callaghan?
22 Who was the first Spice Girl to announce her engagement?
23 *St Elsewhere* was set in which US city?
24 In which country could you watch Rennes playing Sedan at soccer?
25 What was the middle name of Ronnie Barker's character Norman Fletcher in TV's *Porridge*?
26 What did Jimmy Carter farm before becoming US President?
27 Coal is composed from which element?
28 What was the profession of Georges Auguste Escoffier?
29 President Mobutu fled in 1997 after more than 30 years in office in which country?
30 What year was the "New York Mining Disaster" according to the Bee Gees?

POT LUCK 16 *See quiz 35, page 131*

1 Big Bang. 2 Sonny Crockett. 3 Gina G. 4 Ricki Lake. 5 0.54. 6 The eyes.
7 Drugs. 8 PE teacher. 9 Michelle Pfeiffer. 10 McLaren. 11 Princess Anne.
12 Beirut. 13 Barbara. 14 Johnny Fontane. 15 Sir Matt Busby.
16 "Would I Lie To You"?. 17 Anatomy. 18 Michael Foot. 19 1. 20 *The Bodyguard*.
21 17th. 22 Variegated. 23 Holly. 24 "Fairground". 25 Raisa. 26 Light years.
27 Devon. 28 Boyz II Men. 29 Bull. 30 1894.

QUIZ 34 CRICKET

Answers - see Quiz 36, page 132

1 In addition to Leicestershire, which county did David Gower play for?
2 Who was the first cricketer to be awarded a knighthood while still playing Test cricket?
3 In which century was the MCC founded?
4 Which country was readmitted to the Test tour in 1992 along with South Africa?
5 On which ground did Brian Lara hit his record 501 not out?
6 Desmond Hayes earned 116 caps for which side?
7 In which decade did Allan Border make the first of his record breaking 11,174 runs for Australia?
8 In which Gallery at Lord's are the Ashes kept?
9 What is another name for backward point?
10 What did the first C stand for in TCCB?
11 If an umpire raises his index finger in front of his body, or above his head, what does it mean?
12 Which South African captain was suspended under suspicion of taking bribes?
13 Which country scored the highest single innings total in a Test, in 1997?
14 Which future cricket knight partnered Peter May to a partnership of 411 in 1957?
15 What was the AXA Life League called between 1969 and 1986?
16 Which Test cricketer has regularly captained a team on They Think It's All Over?
17 Against which county did Gary Sobers hit his amazing six sixes in an over?
18 Which side won the County Championship in 2001?
19 Test matches are the highest standard of what type of cricket?
20 How many Tests did Geoff Boycott play for England?
21 In 1986 which southern African born player was the youngest to make 2,000 runs in a season?
22 Against which side did Ian Botham make his Test debut?
23 What was Graham Gooch's score on his very first Test match?
24 Which was the first English county side to sign Brian Lara?
25 Which side won the Second Division of the County Championship in 2001?
26 Which South African bowler played a memorable match against Mike Atherton in the summer of 1999?
27 How long are each of the two pieces of wood which make up the bails?
28 In which decade did Gary Sobers first play for the West Indies?
29 In which century did England play her first test match?
30 Alphabetically, which is the first of the first class English county sides?

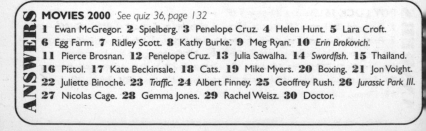

MOVIES 2000 *See quiz 36, page 132*

1 Ewan McGregor. 2 Spielberg. 3 Penelope Cruz. 4 Helen Hunt. 5 Lara Croft.
6 Egg Farm. 7 Ridley Scott. 8 Kathy Burke. 9 Meg Ryan. 10 *Erin Brokovich*.
11 Pierce Brosnan. 12 Penelope Cruz. 13 Julia Sawalha. 14 *Swordfish*. 15 Thailand.
16 Pistol. 17 Kate Beckinsale. 18 Cats. 19 Mike Myers. 20 Boxing. 21 Jon Voight.
22 Juliette Binoche. 23 *Traffic*. 24 Albert Finney. 25 Geoffrey Rush. 26 *Jurassic Park III*.
27 Nicolas Cage. 28 Gemma Jones. 29 Rachel Weisz. 30 Doctor.

QUIZ 35 POT LUCK 16

Answers - see Quiz 33, page 129

1 Which explosive theory explains the formation of the universe?
2 Who did Don Johnson play in Miami Vice?
3 Who sang the British Eurovision Song Contest entry the year before Katrina and the Waves won?
4 Which talk show hostess made her movie debut in *Hairspray*?
5 How would 27% doubled be shown as a decimal?
6 Where in the body are there rods and cones?
7 Home Secretary Jack Straw took his own son to a police station in 1997 after allegations involving what?
8 What was the profession of Zoe in the TV sitcom *May to December*?
9 Who was Oscar-nominated for *Dangerous Liaisons* and *The Fabulous Baker Boys*?
10 Which Malcolm was manager of the punk band The Sex Pistols?
11 Who was the first child of a reigning British monarch to be brought before a criminal court?
12 In which war-torn city was Terry Waite kidnapped?
13 In the White House who went after Nancy and came before Hillary?
14 Which character was supposedly based on Frank Sinatra in *The Godfather*?
15 Who was the first manager to win the European Champions Cup with an English club?
16 Which title links the Eurythmics to a Charles and Eddy No 1?
17 Which branch of biology deals with the structure of animals?
18 Who succeeded James Callaghan as leader of the Labour Party?
19 What is the chemical symbol for iodine?
20 Which film featured the song that gave Whitney Houston her fourth UK No 1?
21 In which century was Blaise Pascal working on his calculating machine?
22 What term describes a leaf with two or more colours?
23 Which species of trees and shrubs come from the genus Ilex?
24 What was Simply Red's first UK No 1?
25 What was Soviet leader Mikael Gorbachev's wife called?
26 Which years measure distance in space?
27 Which English county was part of the name of the horse that collapsed in sight of victory in the Grand National?
28 Who sang with Mariah Carey on "One Sweet Day"?
29 Which animal name was given to the wild Bronx boxer Jake La Motta?
30 When was Blackpool Tower built – 1834, 1894 or 1924?

POT LUCK 15 *See quiz 33, page 129*

ANSWERS

1 Tax fraud. 2 France. 3 Damien Hirst. 4 *Braveheart*. 5 Black & white. 6 *After Henry*.
7 Ascot. 8 Beaulieu. 9 32. 10 Easy. 11 Kensington. 12 Annual. 13 Monopoly.
14 Field hockey. 15 Japan. 16 Pottery. 17 Middlesbrough. 18 Housemartins.
19 New York. 20 Hinge & Bracket. 21 Leonard. 22 Victoria Adams. 23 Boston.
24 France. 25 Stanley. 26 Peanuts. 27 Carbon. 28 Chef. 29 Zaire. 30 1941.

QUIZ 36 MOVIES 2000

Answers - see Quiz 34, page 130

1 Who was Nicole Kidman's co-star in *Moulin Rouge*?
2 Who directed *AI: Artificial Intelligence*?
3 Who played opposite Nicolas Cage in *Captain Corelli's Mandolin*?
4 Who plays Darcy Maguire in *What Women Want*, with Mel Gibson?
5 Who was the star of the computer-animated *Tomb Raider*?
6 What sort of farm features in *Chicken Run*?
7 Who directed *Gladiator*?
8 Who co-starred with Harry Enfield in *Kevin and Perry Go Large*?
9 Who became romantically linked with Russell Crowe during the making of *Proof of Life*?
10 For which movie did Julia Roberts win her first Oscar?
11 Who played the title role in Richard Attenborough's *Grey Owl*?
12 Who plays Johnny Depp's wife in *Blow*?
13 Which *Absolutely Fabulous* star was the voice of Ginger in *Chicken Run*?
14 Which movie starred Hugh Jackman as a computer hacker and John Travolta as a counter terrorist?
15 In which country was *The Beach* filmed?
16 In *The Mexican*, what is the Mexican?
17 Who is the female corner of the love triangle in *Pearl Harbor*?
18 In *Meet The Parents* which animals is Robert De Niro particularly fond of?
19 Who was the voice of Shrek?
20 Which classes should Billy Elliot be going to when he is doing ballet?
21 Who played Lara Croft's father in the *Tomb Raider* film and in real life too?
22 Who plays the single mum in *Chocolat*?
23 Which new millennium movie on the drugs trade starred Michael Douglas?
24 Which English actor played the lawyer in *Erin Brokovich*?
25 Who plays the Marquis de Sade in *Quills*?
26 What was the sequel to *The Lost World* in the *Jurassic Park* films?
27 Who is the star of *The Family Man*, a remake of *It's A Wonderful Life*?
28 Who played Bridget's mum in *Bridget Jones's Diary*?
29 Which actress is the object of Jude Law and Joseph Fiennes affections in *Enemy At The Gates*?
30 What is John Hurt's profession in *Captain Corelli's Mandolin*?

CRICKET *See quiz 34, page 130*

ANSWERS

1 Hampshire. 2 Richard Hadlee. 3 18th. 4 Zimbabwe. 5 Edgbaston. 6 West Indies.
7 1970s. 8 Memorial Gallery. 9 Gully. 10 County. 11 The batsman is out.
12 Hansie Cronje. 13 Sri Lanka. 14 Colin Cowdrey. 15 John Player Sunday League.
16 David Gower. 17 Glamorgan. 18 Yorkshire. 19 First class. 20 108.
21 Graeme Hick. 22 Australia. 23 Duck. 24 Warwickshire. 25 Sussex.
26 Alan Donald. 27 Just under 5 inches. 28 1950s. 29 19th. 30 Derbyshire.

QUIZ 37 POT LUCK 17

Answers - see Quiz 39, page 135

1 Which character in *The Bill* was played by the late Kevin Lloyd?
2 Which branch of physics deals with motion of objects?
3 Which 1997 cartoon movie featured the voices of Meg Ryan and John Cusack?
4 What type of belts are awarded to British champions in boxing?
5 Eton school is in which English county?
6 In sport, what word can go after Trent and Stamford?
7 How is Mary O'Brien who died in March 1999 better known?
8 In which country is Malpensa international airport?
9 Which great Test cricketer's forename initials are the same as the abbreviation for Information Technology?
10 What does fibrian cause the blood to do?
11 Which late great duetted with kd lang on his mega hit "Crying"?
12 How would four-fifths be shown as a decimal?
13 Which sport did Marco Van Basten play?
14 Whose life story was recreated in the biopic *Sweet Dreams*?
15 Which country celebrated its bicentenary in 1988?
16 How many stomachs does a cow have?
17 Which Marx Brother's name is also the name of Oprah Winfrey's production company?
18 Cu is the chemical symbol for which element?
19 Which country was first to host both the Summer and Winter Olympics in the same year?
20 What was the first name of Stephen Tomkinson's character in *Drop the Dead Donkey*?
21 The late Brian Connolly fronted which glam band?
22 What is the name of the cat in *Sabrina The Teenage Witch*?
23 Pop star Billie married in May 2001 in which US city?
24 Who was the body-snatching partner of Hare?
25 Which entertainer said, "George, don't do that"?
26 Which murder victim was mentioned in the trailers for *Twin Peaks*?
27 In which country would you watch Grasshoppers play a home soccer match?
28 What is the minimum score in an over if alternate deliveries are hit to the boundary?
29 Which pop superstar's first wife was Cynthia Powell?
30 Patrick Troughton followed William Hartnell to play which character in a long running TV series?

ANSWERS

ANIMALS See quiz 39, page 135
1 Monkey. 2 Australia. 3 Chick. 4 Marsupial. 5 Umbilical. 6 India. 7 Dodo.
8 African elephant. 9 Cat. 10 Herbivorous. 11 Squirrel. 12 Trees. 13 40%.
14 Smell. 15 Chimpanzee. 16 Alone. 17 Borneo. 18 Reptiles. 19 Hood.
20 Clawed. 21 Border collie. 22 Tapeworm. 23 Whale. 24 Indian cobra.
25 Spawn. 26 Hare. 27 Starfish. 28 Thumb. 29 Cobra. 30 Grizzly bear.

QUIZ 38 SOUNDS OF THE 70S

Answers - see Quiz 40, page 136

1 What was on the other side of Boney M's "Brown Girl in the Ring"?
2 Which Dawn single was in the charts for 39 weeks in the 1970s?
3 Which film did You're the "One That I Want" come from?
4 Which 1970s hit by Wings was the first UK single to sell two million copies?
5 Who made the album *Don't Shoot Me I'm Only The Piano Player*?
6 Which solo singer who died in 2001 recorded the album "And I Love You So"?
7 Who did Elton John have a No 1 single with in 1976?
8 Julie Covington had a UK No 1 with a song from which Andrew Lloyd Webber/Tim Rice musical?
9 Who was the most successful solo star from the group which had a No 1 with "Message In A Bottle"?
10 "Matchstalk Men and Matchstalk Cats and Dogs" was about which artist?
11 With which song did Brotherhood of Man win the Eurovision Song Contest?
12 Who had the original hit with "Seasons in the Sun"?
13 Who had "Breakfast In America"?
14 How many times is Annie's name mentioned in John Denver's "Annie's Song"?
15 Who was the first Beatle to have a solo No 1 in the 1970s?
16 Which member of the cast of *Dad's Army* had a No 1 hit record?
17 Who hit No 1 with "Cum On Feel The Noize"?
18 Who declared that he was the Leader of the Gang?
19 Which star of the stage show Evita had a hit with "Hold Me Close"?
20 What was the title of the England World Cup squad's anthem of 1970?
21 On which new record label was Mike Oldfield's *Tubular Bells* released?
22 Which Tony featured on Dawn's "Tie A Yellow Ribbon"?
23 Which instrument did Suzi Quatro play on "Can The Can"?
24 Who had a hit with Nilsson's "Without You" 20 years later?
25 Which band made the super selling "Rumours"?
26 Which band did Roy Wood lead in "Angel Fingers"?
27 Whose "Sailing" was describes by its performer as "one for the terraces."?
28 Which band's very first hit was "Debora"?
29 "I'd Like To Teach the World to Sing" was later used to advertised which drink?
30 Who recorded the album *Arrival*?

POT LUCK 18 *See quiz 40, page 136*

1 "I Heard It Through the Grapevine". 2 1896. 3 God. 4 *Ballykissangel*. 5 Aubretia.
6 16. 7 Nile. 8 Francis Ford Coppola. 9 At a walking pace. 10 Nesta. 11 Hooves.
12 Meridiem. 13 Portugal. 14 16th. 15 Wren. 16 Elizabeth. 17 1960s.
18 *Mr Men*. 19 Codes. 20 St Denis. 21 Iron. 22 Swedish. 23 Alan Shearer.
24 Grizabella. 25 1920s. 26 Canada. 27 Busy Lizzy. 28 Five.
29 The Three Degrees. 30 Rhubarb.

ANSWERS

QUIZ 39 ANIMALS

Answers - see Quiz 37, page 133

1 What type of creature is a mandrill?
2 The bandicoot is a marsupial from which country?
3 What is a young penguin called?
4 What sort of creature is a Tasmanian devil?
5 Which cord connects the placenta to the embryo in mammals?
6 Which country has the most Asian elephants in their natural habitat?
7 Which extinct flightless bird has the Latin name Didus ineptus?
8 Which weighs the most – African elephant, hippopotamus or white rhinoceros?
9 What can be Persian long hair, British short hair or Oriental short hair?
10 Which word would describe a wombat's diet?
11 The chipmunk is related to which creature?
12 Where do sloths live?
13 What percentage of all living mammals are rodents?
14 Which of the primates senses is the weakest?
15 Which is the most intelligent – baboon, chimpanzee or gorilla?
16 How does a tiger hunt?
17 The orang utan in the wild is restricted to Sumatra and where?
18 Who has the most teeth, reptiles, fish or mammals?
19 What is the neck region of the cobra called?
20 What sort of feet do tortoises have?
21 Which is the most intelligent breed of dog?
22 Which of the following animals has the greatest length or height – African elephant, giraffe or tapeworm?
23 What can be minke, grey or bowhead?
24 Which snake is traditionally used by snake charmers?
25 What are the fertilised eggs of amphibians called?
26 Which is the fastest – hare, horse or greyhound?
27 Which fish are members of the class Asteroidea?
28 Which is the only 'finger' of a bat that is free from the membrane that forms its wing?
29 Which deadly snakes can be Egyptian, Indian or Forest?
30 Which is the heaviest – black bear, grizzly bear or polar bear?

POT LUCK 17 *See quiz 37, page 133*

ANSWERS

1 'Tosh' Lines. 2 Mechanics. 3 Anastasia. 4 Lonsdale. 5 Berkshire. 6 Bridge.
7 Dusty Springfield. 8 Italy. 9 Botham. 10 Clot. 11 Roy Orbison. 12 0.80.
13 Soccer. 14 Patsy Cline. 15 Australia. 16 Four. 17 Harpo. 18 Copper.
19 France. 20 Damien. 21 Sweet. 22 Salem. 23 Las Vegas. 24 Burke.
25 Joyce Grenfell. 26 Laura Palmer. 27 Switzerland. 28 12. 29 John Lennon.
30 Dr Who.

QUIZ 40 POT LUCK 18

Answers - see Quiz 38, page 134

1 Which Marvin Gaye hit got into the top ten again after his murder?
2 When were the first Modern Olympic Games held?
3 What are you afraid of if you suffer from theophobia?
4 Father Peter Clifford appeared in which TV series?
5 Which plant was named after Claude Aubriet?
6 How many pawns start off a chess game?
7 The Aswan Dam was built on which river?
8 Who directed all *The Godfather* series of movies?
9 What does the musical term andante mean?
10 What was Bob Marley's middle name?
11 What does an ungulate animal have?
12 What does the letter m in the time abbreviation pm. stand for?
13 The Azores belong to which country?
14 In which century was William Shakespeare born?
15 Which bird was on the old coin the farthing?
16 What is John Major's daughter called?
17 In which decade did the Victoria line open on the London Underground?
18 Roger Hargreaves created which Men – *The Flowerpot Men*, *The Four Just Men* or *Mr Men*?
19 Cryptography is the study of what?
20 Who is the patron saint of France?
21 What do ferrous metals contain?
22 What nationality was chemist Alfred Nobel?
23 Who was the was the first player to score 100 goals in the Premier League?
24 In the musical *Cats* which cat sings "Memory"?
25 In which decade was the first FA Cup Final played at Wembley?
26 As well as being an animal, the Red Deer is a river in which country?
27 How is the plant Impatiens more usually known?
28 In the movie *Alien*, how many crew members were there in the craft Nostromo?
29 How were Ferguson, Thompson and Pickney known collectively?
30 Hawk's Champagne and Prince Albert are types of what?

QUIZ 41   NEWSWORTHY

Answers - see Quiz 43, page 139

1   Who were the two final contenders for the Tory leadership contest 2001?
2   In which month of 2001 was Jeffrey Archer convicted and sentenced to a jail sentence?
3   Bakelite was the first important what?
4   In which decade did John Logie Baird first demonstrate television?
5   Bangladesh was created from which former territory?
6   Which political leader had a villa retreat at Berchtesgaden?
7   Who succeeded Harold Wilson as Prime Minister and suffered the 'winter of discontent'?
8   Bill Clinton appointed his wife Hillary to carry out reforms in which social service?
9   What was the Democratic Republic of Congo called between 1971 and 1997?
10   Who did George W Bush defeat to become President in 2000?
11   Inkatha was set up to promote the interests of which South African race?
12   What does the M stand for in IMF?
13   Where in London was a memorial service held three days after the New York and Washington terrorist attacks of Sept 2001?
14   What does A stand for in IRA?
15   Which Israeli leader was assassinated in 1995?
16   Silvio Berlusconi became which country's Prime Minister in 1994?
17   Who was the first British writer to receive the Nobel Prize for Literature?
18   Who headed the US committee investigating Communist infiltration in public life?
19   Which country has a news agency called TASS?
20   What did Joseph Pulitzer give a Prize for?
21   Who interviewed Princess Diana on *Panorama* when she frankly discussed her marriage?
22   Which Moors were the scene of the so called Moors Murders?
23   Where did the Earl and Countess of Wessex marry?
24   Where was the rail crash which caused long delays from late 2000 to mid-2001?
25   In 2001 which country had three kings in as many days when many royals were machine gunned to death?
26   In 2001 where was John Prescott campaigning when he hit an egg-throwing protester?
27   Who is George W Bush's brother who was Governor of Florida at the time of the 2000 election?
28   Which journalist Diamond, husband of Nigella Lawson, lost his cancer battle in 2001?
29   Peter Mandelson's first Cabinet post was as Secretary for what?
30   The Black and Tans were an auxiliary force of which Constabulary?

FAMILIES *See quiz 43, page 139*

1 Phil Vickery. 2 Mary. 3 George Bush. 4 Siamese twins. 5 Les Dennis. 6 Angie.
7 Rosie. 8 Stella. 9 *The Archers.* 10 Nigel. 11 Emilia Fox. 12 Philip. 13 Jonathan.
14 Jennifer Saunders. 15 Janet Ellis. 16 David Frost. 17 Hardie. 18 Libby Purves.
19 Wendy Turner. 20 Bobby Brown. 21 Fifi Trixibelle. 22 Joe. 23 Jane.
24 Emma Noble. 25 Zoe Ball. 26 Sarah. 27 Dylan. 28 Kent. 29 Arthur Miller.
30 Mel B.

QUIZ 42 POT LUCK 19

Answers - see Quiz 44, page 140

1 What is petrology the study of?
2 In which decade was the record-breaking *Guinness Book of Records* first published?
3 What number of *Doctor Who* was Tom Baker?
4 Which country did Nana Mouskouri come from?
5 What was the name of the Marlon Brando character in *The Godfather*?
6 Quindeca is a prefix indicating which number?
7 What is the chemical symbol for lead?
8 Which garden fruit has poisonous leaves and edible stems?
9 In the song from *The Music Man*, 76 of what type of instrument led the big parade?
10 Which lady's Vineyard is an island off Cape Cod?
11 The Dead Sea is in Israel and which other country?
12 What is the scientific study of inheritance called?
13 Which country did the composer Chopin come from?
14 What does a sufferer from alopecia lose?
15 What percentage is an eighth?
16 According to the words of a Noel Coward song, who "goes out in the midday sun" with "Mad dogs"?
17 In which London Square is the US Embassy?
18 The movie *Saving Private Ryan* dealt with events in which country?
19 In the 1960s, what was the name of Wayne Fontana's backing group?
20 Photosynthesis is the process by which plants use light to make what?
21 The site of ancient Babylon is today in which country?
22 Which 1980s film became the most profitable in Australian movie history?
23 Who was the first English rugby union player to play in 50 internationals?
24 Which glands produce white blood cells?
25 Juliette Binoche and Kristin Scott Thomas first co-starred in which movie?
26 Which Derbyshire town is famous for its church with a crooked spire?
27 Which Bells helped launch the Virgin label?
28 The Parthenon in Athens was built as a temple to which goddess?
29 The song "On My Own" features in which stage show?
30 A guillemot is what sort of creature?

TV CLASSICS See quiz 44, page 140

1 Vince & Penny. 2 Anthony Andrews. 3 Derek. 4 Jane Marple. 5 Thora Hird.
6 Fforbes Hamilton. 7 Jim Bergerac. 8 South Africa. 9 *Come Dancing*. 10 Stripes.
11 1950s. 12 Liz. 13 Queen's coronation. 14 Music Hall. 15 Panorama.
16 Robin Hood. 17 Early evening. 18 Hughie Green. 19 Percy Thrower. 20 Keys.
21 *The Lone Ranger*. 22 Alan Whicker. 23 25. 24 Michael Bentine. 25 77.
26 Eric Morecambe. 27 *The Rag Trade*. 28 Finlay. 29 Roger Moore. 30 Alma.

ANSWERS

QUIZ 43 FAMILIES

Answers - see Quiz 41, page 137

1 Which TV chef did Fern Britton marry?
2 What is the first name of Mrs Michael Parkinson?
3 Which US president married Barbara Pierce?
4 Chang and Eng Bunker were famous as what type of siblings?
5 Which TV presenter did Amanda Holden marry?
6 What is the first name of the former Mrs George Best who wrote George & Me?
7 What is Lorraine Kelly's young daughter called?
8 Which McCartney became 30 in 2001?
9 On which radio show is Jasper Carrott's daughter a regular voice?
10 Which actor is *This Life*'s Jack Davenport's father?
11 Which actress, who starred in the revival of *Randall & Hopkirk (Deceased)*, is the daughter of Joanna David?
12 Which Prince is the grandson of Prince Louis of Battenberg?
13 Which Dimbleby married writer Bel Mooney?
14 Which comedy actress is Mrs Adrian Edmondson?
15 Which former *Blue Peter* presenter is the mother of chart topping Sophie?
16 Which TV presenter is married to the daughter of the 17th Duke of Norfolk?
17 Which actress Kate is the daughter of Goodie Bill Oddie?
18 Which radio presenter is Mrs Paul Heiney?
19 Which TV presenter with a TV presenter sister married *Minder* actor Gary Webster?
20 Which R & B star married Whitney Houston in 1992?
21 Who is Peaches Geldof's oldest sister?
22 Who is the oldest of the acting McGann brothers?
23 What is Lord Paddy Ashdown's wife called?
24 Which actress/model did ex PM's son James Major marry?
25 Who is Woody Cook's mum?
26 What were Andrew Lloyd Webber's first two wives called?
27 What is the name of the son of Catherine Zeta Jones and Michael Douglas?
28 Lady Helen Taylor is the daughter of which Duchess?
29 Which playwright is Daniel Day Lewis's father in law?
30 Which Spice Girl had a daughter called Phoenix Chi?

NEWSWORTHY *See quiz 41, page 137*
1 Kenneth Clarke and Iain Duncan Smith. 2 July. 3 Plastic. 4 1920s. 5 East Pakistan.
6 Adolph Hitler. 7 James Callaghan. 8 Health. 9 Zaire. 10 Al Gore. 11 Zulus.
12 Monetary. 13 St Paul's. 14 Army. 15 Yitzhak Rabin. 16 Italy. 17 Rudyard Kipling.
18 Senator Joseph McCarthy. 19 Russia. 20 Literature/journalism. 21 Martin Bashir.
22 Saddleworth. 23 St George's Chapel Windsor. 24 Hatfield. 25 Nepal. 26 Rhyl.
27 Jeb. 28 John. 29 Trade and Industry. 30 Royal Ulster.

QUIZ 44 TV CLASSICS

Answers - see Quiz 42, page 138

1 Who were *Just Good Friends*?
2 Who shot to stardom with Jeremy Irons in *Brideshead Revisited*?
3 Which *Coronation Street* character died in his car after a road rage attack?
4 Which detective did Joan Hickson play on TV?
5 Which veteran actress presented *Praise Be!* for many years?
6 What was the surname of Audrey in *To The Manor Born*?
7 Which detective did John Nettles play before becoming involved in *The Midsomer Murders*?
8 Where did Kathy leave for when she first left *EastEnders*?
9 Which dance show's presenters have included Terry Wogan, Angela Rippon and Rosemarie Ford?
10 What was the pattern on Andy Pandy's suit?
11 In which decade was one of TV's first panel games *What's My Line?* first shown?
12 What was Beverley Callard's character called in *Coronation Street*?
13 For which event were TV cameras first installed in Westminster Abbey?
14 What was the supposed setting for *The Good Old Days*?
15 Which long running current affairs programme began in 1953?
16 Which legendary hero played by Richard Greene achieved great success on both sides of the Atlantic?
17 At what time of day was *Crackerjack* broadcast?
18 Who hosted *Double Your Money* throughout its 13 year run?
19 Which famous TV gardener started *Gardening Club*?
20 On *Take Your Pick* what did contestants have to win to open boxes?
21 Which children's show had a masked hero seeking justice in America's wild west?
22 Which travelling journalist with trademark glasses and moustache was famous for presenting his *World*?
23 *All Our Yesterdays* showed film footage of events how many years previously?
24 Which member of *The Goons* presented the zany *It's A Square World*?
25 What number went before Sunset Strip in the title of the US private eye series?
26 Whose catchphrases included "You can't see the join," and "Get out of that!"?
27 Which sitcom was set in Fenners Fashions?
28 Which *Dr* opened his *Casebook* between 1962 and 1971?
29 Which James Bond played *The Saint*?
30 In *Coronation Street*, who was Mike Baldwin's wife immediately before Linda?

QUIZ 45 POT LUCK 20

Answers - see Quiz 47, page 143

1 Which worker gave Ken Barrie a hit – Bob The Builder, Postman Pat or The Singing Postman?
2 Who was the President of Argentina during the Falklands conflict?
3 What is the main island of Japan?
4 Saxifrage is a type of what?
5 On the radio, what is the name of the church in *The Archers*?
6 Which animal was used by Jenner when developing a vaccine against smallpox?
7 The song "I Feel Pretty" comes from which musical?
8 A snake's cast off skin is known as a what?
9 Where is Britain's National Horseracing Museum?
10 Which group thought it was fun to stay at the "YMCA"?
11 What city is the largest in Nevada?
12 Who played Wales at rugby in the inaugural match at the new Millennium Stadium?
13 Which playwright is married to Maureen Lipman?
14 Which member of Gianni Versace's family took over his fashion empire after his death?
15 In 1998, who married millionaire hairdresser Stephen Way?
16 Which Brothers were Scott, John and Gary?
17 Where did Peter and Annie Mayle spend a year?
18 If New Year's day was a Thursday what day would Valentine's Day be?
19 Sarah Brightman was which number wife to Andrew Lloyd Webber?
20 Ruby is linked to which wedding anniversary?
21 In the traditional song, which herb goes with parsley, rosemary and thyme?
22 Who composed the opera "Norma"?
23 Who was the first member of the Royal Family to be interviewed on British TV?
24 A Blue Orpington is a type of what?
25 Which spirit forms the basis for Pimm's No 1?
26 Marty Wilde's name has become cockney rhyming slang for what?
27 Which Prime Minister had a wife who wrote a biography of Joan Sutherland?
28 Which store owner first said, "The customer is always right"?
29 Which group had hits with "The Logical Song" and "Dreamer"?
30 The Sargasso Sea forms part of which ocean?

POT LUCK 21 See quiz 47, page 143
1 A. 2 Ear. 3 Seven. 4 Nut. 5 Trombone. 6 Mrs Beeton. 7 Nervous system.
8 Their feet. 9 Three. 10 Lynda LaPlante. 11 Foxglove. 12 *Fiddler On the Roof.*
13 Miss Marple. 14 Michel Platini. 15 Common. 16 Rugby. 17 None. 18 Helium.
19 Cawley. 20 The Supremes. 21 Friday. 22 *Star Trek.* 23 Athletics. 24 Bad breath.
25 Starsky & Hutch. 26 Ice hockey. 27 Eclipse. 28 The Grateful Dead.
29 Football (Shrewsbury Town). 30 Shape.

QUIZ 46 FOOD AND DRINK

Answers - see Quiz 48, page 144

1 If bread is left to 'prove' what does it do?
2 Which initials indicate the highest quality brandy – AC, RSVP or VSOP?
3 What is a chanterelle?
4 What is aioli flavoured with?
5 What type of sauce was named after the Marquis de Bechamel?
6 What would you be eating if you were served calamari?
7 Enchiladas were originally part of which country's cooking?
8 What shape is the pasta called fusilli?
9 Mozzarella was originally made from which type of milk?
10 Which herb is usually used in gremolata?
11 Which pulses are used to make hummus?
12 Other than tomatoes and onions which is the main vegetable used in moussaka?
13 In which country is the famous wine growing area of the Barossa valley?
14 Chianti comes from which area of Italy?
15 If a dish is cooked en papillote what is it cooked in?
16 Passata is pureed what?
17 A brochette is another word for what?
18 What is prosciutto?
19 What flavour do ratafia biscuits have?
20 What makes a salsa verde green – celery leaves, herbs or spinach?
21 Schnapps is distilled from what?
22 What type of white wine is Barsac famous for?
23 What type of oven is traditionally used for a tandoori?
24 Which Japanese dish is made from rice, seaweed and raw fish?
25 Which herb is usually used in a pesto sauce?
26 What type of dough is calzone made from?
27 What is a bisque?
28 When would antipasto be served?
29 What does baking powder produces when water is added, which makes dough rise?
30 How is something cooked if it is saute?

MOTOR SPORTS *See quiz 48, page 144*

1 Ferrari. 2 500 miles. 3 Automobile. 4 Michael Schumacher. 5 Great Britain.
6 Twice. 7 Luxembourg. 8 Bernie Ecclestone. 9 29. 10 Silverstone. 11 June.
12 Williams. 13 1970s. 14 San Marino. 15 Le Mans 24 Hour race. 16 McLaren.
17 Motorcycling 18 USA. 19 Renault. 20 Never. 21 Twice. 22 Brazil.
23 Michael Schumacher. 24 Monte Carlo. 25 Belgium. 26 May. 27 San Marino.
28 Twice. 29 1910s.. 30 Japan.

ANSWERS

QUIZ 47 POT LUCK 21

Answers - see Quiz 45, page 141

1 What is the next white note on a keyboard above G?
2 What is examined with an otoscope?
3 How many gold medals did Mark Spitz win in the 1972 Olympics?
4 What type of food is a macadamia?
5 What was Glenn Miller's main instrument?
6 Isabella Mary Mayson became better known as which cook?
7 Which of our body systems controls sight, hearing and touch?
8 For many years the title sequence of *The Bill* featured which part of the police officer's bodies?
9 In music, Police contained how many people?
10 Which writer created TV's Jane Tennison?
11 Which plant produce the drug digitalis?
12 "Sunrise, Sunset comes from which musical?
13 Who was the sleuth in *The Body in the Library*?
14 Which Frenchman was voted European Footballer of The Year three times in a row?
15 L stands for lowest, M stands for multiple, but what does the C stand for in LCM?
16 What are you watching if William Webb Ellis is credited with founding it?
17 How many sides of a scalene triangle are equal?
18 Which element has the atomic number 2?
19 In tennis Miss Goolagong became which Mrs?
20 The late Florence Ballard was a member of which group?
21 The Norse goddess of love gives her name to which day of the week?
22 What is Gene Roddenberry's most famous creation?
23 Decker and Budd crashed into each other in which sport?
24 What do you suffer from if you have halitosis?
25 Dave & Ken were the first names of which TV duo?
26 The American Buffalo Sabres play which sport?
27 What describes the Earth or moon entering the other's shadow?
28 The late Jerry Garcia was vocalist with which band?
29 What sport are you watching if you are at Gay Meadow?
30 What changes when something is metamorphosised?

POT LUCK 20 See quiz 45, page 141

1 Postman Pat. 2 Galtieri. 3 Hokkaido. 4 Rock plant. 5 St Stephen's. 6 Cow.
7 *West Side Story*. 8 Slough. 9 Newmarket. 10 Village People. 11 Las Vegas.
12 Argentina. 13 Jack Rosenthal. 14 His sister. 15 Gloria Hunniford.
16 The Walker Brothers. 17 Provence. 18 Saturday. 19 Second. 20 Fortieth.
21 Sage. 22 Bellini. 23 Prince Philip. 24 Fowl. 25 Gin. 26 Mild. 27 Major.
28 Selfridge. 29 Supertramp. 30 Atlantic.

QUIZ 48 MOTOR SPORTS

Answers - see Quiz 46, page 142

1 Which cars have won more Grand Prix than any other car?
2 How long is Indianapolis's most famous race?
3 What does the A stand for in FIA?
4 Which European was the second youngest World Champion of all time in 1994?
5 At the beginning of the new millennium which country had the most Grand Prix wins?
6 How many times was a Finn F1 World Champion in the 1990s?
7 Which Grand Prix was held at the Nurburgring in 1998?
8 Who was the head of F1 at the end of the 20th century?
9 How old was James Hunt when he became World Champion – 24, 29 or 33?
10 Where did Damon Hill drive his first F1 race?
11 In which month does the Isle of Man TT race take place?
12 Who did Damon Hill race for when he became World Champion in 1996?
13 In which decade was Barry Sheene world 500cc champion twice?
14 During which Grand Prix did Ayrton Senna meet his death?
15 Which race is run on the Circuit de la Sarthe?
16 Which was Mika Hakkinen's team when he announced in 2001 he was going to take a year out of racing?
17 Which motor sport has the governing body the AMA?
18 Kevin Schwartz from which country was a 1991 World Champion on a Suzuki?
19 Which French constructor raced with Williams and Benetton in the 1990s?
20 How many times did Stirling Moss win the World Championship?
21 How many times was Graham Hill World Champion in the 1960s?
22 Which country was Nelson Piquet from?
23 Which driver was the highest earning sportsman of 1999?
24 What is the first rally of the World Rally Championship?
25 Where is the Francorchamps circuit?
26 In which month does the Indianapolis 500 take place?
27 Which Grand Prix is held at Imola?
28 How many times was a Briton F1 World Champion in the 1990s?
29 In which decade was the Indianapolis 500m inaugurated?
30 Where is the Suzuka circuit?

FOOD AND DRINK See quiz 46, page 142
1 Rise. 2 VSOP. 3 Mushroom. 4 Garlic. 5 White sauce. 6 Squid. 7 Mexico.
8 Spirals. 9 Buffalo's. 10 Parsley. 11 Chick peas. 12 Aubergine. 13 Australia.
14 Tuscany. 15 Paper. 16 Tomatoes. 17 Kebab. 18 Ham. 19 Almond. 20 Herbs.
21 Potatoes. 22 Sweet. 23 Clay. 24 Sushi. 25 Basil. 26 Pizza. 27 Soup.
28 Before a meal. 29 Carbon dioxide. 30 Fried.

ANSWERS

QUIZ 49 POT LUCK 22

Answers - see Quiz 51, page 147

1 What was Radiohead's first top ten single?
2 In America the Stanley Cup is awarded in which sport?
3 There are 6,080 feet in what?
4 Where did the Norse gods reside?
5 On radio, what did the A stand for in the programme known as *ITMA*?
6 In snooker how many reds are there on a table when one third of them have been potted?
7 Which musical instrument did the late Karen Carpenter play?
8 There are 78 cards in what type of pack?
9 Jimmy Case and Brian Horton have both managed which soccer club?
10 How many edges does a cube have?
11 What was the setting for the TV series *Within These Walls*?
12 On a relief map, which lines connect points of the same height?
13 Gossima was a game that developed into which sport?
14 What green coloured item goes to the winner of the US Masters?
15 What is family name of the main characters in *Sabrina the Teenage Witch*?
16 What type of word reads the same backwards as forwards?
17 Which American gave her name to an item of underwear?
18 Richard Beckinsale played Godber in which classic sitcom?
19 The final of the US Tennis Open is played at which Meadow?
20 Which Irish city do pop band OTT come from?
21 How many letters in our alphabet can be written with one straight line?
22 In which decade were satellite pictures first sent across the Atlantic?
23 How many bones are there in total in the human body?
24 On which island was the TV detective series *Bergerac* set?
25 Which is the biggest planet in our Solar System?
26 Whose leaving Genesis led to Phil Collins becoming the main man for vocals?
27 What type of TV programme was broadcast from Barnsdale?
28 Helvetia features on stamps that come from which country?
29 Which Bob first presented *Blockbusters*?
30 In which decade was Amnesty International established?

ANSWERS

POT LUCK 23 *See quiz 51, page 147*
1 *High Society* 2 Cardigan. 3 15 minutes. 4 Margaret Thatcher. 5 Feast of Tabernacles.
6 Oasis. 7 Kennedy assassination. 8 Australia. 9 1960s. 10 Vietnam War. 11 Gold.
12 Fraternity. 13 Egypt. 14 Roxy Music. 15 Brother. 16 West Bromwich Albion.
17 Philippines. 18 *Eagle*. 19 Luddites. 20 "Looking Up". 21 Iran. 22 Horticultural.
23 Badminton. 24 Horror. 25 Peter Andre. 26 Hitler. 27 Genetically. 28 1910s.
29 Teddy Bear. 30 Four o'clock.

QUIZ 50 MOVIES – HEROES & HEROINES

Answers - see Quiz 52, page 148

1　How many times in the 20th century did Sean Connery play James Bond?
2　Who played hero Fletcher Reede in *Liar Liar*?
3　Which Sheffield boy starred in *Essex Boys*?
4　Who played the queen to Sid James' King Henry in *Carry On Henry*?
5　In the movie *M*A*S*H* who played the role Alan Alda played on TV?
6　Which Hollywood superstar was the subject of *Mommie Dearest*?
7　In which movie did Tom Hanks play Chuck Noland?
8　Who played Morticia to Raul Julia's Gomez in *The Addams Family*?
9　In what type of place is *The Green Mile* set?
10　Which Tom Cruise movie had the line, "'Show me the money!'"?
11　Who is Julia Roberts' love rival in *My Best Friend's Wedding*?
12　Who was chosen to play Harry Potter?
13　Which star of *Singin' In The Rain* appeared with Judy Garland in *Me & My Gal*?
14　Which star of *The Perfect Storm* also starred in *The Thin Red Line*?
15　Which Bridges was *The Big Lebowski*?
16　Who played Estella in the New York-based 1990s version of *Great Expectations*?
17　Which King was played by Leonardo DiCaprio in *The Man in the Iron Mask*?
18　Who plays Annie MacLean in *The Horse Whisperer* with Robert Redford?
19　Who played space hero Harry Stamper in *Armageddon*?
20　Who played Sidney in *Scream* and *Scream 2*?
21　Who plays Gaz in *The Full Monty*?
22　What is Tom Cruise's job in *Mission: Impossible*?
23　Which Redgrave played the astrologer in the life of David Helfgott in *Shine*?
24　Who played airline pilot Steven Hiller in *Independence Day*?
25　Who was the fourth 007?
26　Which historical figure was *Braveheart*?
27　What is the profession of the hero in *The Client*, based on John Grisham's novel?
28　What was the name of Andie McDowell's character in *Four Weddings and a Funeral*?
29　In which film did Tom Hanks play a simple hero with a heart of gold?
30　Who played Steve Biko in *Cry Freedom*?

QUIZ 51 POT LUCK 23

Answers - see Quiz 49, page 145

1 The song "Who Wants To Be A Millionaire?" comes from which musical?
2 Which Earl gave his name to a jacket?
3 Andy Warhol thought that everyone would be famous for how long?
4 Who described President Gorbachev as, "a man we can do business with."?
5 How is the Jewish Feast Sukkot also known?
6 Which chart topping band had Paul McGuigan playing bass?
7 What did the Warren Commission investigate in the 1960s?
8 Composer Percy Grainger came from which country?
9 "Love Is All Around" was a huge 1990s hit but in which decade was the original released?
10 The My Lai massacre took place during which war?
11 What was discovered in Rabbit Creek, Klondike in 1896?
12 What goes with Liberty and Equality in the motto adopted by the French republic?
13 Farouk was the last King of which country?
14 The 1996 rerelease of "Love is the Drug" was a remix from which band's 1970s hit?
15 What relation was Edward VIII to George VI?
16 Ron Atkinson and Bobby Gould have both managed Coventry City and which other soccer club?
17 Corazon Aquino was President of which country?
18 In which comic did Dan Dare first appear?
19 In England which protesters smashed spinning and weaving machines in factories?
20 What was the first hit single for *EastEnders*' Michelle Gayle?
21 The Ayatollah Khomeini returned home to take power in which country in 1979?
22 What does the letter H stand for in gardening's RHS?
23 Which sport takes its name from the Duke of Beaufort's House?
24 What type of book does Clive Barker write?
25 "Flava" and "I Feel You" were the first two No 1s for which singer?
26 Which fanatical leader was born with the surname Schicklgruber?
27 What does the G stand for in the GM referring to crops?
28 In which decade was the first non stop transatlantic flight?
29 What has been named after a nickname of US President Theodore Roosevelt?
30 In "Rock Around The Clock" what time has been reached when rock is first sung?

QUIZ 52 SCIENCE

Answers - see Quiz 50, page 146

1 Which spacecraft launched the Hubble telescope?
2 What does the letter d stand for in radar?
3 Pythagoras's most famous theorem is about which geometric shape?
4 Which part of London is associated with Mean Time?
5 Which German psychiatrist gave his name to a disease of senile dementia?
6 Famous for demonstrating TV, John Logie Baird also developed what type of sound?
7 The study of oncogenes is crucial in the treatment of which disease?
8 Portsmouth born Isambard Kingdom Brunel was responsible for the construction of tunnels, bridges and viaducts on which railway's line?
9 Who were the main opponents of Copernicus's assertion that the Sun was at the centre of the Universe?
10 How is the lady born Manya Sklodowska better known?
11 Which dog gave its name to Darwin's explorer ship?
12 What improvement did Edison make to Bell's telephone?
13 What did Geiger's counter measure?
14 Which scientist wrote A Brief History of Time?
15 In 1898 Marconi transmitted radio signals across where – Atlantic. English Channel or the USA?
16 Which physician gave his name to the disease of paralysis agitans?
17 What process is involved in pasteurisation in order to kill bacteria, as researched by Pasteur?
18 Seismologist Charles Richter studied what?
19 What makes acid rain acid – high temperatures, low temperatures or pollution?
20 In what type of atmosphere do algae live – dry, high altitude or wet?
21 Carbohydrates are made up of carbon, hydrogen and what?
22 If a disease is congenital when does it date from?
23 What is the minimum number of species in a hybrid?
24 What does the V stand for in the fertility treatment IVF?
25 A perennial is a plant which lives longer than how long?
26 Dry ice is solid or frozen what?
27 What is a defensive substance produced as a reaction to a foreign body called?
28 Irish naval officer Sir Francis Beaufort gave his name to measurement of what?
29 Sir Humphry Davy discovered that laughing gas has which effect?
30 What was the nationality of Archimedes?

MOVIES – HEROES & HEROINES See quiz 50, page 146

ANSWERS

1 Seven. 2 Jim Carrey. 3 Sean Bean. 4 Joan Sims. 5 Donald Sutherland.
6 Joan Crawford. 7 Cast Away. 8 Anjelica Houston. 9 Prison. 10 Jerry Maguire.
11 Cameron Diaz. 12 Daniel Radcliffe. 13 Gene Kelly. 14 George Clooney. 15 Jeff.
16 Gwyneth Paltrow. 17 Louis XIV. 18 Kristin Scott Thomas. 19 Bruce Willis.
20 Neve Campbell. 21 Robert Carlyle. 22 Spy. 23 Lynn. 24 Will Smith.
25 Timothy Dalton. 26 William Wallace. 27 Lawyer. 28 Carrie. 29 Forrest Gump.
30 Denzel Washington.

QUIZ 53 MUSIC – CLASSICS

Answers - see Quiz 55, page 151

1 During which part of Handel's *Messiah* does the audience stand?
2 "Morning" comes from which piece of music by Grieg?
3 Which music by Wagner was used as the theme for *Apocalypse Now*?
4 What was the nationality of Bela Bartok who died at the end of WWII?
5 Rachmaninov wrote a "Rhapsody" on whose theme?
6 What type of work is *Pelleas and Melisande* by Debussy?
7 Which religious song about Jerusalem begins "Last night I lay a sleeping'?
8 Dvorak's famous Symphony No 9 is called what?
9 Mendelssohn's "Fingal's Cave" is from which Overture?
10 About which romantic pair did Berlioz write a symphony?
11 "Take A Pair of Sparkling Eyes" comes from which Gilbert & Sullivan opera?
12 Which birthplace of Handel shares its name with a Manchester based orchestra?
13 Rodrigo's Concerto d'Aranjuez is played on which instrument?
14 Chopin wrote music almost exclusively for which musical instrument?
15 The music "Crimond" is usually sung to which psalm?
16 What range of voice did Kathleen Ferrier have?
17 Which Gilbert & Sullivan opera is set in the Tower of London?
18 Which of Beethoven's Symphonies is the *Choral Symphony*?
19 "One Fine Day" comes from which Puccini opera?
20 Which words were put to Elgar's "Pomp and Circumstance March No 1 in D Major"?
21 What type of work by Beethoven has the title "Moonlight"?
22 "The Dance of the Sugar Plum Fairy" is from which Tchaikovsky ballet?
23 Which Handel composition about anointing Solomon King is sung at English coronations?
24 "Nimrod" is from which Elgar composition?
25 In which English county was Sir Harrison Birtwistle born?
26 Where was Rossini's famous *Barber* from?
27 Which aria can be translated as "None Shall Sleep"?
28 What type of voice normally sings "O For the Wings of a Dove"?
29 How is Bizet's *Les Pecheurs de Perles* also known?
30 What goes with "Peasant" in the Overture by Suppe?

HEADLINES See quiz 55, page 151
1 Donald Campbell. 2 Kiev. 3 Cuban Missile. 4 Galtieri. 5 Gerald Ford.
6 Anthrax. 7 Pennsylvania. 8 Ayatollah Rafsanjani. 9 Elton John. 10 Lyndon Johnson.
11 Australia. 12 West German. 13 November. 14 Oklahoma. 15 Harold.
16 The Philippines. 17 East Sussex. 18 Martin McGuinness. 19 Stephen Lawrence.
20 Donald Dewar. 21 *The Guardian*. 22 President Akihito. 23 Welsh Guards.
24 Tony Banks. 25 Boris Yeltsin. 26 *Panorama*. 27 Josie. 28 Hyde. 29 Viagra.
30 Battle of Britain.

QUIZ 54 POT LUCK 24

Answers - see Quiz 56, page 152

1 What was Jamiroquai's first UK Top Ten hit?

2 Which of these is a sport that is very similar to ice hockey – bandy, gandy or handy?

3 What does a barometer measure?

4 What was Frank Spencer's daughter called?

5 Who or what was the dauphin?

6 Who was the last Prime Minister directly before Margaret Thatcher?

7 Copernicus is often cited as being the father of modern what?

8 Which song gave The Shamen their first No 1?

9 Which Wimbledon singles champion was related by marriage to sports tycoon David Lloyd?

10 Chris Patten was the last British Governor of where?

11 How many dresses did Princess Diana auction at Christie's in 1997 – around eight, around 80 or around 800?

12 Which household item was developed by Harry Pickup?

13 Fanny Blankers-Koen was the first woman to win how many Olympic gold medals?

14 What was Cherie Blair's maiden name?

15 Which of Queen Elizabeth II's children was the first to marry?

16 What did Clarice Cliff make?

17 In which month of the year is Mother's Day celebrated in America?

18 Cinnamon comes from which part of a tree?

19 What colour is paprika?

20 Which sought-after clothing items went on sale in the UK for the first time in 1941?

21 Shirley Conran said, "Life is too short to stuff a ..." what?

22 The Sierra Nevada mountains are in which American state?

23 Which Joe was a world champion at both snooker and billiards?

24 Paul Merson was at which club when he made his league debut?

25 Which politician said, "All babies look like me" – Iain Duncan Smith, William Hague or Winston Churchill?

26 What does the second s mean in the knitting term psso?

27 *Cagney and Lacey* was set in which city?

28 Hippophobia is a fear of what?

29 Why was the 1994 Baseball World Series cancelled?

30 What was named after Captain Becher?

POT LUCK 25 *See quiz 56, page 152*

ANSWERS

1 The moon. 2 Carbon. 3 *Prisoner Cell Block H.* 4 Sydney. 5 Equilibrium.
6 Diana Rigg. 7 Facsimile. 8 Richard Nixon. 9 Waitangi Day. 10 Z Cars. 11 Acute.
12 Dr Livesey. 13 Seaside postcard. 14 Lotus. 15 Quakers. 16 Beach Boys.
17 Cockerel. 18 Queen Victoria. 19 Sopwith. 20 Hobby. 21 Milk. 22 Melbourne.
23 Rossini. 24 *Porridge.* 25 Softer. 26 1950s. 27 Albatross. 28 *Between The Lines.*
29 Africa. 30 Tottenham Hotspur.

QUIZ 55 HEADLINES

Answers - see Quiz 53, page 149

1 In 2001 whose car was found in Lake Coniston, 30 years after an attempt on the water speed record?
2 Which city of the Ukraine was closest to Chernobyl?
3 Which crisis brought about the hot line between the White House and the Kremlin?
4 Who led the Argentinians in the Falklands War?
5 Who replaced President Nixon after Watergate?
6 In October 2001, the US's Senate Majority leader received what in the post?
7 In the Sept 11th 2001 terrorist attacks on the US, in which state did the plane crash which did not crash into a building?
8 Who succeeded Ayatollah Khomeini as president of Iran?
9 In 1979 who was the first western rock star to visit the USSR?
10 Who succeeded JF Kennedy after his assassination?
11 Paul Keating, famous for his views on Republicanism, became Prime Minister of where?
12 To which Parliament was militant Petra Kelly elected in 1983?
13 In which month did JFK die?
14 Which US city was the scene of a terrorist bomb in 1995?
15 What was spy Kim Philby's real first name?
16 Where did Corazon Aquino become president after the death of her husband?
17 In which county was Piltdown Man discovered in the early years of the 20th century?
18 Which Sinn Fein politician became Minister of Education after the Good Friday agreement?
19 Neil and Jamie Acourt were named as two of six suspects of the murder of whom?
20 Who was the first leader of the Scottish Parliament?
21 Jonathan Aitken was imprisoned after a failed libel case against which newspaper?
22 Which Japanese leader visited Britain amid great controversy in 1998?
23 Simon Weston, who was badly burned in the Falklands War served in which regiment?
24 Who was Tony Blair's first Minister for Sport?
25 Who preceded Vladimir Putin as Russian leader?
26 On which programme did ex nanny Louise Woodward explain her case on British TV?
27 Which member of the Russell family survived a murderous attack where her mother and sister perished?
28 Where in Greater Manchester did Dr Harold Shipman practise?
29 Which drug was launched in the late 1990s as a cure for impotence?
30 In which Battle did Britain use radar for the first time?

MUSIC CLASSICS See quiz 53, page 149

ANSWERS

1 "Hallelujah Chorus". 2 *Peer Gynt*. 3 "Ride of the Valkyries". 4 Hungarian. 5 Paganini.
6 Opera. 7 "The Holy City". 8 "From The New World". 9 "Hebrides".
10 Romeo & Juliet. 11 *The Gondoliers*. 12 Halle. 13 Guitar. 14 Piano.
15 23, "The Lord's My Shepherd". 16 Contralto. 17 *Yeomen of the Guard*. 18 Ninth.
19 *Madame Butterfly*. 20 "Land of Hope and Glory". 21 Sonata. 22 *Nutcracker*.
23 "Zadok The Priest". 24 *Enigma Variations*. 25 Lancashire. 26 Seville.
27 "Nessun Dorma". 28 (Boy) Soprano. 29 *The Pearl Fishers*. 30 Poet.

QUIZ 56 POT LUCK 25

Answers - see Quiz 54, page 150

1 Where does a plaque read: "We came in peace for all mankind. July 1969"?
2 A diamond is made up of which element?
3 Which TV series featured the Wentworth Detention Centre?
4 Michael Hutchence was born in and died in which city?
5 What word describes a state of complete balance?
6 Who played the TV Avengers role taken by Uma Thurman in the 1990s movie?
7 The word fax is an abbreviation of which word that means a copy?
8 Who was the first US President to resign from office?
9 What is New Zealand's National Day called?
10 In which police TV series did the character Charlie Barlow first find fame?
11 What name is given to an angle of less than 90 degrees?
12 The adventure yarn Treasure Island is narrated by Jim Hawkins and who else?
13 Where would you be most likely to see the artwork of Donald McGill?
14 Which motor racing team has the name of a flower that is sacred in India?
15 Which religious group founded the city of Philadelphia?
16 Carl Wilson of which legendary band died in 1998?
17 In the sitcom The Good Life, Lenin was what kind of creature?
18 Who was the first British monarch to travel by train?
19 Who was the designer of the Sopwith Camel – was it Camel, Sopwith or Sopwith Camel?
20 What can be a small horse or a small falcon?
21 Which everyday food item includes the protein casein?
22 What was Australia's capital before Canberra?
23 Who composed the opera William Tell?
24 Going Straight was the sequel to which TV sitcom?
25 If music is diminuendo it gradually becomes what?
26 In which decade were Duke of Edinburgh awards first presented?
27 Which creature provided Fleetwood Mac with a worldwide hit?
28 In which TV series did Neil Pearson play Det Sup Tony Clark?
29 Mungo Park is famous for exploration in which part of the world?
30 Gerry Francis and George Graham have both managed which soccer club?

POT LUCK 24 See quiz 54, page 150

1 "Too Young to Die". 2 Bandy. 3 Atmospheric pressure. 4 Jessica.
5 Title of a French prince. 6 James Callaghan. 7 Astronomy. 8 "Ebeneezer Goode".
9 Chris Evert. 10 Hong Kong. 11 80. 12 Harpic. 13 Four. 14 Booth.
15 Princess Anne. 16 Pottery. 17 May. 18 Bark. 19 Red. 20 Nylon stockings.
21 Mushroom. 22 California. 23 Joe Davis. 24 Arsenal. 25 Winston Churchill.
26 Stitch. 27 New York. 28 Horses. 29 Strike by the players.
30 The fence at Aintree Becher's Brook.

QUIZ 57 THE FAMOUS

Answers - see Quiz 59, page 155

1 Chad Varah founded which charity?
2 The Queen's residence of Balmoral is on which river?
3 Which Princess is nearest in line to the throne?
4 Who was the only Irish author to win the Nobel Prize for Literature in the 1990s?
5 Which Richard designed the Thrust, the fastest land vehicle of its day?
6 Millvina Dean was the youngest survivor of which ship?
7 What type of radio did Trevor Bayliss invent?
8 Athina Onassis Roussel will inherit millions due to the fortune her grandfather made in what?
9 Sam Walton founded which US based chain of stores?
10 Which child of a rock star inherited nearly £80 million – Frances Cobain, Sean Lennon or Lisa Marie Presley?
11 Which supermodel is dubbed 'The Body'?
12 Which religious figure broadcasts regularly on a radio show called *Decision Hour*?
13 What relation is Jemma Redgrave to Vanessa Redgrave?
14 Which job does George Carey have?
15 How was Lesley Hornby better known?
16 Which of the following is not left handed – Tim Henman, Brian Lara or Martina Navratilova?
17 Alan Ayckbourn famously stages his plays at which seaside resort?
18 Who succeeded Gaby Roslin on Channel 4's *The Big Breakfast*?
19 Who was Tony Blair's first Press Secretary when he became Prime Minister?
20 Jimmy McGovern and Alan Bleasdale are famous names as what?
21 Which First Lady had the maiden name Roddam?
22 What is the first name of Mrs Gordon Brown?
23 How tall was Prince William when he went to university – 6ft 3", 6ft or 5'10"?
24 Prince Albert is heir to which Principality?
25 What do Victor Edelstein and Catherine Walker design?
26 Who was elected to Alan Clark's constituency after his death?
27 What is the first name of the first Mrs Robin Cook?
28 What was Tony Blair's first constituency?
29 The Lauder brothers inherited from their mother Estée who made a fortune in what?
30 Which Princess has middle names Elizabeth Mary?

TV SITCOMS See quiz 59, page 155
1 *Chambers*. 2 Brabinger. 3 Seattle. 4 *Absolutely Fabulous*. 5 Victor Meldrew. 6 Tom.
7 Richard Wilson. 8 Sarah Lancashire. 9 Robert Lindsay. 10 Bollinger.
11 "Listen very carefully". 12 Calista Flockhart. 13 *Are You Being Served?*. 14 White.
15 Julia Roberts. 16 Harold Steptoe. 17 Stephen Tomkinson. 18 Paul Eddington.
19 Samantha. 20 Garth. 21 Nurse. 22 *Cheers*. 23 Captain Mainwaring.
24 Father Jack. 25 *Fawlty Towers*. 26 Ruby Wax. 27 Draughtsman. 28 Richard.
29 Ivy. 30 North east.

QUIZ 58 POT LUCK 26

Answers - see Quiz 60, page 156

1 James Logan gave his name to a type of what – danceband, fruit or road race
2 What was Henri Paul doing to be involved in the crash in which Princess Diana died?
3 Which Day was inaugurated by Miss Anna Jarvis in Philadelphia in 1907?
4 What was Walt Disney's first TV programme called?
5 What did William Herschel discover?
6 What term describes a plant created from crossing different species?
7 In which decade of last century was Margaret Thatcher born?
8 Which Brontë wrote the novel *Jane Eyre*?
9 Charles Babbage was involved in the early development of what?
10 Who found fame after appearing on the docu soap *The Cruise*?
11 What was tennis player Margaret Smith's married name that was linked to her sport?
12 When was the movie *Enigma* set?
13 Steve Bruce and Nigel Spackman have both managed which soccer club?
14 Princess Anne's second marriage took place near which royal residence?
15 What sort of *Days* was the title of Robson & Jerome's Best of album?
16 What sort of car did *Avenger* Emma Peel drive?
17 What was the real first name of Curly Watts in *Coronation Street*?
18 What would you do with a burrito?
19 What is the English name of the lunar sea Lacus Mortis?
20 Which American state is directly below North Carolina?
21 Warrumbungle is found in Australia, but what is it?
22 Dean Martin's "Memories Are Made of This" was used in an ad for which make of car?
23 What number does Thomas display on his Tank Engine?
24 What is another name for your clavicle?
25 Which Mr Miller married Marilyn Monroe?
26 What did Grover live in *Sesame Street*?
27 In which branch of mathematics do letters replace unknown quantities?
28 *The Rose* was a Bette Midler movie based on the life of which singer?
29 Which Diane has been Sean Connery's wife?
30 Del Boy Trotter's catchphrase was "Lovely" what?

POT LUCK 27 *See quiz 60, page 156*

ANSWERS
1 911. 2 Calamity Jane. 3 Scotland. 4 Alexander the Great. 5 *Silent Witness*.
6 Channel 5. 7 Limestone. 8 Three. 9 *Neighbours*. 10 Scripts. 11 Lower arm.
12 Golf's US Masters. 13 Ceefax. 14 Kamikaze. 15 60 degrees. 16 Surrey.
17 Colony. 18 Toes and fingers. 19 Hungary. 20 297. 21 Oyster. 22 The Saint.
23 Rita. 24 Wavelengths of light. 25 Ron Atkinson. 26 Swim the English Channel.
27 Three. 28 Des O' Connor. 29 Processing. 30 Sunday.

QUIZ 59 TV SITCOMS

Answers - see Quiz 57, page 153

1 Which series with John Bird was set in a legal practice?
2 In *To The Manor Born* what was the name of Audrey's butler?
3 Where is *Frasier* based?
4 Which show introduced a character called Katy Grin?
5 Whose catchphrase was, "I don't believe it!?
6 Which character appeared with Linda in *Gimme Gimme Gimme*?
7 Who played opposite Stephanie Cole in *Life As We Know It*?
8 Which ex *Coronation Street* actress starred in *Blooming Marvellous* with Clive Mantle?
9 Who played Ben to Zoe Wanamaker's Susan in *My Family*?
10 In *Absolutely Fabulous*, what was Patsy's favourite champagne?
11 In *Allo Allo*, which three words come before "I shall say this only once!"?
12 Who played Ally McBeal?
13 Beane's of Boston was a US version of which UK sitcom set in the retail business?
14 What colour were Seinfeld's shoes?
15 Which 2001 Oscar-winning actress guested on *Friends*?
16 Whose catchphrase was "You dirty old man!"?
17 Which ex *Ballykissangel* star appeared in *Bedtime*?
18 Who found fame as Jerry Leadbetter?
19 Which witch was played by Elizabeth Montgomery in *Bewitched*?
20 Who was Wayne's sidekick in *Wayne's World*?
21 What was Dorothy's profession in *Men Behaving Badly*?
22 Which US programme was the then most watched TV show when it aired for the last time in 1993?
23 Who was in charge of the Walmington On Sea Home Guard?
24 In *Father Ted*, which priest was almost permanently drunk?
25 Which sitcom saw Polly, Miss Tibbs and Major Gowen?
26 Which American played the American flatmate in *Girls On Top*?
27 What was Tom Good's job before he gave everything up for *The Good Life*?
28 What was Hyacinth Bucket's husband called?
29 Who was the cafe proprietress in *Last of the Summer Wine*?
30 Where in the UK was *The Likely Lads* set?

THE FAMOUS *See quiz 57, page 153*

1 The Samaritans. 2 Dee. 3 Beatrice. 4 Seamus Heaney. 5 Noble. 6 "Titanic".
7 Clockwork. 8 Shipping . 9 Wal Mart. 10 Lisa Marie Presley. 11 Elle MacPherson.
12 Billy Graham. 13 Niece. 14 Archbishop of Canterbury. 15 Twiggy.
16 Tim Henman. 17 Scarborough. 18 Zoe Ball. 19 Alastair Campbell.
20 Playwrights. 21 Hillary Clinton. 22 Sarah. 23 6ft 3". 24 Monaco. 25 Clothes.
26 Michael Portillo. 27 Margaret. 28 Sedgefield. 29 Cosmetics. 30 Beatrice.

ANSWERS

QUIZ 60 POT LUCK 27

Answers - see Quiz 58, page 154

1 In the USA which of these numbers do you ring in an emergency, 999, 606, 911?
2 How was the famous American Martha Jane Burke better known?
3 Prince William went to a university in which country?
4 Which of the following did Shakespeare not write a play about – Alexander the Great, Julius Caesar or Macbeth?
5 Amanda Burton played forensic scientist Sam Ryan in which series?
6 Which TV launch was connected with the Spice Girls?
7 Which rock is chiefly made from calcium carbonate?
8 In going for a maximum break in snooker, how many times must the black ball be potted to reach 20 points?
9 In which TV show did the kids attend Erinsborough High School?
10 What did Ray Galton and Alan Simpson produce – scripts, shoes or songs?
11 Where in the human body is the ulna?
12 Which of these sporting events is held most frequently – golf's US Masters, golf's Ryder Cup or football's World Cup?
13 What was the BBC's first teletext service called?
14 Which Japanese word actually means 'divine wind'?
15 In an equilateral triangle, how many degrees does each angle measure?
16 Wentworth golf course is in which English county?
17 What is the collective name for a group of beavers?
18 What are your phalanges?
19 In which country could you watch Ferencvaros playing Vasas at soccer?
20 A4 paper is 210mm by how many mm?
21 The Essex town of Colchester is famous for what kind of Festival?
22 In fiction how was the character Simon Templar known?
23 What was Alf Garnett's daughter called?
24 What does the angstrom unit measure?
25 Who did Alex Ferguson replace at Man Utd?
26 Captain Matthew Webb was the first person to do what?
27 When the prefix kilo is used to describe an amount, how many noughts would be written in digits?
28 Who first presented the 1990s revival of the TV game show *Take Your Pick*?
29 In computing, what does the P stand for in CPU?
30 The Prix De L'Arc de Triomphe is run on which day of the week?

POT LUCK 26 *See quiz 58, page 154*

ANSWERS

1 Fruit. 2 Driver. 3 Mother's Day. 4 *Disneyland*. 5 A planet. 6 Hybrid. 7 1920s.
8 Charlotte. 9 The computer. 10 Jane MacDonald. 11 Court. 12 WWII.
13 Sheffield United 14 Balmoral. 15 *Happy Days*. 16 Lotus Elan. 17 Norman.
18 Eat it. 19 Lake of Death. 20 South Carolina. 21 National Park. 22 Peugeot.
23 1. 24 Collar bone. 25 Arthur Miller. 26 Trashcan (dustbin/rubbish bin).
27 Algebra. 28 Janis Joplin. 29 Cilento. 30 Jubbly.

QUIZ 61 BOOKS

Answers - see Quiz 63, page 159

1 Which Ballard wrote *Empire of the Sun*?
2 Which musical instrument was Captain Corelli famous for?
3 Who wrote the *Mary Ann* series of romantic novels?
4 What was the surname of Richmal Crompton's most famous schoolboy hero?
5 Who wrote *The Day of the Jackal*?
6 Who wrote the book originally published in the UK as *The Diary of a Young Girl*?
7 Nadine Gordimer hails from which country?
8 Who wrote *The Female Eunuch*?
9 Who is the author of *Riders of the Purple Sage*?
10 Which writer famous for her historical fiction wrote *Regency Buck*?
11 What is Ripley's first name in Patricia Highsmith's *The Talented Mr Ripley* and *Ripley Under Water*?
12 In which language did Czech-born Franz Kafka write?
13 Whose *Guns of Navarone* was made into a film?
14 Whose autobiography was called *Learning to Fly*?
15 Which Josephine wrote *Tonight Josephine*?
16 Which ex jockey wrote *Shattered*?
17 Which thriller writer penned *The Shape of Snakes*?
18 Which word completes the title of Rick Stein's cookery book, *Rick Stein's Seafood ...*?
19 Whose memoir was called *Bad Blood*?
20 What sort of guide did Leslie Halliwell found?
21 In which city was Barbara Taylor Bradford born?
22 Whose *Death in Holy Orders* was set on the coast of East Anglia?
23 Whose autobiography was called *Himoff!*?
24 Who wrote the novels on which the *Touch of Frost* TV character was based?
25 In which Stephen King novel does the character Annie Wilkes feature?
26 In Ruth Rendell's Wexford novels what is Reg's wife called?
27 Which Alfred wrote many books about walks in his beloved Lake District?
28 Who created the characters Dalziel and Pascoe?
29 Whose cookery book had a title which began with *Happy Days*?
30 Was Richard Branson's autobiography called Like A Virgin, Losing My Virginity or The Moon's A Balloon?

RUGBY See quiz 63, page 159
1 Australia. 2 Brian Baister. 3 Professional. 4 Lebanon. 5 Romania. 6 Dennis John.
7 Mike Catt. 8 1996. 9 1980s. 10 Lawrence Dallaglio. 11 Paul Newlove.
12 Rugby Union World Cup. 13 Sydney. 14 David Campese. 15 England.
16 Pay (Broken time payments). 17 1920s. 18 South Africa. 19 Pilkington Cup.
20 Bill Beaumont. 21 Hunslet. 22 Wales and South Africa. 23 Leeds Rhinos.
24 (Stade de) France. 25 South Africa. 26 Cambridge. 27 Blue Sox. 28 Swalec Cup.
29 Australia. 30 Wigan.

ANSWERS

QUIZ 62 POT LUCK 28

Answers - see Quiz 64, page 160

1 Which word describes the brightness of stars?
2 What did Croft and Perry create between them?
3 Which country was first to win soccer's World Cup four times?
4 In which country is La Coruña international airport?
5 Which are there most of – birds, fish or insects?
6 In MODEM, MO stands for Modulator, what does DEM stand for?
7 The Tour of Spain in cycling takes place how often?
8 A mandrill's bottom is coloured red and what else?
9 After a drugs test Ben Johnson was stripped of Olympic gold in which race?
10 Carbohydrates consist of carbon, hydrogen and which other element?
11 What is the highest number on the Richter scale?
12 Trevor Francis and Gerry Francis have both managed which soccer club?
13 What shape is a swallow's tail?
14 The Philippines lie in which ocean?
15 147 is a maximum continuous score in which game?
16 What name describes a component that will transmit electricity or heat?
17 How many legs does a flatworm have?
18 Which instrument did jazzman Charlie 'Bird' Parker play?
19 The flower edelweiss is what colour?
20 What does C stand for in the abbreviation VCR?
21 Which soccer team recorded "Come On You Reds"?
22 *Fidelio* was the only opera of which German composer?
23 What type of leaves does a koala eat?
24 Who had chart success with the album *Fever* in 2001?
25 In which country is Rawalpindi?
26 The clock on Big Ben's tower has how many faces?
27 The Channel Island Sark is noted for its ban on what?
28 Which of the Bee Gees is not a twin?
29 What did Lewis E. Waterman invent?
30 What is the name for a camel with two humps?

POT LUCK 29 See quiz 64, page 160

ANSWERS

1 Capability Brown. 2 Cats. 3 F. 4 Vicar. 5 Engineering. 6 Turkey. 7 Yvonne.
8 Jacques. 9 A1. 10 Bird. 11 Paul McCartney. 12 Three. 13 White. 14 Glasgow.
15 Victoria Wood. 16 Brain. 17 Lower arm. 18 Fool's gold. 19 Cambodia.
20 Two. 21 Wolves. 22 Belgium. 23 Two. 24 Harry. 25 Tuesday. 26 New York.
27 Three. 28 *To The Manor Born.* 29 Prime Minister. 30 Red.

QUIZ 63 RUGBY

Answers - see Quiz 61, page 157

1 In which country do Parramatta play?
2 Who replaced Cliff Brittle as chairman of the RFU?
3 What does the P stand for in RFAPC?
4 Hazen El Masri represented which international side?
5 Which side did Philippe Sella face in his first international?
6 Who was Wales' caretaker coach when they were beaten 96–13 by South Africa in 1998?
7 Who scored all of England's points in their 15–15 draw with Australia in November 1997?
8 In what year was the Regal Trophy discontinued – 1986, 1990 or 1996?
9 In which decade of the 20th century did Ireland last win the Five Nations?
10 Who became England captain for the first time in 1997?
11 Who was the youngest League player in an international in the 20th century?
12 What is another name for the Webb Ellis Trophy?
13 Which city's University had the first Rugby Club in Australia?
14 In 1996 which Australian received a UNESCO award as one of the most outstanding sportsmen of the century?
15 By 2000 which country had won the Rugby International Championships outright most times?
16 Rugby League was formed after a dispute with the Rugby Football Union about what?
17 In which decade was the first Challenge Cup Final at Wembley?
18 Who were the third winners of the Rugby Union World Cup after New Zealand and Australia?
19 Which Cup was called the John Player Cup until 1988?
20 Which English Rugby star was a regular team captain on A Question of Sport?
21 Which side became Hawks in the 1990s?
22 Which sides met in the first game at Cardiff's Millennium Stadium?
23 Who won the last Challenge Cup of the 20th century?
24 Which was the only Five Nations side to have its country's name in its home ground?
25 Who joined Australia and New Zealand in the 1998 Tri Nations series?
26 By the end of the millennium, who had won most Varsity matches?
27 What did Halifax add to their name in the 1990s?
28 Which Cup was previously called the Schweppes Welsh Cup?
29 Which was the first team to win the Rugby World Cup twice?
30 Who were the last winners of the Regal Trophy?

BOOKS See quiz 61, page 157

ANSWERS
1 JG. 2 Mandolin. 3 Catherine Cookson. 4 Brown. 5 Frederick Forsyth.
6 Anne Frank. 7 South Africa. 8 Germaine Greer. 9 Zane Grey. 10 Georgette Heyer.
11 Tom. 12 German. 13 Alistair Maclean. 14 Victoria Beckham. 15 Cox.
16 Dick Francis. 17 Minette Walters. 18 Odyssey. 19 Lorna Sage. 20 Film.
21 Leeds. 22 PD James. 23 Richard Whiteley. 24 RD Wingfield. 25 Misery.
26 Dora. 27 Wainwright. 28 Reginald Hill. 29 Jamie Oliver. 30 Losing My Virginity.

QUIZ 64 POT LUCK 29

Answers - see Quiz 62, page 158

1 How did Lancelot Brown become better known – Arthur Brown, Capability Brown or James Brown?
2 Allurophobia is a fear of which creature?
3 What is the fourth note in the scale of C?
4 What was the occupation of the sitcom character named Geraldine Grainger?
5 What does Carol Vorderman have a degree in?
6 In which country could you watch Besiktas play a home soccer match?
7 Who was Gary's 1990s wife in TV's *Goodnight Sweetheart*?
8 EC Presidents Delors and Santer both shared which forename?
9 What is the chemical symbol for aluminium?
10 What type of creature is a kookaburra?
11 Who is the only Beatle not to have been divorced?
12 How many different countries did Alfredo di Stefano play international soccer for?
13 What is the colour of a baby grey seal's coat?
14 In which city are you if you walk along Sauchiehall Street?
15 Which writer/comedienne is Mrs Geoffrey Durham?
16 Which part of his body did Einstein leave to Princeton University?
17 Where in the human body is the radius?
18 Iron pyrites are known as what type of gold?
19 What is Kampuchea also known as?
20 How many main islands is New Zealand made up of?
21 Graham Taylor and Dave Jones have both managed which soccer club?
22 Waterloo, scene of a famous battle, is in which country?
23 Which number can be typed using only letters on the top row of a keyboard?
24 Which Corbett created Sooty the bear?
25 If the December 1 is a Saturday what day is January 1?
26 Where did the Jumbo jet leave from on its first transatlantic flight?
27 Liam Gallagher was what number of husband for Patsy Kensit?
28 In which sitcom did Richard De Vere marry Audrey?
29 William Pitt became the youngest British what?
30 What colour are the hotels in Monopoly?

POT LUCK 28 See quiz 62, page 158
1 Magnitude. 2 TV shows, chiefly sitcoms. 3 Brazil. 4 Spain. 5 Insects.
6 Demodulator. 7 Annually. 8 Blue. 9 100m. 10 Oxygen. 11 9.
12 Queens Park Rangers (QPR). 13 Forked. 14 Pacific Ocean. 15 Snooker.
16 A conductor. 17 None. 18 Saxophone. 19 White. 20 Cassette.
21 Manchester United. 22 Beethoven. 23 Eucalyptus. 24 Kylie Minogue.
25 Pakistan. 26 Four. 27 Cars. 28 Barry. 29 Fountain pen. 30 Bactrian.

QUIZ 65 MOVIE MEMORIES

Answers - see Quiz 67, page 163

1 Who played Anne Heche's husband in *Donnie Brasco*?
2 Who played Quasimodo in the 1923 version of *The Hunchback of Notre Dame*?
3 How many sound movies did the legendary DW Griffith make?
4 Which category did Disney's *Snow White* have when it first opened?
5 Which wife of Clark Gable was one of Mack Sennett's bathing beauties?
6 Which western with Gary Cooper made Grace Kelly a star?
7 Which 1990s Dreamworks movie is about Moses?
8 What was Quentin Tarantino's first film?
9 Who played Stanley Kowalski in *A Streetcar Named Desire*?
10 What is Nicole Kidman's job in *To Die For*?
11 Who are the musical duo in *Topsy Turvy*?
12 The movie *Thirteen Days* is about which crisis?
13 What was the sequel to *Ace Ventura Pet Detective*?
14 What was the most expensive film of the 20th century?
15 Which sci fi film of 1999 starred Keanu Reeves?
16 Which of the following movies did not have a dog or dogs as their stars – *Babe*, *Beethoven* or *Homeward Bound*?
17 Of the following stars of *Ghostbusters*, who did not also write it – Dan Aykroyd, Bill Murray or Harold Ramis?
18 Who plays the widowed hero in *The American President*?
19 Back in the 1960s who was the *Girl on a Motorcycle*?
20 After making *Some Like It Hot*, Tony Curtis reputedly said that kissing who was like kissing Hitler?
21 Which Richardson co starred with Hugh Laurie in *Maybe Baby*?
22 What is Hugh Grant's profession in *Notting Hill*?
23 In which movie did Eddie Murphy play Sherman Klump?
24 How many films did Bogart make with Bacall – was it two, four or six?
25 In which movie did Audrey Hepburn play Holly Golightly?
26 In which city is *Dirty Harry* set?
27 Who does Jack Nicholson play in *The Witches of Eastwick*?
28 In which part of New York is Martin Scorsese's semi-autobiographical movie *Mean Streets* set?
29 What was Wallace & Gromit's first adventure?
30 Which movie classic features Rick and Renault?

NATURAL PHENOMENA *See quiz 67, page 163*
1 Quicklime. 2 Jupiter. 3 Pluto. 4 Indian. 5 Amazon. 6 Loch Lomond. 7 Canada.
8 North Atlantic (Great Britain). 9 Balmoral. 10 Turkey. 11 Angola. 12 Cornwall.
13 Hydrogen. 14 Plutonium. 15 Ullswater. 16 Calcium carbonate. 17 China clay.
18 500. 19 Mouont McKinley. 20 Russia. 21 Washington. 22 Carbon. 23 Iceland.
24 Kobe. 25 Emerald. 26 Charles. 27 10%. 28 Yellow. 29 Indonesia. 30 Winnebago.

ANSWERS

QUIZ 66 POT LUCK 30

Answers - see Quiz 68, page 164

1 Which of these words is made from letters on the top row of a keyboard – part, pile or pour?
2 The aria "One Fine Day" comes from which opera?
3 Where were satsumas originally grown?
4 Who was famous for his Theory of Evolution?
5 How many faces does a pyramid with a triangular base have?
6 George Ferris gave his name to which fairground attraction?
7 On which group of islands is Mount Fuji?
8 In music how many lines are there for notes to be written on?
9 Which building was constructed on the orders of Shah Jehan?
10 Lacrosse was invented in which country?
11 Which was London's first railway station?
12 What was the name of Jim Hacker's wife in *Yes Minister*?
13 In blackjack the maximum score is equivalent to potting how many blacks at snooker?
14 Who was the first Scot to be voted European Footballer of The Year?
15 Where would you find your ventricle and atrium?
16 Which creatures live in a formicary?
17 What does the M stand for in the radio abbreviation FM stand for?
18 What was the first name of the commentator who famously said, "They think it's all over."?
19 The Derby at Epsom is run in which month?
20 Which fellow guitarist joined Brian May for a 1990s version of "We Are the Champions"?
21 The movie *The China Syndrome* deals with what type of accident?
22 A male fencer needs how many hits for a victory?
23 Maddy Magellan is the partner of which fictional detective?
24 Whose 1990s greatest hits album was modestly called *Modern Classics*?
25 How many bytes are there in a kilobyte?
26 In which country did speed skating originate?
27 Which ship sent out the the first S.O.S?
28 Richie Richardson captained which country at cricket?
29 Which office machine can be flat bed or hand held?
30 What song does Elton John sing on the tribute album *Tammy Wynette Remembered*?

POT LUCK 31 *See quiz 68, page 164*
1 Head. 2 Silicon Valley. 3 Haiti. 4 Circle. 5 Refraction. 6 Harvey. 7 Hearn.
8 St Valentine's Day. 9 St Andrews. 10 A Tolkien novel title. 11 Four.
12 "Man In Black". 13 Pink Floyd. 14 Nick Leeson. 15 Eskimo. 16 Marzipan.
17 Snake. 18 Coventry. 19 1990. 20 Leeds United. 21 Sandy Lyle.
22 Simnel cake. 23 Isle of Wight. 24 *Live and Let Die*. 25 *Class*. 26 Ipswich Town.
27 Cheese. 28 The bereaved. 29 "Talk". 30 Pakistan.

QUIZ 67 NATURAL PHENOMENA

Answers - see Quiz 65, page 161

1   What is another name for calcium oxide?
2   What is the next largest body in our solar system after the Sun?
3   What is the only planet to have been discovered by an American – Mars, Pluto or Venus?
4   What is the next deepest ocean after the Pacific?
5   What is the longest river on the American continent?
6   Which is the largest lake on the UK mainland?
7   Which country has the largest area of inland water?
8   In which waters is the EEC's largest island?
9   Which home of the Queen is one of the coldest places in the UK?
10 Where did the second worst earthquake of the 1990s occur, in August 1999?
11 The Congo river is in the Democratic Republic of Congo and where else?
12 Which county of mainland England is the warmest?
13 What is the most common element in the universe?
14 Which is the heaviest, plutonium, gold or uranium?
15 What is England's second largest lake?
16 What is the chemical name for chalk?
17 Kaolin is what type of clay?
18 Denmark comprises how many islands – 26, 300 or 500?
19 Which mountain is the highest in the Alaska Range?
20 The Caucasus Mountains divide Georgia and Azerbaijan from where?
21 In which US state is the volcanic mountain of Mount St Helens which erupted in 1980?
22 A diamond is formed from which element?
23 In which country are most of Europe's volcanoes?
24 Where in Japan did a massive earthquake kill over 5,000 people in 1995?
25 What is the most popular form of green beryl called?
26 What was the first name of Richter whose scale measures the intensity of an earthquake?
27 How much of the Earth's area is covered in ice – 5%, 10% or 20%?
28 What colour is the quartz known as citrine?
29 Where is the volcanic island of Sumatra?
30 Which lake of Wisconsin shares its name with a mobile home?

MOVIE MEMORIES See quiz 65, page 161

ANSWERS

1 Johnny Depp. 2 Lon Chaney. 3 Two. 4 A. 5 Carole Lombard. 6 *High Noon.*
7 *The Prince of Egypt.* 8 *Reservoir Dogs.* 9 Marlon Brando. 10 TV weather presenter.
11 Gilbert & Sullivan. 12 Cuban missile. 13 *When Nature Calls.* 14 *Titanic.*
15 *The Matrix.* 16 *Babe.* 17 Bill Murray. 18 Michael Douglas. 19 Marianne Faithfull.
20 Marilyn Monroe. 21 Joely. 22 Bookshop owner. 23 *The Nutty Professor.* 24 Four.
25 *Breakfast At Tiffany's.* 26 San Francisco. 27 The Devil. 28 Little Italy.
29 *A Grand Day Out.* 30 *Casablanca.*

QUIZ 68 POT LUCK 31

Answers - see Quiz 66, page 162

1 What part of the human body is measured using the cephalix index?
2 What nickname is given to the Santa Clara valley in America?
3 In which country did the private security force the Tontons Macoutes operate?
4 The shot, hammer and discus are thrown from an area that is which shape?
5 What word describes the bending of light passing from one medium to another?
6 Who is Sabrina's boyfriend in Sabrina The Teenage Witch?
7 Which Barry managed snooker's Steve Davis through his winning years?
8 On which special day were seven of Bugs Moran's gang murdered in America?
9 Where could Prince William have a round of golf at the local club for his university?
10 What did the group Marillion base their group name on – a Tolkien novel, Marilyn Monroe or a nightclub?
11 What is the minimum number of times the racket must hit the ball in a tennis game?
12 Darts player Alan Glazier and singer Johnny Cash have been both known as what?
13 Who released the classic Ummagumma album?
14 Who was responsible for the crime recounted in the film Rogue Trader?
15 From which language does the word anorak – a hooded jacket – come?
16 What is on the outside of a Battenburg cake?
17 A taipan is a type of what?
18 Which of these English cities is the furthest south – Birmingham, Coventry or Leicester?
19 In what year was Nelson Mandela released from prison?
20 Eric Cantona joined Manchester United from which club
21 Who was the first Briton to win golf's US Masters?
22 Which cake was originally made for Mothering Sunday?
23 On which Isle was Queen Victoria's residence Osborne House?
24 In which film did Roger Moore first play James Bond?
25 Pulp's debut album was called Different what?
26 Who was on the wrong side of Manchester United's record nine goals Premier League win?
27 What is the main ingredient in a traditional fondue?
28 The organisation CRUSE was set up to help who?
29 What was "Happy" in the title of Captain Sensible's only No 1 hit?
30 Which country won cricket's 1992 World Cup Final?

POT LUCK 30 See quiz 66, page 162
1 Pour. 2 Madam Butterfly. 3 Japan. 4 Charles Darwin. 5 Four. 6 Big wheel.
7 Japan. 8 Five. 9 Taj Mahal. 10 Canada. 11 Euston. 12 Annie. 13 Three.
14 Denis Law. 15 Heart. 16 Ants. 17 Modulation. 18 Kenneth. 19 June.
20 Hank Marvin. 21 Nuclear. 22 Five. 23 Jonathan Creek. 24 Paul Weller.
25 1024. 26 Holland. 27 "Titanic". 28 West Indies. 29 Scanner.
30 "Stand By Your Man".

ANSWERS

QUIZ 69 MUSIC SUPERSTARS

Answers - see Quiz 71, page 167

1 Who won the Brit Award for Best Single and Best Video in 1999 and 2000?
2 Which lady sang the soul album *I Never Loved A Man (the Way I Love You)*?
3 Who killed Marvin Gaye?
4 Why was Bob Dylan booed at the Albert Hall in 1966?
5 How many people were on the cover of Michael Jackson's *Thriller* album cover?
6 Which Beatle was the first to have a solo No 1 in the US?
7 How old was Elton John when he hit No 1 with the single in memory of Diana Princess of Wales – 46, 51 or 56?
8 Who had a best selling album *No Jacket Required* in 1985?
9 Which US solo singer had a successful album of *Love Songs* in the 1980s?
10 Which American singer had 35 consecutive UK Top Ten Hits between 1984 and 1994?
11 How many years do Cher's No 1 UK hits span – 25, 33 or 39?
12 Which country superstar has had most solo album sales in the USA – Garth Brooks, Dolly Parton or Kenny Rogers?
13 Which superstar band wrote Diana Ross's "Chain Reaction"?
14 In which part of New York was Barry Manilow born?
15 Which superstar played the title role in the 1980s *The Jazz Singer*?
16 Which country singer won a Lifetime Achievement Grammy in 2000?
17 With which late star did opera's Monserrat Caballe sing at the Barcelona Olympics?
18 Who recorded *Ten Summoner's Tales* in 1993?
19 Paul McCartney's *Standing Stone* premiered in New York and at which London venue?
20 Who was the first singer to have No 1 hits in five decades?
21 Who wrote the Mariah Carey/Westlife hit "Against All Odds"?
22 Which character in radio's *The Archers* shares her name with a Dolly Parton hit?
23 Which female vocalist duetted with George Michael on "If I Told You That"?
24 Which former Motown star had a new millennium hit with "Not Over Yet"?
25 Which rock star of Scottish parentage was inducted into the Rock and Roll Hall of Fame in 1994?
26 Which James Bond theme did Tina Turner sing?
27 Who is Britain's most successful female chart artist, who became a Dame in 2000?
28 Who sang in a benefit concert following the New York atrocity after suffering her own health problems in 2001?
29 Who was the first major star to make a full album available for downloading?
30 Which Frank Sinatra single won him a Grammy, only the ninth ever awarded?

TECHNOLOGY & INDUSTRY See quiz 71, page 167

ANSWERS

1 Consignia. 2 Red & white. 3 Woolwich. 4 Books. 5 *Express*.
6 London Underground. 7 Colgate. 8 Vodaphone. 9 Railtrack. 10 Marks & Spencer.
11 Disneyland Paris. 12 Tesco. 13 Seattle. 14 Mothercare. 15 Honda.
16 Mobile phones. 17 Benjamin Guinness. 18 Apple. 19 Sony. 20 Charles Rolls.
21 Asda. 22 Ginger Productions. 23 Washing machine. 24 Sugar. 25 Sabena.
26 MGM. 27 Henry Royce. 28 Winfield. 29 Ships. 30 Marks & Spencer.

QUIZ 70 POT LUCK 32

Answers - see Quiz 72, page 168

1 Which of the *Monty Python Flying Circus* team was called Michael?
2 Who made the album *Songs From the West Coast*?
3 What did Lord Gyllene win on a Monday in 1997 that would have been on Saturday but for a bomb threat?
4 Robben Island was a prison located near which city?
5 What is the fruit flavour of Cointreau?
6 How old was Billy The Kid when he died?
7 On a computer keyboard where is the letter O in relation to the L – above it, below it or next to it?
8 In rhyme, on what day of the week was Solomon Grundy married?
9 Which *Little* book by Louisa May Alcott became a best seller?
10 Julia Smith married and became the estranged wife of which top sportsman?
11 Which two colours are most often confused in colour blindness
12 Which Abba album was No 1 again in 1999 seven years after its release?
13 Which entrepreneur owns The Ritz in Paris?
14 Which stately home and safari park is owned by the Marquis of Bath?
15 Which ex Tory MP once said, "Only domestic servants apologise"?
16 Which Spanish club side were the first winners of the European Champions Cup?
17 What type of animal can be Texel and Romney Marsh?
18 The Bee Gees were born on which island?
19 Theatre impresario Bill Kenwright is connected with which soccer club?
20 What was Jemima Khan's maiden name?
21 In the judiciary, what does the D in DPP stand for?
22 Who became the face of Estée Lauder in the mid 1990s?
23 Which is the nearest city to the Tay road bridge?
24 How many different Popes were there in the year of 1978?
25 In which decade of last century did Constantinople change its name to Istanbul?
26 How many bridesmaids attended Princess Diana?
27 Which designer was once a partner of Malcolm McLaren?
28 Genesis's debut was called *Genesis To* what?
29 In which century was the last execution at the Tower of London?
30 In which group of islands is Panay?

QUIZ 71 TECHNOLOGY AND INDUSTRY

Answers - see Quiz 69, page 165

1 What did The Post Office change its name to at the beginning of the new millennium?
2 What colours are in the logo of the Internet banking company First Direct?
3 Which building society merged with Barclays Bank in 2000?
4 What do Amazon.com chiefly sell?
5 Which newspaper did Lord Beaverbrook take over in the 20th century?
6 Ken Livingstone appointed Bob Kiley to oversee the reform of what?
7 Which brand of toothpaste gave its company a huge boost when George W Bush and Tony Blair both admitted using it?
8 In 2001 what was the world's biggest mobile phone company?
9 Which UK transport company went into receivership in October 2001?
10 Which retailer introduced the brand Per Una to boost flagging sales?
11 Where was Yves Gerbeau working when he took over as chief executive of the Millennium Dome?
12 Which was the first UK supermarket to achieve profits of more than £1bn?
13 In which city associated with the technology industry was Bill Gates born?
14 Habitat founder Terence Conran has also been involved in the management of which store catering for young families?
15 Which car and motor cycle manufacturer had the first name Soichiro?
16 What did Virgin trains ban from all but designated carriages from the autumn of 2001?
17 Which industrialist, whose name is known all over the world, was the first Lord Mayor of Dublin?
18 Which company did Steven Jobs leave prior to setting up NeXT Inc?
19 Akio Morita and Masaru Ibuka founded which electronics company?
20 Which motor manufacturer made the first non stop double crossing of the English Channel by plane?
21 Which supermarket chain introduced the fashion label George?
22 What was the name of Chris Evans' company which bought Virgin radio?
23 What type of motor did Sinclair use in his personal transport C5?
24 The donor of the Tate Gallery made his fortune in which commodity?
25 Which Belgian airline effectively went bust after the World Trade Center atrocity?
26 Which company's chain of high street cinemas did Richard Branson buy in 1995?
27 Which motor manufacturer designed Spitfire and Hurricane engines in WWII?
28 What was Frank Woolworth's middle name which was used for the store's own brand?
29 What did Cammell Laird manufacture?
30 Which company announced it was closing all its European stores in April 2001?

MUSIC SUPERSTARS See quiz 69, page 165
1 Robbie Williams. 2 Aretha Franklin. 3 His father (Marvin Gaye Sr).
4 He played an electric guitar. 5 One. 6 George Harrison. 7 51. 8 Phil Collins.
9 Barbra Streisand. 10 Madonna. 11 33. 12 Garth Brooks. 13 Bee Gees.
14 Brooklyn. 15 Neil Diamond. 16 Willie Nelson. 17 Freddie Mercury. 18 Sting.
19 Albert Hall. 20 Cliff Richard. 21 Phil Collins. 22 "Jolene". 23 Whitney Houston.
24 Diana Ross. 25 Rod Stewart. 26 *Goldeneye*. 27 Shirley Bassey.
28 Mariah Carey. 29 David Bowie. 30 "Strangers In The Night".

QUIZ 72 POT LUCK 33

Answers - see Quiz 70, page 166

1 How is Joyce Frankenberg better known as a movie actress – Jane Seymour, Julia Roberts or Jodie Foster?
2 In which profession did Marco Pierre White find fame?
3 Which vessel went down on the Seven Stones reef off Land's End?
4 What was the surname of Scot Charles Rennie of the Art Nouveau movement?
5 Who were Liverpool playing when Gerard Houllier was taken ill in October 2001?
6 On TV, which real crime series was based on the German *File XY Unsolved*?
7 Hull and Leeds are linked by which motorway?
8 In which film did Michael Douglas live by the maxim that "Greed is good"?
9 In which country is Peterson Field international airport?
10 Which Jimi Hendrix song hit No 1 a few weeks after the singer's death?
11 The news agency TASS is based in which city?
12 In which country was Edith Cresson PM in the 1990s
13 Which of the following is not a crustacean – crab, lobster or toad?
14 In the 1990s single title what did Meat Loaf add to "I'd Lie For You"?
15 In fiction, what was the name of Perry Mason's secretary
16 Which A road links London with East Anglia?
17 In which Brighton Hotel did an IRA bomb explode in 1984 at the Tory Conference?
18 When did the Pony Express ride into the sunset and close down its service – was it 1791, 1861 or 1921?
19 How many times did Gagarin orbit the Earth on his first journey into space?
20 Who was the first actress to be paid $1 million for a single film?
21 What did the Falstead Act aim to control in the US?
22 The northern terminus of the Pan American highway is in which state?
23 What is Daley Thompson's first name?
24 In which city did Louise Woodward's trial take place after a baby died in her care?
25 What did Dionico Ceron win three years in a row in the 1990s?
26 Which radio programme celebrated its 50th birthday in 2001?
27 What was the USA's first public television service?
28 What was Fitz's full name in Cracker?
29 What is Britain's third largest airport?
30 What is the main subject of the play *The Crucible* – chemistry, snooker or witchcraft?

ANSWERS

POT LUCK 32 See quiz 70, page 166

1 Palin. 2 Elton John. 3 Grand National. 4 Cape Town. 5 Orange. 6 21. 7 Above it.
8 Wednesday. 9 *Little Women*. 10 Will Carling. 11 Green and red. 12 *Abba Gold*.
13 Mohammed Al-Fayed. 14 Longleat. 15 Alan Clark. 16 Real Madrid. 17 Sheep.
18 The Isle of Man. 19 Everton. 20 Goldsmith. 21 Director. 22 Elizabeth Hurley.
23 Dundee. 24 Three. 25 1930s. 26 Five. 27 Vivienne Westwood. 28 *Revelation*.
29 20th. 30 Philippines.

QUIZ 73 LEADERS

Answers - see Quiz 75, page 171

1   What was Vaclav Havel's profession before he became President of the Czech Republic?
2   In 1985 Oxford University refused to give an honorary degree to which PM?
3   Assassinated Prime Minister Olof Palme led which country?
4   Who called the USSR an 'evil empire'?
5   Which Prime Minister of Australia wept on TV when he confessed to marital misdemeanours?
6   Who did John Hinckley Jr shoot?
7   Lord Carrington resigned as Foreign Secretary during which conflict?
8   How many leaders did the Labour Party have in the 1990s?
9   Who did Nelson Mandela succeed as head of the ANC?
10 On which day does the US President give his weekly talk to the American people?
11 Who became Secretary of State for Culture Media & Sport after the 2001 election?
12 Betty Boothroyd had which famous position of responsibility?
13 At the turn of the millennium which queen – other than Victoria – had reigned longest?
14 Which of the following Prime Ministers were in their nineties when they died – Clement Attlee, William Gladstone and Harold Macmillan?
15 How many years was Margaret Thatcher British Prime Minister – 9, 11 or 15?
16 Newt Gingrich was a respected politician in which country?
17 Who did Jack Straw replace as Foreign Secretary?
18 In 1999 Ehud Barak became Prime Minister of which country?
19 Who was Bill Clinton's first Vice President?
20 Prince Rainier III has ruled where for over 50 years?
21 Who did Gerhard Schroeder replace as German Chancellor?
22 Who was Mayor of New York at the time of the World Trade Center disaster?
23 Who did Paddy Ashdown replace as Liberal leader?
24 How many leaders did the Conservative Party have in the 1990s?
25 Which British Queen had 17 children?
26 Who did Tony Blair replace as Labour leader?
27 Which monarch succeeded King Hussein of Jordan?
28 Who became French Prime Minister in 1997?
29 Queen Wilhelmina led which country?
30 Who was George W Bush's first Secretary of State?

ANSWERS

TV DRAMA *See quiz 75, page 171*
1 Detective. 2 WWII. 3 *Casualty*. 4 Emilia Fox. 5 *Goodnight Mister Tom*. 6 Colin Firth.
7 Peter. 8 Merseyside. 9 *This Life*. 10 Miss Marple. 11 Forensic. 12 England & USA.
13 *Martin Chuzzlewit*. 14 Lindsay Duncan. 15 *Cardiac Arrest*. 16 *Love in a Cold Climate*.
17 Sean Bean. 18 *Hearts & Bones*. 19 Poirot. 20 Bradford. 21 *Bergerac*.
22 Ewan McGregor. 23 Cherie Lunghi. 24 *Northern Exposure*. 25 Philadelphia.
26 Jack Frost. 27 Edward VII. 28 Wednesday. 29 *Cracker*. 30 *Holby City*.

QUIZ 74 POT LUCK 34

Answers - see Quiz 76, page 172

1 Which drug took its name from the Greek god of dreams?
2 Which is the largest borough in the city of New York?
3 Which Grand National course fence, other than Becher's, contains the name Brook?
4 Stephen Cameron's 1996 death was a tragic first in which circumstances?
5 Which American was the first to achieve tennis's Men's Singles Grand Slam?
6 In song lyrics, where did Billie Jo Spears want to lay her blanket?
7 Which Roger was drummer with Queen?
8 Along with Doric and Corinthian, what is the third Greek order of architecture?
9 Who was the first British woman to win a world swimming title?
10 Which northern city has the dialling code 0113?
11 What nationality is Salman Rushdie?
12 What was the previous title of Raine, Comtesse de Chambrun?
13 Which population was devastated by myxomatosis?
14 Which is the brightest planet as seen from the Earth?
15 What do three horizontal lines represent in mathematics?
16 Which English King was the last to die in battle?
17 In rock opera, Tommy was deaf, dumb and what else?
18 How many times does the letter A appear in the first name of singer/actress Streisand?
19 Who recorded the album *Sweet Baby James*?
20 What is the next prime number above 100?
21 What is a quadrilateral with one pair of opposite sides parallel called?
22 Which telephone link service was established in July 1937?
23 What is lowered by a beta-blocker?
24 Which country has the greatest number of telephone subscribers?
25 In the song "Country Roads", which place is described as "almost heaven"?
26 Who was the most famous inhabitant of the fictitious village St Mary Mead?
27 Which composer's "6th Symphony" is known as the "Pathètique?
28 Who called his autobiography From *Drags to Riches*?
29 Boxer Jack Dempsey was nicknamed which Mauler?
30 What killed Sir Francis Drake?

QUIZ 75 TV DRAMA

Answers - see Quiz 73, page 169

1 What was the occupation of the person in the title role in *Rebus*?
2 Which War did *Foyle's War* deal with?
3 Ian Kelsey left *Emmerdale* for which hospital drama?
4 Who played Jeannie in the revival of *Randall & Hopkirk (Deceased)*?
5 In which drama did John Thaw play an elderly man who takes in a London evacuee?
6 Who was a memorable and different Mr Darcy on the large and small screen?
7 What was the name of the priest played by Stephen Tompkinson in *Ballykissangel*?
8 Where was the classic *Boys From the Blackstuff* set?
9 Which series featured Miles, Anna and Egg?
10 The late Joan Hickson played which famous sleuth on TV?
11 What type of surgeon was Dangerfield?
12 In which two countries was *The Buccaneers* set?
13 Which 1990s Dickens adaptation had Paul Scofield in the title role?
14 Who played Mrs Peter Mayle in the ill fated *A Year in Provence*?
15 In which series did Helen Baxendale play Claire Maitland?
16 Which Nancy Mitford novel was a lavish adaptation at the beginning of the millennium?
17 Who played Mellors in the 1993 TV adaptation of *Lady Chatterley's Lover*?
18 Which 'thirtysomething' drama series starred Amanda Holden and Dervla Kirwan?
19 Which sleuth had a secretary called Miss Lemon?
20 Where was *Band of Gold* set?
21 Which TV detective worked for the Bureau des Etrangers?
22 Which future co-star of Nicole Kidman starred in Dennis Potter's *Lipstick on Your Collar*?
23 Which actress, who made a brief appearance in *EastEnders* in 2001, starred as *The Manageress*?
24 Which series had Dr Joel Fleishmann In the Alaskan town of Cicely?
25 In which state was *Thirtysomething* set?
26 Which TV detective was created in the books of RD Wingfield?
27 Which monarch was on the throne at the time *Upstairs Downstairs* was set?
28 Which day of the week was famous for having a weekly play in the late 1960s?
29 In which series did Robbie Coltrane play Fitz?
30 Which *Casualty* spin-off proved more popular than the original?

QUIZ 76 POT LUCK 35

Answers - see Quiz 74, page 170

1 Which was the world's first country to introduce a driving test?
2 What are Bill Gates's two first names?
3 "When The Lights Go Out" was the first top ten hit for which band?
4 What does the letter B stand for in SCUBA?
5 In the 1920s which American sportsman said, on being told he was earning more than the US President, said, "Well, I had a better year than he did."?
6 In which country was England cricket captain Ted Dexter born?
7 Which language does the word ombudsman derives from?
8 Leslie Thomas wrote a novel about what kind of *Soldiers*?
9 Which island lies in the Bay of Naples?
10 Cyril Mead became known as which half of a comic duo?
11 Which country produced the first Miss World contest winner?
12 Florence Nightingale was given the Freedom of which city?
13 How many top ten hits did Kate Bush have in the last decade of the old millennium?
14 Rhodes is the largest of which group of islands?
15 The Battle of Britain is remembered on which date?
16 Which of these comics died the youngest – Tony Hancock, Eric Morecambe or Peter Sellers?
17 Which US national park has a highway called Alligator Alley?
18 Which invention affecting trousers was patented in Chicago in 1913?
19 Which director started off the *Scream* series of movies?
20 What animal appears on the cover of the Beach Boy's album *Pet Sounds*?
21 Who won the Best Actress Oscar for the movie *Misery*?
22 What was the first name of *Valentine* in Willy Russell's play?
23 How is the painting La Gioconda also known?
24 In the Church of England what is the smallest administrative unit?
25 Which letter identified Tommy Lee Jones' character in the *Men In Black* movie?
26 In which London building does the Lutine Bell hang?
27 Which male singer called his debut solo album *Faith*?
28 Donna Reed replaced Barbara Bel Geddes in which US TV series?
29 Which of these is furthest south – Bath, Bristol or Southampton?
30 What was the first top ten hit for the Chemical Brothers?

POT LUCK 34 *See quiz 74, page 170*
1 Morphine. **2** Queens. **3** Valentine's. **4** Road rage attack. **5** Donald Budge.
6 On the ground. **7** Taylor. **8** Ionic. **9** Karen Pickering. **10** Leeds. **11** British.
12 Countess Spencer. **13** Rabbit. **14** Venus. **15** Identically equal to. **16** Richard III.
17 Blind. **18** Twice. **19** James Taylor. **20** 101. **21** Trapezium. **22** 999 service.
23 Heart rate and/or blood pressure. **24** USA. **25** West Virginia. **26** Miss Marple.
27 Tchaikovsky. **28** Danny La Rue. **29** Manassa. **30** Dysentery.

ANSWERS

QUIZ 77 HOBBIES

Answers - see Quiz 79, page 175

1 Which company created the computer game Shenmue?
2 In which decade were books issued as CD Roms?
3 Which comic is older, Beano or Dandy?
4 Which best selling toys do Steiff make?
5 Where in the UK is the Kelvingrove art gallery?
6 How many counters does each backgammon player have at the start of play?
7 Which fiction writer has sold more books than any other?
8 Pokemon Yellow was created by which manufacturer?
9 What is a round of play called in a hand of bridge?
10 In which county is Alton Towers?
11 What is the number to aim for in a game of cribbage?
12 In which decade was the first Home Video System produced?
13 What colour are Scrabble tiles?
14 Which computer games can be Red, Yellow and Pikachu?
15 What type of needlework requires aida fabric?
16 Where was shuffleboard originally played?
17 Which company created the Gran Turismo Real Driving Simulator?
18 Ikebana is the art of what?
19 What are satin, stem and lazy daisy?
20 EasyEverything is the world's biggest what?
21 Which colour do Morris dancers predominantly wear?
22 Where in the UK is the Blackgang Chine Clifftop Theme Park?
23 Which special piece of equipment is needed to do crochet?
24 Who wrote the spy thriller Without Remorse?
25 How many dice are used in a craps game?
26 Which company produced the first battery powered cassette recorder?
27 How many packs of cards are used in a game of canasta?
28 What is the world's most widely played board game?
29 Which company created the MS Flight Simulator?
30 In draughts when can a piece move forwards or backwards?

SPORTING LEGENDS See quiz 79, page 175

ANSWERS

1 Severiano Ballesteros. 2 Doctor. 3 Manchester United. 4 1970s. 5 Four.
6 Sheffield Wednesday. 7 1950s. 8 Aberdeen. 9 Chelsea. 10 1970s.
11 400m hurdles. 12 14. 13 Stephen Hendry. 14 Tony Jacklin. 15 Barry John.
16 Michael Johnson. 17 Kapil Dev. 18 Chess. 19 Hamburg. 20 Squash. 21 20.
22 Bjorn Borg. 23 452. 24 Australian. 25 Ravel's "Bolero". 26 Ipswich Town.
27 Baseball. 28 Refused to do military service. 29 French. 30 Willie Carson.

QUIZ 78 POT LUCK 36

Answers - see Quiz 80, page 176

1 Usually meaning extra terrestrial, where is a car from with the registration letters ET?
2 Which football ground has a Matthew Harding Stand?
3 Which method did John Haigh use to dispose of his victims' bodies?
4 Ralph Scheider was an inventor credited with developing which daily used item?
5 In which country was Europe's first motorway built?
6 What does the reference ibid mean?
7 Which creepy horror movie features the character Jack Torrance?
8 What does the C stand for in COBOL?
9 What is the nationality of Jennifer Lopez's parents?
10 In which city should you "be sure to wear some flowers in your hair"?
11 In which country was the musician Bela Bartok born?
12 In 1918 in Britain women over what age were given the vote?
13 Which Royal first sat in the House of Lords in 1987?
14 Baroness de Laroche was the first woman to be awarded what licence?
15 Which George produced records for the Beatles?
16 In which London street did Selfridge's first open?
17 Michael Steele was in which all-girl group?
18 Which culinary ingredient can be Extra Virgin?
19 On TV, who was the first regular female presenter of *Points Of View*?
20 Who composed the comic opera *The Gondoliers*?
21 Which picnic aid did James Dewar invent?
22 "The Most Beautiful Girl In The World" was the first UK No 1 single for which artist?
23 Which sisters used Bell as a pseudonym?
24 Whose dying words were, "My neck is very slender"?
25 "Goodbye England's Rose" was the first line of which song?
26 Oyster and Morel are both types of which vegetable?
27 How is actress/model Lesley Hornby better known?
28 What is the earliest date you can eat an Easter egg on Easter Day?
29 How was designer Laura Mountney better known?
30 ABTA represents which group of people?

POT LUCK 37 *See quiz 80, page 176*

1 Four Tops. 2 Cheltenham. 3 A clove. 4 George VI. 5 Women's Institute. 6 Bikini.
7 Richard I. 8 Colditz. 9 *News of the World*. 10 Champion Jockey. 11 Michaelmas Day.
12 Neneh Cherry. 13 Axis. 14 1,000 Guineas. 15 Argentina. 16 Duchess of York.
17 Peru. 18 Duke of Bedford. 19 Norfolk. 20 Charterhouse. 21 Walt Disney.
22 The Duchess of Windsor. 23 Pankhurst. 24 Stonehenge. 25 Test tube baby.
26 Belgium. 27 Manchester. 28 Julienne. 29 Greek kilt. 30 Jon Lindsay.

QUIZ 79 SPORTING LEGENDS

Answers - see Quiz 77, page 173

1 Which Spaniard became the youngest golfer to win the British Open in the 20th century?
2 What was Roger Bannister's 'day job'?
3 Which English club did George Best join immediately after leaving school?
4 In which decade did Ian Botham make his Test debut?
5 How many times did Will Carling lead England to the Five Nations Championships?
6 Which Yorkshire club did Jack Charlton manage before he managed the Republic of Ireland?
7 In which decade did Henry Cooper win his first British heavyweight championship?
8 Which side did Alex Ferguson manage before he went to Manchester United?
9 For which club did Jimmy Greaves make his Football League debut as a striker?
10 In which decade did Wayne Gretzky make his professional debut?
11 What was Sally Gunnell's Olympic gold medal winning event?
12 Mike Hailwood won a record how many Isle of Man TT races between 1961 and 1979?
13 Who was the first snooker player to win all nine world ranking tournaments?
14 Who was the European Ryder Cup team's non-playing captain from 1983 to 1989?
15 Which Welsh Rugby player scored a record 90 points for his country between 1966 and 1972?
16 Who was the first man to hold the world record at 200m and 400m simultaneously?
17 Who led India to victory in the Cricket World Cup in 1983?
18 Anatoli Karpov was world champion in what?
19 Which team on the European mainland did Kevin Keegan play for?
20 Which sport did Jahangir Khan play?
21 How many Wimbledon titles did Billie Jean King win?
22 Who broke Fred Perry's record of three consecutive Wimbledon titles?
23 To the nearest 50 how many runs did Don Bradman make on his first innings for New South Wales?
24 In 1990 John McEnroe was expelled from which Grand Slam Open for swearing?
25 Which music did Torvill & Dean use when they scored a full hand of perfect scores at the 1984 Olympics?
26 Which team did Alf Ramsey take to the First Division Championship?
27 Which sport did Hank Aaron play?
28 Why was Muhammad Ali stripped of his World Heavyweight tile in 1967?
29 Which was the only Grand Slam title Pete Sampras has not won?
30 Which former Scottish jockey has the first names William Hunter Fisher?

ANSWERS

HOBBIES See quiz 77, page 173
1 Sega. 2 1990s. 3 *Beano*. 4 Teddy bears. 5 Glasgow. 6 15. 7 Agatha Christie.
8 Nintendo Game Boy. 9 Trick. 10 Staffordshire. 11 31. 12 1970s.
13 Cream/white. 14 Pokemon. 15 Embroidery. 16 On board ship.
17 Sony Play Station. 18 Flower arranging. 19 Embroidery stitches. 20 Internet cafe.
21 White. 22 Isle of Wight. 23 Hook. 24 Tom Clancy. 25 Two. 26 Philips.
27 Two. 28 Monopoly. 29 Microsoft. 30 When it becomes a king.

QUIZ 80 POT LUCK 37

Answers - see Quiz 78, page 174

1 Levi Stubbs was lead singer with which Tamla Motown group?
2 Which Gloucestershire town had the first public school for girls?
3 What is a small segment of garlic called?
4 Who was the first reigning monarch to visit the USA?
5 Which women's organisation was founded by Mrs Hoodless in 1897?
6 Which fashion statement was created by Louis Reard in 1946?
7 Who was king of England at the time that Robin Hood was said to have lived in Sherwood Forest?
8 How was the prison camp Oflag IVC better known?
9 Which Queen album had the name of a national newspaper?
10 What did Gordon Richards become a record 26 times between 1925 and 1953?
11 On a calendar, what is the third quarter day in England?
12 Which female singer had hits with "Manchild" and "Buffalo Stance"?
13 What was the name of the alliance between Germany and Italy in World War II?
14 Which Classic horse race was the first to be run on a Sunday in England?
15 In which country did Carlos Menem become President in 1989?
16 Who was the first female Royal to receive her pilot's licence?
17 In which country does the Amazon begin?
18 Which Duke has an ancestral home at Woburn Abbey?
19 In which county is the Queen's home Sandringham House?
20 All the members of Genesis were ex pupils of which school?
21 Who said, "I love Mickey Mouse more than any woman I've ever known."?
22 Who said, "No woman can be too rich or too thin."?
23 What was Emmeline Goulden's married name?
24 Amesbury, southern England, has which world heritage site close by?
25 Why was Louise Joy Brown's birth a first in 1978?
26 In which country was the first beauty contest held? .
27 In which city did the first Marks & Spencer store open?
28 What term describes thinly cut vegetables slowly cooked in butter?
29 What sort of garment is a fustanella?
30 In *Coronation Street* what was the name of the conman who landed Deirdre Rachid in court for fraud?

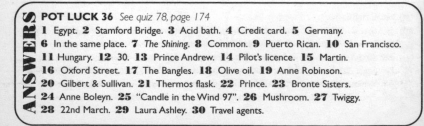

POT LUCK 36 *See quiz 78, page 174*

1 Egypt. 2 Stamford Bridge. 3 Acid bath. 4 Credit card. 5 Germany.
6 In the same place. 7 *The Shining.* 8 Common. 9 Puerto Rican. 10 San Francisco.
11 Hungary. 12 30. 13 Prince Andrew. 14 Pilot's licence. 15 Martin.
16 Oxford Street. 17 The Bangles. 18 Olive oil. 19 Anne Robinson.
20 Gilbert & Sullivan. 21 Thermos flask. 22 Prince. 23 Bronte Sisters.
24 Anne Boleyn. 25 "Candle in the Wind 97". 26 Mushroom. 27 Twiggy.
28 22nd March. 29 Laura Ashley. 30 Travel agents.

QUIZ 81 MEDICINE & HEALTH

Answers - see Quiz 83, page 179

1 What are the initials for the human form of BSE?
2 Oncology is the study of which disease?
3 A hysterectomy involves removal of what?
4 Osteoporosis is a weakness and brittleness of what?
5 In which decade did a report first appear in the US saying smoking could damage health?
6 What was the nationality of the founder of the Red Cross?
7 Penicillin was the first what?
8 Ebola is also known as which disease?
9 What does S stand for in AIDS?
10 Appendicitis causes pain where?
11 Which insects cause bubonic plague?
12 Which disease – more common in children – is also called varicella?
13 What causes cholera – contaminated water, insects or malnutrition?
14 Which part of the body is affected by conjunctivitis?
15 The infection of wounds by what can bring on tetanus?
16 Which of the following is not a blood group – AB, O or T?
17 What sort of flies transmit sleeping sickness?
18 Cranial osteopathy involves the manipulation of which bones?
19 Reflexologists massage which part of the body?
20 Shiatsu is a massage technique from which country?
21 Anabolic steroids are used to repair or build what?
22 What does an analgesic drug do?
23 What does the H stand for in HIV?
24 In which part of the body is the human's longest bone?
25 Hypertension is another name for what?
26 What is the most common element in the human body?
27 After the skin, what is the next largest human organ?
28 What is another name for the sternum?
29 Hydrotherapy involves the use of what in treatment?
30 Where was the first ambulance used?

ANSWERS

THE OSCARS See quiz 83, page 179

1 *American Beauty*. 2 Seven. 3 Gwyneth Paltrow. 4 *West Side Story*. 5 *American Beauty*.
6 *Boys Don't Cry*. 7 Tommy Lee Jones. 8 *The Cider House Rules*. 9 *The Piano*. 10 March.
11 James Whale. 12 Julia Roberts. 13 Ang Lee. 14 *Creature Comforts*.
15 John Williams. 16 *The Madness of King George*. 17 *As Good As It Gets*. 18 Tom Hanks.
19 Sally Field. 20 *Moonstruck*. 21 Shirley MacLaine. 22 American Civil War.
23 Oliver Reed. 24 Jane Fonda. 25 Jon Voight. 26 Hayley Mills. 27 Geoffrey Rush.
28 Jeremy Irons. 29 New York. 30 Sam Mendes.

QUIZ 82 POT LUCK 38

Answers - see Quiz 84, page 180

1 In which country did the Women's Institute begin?
2 Who was the first woman to speak in the British Parliament?
3 The French President occupies which official residence?
4 In which country is Archangel international airport?
5 On which Greek island was Prince Philip born?
6 Who was backed by The Dakotas?
7 In which ocean is the Sargasso Sea – Atlantic, Indian or Pacific?
8 French designer Christian Dior created what kind of Look in the late 1940s?
9 Which John made the best selling album *Rhymes and Reasons*?
10 The Fosse Way links which two English cities?
11 In which capital city was jazz's Hot Club?
12 Prince Edward resigned from which branch of the services in 1987?
13 Who is the oldest of The Three Tenors?
14 In which song were "them good old boys drinkin' whisky & rye"?
15 How is Formosa now known?
16 Who introduced the very first edition of *Countdown* on TV?
17 What did the Penny Bazaar opened by Michael and Tom in Manchester grow into?
18 In what year did *Blue Peter* first set sail on the airwaves of TV?
19 Viscount Linley was the first British Royal to be banned from doing what?
20 Peter Sutcliffe became better known under which graphic name?
21 Which month was in hit titles by Pilot and Barbara Dixon?
22 In which mountain range is the Simplon Pass?
23 Marie Curie was the first woman to win which notable prize?
24 Who had an instrumental hit with "Don't Cry For Me Argentina"?
25 In which year did Queen Elizabeth and the Duke of Edinburgh celebrate their Golden Wedding?
26 What is the chief shopping street in Edinburgh?
27 How did the second wife of *Coronation Street*'s unlucky-in-love Ken Barlow meet her demise?
28 René Lalique used which material when making ornaments?
29 Which city is named after US frontiersman Kit Carson?
30 Kurt Cobain's farewell note in 1995 read, "It's better to burn out than" do what?

QUIZ 83 THE OSCARS

Answers - see Quiz 81, page 177

1 For which movie did Kevin Spacey win his second Oscar?
2 How many Oscars did *Schindler's List* win?
3 Who played Viola in *Shakespeare in Love*?
4 Which musical won most Oscars?
5 Which movie was the last Best Picture winner of the 1990s?
6 For which movie did Hilary Swank win her first Oscar?
7 Who played the marshal in an Oscar winning performance in *The Fugitive*?
8 For which movie did Michael Caine win his second Oscar?
9 For which movie did the 11 year old Anna Paquin win an Oscar in 1993?
10 In which month does the Oscars ceremony usually take place?
11 Which director is the subject of *Gods and Monsters*?
12 Who won the Best Actress Oscar in 2001?
13 Who directed *Crouching Tiger Hidden Dragon*?
14 For which movie did Nick Park win his first Oscar?
15 Who wrote the music for *Jaws*?
16 Which Nicholas Hytner movie had Nigel Hawthorne in the title role?
17 Which 1997 movie with Oscar winning performances had the ad line, "Brace yourself for Melvin!"?
18 Who 'outed' his drama teacher at an Oscars ceremony where he won for the AIDS issue movie *Philadelphia*?
19 Who played Oscar nominated Julia Roberts' mother in *Steel Magnolias*?
20 For which movie did Cher receive her Oscar in a dress which caused more uproar than the film?
21 Which actress, who had her 67th birthday in 2001, said "I deserve this" on receiving her Oscar in 1983?
22 Against which conflict is *Dances with Wolves* set?
23 Which actor died during the making of the Oscar-winning *Gladiator*?
24 Between Glenda Jackson's two Best Actress Oscars, Liza Minnelli and who else won?
25 Which father of Angelina Jolie won an Oscar for *Coming Home*?
26 Which English actress won an Oscar as a child in 1960?
27 Which star of *Quills* won an Oscar for *Shine*?
28 Who was the only English Best Actor of the 1990s?
29 Where did Woody Allen set *Hannah and Her Sisters*?
30 Which British director directed *American Beauty*?

QUIZ 84 POT LUCK 39

Answers - see Quiz 82, page 178

1 Which Ruth was the last woman to be hanged in British history?
2 The Transandine railway tunnel links which two countries?
3 Which wedding anniversary is linked to tin?
4 Who or what was Dolly Varden?
5 What was the motto of Tesco founder Sir Jack Cohen?
6 How was dancer and spy Margarete Gertrude Zelle better known?
7 Which US President was married to Rosalynn Smith?
8 Which Cat sang that he loved his dog?
9 The Great Barrier Reef is off which Australian state?
10 Which Richard played TV's Dr Kildare?
11 Which British monarch's name does Princess Eugenie have?
12 What is the first name of MEP Mrs Kinnock?
13 How did singer Mark McLoughlin become better known?
14 Ruthie Henshall and Ute Lemper were the first West End stars of which musical?
15 Which Walter Hunt invention of 1849 has Liz Hurley used as a fashion statement?
16 Which 1950s singer Rosemary is aunt of a popular actor George with the same surname?
17 Baker, Bruce and Clapton made up which group?
18 In the late 1990s, which celebs chose Beauregard among their baby son's names?
19 What are the first two words of "My Way"?
20 "Hopelessly Devoted To You" comes from which musical?
21 Connee, Martha and Helvetia were which close harmony singing Sisters?
22 Which part of the body is studied by a phrenologist?
23 What was Frank Sinatra's middle name?
24 Which shopping chain advertised 'nothing over sixpence'?
25 Who was the female leader of the Baader Meinhof terrorist group?
26 Where is the Masai Mara game reserve?
27 What are a banoffee pie's main two ingredients?
28 Who was the first British monarch seen on a moving picture?
29 Jack Charlton played all his League football with which club side?
30 How many UK No 1s did Buddy Holly have during his lifetime?

POT LUCK 38 *See quiz 82, page 178*
1 Canada. 2 Lady Astor. 3 Elysee Palace. 4 Russia. 5 Corfu. 6 Billy J Kramer.
7 Atlantic. 8 New Look. 9 Denver. 10 Lincoln & Exeter. 11 Paris.
12 Royal Marines. 13 Luciano Pavarotti. 14 "American Pie". 15 Taiwan.
16 Richard Whiteley. 17 Marks and Spencer. 18 1958. 19 Driving.
20 The Yorkshire Ripper. 21 "January". 22 Alps. 23 Nobel Prize. 24 The Shadows.
25 1997. 26 Princes Street. 27 He committed suicide. 28 Glass. 29 Carson City
30 "Fade away."

QUIZ 85 MUSIC WHO'S WHO?

Answers - see Quiz 86, page 182

1 Which female band had a No 1 with "Independent Women Part 1"?
2 Who wrote the *Liverpool Oratorio* with Paul McCartney?
3 Whose album had the invitation *Come On Over* in 1998?
4 Who sang "I Walk the Line" and "A Boy Named Sue"?
5 What did Leo Fender make?
6 Which Australian had 13 consecutive UK Top Ten hits between Jan 1988 and June 1991?
7 Which duo had a multi-million seller with "Unchained Melody" in 1995?
8 Whose best-selling posthumous album was called *Legend*?
9 Who made the solo albums *Watermark* and *Shepherd Moons*?
10 How were John McDermott, Anthony Kearns and Ronan Tynan styled?
11 Whose albums include *Sogno, Romanza* and *Sueno*?
12 What type of musician was conductor Daniel Barenboim's wife Jacqueline?
13 How was Nathaniel Adams Coles better known?
14 Which Harry won a Lifetime Achievement Grammy in 2000?
15 Which 'title' did bandleader Basie have?
16 Which Harry made the albums *We Are In Love* and *Blue Light, Red Light*?
17 With which orchestra did Simon Rattle make his name?
18 Which veteran country singer had two best-selling albums recorded in prisons?
19 Who featured in the movie *Purple Rain*?
20 Who sang the theme song from the Bond movie *Tomorrow Never Dies*?
21 Who won a Grammy in 1992 for "Tears In Heaven"?
22 Who wrote the musical *Oliver!*?
23 Which instrument did Stan Getz play?
24 How many members of boy band A1 are there?
25 Which country do the band Modjo come from?
26 Which English city does Craig David come from?
27 Who recorded the song which the Labour Party used in their 1997 campaign?
28 Who played keyboards with the Strawbs and Yes?
29 Who won a Grammy with her unforgettable late dad in 1991?
30 In which musical did Ruthie Henshall open in the West End in August 2001?

QUIZ 86 POT LUCK 40

Answers - see Quiz 85, page 181

1 Which European city has the same name as an archer in mythology?
2 Which month comes after the month containing Saint Andrew's Day?
3 Which fruit includes the variety Ellison's Orange?
4 Princess Margaret was born in which country?
5 Aduki, borlotti and cannellini are all types of what?
6 Where would a Spanish lady wear her mantilla?
7 In which decade was Little Jimmy Osmond born?
8 Who was the first woman General of the Salvation Army?
9 Who was the first singer to have seven consecutive singles reach No 1 in the US?
10 Which English cricket captain had a bust up with umpire Shakoor Rana in Faisalabad?
11 "Rhythm Of Life" comes from which musical?
12 Svetlana Savitskaya was the first woman to walk where?
13 In the 1990s which US property scandal involved the Clintons?
14 The frittata is an Italian version of what popular egg dish?
15 What was the highest ranking job that the fictitious Jim Hacker achieved?
16 How many beats to the bar does a traditional waltz have?
17 Which sweet delicacies have a name meaning 'little ovens'?
18 Which title did Hillary Clinton prefer to First Lady?
19 In France what would you buy if you asked for pamplemousses?
20 Which Royal's motto is "Ich dien" or "I serve"?
21 Which flavouring used in tonic water is taken from a cinchona tree?
22 Why might you be embarrassed by your lentigines?
23 Which jazz singer is Mrs Johnny Dankworth?
24 What colour is the background of the flag of the European Union?
25 Kim Carnes sang about which film star's eyes?
26 Who should Scotland have played when they went on the pitch for a World Cup qualifier but the opponents didn't?
27 How many sharps and flats are there in the key of C major?
28 Syd Barrett was a founder of which group?
29 How is the volcanic Mongibello also known?
30 At which English club did Ian Wright end his soccer playing career?

THE HARD QUESTIONS

Ask a full round of these questions and you will be greeted by a stunned silence and much scratching of foreheads and a furrowing of brows. These questions are designed to sort the men from the boys.

These 'hard' questions are perfect for wiping the grin off the face of the smart alec, know-it-all at the end of the bar. However, you are advised to use them sparingly and allow plenty of time for your contestants to mull over the answers, otherwise you will send the punters home frustrated and humiliated, muttering vows never to take part in another pub quiz as long as they live. If you see smoke issuing from the contestants ears during a 'hard' round suggest a quick bar break to cool down their overworked cerebrums and calm their frayed nerves.

QUIZ 1 NEWSWORTHY

Answers - see Quiz 3, page 187

1 The first shorn fleece of Dolly the cloned sheep was donated to which charity?
2 The Prometheus was the first of which type of kitchen equipment?
3 Which US state was acquired from the Badsen Purchase?
4 Where was "God Save The King" first sung in public?
5 Who was the first British Foreign Secretary to visit Iran after the fall of the Shah?
6 Who founded Amazon.com?
7 In 1992 Don Hollister and Don Pelazzo were responsible for developing what?
8 Who was Germany's longest-serving post-war Chancellor?
9 When did the first Page Three girl appear in the The Sun?
10 Which distress signal did SOS replace?
11 Where was the first gold rush in Western Australia in 1885?
12 Which film holds the record as having three of its actors being Oscar nominated?
13 In 2000 how many sovereign countries were there in the world?
14 Which was the first regiment to wear khaki?
15 What is the world's largest conservation charity?
16 What was the name of the first balloon to circumnavigate the globe non stop?
17 Who became chairman of the KGB in 1967?
18 What date was the first Penguin book published – the same date that England won the World Cup 31 years later?
19 Who was Hitler's propaganda chief?
20 When was PAYE Income Tax introduced?
21 In the 1980s, laser surgery was pioneered by Ludwig Demling who first used it to destroy what?
22 What is the largest CD edition of a talking book?
23 At which golf club was the Jack Nicklaus Online Golf Championship played in December 1999?
24 About how many mountaineers scale Everest each year?
25 Who took part in the USA's first manned orbital flight?
26 Where was the tanker registered, which spilt millions of gallons of oil off the French coast in March 1978?
27 Where was the on line bookstore Amazon first based?
28 John F Kennedy said the Apollo programme would land a man on the Moon and what else?
29 Who was the first elected President of Argentina after the Falklands War?
30 What is the correct name of the World Bank?

ANSWERS

TV SOAPS See quiz 3, page 187

1 Twice. 2 Hairdresser. 3 Maggie (*ER*). 4 Ken Jackson. 5 Luke. 6 *Melrose Place*.
7 Viv Martell. 8 Five. 9 Dennis. 10 *Black Forest Clinic*. 11 Ricky Tomlinson.
12 Derek Thompson. 13 Fallon. 14 Julie Goodyear. 15 Meadowcroft.
16 Leonard Swindley. 17 QE2. 18 "Conundrum". 19 Chadwick. 20 Mal Young.
21 Fred. 22 *Dynasty*. 23 Thaw. 24 *The Brothers*. 25 Liam. 26 Peggy. 27 Thomas.
28 *Compact*. 29 *Dynasty*. 30 Hannah Waterman (dad Dennis played Alfred Dolittle).

QUIZ 2 POT LUCK I

Answers - see Quiz 4, page 188

1   Who was the first US President to ride in a car?
2   The drink Kir was named after the mayor of which town?
3   Where was the SALT II treaty signed?
4   Who was the leader of the Taliban at the beginning of the raids on Afghanistan in October 2001?
5   Who said there were three stages for a Hollywood actress, Babe, District Attorney and Driving Miss Daisy?
6   In the US what were 'swift walkers'?
7   Where was the first sugar beet extraction factory built?
8   In which city was Britain's Independent Labour Party founded?
9   Which Oscar winning actor links *Tomb Raider* and *Pearl Harbor*?
10 In what year were dog licenses abolished in the UK?
11 Of the three top names in the US's Ivy League which is the middle one alphabetically?
12 On which river is the state capital of Mississippi?
13 Which Pope excommunicated Martin Luther?
14 Who made jasperware?
15 Who committed suicide after being charged with living off the immoral earnings of Christine Keeler and Mandy Rice Davies?
16 Which future party leader was the then youngest-ever government minister when he became Under-Secretary to the Navy on his 30th birthday?
17 During which months did Jack the Ripper kill five prostitutes?
18 Jatakas are stories of the previous lives of whom?
19 Which US President pardoned the first US President to have resigned from office?
20 Which monarch knighted Isaac Newton?
21 Which state is to the south west of Rajashan in India?
22 What colour is the head and neck of the jabiru?
23 Which rock star died two years to the day after the death Rolling Stone Brian Jones?
24 Where was Europe's oldest university founded?
25 Where were emeralds first mined?
26 Which dams in the Ruhr were hit by the Dam Busters in 1943?
27 In which city was Chop Suey invented?
28 Where was the world's first electric power station?
29 A strophium was an early prototype of which garment?
30 Who wickedly said to Jeffrey Archer, "Is there no beginning to your talents?"?

ANSWERS

PLANTS *See quiz 4, page 188*
1 Alaska. 2 Chlorophyll. 3 Dead matter. 4 New Zealand. 5 0.9%.
6 Barley. 7 Lamina. 8 Gymnosperm. 9 Hollies. 10 Epiphyte. 11 Cork.
12 Forget Me Not. 13 Small stalk. 14 Myrtle sprig. 15 Honesty. 16 Azalea.
17 Pink. 18 Autumn crocus. 19 Rosa gallica. 20 Carnations. 21 Saffron.
22 Glory of the snow. 23 South Africa. 24 Sap. 25 Boston. 26 Root.
27 Aubretia. 28 Parsley. 29 Daffodil. 30 Flemish.

QUIZ 3 TV SOAPS

Answers - see Quiz 1, page 185

1 How many times a week was *Coronation Street* originally broadcast?
2 Which profession did Helen Shapiro's character play in *Albion Market*?
3 For which character did Sally Field win an Emmy in 2000?
4 Which police character did George Irving play before joining *Holby City*?
5 What was 'Nora Batty's' surname in the revival of *Crossroads*?
6 What was the spin off of *Beverly Hills 90210*?
7 Which character did the barmaid from *Only Fools and Horses* play in *The Bill*?
8 How many members of the family were there which was created on *Soapstars*?
9 In *Coronation Street* who was Elsie Tanner's son?
10 Which overseas soap had the character Klaus Brinkmann?
11 In *Brookside* which actor who had been a striker in real life played a builder on strike?
12 Which member of the *Casualty* cast played an IRA terrorist in *The Long Good Friday*?
13 In *The Colbys* who shared her name with a youngster in *The Archers*?
14 Which *Coronation Street* barmaid was given an OBE?
15 What was the original title of *Brookside* to have been?
16 *Pardon the Expression* was a spin off series about which *Coronation Street* character?
17 In *Crossroads*, where was Meg when the motel burned down?
18 What was the final episode of *Dallas* called?
19 What did the actress who plays Linda Baldwin change her surname to in real life?
20 Which producer of *Brookside* took over the same year that the set expanded to include the shopping centre?
21 Which character became Mike Baldwin's step-father-in-law in 2001?
22 In which soap did the voice of Charlie in *Charlie's Angels* appear?
23 What is the married name of the actress who played Steve Owen's mum in *EastEnders*?
24 Which soap/drama centred on Hammond Transport Services?
25 Who did Bianca leave *EastEnders* with?
26 Which *EastEnders* character's one time real husband was jailed for the 1983 Security Express Robbery?
27 What was Sinbad's real name?
28 Which soap had *Crossroads*' creators previously created?
29 Which soap boasted appearances by Gerald Ford and Henry Kissinger?
30 Martine McCutcheon left *EastEnders* for *My Fair Lady*, but which other actress has a link with the show which was restaged in 2001?

NEWSWORTHY See quiz 1, page 185

ANSWERS

1 Cystic Fibrosis Fund. 2 Electric kettle. 3 Arizona. 4 Theatre Royal Drury Lane.
5 Jack Straw. 6 Jeff Bezos. 7 High tech light bulb. 8 Helmut Kohl. 9 1970. 10 CQD.
11 Halls Creek. 12 *Mutiny On The Bounty*. 13 192. 14 Oxford Light Infantry.
15 World Wildlife Fund. 16 Breitling Orbiter. 17 Yuri Andropov. 18 30th July.
19 Josef Goebbels. 20 1944. 21 Gallstones. 22 The Bible. 23 Pelican Hill. 24 750.
25 John Glenn. 26 Cyprus (Amoco Cadiz). 27 Seattle. 28 Return him safely to Earth.
29 Raul Alfonsin. 30 International Bank For Reconstruction & Development.

QUIZ 4 PLANTS

Answers - see Quiz 2, page 186

1 In which US state is the Tongass National Forest?
2 Which of the following do algae have – chlorophyll, roots and stems?
3 What does a saphrophyte feed on?
4 Urtica ferox is a deadly tree nettle native to where?
5 How much chlorophyll does spinach have – 0.9%, 0.12% or 0.17%
6 Which of the following originated in the Middle East – barley, maize or millet?
7 What is another name for the blade of a plant?
8 What name is given to a plant whose seed is not enclosed in an ovary?
9 Which of the following are in the Aquilfoliacae group – conifers, hollies or ivies?
10 What name is given to a plant which grows on another without damaging it?
11 The Whistler Tree is what type of tree?
12 Myosotis is another name for which flower?
13 What is a funicle?
14 According to legend which plant did Adam take from the Garden of Eden?
15 How is lunaria biennis better known?
16 What type of plant is a Silver Slipper?
17 What colour are the blooms of the Zephirine Drouhin?
18 What is another name for the meadow saffron?
19 What is the rose of Lancaster also called?
20 What are Alice Forbes and Bailey's Delight?
21 What is crocus sativus?
22 How is chionodoxa also known?
23 The agapanthus is native to where?
24 Which part of asafoetida is used?
25 The borlotti bean also takes its name from which city?
26 Which part of a mooli is edible?
27 How is rock cress better known?
28 Which herb reputedly travels seven times to the devil before it will emerge?
29 The amaryllis is related to which popular spring flower?
30 What is the nationality of the man who gave his name to the plant Lobelia?

QUIZ 5 POT LUCK 2

Answers - see Quiz 7, page 191

1 Which John won the Best Director Oscar for the movie *The Informer*?
2 The world's first known drilling for oil took place in which US state?
3 At what number Cromwell Street was the West's so-called "House of Horror"?
4 The Kate Bush album *Never For Ever* featured a song about which classical composer?
5 On which special day was William the Conqueror crowned King of England?
6 Which day of the week was dubbed the 'Black' day of the 1929 Wall Street Crash?
7 The first kindergarten was established in which country?
8 Ingemar Johansson became Sweden's first champion in which sport?
9 Roger Moore played 007 in how many films?
10 Matching the date of the French Revolution, how many steps are there to the top of the Eiffel Tower?
11 In which US state was John Travolta born?
12 Which security item was Joseph Farwell Glidden's patent in 1873?
13 In which city was the first Model T Ford produced in Britain?
14 In which country would you watch Jazz Pori play a home soccer match?
15 Which England cricket captain was born in Italy?
16 King Michael abdicated which European throne in 1947?
17 Which Mr Smith was the main character of 1984?
18 *A Man For All Seasons* was set in the 16th century but was written in which century?
19 The first prime minister of Australia shared his surname with which fictional detective?
20 Which country did 1990s group Whale come from?
21 Which country owns the Kuril Islands?
22 If 12 January falls on a Friday, on what day does 12 February fall?
23 How old was Mozart when he wrote his first musical composition?
24 How many hurdles are there in total in a six-lane 400 metre hurdle race?
25 Which paper did Superman work on?
26 In which year did Shirley Bassey, the Tigress of Tiger Bay, first have a top ten single
27 The first heart transplant patient survived for how long after the operation?
28 Which actor links the movies *Sliding Doors* and *Pandaemonium*?
29 In which country is the city of Londrina?
30 What is the first word of "My Heart Will Go On"?

ANSWERS

POT LUCK 3 *See quiz 7, page 191*

1 Prince Edward. 2 The Blind Beggar. 3 Doug Mountjoy. 4 Friendship 7.
5 Charles Blondin. 6 Painting. 7 Portugal. 8 46 years. 9 Argentine. 10 Sued.
11 Selhurst Park. 12 Farce. 13 Dolly Parton. 14 Vanbrugh. 15 Belgium. 16 Henry.
17 The "Forfarshire". 18 Tonga. 19 White Town. 20 Pope. 21 Bruton Street.
22 Norway. 23 Soccer club. 24 Paddington. 25 Brazil. 26 Frank Coraci.
27 France. 28 Coca Cola. 29 Brazil. 30 Pointer Sisters.

QUIZ 6 SOUNDS OF THE 80S

Answers - see Quiz 8, page 192

1. Who was the only American lady to have a million-seller in the UK in the 1980s?
2. Who directed Michael Jackson's best-selling album?
3. Whose album of *Love Songs* was the top selling album of 1982?
4. Who was the first country artist to have two UK No 1s?
5. What was Blondie's third single from the *Eat To The Beat* album?
6. Who wrote the first double A side of the 1980s to debut at No 1?
7. What were the Detroit Spinners called in the UK before using this name?
8. Who was the star of the movie from which the best-selling single of the 1980s in the US came?
9. The writer of Kelly Marie's "Feels Like I'm In Love" was a member of which 1970s band?
10. Who was the last Australian with a UK No 1 before Men At Work's first No 1?
11. What was the only song from *Thriller* to reach No 1 in the UK?
12. The brother of the writer of "True" starred in which TV soap?
13. Who was Billy Joel's 1983 No 1 dedicated to?
14. Which album did Lionel Richie's first No 1 of 1984 come from?
15. Which soap star had the best selling single of 1986?
16. Who was the only American man to have a million seller in the UK in the 1980s?
17. Which top selling hit of 1985 was a hit for a Canadian singer in the 1990s?
18. Which movie gave ELO their only UK No 1?
19. What colour shirt is Michael Jackson wearing on the cover of *Thriller*?
20. Which record of John Lennon's went to No 1 almost immediately after his murder?
21. What was the fourth British Eurovision Song Contest winner, which charted in this decade?
22. Which song did Smokey Robinson release to celebrate his silver anniversary in show business?
23. Under what name did Mary Sandeman have an 1980s No 1?
24. Who was the first white singer to have No 1 on the Motown label?
25. Where did Paul McCartney and Stevie Wonder record their No 1 duet?
26. Which big 1980s band were once called In Praise of Lemmings?
27. With whom did George Michael have his second No 1 as part of a duo?
28. Who directed the video for the Pet Shop Boys second No 1?
29. Which band topped the charts in the 1980s, as well as the 1960s and 1970s?
30. What was the surname of the singer who sang "Orinoco Flow"?

QUIZ 7 POT LUCK 3

Answers - see Quiz 5, page 189

1 Who was Prince Andrew's best man for his wedding to Sarah Ferguson?
2 Ronnie Kray shot George Cornell in which East End pub?
3 Who did Steve Davis beat to win his first World Snooker Championship?
4 John Glenn orbited the Earth in 1962 in which craft?
5 How did daredevil stuntman Jean Francois Gravelet become known?
6 John Sell Cotman became famous for doing what?
7 In which country is the Penina golf course?
8 How long was the Nazi Rudolf Hess in prison?
9 What was the nationality of Cuban revolutionary leader Che Guevara?
10 Satirical editor Richard Ingrams suggested his motto should be "Publish and be " what?
11 At which ground did Cantona perform his wild kung fu kick at a spectator?
12 What kind of theatrical play was the speciality of Brian Rix?
13 Who said, "It costs a lot to make me look so cheap!" – Dolly Parton, Madonna or Jeffrey Archer?
14 Which Sir John was the designer of Castle Howard and Blenheim Palace?
15 Albert became a king of which country in 1993?
16 What is Warren Beatty's other Christian name?
17 The crew of which boat were saved by the heroics of Grace Darling?
18 In which country did Queen Salote Tupou III rule for nearly 50 years?
19 Under which name did producer Jyoti Mishra have a No 1 hit?
20 Nicholas Breakspear was the first British what?
21 In which London Street is the residence where Princess Elizabeth – later Elizabeth II – was born?
22 In which country would you watch Tromso playing Molde at soccer?
23 What was the setting of the 1960s soap United!?
24 Michael Hordern provided the voice over for which TV bear?
25 Djalma Santos played soccer 100 times for which country?
26 Who directed the movie The Wedding Singer?
27 After abdicating, in which country did the former Edward VIII marry?
28 Dr John Pemberton invented which world famous drink?
29 In which country is the city of Recife?
30 How were June, Anita, Ruth and Bonnie known collectively?

POT LUCK 2 *See quiz 5, page 189*

QUIZ 8 UK TRAVEL

Answers - see Quiz 6, page 190

1   In which Square is the UK's highest building?
2   How many capsules or pods does the London Eye have?
3   What did the Theatre of Small Convenience in Malvern used to be?
4   Where is the National Library of Wales?
5   Where does the Avon flow into what the French call La Manche?
6   Which Bridge spans the Beauly Firth?
7   What was London's first new underground railway line to open in the second half of the 20th century?
8   Which Welsh city is near the old Roman fort of Segontium?
9   What was Lord Camden's name before he became a Lord and before the London borough was named after him?
10 How many miles is it from Land's End to John O'Groats?
11 Which county is to the west of Hereford & Worcester?
12 What is the official name of Brighton Pier?
13 In which county is the Cerne Giant?
14 Which of the Cinque Ports is nearest the beginning of the alphabet?
15 One of the founders of Fortnum and Mason was a footman in the service of which monarch?
16 Who inaugurated the Glyndebourne Festival?
17 Which is the UK's tallest structure built before the 20th century?
18 Where is the Cranfield Institute of Technology?
19 Where in Wales is the Royal Mint?
20 How long is Britain's longest river?
21 Which county is the largest to the east of Perth & Kinross?
22 When were the Broads designated a National Park?
23 Constable country is along which river?
24 What is the local name of the river which runs through Cambridge?
25 In what year were marriages at the famous blacksmith's shop in southern Scotland made illegal?
26 The founder of Guy's Hospital followed which profession?
27 Which county is to the south of Oxfordshire?
28 Where is the second largest castle in England and Wales?
29 What was Arsenal tube station called before it was called Arsenal?
30 Where did Britain's first nudist beach open in 1979?

SOUNDS OF THE 80S *See quiz 6 page 190*

1 Jennifer Rush. 2 Quincey Jones. 3 Barbra Streisand. 4 Kenny Rogers. 5 "Atomi"c.
6 Paul Weller. 7 Motown Spinners. 8 Richard Gere (*American Gigolo*). 9 Mungo Jerry.
10 Rolf Harris. 11 "Billie Jean". 12 *EastEnders* (the Kemps). 13 Christie Brinkley.
14 *Can't Slow Down*. 15 Nick Berry. 16 Stevie Wonder. 17 "The Power of Love".
18 "Xanadu". 19 Cream. 20 "(Just Like) Starting Over". 21 "Making Your Mind Up".
22 "Being With You". 23 Aneka. 24 Charlene. 25 Montserrat. 26 Culture Club.
27 Aretha Franklin. 28 Derek Jarman. 29 Bee Gees. 30 Brennan.

QUIZ 9 POT LUCK 4

Answers - see Quiz 11, page 195

1 Chester Carlson invented a machine that produces what?
2 Jobs and Wozniak pioneered development in which field?
3 In which country would you watch Karpaty playing Krivbas at soccer?
4 One language is spoken in more countries of the world than any other – which is it?
5 General Choi Hong Hi developed which martial art?
6 What position does the canoeist adopt in Canadian canoeing?
7 What did Wilhelm Rontgen discover to help medical science?
8 Which movement did George Williams found in 1844?
9 How is St Kentigern, patron saint of Glasgow also known?
10 Brigham Young was a leader of which religious movement?
11 Who first chaired *Mastermind* when it moved regularly to radio?
12 In 1989, who became the first US male tennis player in over 30 years to win the French Open?
13 What was the occupation of writer D.H.Lawrence's father?
14 In 1987 Lindy Chamberlain said her baby had been snatched by what?
15 How many track races are included in the decathlon?
16 Despite allegations of past Nazi activities, Kurt Waldheim became President of where in 1986?
17 Which film soundtrack topped the first classified UK album chart?
18 Who was convicted of murdering nanny Sandra Rivett?
19 In which country is the city of San Cristobal?
20 Who was the first US President not to be elected into office and who subsequently failed to win a presidential election?
21 Polly Nicholas was the first victim of which killer?
22 Which Cabinet minister's affair with Sara Keays brought about his resignation?
23 Who was the first rock star from the West to play in the USSR?
24 France, Great Britain and which other country competed in every Winter Olympic Games of the 20th century?
25 William Kemmler was the first man to die in what?
26 What is Japan's highest peak?
27 Who won the Best Actress Oscar for the movie *Blue Sky*?
28 The Galapagos Islands belong to which country?
29 What was the only top ten hit for West End featuring Sybil?
30 What was the name of Franco's fascist party in Spain?

ANSWERS

POT LUCK 5 See quiz 11, page 195

1 25 March. 2 Dixie Dean. 3 Harold Macmillan. 4 1994. 5 *Hi-De-Hi!*. 6 Norwegian.
7 1914. 8 Armani. 9 Henry I. 10 India. 11 *Godzilla*. 12 Colchester. 13 Adams.
14 Bay. 15 Ajax. 16 Chicago. 17 Jeffrey Archer. 18 144. 19 *Unchained*.
20 *Transformer*. 21 Alexander. 22 Swimming. 23 British Empire Exhibition.
24 Rievaulx. 25 21. 26 "If U Can't Dance". 27 Rafsanjani. 28 20 mins.
29 Silk screen. 30 Blythe Danner.

QUIZ 10 SOCCER

Answers - see Quiz 12, page 196

1 Who first coined the name soccer?
2 In the penultimate World Cup Final of last century, what was the score at 90 minutes?
3 Which of FIFA's original member countries came nearest the end of the alphabet?
4 Why did India pull out of the fourth World Cup?
5 When did West Germany win their second European Championship ?
6 Which was the most northerly club Peter Shilton played for in his record 1390 senior appearances?
7 In July 2000 which club owned the world's most expensive footballer?
8 Which was the first indoor arena used in a World Cup Final?
9 Which is the only club to have competed each year in Europe since European competition began?
10 For how much did the first hat trick scorer in a World Cup final sell his shirt in 2000?
11 In which 2001 movie did Pele make an appearance?
12 Whose World Cup medal was sold for almost £125,000 in 2001?
13 For how many years was the League Cup the Rumbelows League Cup?
14 The Football League Cup was a two-legged final until which year?
15 Who won the FA Cup the year Prince William was born?
16 The world's second most expensive goalie at the beginning of 2001 had been transferred from which club?
17 Who won the first post WWII Scottish FA Cup?
18 In which country did West Germany win their first World Cup?
19 The oldest man to play in the World Cup finals won the French Cup with which club?
20 Who were the first runners up of the Milk Cup?
21 Which was the first country to have players who scored more than once in a World Cup Final?
22 Who was Tommy Lawton playing for when he scored his first League hat trick?
23 Who was the first player to score twice in the final of the European Championships?
24 The first Yorkshire side to win the Fairs Cup in the 1960s beat which side in the final?
25 Which was the first side to win the UEFA Cup on penalties?
26 Who were runners up in the first FA Cup final played at Wembley?
27 Who were the last runners up of the old First Division?
28 At the end of the millennium who was the world's most expensive goalkeeper?
29 In which stadium was the sixth World Cup Final held?
30 In the last World Cup Final of the 20th century played outside Europe, what colour shirts did the winners wear?

QUIZ 11 POT LUCK 5

Answers - see Quiz 9, page 193

1 Before the Calendar Act of of 1752 what date was New Year's Day?
2 Which English goal scorer had the first names William Ralph?
3 Who described Margaret Thatcher's privatisation policy as "selling the family silver"?
4 In which year did Ayrton Senna die in a Grand Prix accident?
5 Crimpton-on-Sea was the location for which sitcom?
6 What was the nationality of the first team to reach the South Pole?
7 When was the Panama Canal opened?
8 Which designer made clothes for younger people under the Emporio label?
9 Which monarch was responsible for founding the first English zoo?
10 In which country was there a major earthquake in January 2001?
11 In which monster movie film did the character Dr Niko Tatopoulos appear?
12 Which city was known as Camulodunum in Roman times?
13 Who was the first president to live in the White House?
14 What was the official colour of legendary racehorse Arkle?
15 Which soccer team from Holland is named after a mythological Greek figure?
16 Where is the University of Illinois?
17 Which prominent figure became the youngest ever member of the GLC in 1969?
18 How many tiles are there in a game of mah-jong?
19 Which 1955 movie used "Unchained Melody" as its theme tune?
20 No 1 in the 1990s, "Perfect Day" first appeared on which early 1970s album?
21 What was Cary Grant's middle name?
22 Which sport follows FINA rules?
23 The original Wembley Stadium was costructed for which event?
24 Harold Wilson became Baron of where when he was made a peer?
25 After 'The Flapper Vote' in 1928, women over what age could vote in an election?
26 What was the final track on the Spice Girl's first album *Spice*?
27 In Iran, who succeeded the Ayatollah Khomeini as political leader?
28 In the silent days of cinema how long would a 'two reeler' last?
29 Serigraphy is also known as what type of printing?
30 Who is Gwyneth Paltrow's mother?

QUIZ 12 THE ROYALS

Answers - see Quiz 10, page 194

1 Who was the last person to be born first in line to the British throne?
2 Who did the Queen make the first STD call to?
3 Which Royal's wedding saw the first performance of Mendelssohn's Wedding March?
4 How old was Prince Charles when he became engaged to Lady Diana Spencer?
5 Who in 1934 said, "I can see no reason why women should not wear shorts."?
6 Who was the first British monarch to eat a hot dog?
7 Which royal family is the richest in Europe?
8 What is Prince William's penultimate Christian name?
9 How many interviews did the Queen Mother give in the 20th century?
10 Which Queen of Jordan succeeded Queen Noor?
11 From where did the Duke & Duchess of York leave for honeymoon by helicopter?
12 Where are the offices of the Earl of Wessex's TV production company?
13 Who was the first royal bride to include her family's motto on her personal coat of arms?
14 In 2001, which former member of Princess Diana's staff was charged with robbery?
15 On which soap did cast members 'visit' Duchy Home Farm?
16 In which month did Edward VIII cease to be Edward VIII?
17 Who won the Ladies Singles at Wimbledon just before Charles and Diana married?
18 Which Prince of Wales considered marrying a Lady Diana Spencer before Prince Charles?
19 Where did the Duke and Duchess of York consider having their daughters educated until there was a scandal about that school's principal?
20 Sir William Worsley was the father of which Duchess?
21 What medical treatment did the Queen Mother have shortly before her 101st birthday?
22 At which Cambridge college was Prince Charles educated?
23 What was the name of Diana, Princess of Wales' stepfather?
24 Who is the Queen's second oldest granddaughter?
25 What is the Queen Mother's third Christian name?
26 What was the name of the man who attempted to kidnap Princess Anne in 1974?
27 Whose portrait of Lady Diana Spencer was damaged in the National Portrait Gallery shortly after her wedding to Prince Charles?
28 Who was the first Royal bride to omit the word 'obey' in her marriage vows?
29 Which royal family is the richest in the world?
30 Who was the first Royal to be banned from driving?

SOCCER See quiz 10, page 194

1 Charles Wreford Brown. 2 0–0. 3 Switzerland. 4 They had to wear boots. 5 1980.
6 Bolton Wanderers. 7 Real Madrid. 8 Pontiac Silverdome, Detroit. 9 Barcelona.
10 £91,750. 11 *Mike Bassett: England Manager.* 12 Gordon Banks. 13 Two. 14 1966.
15 Tottenham Hotspur. 16 Monaco (Barthez to Manchester United). 17 Aberdeen.
18 Switzerland. 19 Monaco (Roger Milla, Cameroon). 20 Tottenham Hotspur. 21 Italy.
22 Burnley. 23 Gerd Müller. 24 Ferencvaros. 25 Tottenham Hotspur. 26 West Ham.
27 Manchester United. 28 Angelo Peruzzi. 29 Rasunda (Stockholm). 30 Yellow.

QUIZ 13 POT LUCK 6

Answers - see Quiz 15, page 199

1 Alex James and Dave Rowntree played in which band?
2 The Olympic Games were first televised by the BBC in which year?
3 Where in suburbia was the sitcom _The Good Life_ set?
4 In India what was Suttee?
5 Constantine, Liberius and Sissinius are names of what?
6 What was Abba's only single to make No 1 in the USA?
7 On a keyboard all the letters from F to L are in alphabetical order apart from which one?
8 Who was the Foreign Secretary who lost his seat in the 1997 British General Election?
9 In which country is the city of Douala?
10 Willie Park became the first winner of which sporting trophy?
11 Jane Wyman was the first wife of which famous American?
12 What colour separates the black, red and green bands on the Kenyan flag?
13 If you are misocapnic what do you dislike?
14 Whose first solo album after leaving a chart topping group was _All Things Must Pass_?
15 Before becoming PM, Margaret Thatcher was dubbed "The … Snatcher"?
16 In which year did the first kidney transplant take place?
17 Which first name is derived from Greek for rock or stone?
18 What was the first top ten hit for K-Klass?
19 How many episodes of _Fawlty Towers_ were made in total?
20 Which country was the first to retain soccer's World Cup?
21 How long does the French presidential term in office last?
22 Bruce Willis was born in which country?
23 What was the number of the Earl of Derby who gave his name to the Classic horse race the Derby?
24 In which country is the city of Panshan?
25 In which century was Robbie Burns born?
26 Who links the groups Slik, Visage and Ultravox?
27 Which element has the atomic number one?
28 Solo round-the-world yachtsman Francis Chichester sailed in which craft?
29 Which entertainment pioneer's catchphrase was "Leave' em wanting"?
30 Esperanto actually means one who does what?

THE 20TH CENTURY 1900–1950 _See quiz 15, page 199_
1 Humpty Dumpty Store, Oklahoma. **2** Paris Observatory. **3** 1946. **4** Clyde Tombaugh. **5** Little Boy. **6** First on National Health. **7** Stockings. **8** July. **9** Folkestone. **10** 1900. **11** Popov. **12** Policewomen. **13** Hull. **14** League of German Maidens. **15** 13. **16** Japan. **17** Banting & Best. **18** Ernest. **19** Plymouth. **20** Italy. **21** Bao Dai. **22** Bateman. **23** Beaverbrook. **24** Begin. **25** Abercrombie. **26** Balfour. **27** Gertrude Bell. **28** Poland (Ben Gurion). **29** Virginia Woolf. **30** 1,100.

QUIZ 14 MOVIE CLASSICS

Answers - see Quiz 16, page 200

1 Which company won a Special Oscar for producing 'the pioneer outstanding talking picture'?
2 Which movie classic was remade in the 1950s as *You Can't Run Away From It*?
3 Who won the first ever posthumous Oscar for *Gone With the Wind*?
4 Which studio made the original *King Kong*?
5 Which dance was Fred Astaire and Ginger Rogers' first together on screen?
6 For which movie did James Stewart receive his first Oscar nomination?
7 Which song was Oscar nominated in the Fred Astaire/Ginger Rogers musical of 1935?
8 Which gossip columnist asked for the withdrawal of the movie *Citizen Kane* because its main character bore a passing resemblance to her boss?
9 After being banned for six years, which category of censorship did *The Outlaw* have on its UK release?
10 What was the name of the prostitute played by Ingrid Bergman in *Dr Jekyll & Mr Hyde*?
11 In which movie did Bogart say, "I'm the only cause I'm interested in."?
12 To which studio did George M Cohan sell the movie rights of his life story?
13 Which piece of music ends the movie *Mrs Miniver*?
14 To the nearest 10 minutes how long did *The Wizard of Oz* last?
15 Which leader banned the Marx Brothers' *Duck Soup*?
16 Who plays Judy Garland's mother in *Meet Me in St Louis*?
17 Where is the setting for Lauren Bacall's screen debut?
18 Whose composition accompanied Mickey Mouse's broomstick dance in *Fantasia*?
19 Who was the voice of Snow White in Disney's classic?
20 To who or what did Cary Grant sing "I Can't Give You Anything But Love" in *Bringing Up Baby*?
21 Why does Trevor Howard first assist Celia Johnson in *Brief Encounter*?
22 Where does the climax of the UK's first talkie take place?
23 Who won the only Oscar for *Key Largo*?
24 What was Hitchcock's favourite of his British movies?
25 Which skier was the third screen Tarzan?
26 Who played the fuddy duddy professor in the movie which made Dietrich a star?
27 Whose play was the movie *Harvey* based on?
28 Who was Charlie Chaplin's co star in his last silent movie?
29 Who was Katharine Hepburn's character in *The African Queen*?
30 How old was Elizabeth Taylor when she first kissed Montgomery Clift on screen?

POT LUCK 7 See quiz 16, page 200

1 Switzerland. 2 Haltemprice. 3 Pink Floyd. 4 Warner Brothers. 5 59.4. 6 Everton.
7 Freshwater angling. 8 Canada. 9 Scottish. 10 DDT. 11 "Crazy". 12 1972.
13 *Cabaret*. 14 Jim Davidson. 15 Joanna Lumley. 16 Tim Henman. 17 Japan.
18 Grapes. 19 David Dundas. 20 Winston Churchill. 21 Bruce Willis and Demi Moore.
22 Canada/USA. 23 Venus. 24 *The Accidental Tourist*. 25 Thames. 26 "Going For Gold".
27 Sir Thomas Cullinan, superintendent at Premier Mine. 28 Paris. 29 IMF. 30 Tipp-Ex.

ANSWERS

QUIZ 15 THE 20TH CENTURY 1900–1950

Answers - see Quiz 13, page 197

1 Which store inaugurated supermarket trolleys in 1937?
2 Where was the first speaking clock revealed?
3 In which year did the World Bank open?
4 Who discovered the most recently discovered planet?
5 What was the codename of the bomb which was dropped on Hiroshima?
6 Why was Jean Murray's birth near Wigan in 1948 memorable?
7 In 1942 women were allowed to enter the Vatican without wearing what?
8 In which month was the *Beano* first published?
9 In which UK resort was the first international beauty contest held?
10 When did Coca Cola go on sale in Britain?
11 What was the name of the first pilot killed in warfare?
12 In 1914 Miss Allen and Miss Harburn became the first what?
13 Where was Britain's first crematorium opened?
14 What was the female equivalent of the Hitler Youth called?
15 Which lifeboat did "Titanic" survivor Millvina Dean take when she escaped from the doomed ship aged nine weeks?
16 Who joined the Axis Powers after signing the Anti Comintern Pact?
17 Who first isolated insulin?
18 What was the first name of the Duchess of Windsor's second husband?
19 Britain's first woman MP represented which constituency?
20 The Hoare Laval pact allowed the annexation of which country?
21 Who abdicated as Vietnamese Emperor at the end of WWII?
22 Who developed the *The Man Who ...* cartoons?
23 Who was Minister of Aircraft Production in Winston Churchill's wartime Cabinet?
24 Who was the first head of Israel's Herut Party?
25 Which pioneer town planner drew up plans for green belts in the The Great London Plan of 1935?
26 Who was Foreign Secretary during WWI?
27 Who in her capacity as Oriental Secretary to the British High Commissioner helped negotiate the independence of Iraq in the early 1920s?
28 Where was Israel's first Prime Minister born?
29 Who was Vanessa Bell's famous younger sister?
30 Dying in 1931, how many inventions had Thomas Edison patented in his lifetime?

POT LUCK 6 *See quiz 13, page 197*

1 Blur. 2 1948. 3 Surbiton. 4 Widow sacrifice. 5 Popes. 6 "Dancing Queen". 7 I.
8 Malcolm Rifkind. 9 Cameroon. 10 Golf's British Open. 11 Ronald Reagan.
12 White. 13 Tobacco smoke. 14 George Harrison. 15 Milk Snatcher. 16 1950.
17 Peter. 18 "Rhythm Is A Mystery". 19 12. 20 Italy. 21 Seven years.
22 West Germany. 23 12th. 24 China. 25 18th. 26 Midge Ure. 27 Hydrogen.
28 "Gipsy Moth IV". 29 Fred Karno. 30 Hopes.

ANSWERS

QUIZ 16 POT LUCK 7

Answers - see Quiz 14, page 198

1 In which country would you watch Servette play a home soccer match?
2 Which constituency did MP Alan B'Stard's represent in TV's *The New Statesman*?
3 *Atom Heart Mother* was the first album to top the UK charts by which long lasting group?
4 Which film studio released the first talking film?
5 Roger Bannister's first sub four minute mile was recorded at 3 minutes and how many seconds?
6 Which club did Mark Hughes join when he left Chelsea?
7 In which sport has Bob Nudd been world champion?
8 Which Commonwealth country was the first to issue a special Christmas stamp?
9 What was the nationality of the first manager to win the European Cup with an English club?
10 Which initials are linked to the discovery by Paul Muller?
11 What was the first top ten hit for Seal?
12 When was the last manned moon landing of the last century?
13 Which musical is based on the writing of Christopher Isherwood?
14 TV presenter Alison Holloway became the third wife of which comic?
15 *Stare Back and Smile* was the autobiography of which actress?
16 Who was the first winner on Wimbledon's new No 1 court in the 1990s?
17 In which country is the city of Nara?
18 Concord and Louise Bonne are both types of what?
19 Whose one and only UK top ten hit was "Jeans On"?
20 Who was Queen Elizabeth II's first Prime Minister?
21 Which married couple acted together in *Mortal Thoughts*?
22 Which two countries share the world's longest frontier?
23 Which planet's day is actually longer than its year?
24 For which film did Geena Davis first win an Oscar?
25 Over which river did pioneering aviator Amy Johnson disappear?
26 What was the first top ten hit for Shed Seven?
27 Who or what was the fabulous Cullinan Diamond named after?
28 The first solo transatlantic flight started in New York but where did it finish?
29 Usually known by its initials, what was set up at The Bretton Wood Agreement of 1944?
30 Which office item was registered by Wolfgang Dabisch in 1962?

MOVIE CLASSICS See quiz 14, page 198

ANSWERS
1 Warner Bros. 2 *It Happened One Night.* 3 Writer Sidney Howard. 4 RKO. 5 Carioca.
6 *Mr Smith Goes to Washington.* 7 "Cheek to Cheek" (*Top Hat*). 8 Louella Parsons. 9 U.
10 Ivy Patterson. 11 *Casablanca.* 12 Warner Bros. 13 "Land of Hope & Glory". 14 101.
15 Benito Mussolini. 16 Mary Astor. 17 Martinique (*To Have & Have Not*). 18 Paul Dukas.
19 Adriana Caselotti. 20 Katharine Hepburn's pet leopard. 21 She has grit in her eye.
22 British Museum (*Blackmail*). 23 Claire Trevor. 24 *39 Steps.* 25 Lex Barker.
26 Emil Jannings. 27 Mary Chase. 28 Paulette Goddard. 29 Rose Sayer. 30 17.

QUIZ 17 TV TRIVIA

Answers - see Quiz 19, page 203

1 What was the last answer Judith Keppel gave to win a million on *Who Wants To Be A Millionaire?*?
2 Who was *The Flying Gardener*?
3 Who hosted the US version of *Who Wants To Be A Millionaire?*?
4 How many World Cups had there been before the first one was broadcast in colour?
5 Who presented the BBC's *10 O'Clock News* on September 11th 2001?
6 In which series did Tricky Woo appear?
7 In what type of programmes would Charlotte Uhlenbroek be most likely to appear?
8 What was the first, unsuccessful, spin off of *Baywatch*?
9 Who was the first woman sports presenter on Independent Television?
10 Which character won his actor the highest fee per episode for a TV series?
11 In 1999 who had a TV special called *Just For You*?
12 Which famous football commentator died the same day that England had their memorable World Cup qualifying win over Germany?
13 What is the name of the surgery where Will Preston and Jack Kerruish have worked?
14 With which celebrity golfer did Tiger Woods appear on US TV aged two?
15 Who was the first US President veteran interviewer Barbara Walters interviewed?
16 Which husband and wife presented the Channel 4 programme, *Top Ten TV: Lovers*?
17 How long did the Saturday morning show *Live & Kicking* run?
18 How much was the total prize money on the exploitation show with Ulrika Jonsson?
19 Who was the BBC Sports Personality the Year in 1998?
20 Which of Dennis Potter's dramas was the first he directed himself?
21 What was Britain's first daily TV quiz?
22 What had Giles aka "Watcher" in the series with Sarah Michelle Gellar advertised on UK TV?
23 About which series did a cast member say, "When the show got to No 1, I decided it could only be because none of us wears a bra."?
24 Who were the first Dalziel & Pascoe on TV?
25 What was the name of the company in the US comedy *Designing Women*?
26 What did Richard Arnold look at on GMTV?
27 Which show received the first National Television Award for Comedy?
28 Who wrote the novels on which Lloyd & Hill was based?
29 What was the occupation of the second person to win a million on *Who Wants To Be A Millionaire?*?
30 Who launched the first Pay TV system?

QUIZ 18 POT LUCK 8

Answers - see Quiz 20, page 204

1 What is another name for tungsten?
2 In the Watergate scandal, the Republican Committee to Re elect the President was known as what?
3 Which city was capital of Spain before Madrid?
4 What does a herpetologist study?
5 What type of fruit features in the title of a Chekhov play?
6 Coffee is named after the city of Kaffa in which country?
7 Against orders, what is Epimethius supposed to have opened?
8 Which present day place in the East of England was the centre of the ancient kingdom of Lindsey?
9 Who sailed in "Lively Lady"?
10 What did John Speke and James Grant discover in the 19th century?
11 In Da Vinci's masterpiece the Mona Lisa in which direction is the lady looking?
12 How many titles did Jimmy Connors win in his tennis career?
13 What is the most number of letters in the name of any one calendar month?
14 How many storeys are there in the Empire State Building?
15 Who was the world's richest self made millionaire at the end of the old millennium?
16 Which country did Scotsman Robert Louis Stevenson die in?
17 In which country would you watch Brann playing Bryne at soccer?
18 In the stage farce, where did Charley's Aunt come from?
19 Which of the Beatles has the same name as the patentor of the dental drill?
20 Who wrote An Accidental MP?
21 A liaison with which Donna ended Gary Hart's push to be a US presidential nominee?
22 In 1984 WPC Yvonne Fletcher was shot outside which London Embassy?
23 Who was the first US President to make a visit to China?
24 The first rugby union player to score 50 international tries played for which country?
25 How was Baron Home of the Hirsel known when he was British Prime Minister?
26 What was the first album to make its debut at No 1 in the UK chart?
27 Who was the last British Royal to visit Hong Kong while it was under British rule?
28 Who did Mehmet Ali Agca try to assassinate in 1981?
29 What was the first top ten hit for Simple Minds?
30 In which country would you watch Petrolul playing Astra at soccer?

MUSIC CHARTS See quiz 20, page 204

1 "The Way I Am". 2 "Never Had a Dream Come True". 3 "Bills, Bills, Bills". 4 Oasis.
5 "Written in the Stars". 6 "Summertime of Our Lives". 7 "Wishing I Was Lucky".
8 Arsenal. 9 One week. 10 "Deeper Shade of Blue". 11 "Bohemian Rhapsody".
12 "War of Nerves". 13 Five and Queen. 14 Hercules. 15 Billie. 16 Madison Avenue.
17 Samantha Fox. 18 "Gangster Trippin'". 19 E-17. 20 "Tsunami". 21 Six.
22 Rolf Harris. 23 Westlife. 24 Des O'Connor. 25 "Fairytale of New York". 26 Six.
27 Manchester United. 28 12. 29 "Even After All". 30 "When Doves Cry".

QUIZ 19 ANIMALS

Answers - see Quiz 17, page 201

1 What is the second largest species of fish?
2 What type of animals were space travellers Sam and Miss Sam?
3 Which animals spends the largest amount of time asleep?
4 Who first named the gorilla?
5 Which usually weighs the most – a bison, a moose or a polar bear?
6 What are Pacific leatherbacks and Atlantic leatherbacks?
7 Which of these swims the fastest – marlin, sailfish or swordfish?
8 Kittis's hognosed bat is native to which country?
9 What is Rhincodon typus?
10 The devil's hole pupfish restricts its habitat to an isolated part of which US state?
11 What is a Ruppell's griffon?
12 What has the highest reproductive rate of all marsupials?
13 What is another name for the colugo?
14 Approximately how many domestic breeds of dog are there?
15 What is the most socially organised member of the cat family?
16 Which is the largest – giant African snail, giant clam or giant squid?
17 Which creature is unique in its ability to penetrate the quills of a porcupine?
18 What is the only truly amphibious member of the weasel family?
19 The skunk is a major carrier of which disease?
20 The greatest number of feathers counted on a bird was on a what?
21 Which is the largest of the toothed whales?
22 What is the smallest of the Ratitae order?
23 Which flies the fastest – mallard, pintail or teal?
24 Which sense does the Old World vulture lack?
25 What is the most beautiful part of the bulbul?
26 What does the tuatara have on top of its head?
27 What is the only marsupial which specialises in burrowing?
28 Where is the Bolson tortoise native to?
29 What is the San Joaquin leopard lizard also known as?
30 What is the largest living rodent?

ANSWERS

TV TRIVIA *See quiz 17, page 201*
1 Henry II. 2 Chris Beardshaw. 3 Regis Philbin. 4 Eight. 5 Peter Sissons.
6 *All Creatures Great and Small.* 7 *Wildlife.* 8 *Baywatch Nights.* 9 Rachel Heyhoe-Flint.
10 Dr Mark Greene (*ER*). 11 Boyzone. 12 Brian Moore. 13 The Beeches.
14 Bob Hope. 15 Richard Nixon. 16 Paul Daniels and Debbie McGee. 17 8 years.
18 £10,000. 19 Lennox Lewis. 20 *Blackeyes.* 21 *Blockbusters.* 22 Nescafe.
23 *Charlie's Angels.* 24 Hale & Pace. 25 Sugarbakers. 26 TV. 27 *Men Behaving Badly.*
28 Jill McGown. 29 Teacher. 30 Zenith Radio Corp.

QUIZ 20 MUSIC CHARTS

Answers - see Quiz 18, page 202

1 What was Eminem's chart success between his first two UK No 1s?
2 What was SClub7's second No 1 which went straight to the top spot?
3 What was Beyonce Knowles' band's first US No 1?
4 Which chart topping band's line up has included Tony McCarroll and Gem Archer?
5 What was LeAnn Rimes' first UK hit with another artist?
6 What was A1's follow up to their UK chart debut?
7 Their biggest hit was "Love is All Around" in 1994, what was their first?
8 Which soccer side charted with "Hot Stuff"?
9 For how long was the NME chart a Top 25?
10 What was Steps' first Top Ten hit of the new millennium?
11 Which classic single topped the chart when Mel C was born?
12 What was All Saints' last hit of the 1990s?
13 With whom did "We Will Rock You" first chart?
14 From which movie was Stephen Gately's solo chart debut?
15 Who was the first lady to top the charts three times before being able to vote in the UK?
16 How are chart toppers Andy Van Dorsselaer and Cheyne Coates better known?
17 Who was the only British female to have three US & UK Top Ten singles in the 1980s?
18 What was Fatboy Slim's second single to enter the UK Top Ten?
19 What did Brian Harvey's band change their name to on their return to the charts in 1998?
20 What was the Manic Street Preachers' last hit of the 1990s?
21 What was Mansun's last 1990s hit to have a number in the title?
22 Who had the final chart topper of the 1960s?
23 Which was the first band to have four UK No1's in a single year?
24 Who had a Top Twenty hit in 1969 with "Dick A Dum Dum"?
25 What was the Pogues' follow-up to their first Top Ten hit?
26 How many Top Ten hits did Ocean Colour Scene have in a row in the 1990s?
27 Whose last hit of the 1990s was "Move Move Move"?
28 How many successive Top Twenty singles did Prodigy have by the end of the millennium?
29 What was Finley Quaye's first Top Ten single?
30 Which single was Prince's most successful before "Purple Rain"?

QUIZ 21 POT LUCK 9

Answers - see Quiz 23, page 207

1 What is named after Benjamin Hall?
2 Before making it big as a solo singer who wrote "I'm A Believer" for The Monkees?
3 What is the name for a sentence containing all the letters of the alphabet?
4 How many of the first five letters of Singapore appear on the international car index mark for a car from that country?
5 The time it takes a planet to orbit the sun is called what?
6 What was David Kane's follow up movie to *This Year's Love*?
7 In which decade of last century did Fiji leave the Commonwealth?
8 Which US state has a capital bearing the name of 15th-century explorer Christopher?
9 *Girls On Film* was the first Top Ten hit for which group?
10 A fear of dust is known as what?
11 Which Marc Bolan song features on the soundtrack of *Moulin Rouge*?
12 In which decade did Barbra Streisand first make the UK top 20 charts with a single?
13 What does the musical notation 'pesante' mean – heavy and ponderous, unaffected or lively?
14 Who was the Greek goddess of victory?
15 In which month is Canada Day celebrated?
16 Who wrote the score for the blockbusting movie *Jaws*?
17 In which city did the first Cruft's dog show take place?
18 To the nearest ten, how many minutes did the audience have to scream during the first *Scream* movie?
19 What did Melville Bissell patent in 1881?
20 What was the first film Tom Cruise and Nicole Kidman starred in after their marriage?
21 In which decade was the Brazilian Grand Prix first held?
22 Who coined the name vaccination?
23 In which European country was the leader shot with his wife in December 1989?
24 On which label did Vengaboys first make No 1 – Positiva, Outpost or Skint?
25 The old London Bridge was dismantled, transported and rebuilt in which US state?
26 As a fully grown male which weighs the most – a baboon a mandrill or a proboscis monkey?
27 Which Elvis Presley movie featured the song "Return to Sender"?
28 What was the occupation of John Dunlop of tyre fame?
29 In song lyrics, what – according to Buggles – "Killed the Radio Star"?
30 Which famous artist once said of his work that, "I draw like a child."?

POT LUCK 10 See quiz 23, page 207
ANSWERS
1 Dr Crippen. 2 54. 3 Richard Nixon. 4 Norman Tebbit. 5 Simon. 6 Tenerife.
7 Winchester. 8 *Blue Peter*. 9 Shropshire. 10 200m and 800m. 11 Three.
12 20. 13 "Bohemian Rhapsody". 14 *Face Value*. 15 DeForest. 16 Venezuela.
17 *Goodbye Yellow Brick Road*. 18 1975. 19 Katharine Hepburn. 20 Simian Films.
21 1666. 22 Kenya. 23 Madonna. 24 Belgium. 25 Nobel prizes. 26 Harry James.
27 Jack Ruby. 28 George I. 29 1974. 30 "Vincent".

QUIZ 22 EUROPEAN TRAVEL

Answers - see Quiz 24, page 208

1 Which is the largest province of the country which has Madrid as its capital?
2 Which building houses the Bayeux Tapestry?
3 Cadiz has a ferry link with which location which shares its name with a film title?
4 In which department of Basse Normandie is the village where the famous soft cheese is made?
5 Where are the Bakony Mountains?
6 Where is Switzerland's oldest university?
7 What is Europe's most southerly point?
8 Which country is to the immediate north of the Ukraine?
9 In which Sea are Gotland and Oland?
10 Which language is Euskara?
11 Which city is the burial place of William the Conqueror and Beau Brummel?
12 Which Austrian city was known as Thermae Helveticae to the Romans?
13 Anjou is now part of which French departement?
14 In Austria what is the Fohn?
15 The Campine coalfield is to the east of which country?
16 Which country is to the immediate south of Croatia?
17 Where is the Jotunheimen range of mountains?
18 Which Italian port takes its name from the Greek for elbow?
19 Which language is spoken in Wallonia?
20 What is the capital of Brabant?
21 How many countries border the Federal Republic of Germany?
22 Which country is to the north of Slovakia?
23 What is the currency of Slovenia?
24 What is the capital of the German province to the south of Brandenburg?
25 What is the capital of the province to the west of Abruzzio?
26 In which country are the Pripet Marshes?
27 Which river bisects Andorra?
28 Who designed the Finlandia Concert Hall in Helsinki?
29 In which mountain range is Europe's highest peak?
30 Of the ten largest cities in Europe which three were once part of the Soviet Union?

UNFORGETTABLES See quiz 24, page 208

ANSWERS

1 Brian Jones and Jim Morrison. 2 Lake Tanganyika. 3 13 years. 4 331. 5 Somalia.
6 Montserrat Caballe. 7 Hotel de la Reine. 8 Martha Washington. 9 Victor Gollancz.
10 John Reed. 11 Mrs Ronald Reagan. 12 Bernard Herrmann. 13 Dashiel Hammett.
14 Rex Harrison. 15 Alexander Graham Bell. 16 Marty Melcher. 17 19 May.
18 Three. 19 Agatha Christie. 20 Elizabeth Arden. 21 Clement Attlee. 22 Doctor.
23 Giles Gilbert Scott. 24 Leonard. 25 Bertrand Russell. 26 Jennifer Jones.
27 Where's the Bourbon?. 28 John Paul II. 29 Alfred Hitchcock. 30 Frankie Howerd.

QUIZ 23 POT LUCK 10

Answers - see Quiz 21, page 205

1 Which villain had a mistress called Ethel Le Neve?
2 How old was Lester Piggott when he made his return to racing in 1990?
3 Who was the first US President to visit the USSR?
4 Which Norman said his father "got on his bike and looked for work."?
5 Who was named as being in The Chipmunks along with Alvin and Theodore?
6 On which island were 583 people killed in a 1970s air disaster?
7 Where is Britain's longest cathedral?
8 Leila Williams was the first female presenter of which long running TV show?
9 In which English county was the world's first iron bridge built?
10 100m hurdles and which two other track events are included in the World Championship women's heptathlon?
11 How many of Henry VIII's children followed him to the throne?
12 How old was Mike Tyson when he became boxing's youngest ever heavyweight world champion?
13 Which hit was the first single to be No 1 over two separate Christmasses?
14 What was the first solo No 1 album for Phil Collins?
15 What was the middle name of Humphrey Bogart?
16 In which country is the city of Maracay?
17 Elton John's original "Candle In the Wind" first featured on which album?
18 In what year did Charlie Chaplin eventually receive a knighthood?
19 Ludlow Ogden married which famous Hollywood actress?
20 Which production company was set up by Hugh Grant and Liz Hurley?
21 In which year was fire insurance first pioneered in London – was it 1666, 1812 or 1914?
22 In which country was Mau Mau a nationalist movement?
23 Stephen Bray and Patrick Leonard have both co-written No 1 singles with which solo singer?
24 In which country did the Battle of Passchendaele take place?
25 Which prizes were first awarded in 1901?
26 Which bandleader did Betty Grable marry in 1943?
27 Involved in a famous 20th century murder how was Jacob Rubinstein better known?
28 Which English king could not speak English?
29 In which year was Juan Peron – of *Evita* fame – last in office as President of Argentina?
30 Don McLean's *American Pie* album featured which song that he took to No 1 as a UK single?

QUIZ 24 UNFORGETTABLES

Answers - see Quiz 22, page 206

1. Which two major rock stars died on 3 July, one in 1969 one in 1971?
2. Where did Henry Stanley say, "Dr Livingstone I presume."?
3. For how long were Napoleon and Josephine married?
4. How many weekly radio addresses did Ronald Reagan make to the American people?
5. Which country did Audrey Hepburn visit as a UNICEF Ambassador shortly before her death?
6. Which opera star was born on the late Maria Callas's 10th birthday?
7. In which hotel did John Lennon and Yoko Ono have their famous 'bed in'?
8. Who was the first First Lady of the USA – although the actual phrase had yet to be coined?
9. Which publisher founded the charity War On Want?
10. Who was the first American to be buried in the Kremlin?
11. What was the actress born Anne Frances Robbins most famous married name?
12. To whom did Martin Scorsese dedicate *Taxi Driver*?
13. Which novelist investigated the Fatty Arbuckle assault case when working for the Pinkerton Detective Agency?
14. Which much married actor edited the anthology of romantic poems *If Love Be Love*?
15. Who said on 10th March 1876, "Come here, Watson, I want you."?
16. Which of Doris Day's husbands embezzled her entire life's earnings?
17. On what date did Marilyn Monroe famously sing "Happy Birthday" to John F Kennedy?
18. How many No 1 singles did Roy Orbison achieve in the UK during his lifetime?
19. Mary Westmacott is also known as whom?
20. How is cosmetics queen Florence Nightingale Graham better known?
21. Who was the first Labour PM to have an absolute majority in House of Commons?
22. What was the occupation of the first independent President of Malawi?
23. Who designed Battersea Power Station?
24. What is the first name of Baron Callaghan of Cardiff?
25. Who was the first president of CND?
26. Who was the widow of the producer of *Gone With the Wind*?
27. What was Marilyn Monroe's only line of dialogue in the scene which took 59 takes in *Some Like It Hot*?
28. Who was the youngest Pope of the 20th century?
29. Which film director married Alma Reville?
30. Which late comedian's autobiography was called *On My Way I Lost It*?

EUROPEAN TRAVEL See quiz 22, page 206

ANSWERS
1 Badajoz. 2 William the Conqueror Cultural Centre. 3 Casablanca. 4 Orne.
5 Hungary. 6 Basle. 7 Tarifa Point. 8 Belarus. 9 Baltic. 10 Basque. 11 Caen.
12 Baden. 13 Maine et Loire. 14 Wind. 15 Belgium. 16 Bosnia Herzegovina.
17 Norway. 18 Ancona. 19 French. 20 Brussels. 21 Nine. 22 Poland. 23 Tolar.
24 Dresden. 25 Rome. 26 Belarus. 27 Valira. 28 Alvar Aalto. 29 Caucasus.
30 Moscow, St Petersburg and Kiev.

QUIZ 25 POT LUCK 11

Answers - see Quiz 27, page 211

1 Who wrote Blondie's 1999 chart topper "Maria"?
2 *Tenko* was a popular TV series but what does Tenko mean?
3 The first ever programme of *Top of the Pops* was broadcast from which city?
4 Ed Koch is a former mayor of which American city?
5 What is the nationality of actor William Shatner famous as Captain Kirk?
6 What's the job of Jack Nicholson's character in the movie *Wolf*?
7 In which country is the city of Sorocaba?
8 What was the first top ten hit for Wilson Phillips?
9 On which special day did Dirty Den serve divorce papers on Angie in *EastEnders*?
10 In which department did TV MP Jim Hacker first become a minister?
11 In 1995 which visiting side became the first team in 22 years to win a Test series in the West Indies?
12 What did the letter K stand for in the film company name RKO?
13 What was the first name of the late classically trained actor John Gielgud?
14 Joseph Merlin invented what kind of sporting footwear?
15 Who as a youngster was brought up in disguise in Smallville, USA?
16 In which county did The Great Train Robbery take place?
17 How many neck bones does a giraffe have?
18 Who presented the Rugby World Cup to Francois Pienaar in 1995?
19 Which religious movement was founded by Mary Baker Eddy?
20 What was singer songwriter Hoagy Carmichael's real first name?
21 Which Kenneth devised the London stage sex revue *Oh, Calcutta*?
22 Ray Harford managed Fulham and Blackburn Rovers in that order, but who managed Blackburn Rovers and then Fulham?
23 Kim Campbell was the first woman PM of which country?
24 According to a Henry Kissinger quote what was "the ultimate aphrodisiac."?
25 Elizabeth Garrett Anderson is recognised as being the first British woman to carry out which profession?
26 Which Mike broke Bob Beaman's 23 year long jump record in 1992?
27 Which boxer coached actor Daniel Day-Lewis for his role in *The Boxer*?
28 In which country was escapologist Houdini born?
29 Johann Christophe Denner invented which musical instrument?
30 In which year did Yasser Arafat became PLO chairman?

POT LUCK 12 *See quiz 27, page 211*
1 Dundalk. 2 May. 3 Invincible (adamas). 4 EF Schumacher. 5 Root.
6 Isabella Rossellini. 7 Cuban missile. 8 Ibadan. 9 Fidel Castro. 10 Stephen Dorrell.
11 *The Blue Room*. 12 University College. 13 The Absinthe Fairy. 14 *Private Lives*.
15 Lotte Lenya. 16 Leprosy. 17 Texas. 18 Iberus (hence Iberia) 19 Capricorn.
20 William Rogers. 21 Primo Levi. 22 His mother (Statue of Liberty). 23 Iraq.
24 Steven Spielberg. 25 Margot. 26 Valerie. 27 "What hath God wrought?".
28 Platform shoes. 29 Nancy Griffith. 30 Royal Exchange.

QUIZ 26 MOVIE WHO'S WHO?

Answers - see Quiz 28, page 212

1 Which film director was born on Betty Grable's 31st birthday?
2 Which wife of Robert De Niro appeared in *New York New York*?
3 What is the real name of the actress who played the title role in *Octopussy*?
4 Which role did Lorraine Bracco play in *Goodfellas*?
5 Which pseudonym did Kim Basinger use when she performed as a solo singer in her early career?
6 For which of his movies did Nicolas Cage reputedly swallow a live cockroach?
7 Who was the fourth movie *Batman*?
8 Who traditionally sings the US National Anthem at each season's first home game of baseball team the New York Mets?
9 Who wrote the lyrics for the theme song of the 1960s film *Georgy Girl*?
10 Who was the big screen's first nude Lady Macbeth?
11 Who was known in France as "le sacre monstre"?
12 Which actor competes in rodeo competitions as "The Jewish Cowboy"?
13 Which actress was president of Actors Equity in the US between 1982 and 1985?
14 Who owns the production company TIG?
15 Which star of *Drugstore Cowboy* is a grand nephew of the creator of Flash Gordon?
16 Which profession did the director of *If* play in *Chariots of Fire*?
17 What was Daniel Day Lewis's very first movie at the age of 14?
18 Who set up a production company called Tribeca Films?
19 Whose production company was called Memorial Enterprises?
20 Who was Carrie Fisher's first step mother?
21 Which of the Gabor sisters was the first to move to the US?
22 Which leader did Anthony Hopkins play in *Victory At Entebbe*?
23 What was Jodie Foster's second movie as director?
24 Who prefaced his first book with, "This book is for people who like movies."?
25 John Huston died during the making of which film, due to be directed by his son?
26 Who did Kirstie Alley play in her debut movie?
27 Which star of *The Exorcist* competed in equestrian events as Martha McDonald?
28 What was Bob Hoskins' next film after his first Oscar nomination?
29 Joel and Ethan Coen are said to have written *Raising Arizona* with which actress in mind?
30 Famous daughter Anjelica Huston played opposite the son of which General in *A Walk With Love and Death*?

SPORTING LEGENDS *See quiz 28, page 212*

1 Seven. 2 Reggie Jackson. 3 24. 4 Arnold Palmer. 5 13. 6 Elizabeth Ryan. 7 1966.
8 Seoul (Krisztina Egerszegi). 9 Backstroke. 10 Philippe Sella. 11 112.
12 Tiger Woods. 13 Bruce Sheldon. 14 Gary Player. 15 Natalie Tauziat.
16 Tuberculosis. 17 1959. 18 Brooklyn Dodgers. 19 Merlin Olsen. 20 Nick Faldo.
21 Wimbledon. 22 Liz McColgan. 23 Seamus McDonagh. 24 Billie Jean King.
25 Marvin Hart. 26 Huddersfield. 27 Sabatini. 28 Walter Hagen. 29 Mike Tyson.
30 Knocked overboard on his yacht.

QUIZ 27 POT LUCK 12

Answers - see Quiz 25, page 209

1 Which town do The Corrs hail from?
2 In which month was Britain's first official bank holiday?
3 The word diamond comes from a Greek word meaning what?
4 Who wrote *Small is Beautiful* which stresses that people should come first?
5 What part of the plant does phylloxera vitifoliae attack?
6 Which actress lost her Lancome contract around her 40th birthday?
7 During which crisis did a US politician comment, "We're eyeball to eyeball and I think the other fellow just blinked."?
8 What is the second largest city of Nigeria?
9 Which world leader was excommunicated in 1962?
10 Who was health secretary when the link between BSE and CJD was first admitted?
11 In which play did Elle Macpherson make her stage debut?
12 What is the oldest Oxford college?
13 Which role did the singer of the No 1 "Can't Get You Out of My Head" play in *Moulin Rouge*?
14 In which play did Noel Coward write, "Very flat, Norfolk."?
15 How was the actress and singer Karoline Blamauer better known?
16 What is another name for Hansen's disease?
17 Alaska replaced which state as the USA's largest?
18 What was the Roman name for the River Ebro?
19 What is Mel Gibson's star sign?
20 Which male founder of the SDP had the surname nearest the end of the alphabet?
21 Who recounted his experiences in Auschwitz in *If This is a Man*?
22 Who did FA Bartholdi use as a model for his most famous sculpture?
23 The ancient civilisation of Sumeria is now in which country?
24 Who directed the movie about Gigolo Joe, a robot boy and his teddy bear?
25 What was Anne Frank's older sister called?
26 What was the first name of TS Eliot's widow?
27 What was the first message transmitted by telegraph?
28 What were buskins?
29 Who made the album *Clock Without Hands*?
30 What was the Stock Exchange called when it was first founded?

ANSWERS

POT LUCK 11 *See quiz 25, page 209*
1 Jimmy Destri. 2 Roll call. 3 Manchester. 4 New York. 5 Canadian. 6 Book editor.
7 Brazil. 8 "Hold On". 9 Christmas Day. 10 Administrative Affairs. 11 Australia.
12 Keith. 13 Arthur. 14 Roller skate. 15 Superman. 16 Bedfordshire. 17 Seven.
18 Nelson Mandela. 19 Christian Science. 20 Hoagland. 21 Tynan. 22 Don Mackay.
23 Canada. 24 Power. 25 Doctor. 26 Powell. 27 Barry McGuigan. 28 Hungary.
29 Clarinet. 30 1968.

QUIZ 28 SPORTING LEGENDS

Answers - see Quiz 26, page 210

1 How many times did Jaden Gil Agassi's mum win Wimbledon?
2 Who was the second man, after Babe Ruth, to hit three home runs in one baseball World Series game?
3 For how many years was Matt Busby boss of Manchester United?
4 Who won golf's British Open in its centenary year?
5 How many conversions were among the Six Nations Championship record-breaking total of 35 points Jonny Wilkinson scored at Twickenham in February 2001?
6 Who died on the day that Billie Jean King beat her Wimbledon title record?
7 When did Jack Nicklaus win his third US Masters?
8 Where did the world's most successful Olympic woman swimmer win gold first?
9 Which of backstroke, butterfly or freestyle did Mark Spitz not swim at Munich in 1972?
10 Who won a record 111 international caps for Rugby between 1982 and 1995?
11 How many games were played in Wimbledon's longest match?
12 Who did Nick Faldo hand a green jacket to in April 1997 in Georgia?
13 Who did Mike Tyson beat to win his third world heavyweight championship?
14 Who was the first US Open golf winner to be neither British nor American?
15 Against whom did Jana Novotna play her third Wimbledon Singles Final of the 1990s?
16 Harry Vardon won two British Open golf titles after contracting which illness?
17 Which was Pele's most successful individual year as a goalscorer?
18 Against who did New York Yankees pitcher Don Larson pitch a World Series perfect game?
19 Who completed the Los Angeles Rams' 'Fearsome Foursome' along with Deacon Jones, Lamarr Lundy and Roosevelt Grier?
20 Outside the USA which individual holds the record for most Ryder Cup wins?
21 Of her 24 Grand Slam titles which did Margaret Court win the least?
22 Who was the only female BBC Sports Personality of the Year in the 1990s?
23 Who did Evander Holyfield beat in his first win by a knock out in the 1990s?
24 Who was the first president of the WTA?
25 Who won the first 20th century heavyweight boxing championship to be stopped?
26 For which team did Albert Rosenfield score his record 80 Rugby League tries in 1914?
27 Who did Steffi Graf beat to win her first Wimbledon Singles title of the 1990s?
28 Jack Nicklaus holds the record for most US PGA titles with which golfer?
29 Which boxer was born on the same day, several years later, that Superman first put in an appearance?
30 How did Eric Tabarly meet his death?

MOVIE WHO'S WHO? *See quiz 26, page 210*

1 Steven Spielberg. 2 Diahnne Abbott. 3 Maude Wikstrum. 4 Karen Hill. 5 Chelsea.
6 *Vampire's Kiss.* 7 George Clooney. 8 Glenn Close. 9 Francesca Annis. 10 Jim Dale.
11 Charles Bronson. 12 James Caan. 13 Ellen Burstyn.. 14 Kevin Costner.
15 Matt Dillon. 16 Schoolmaster (Lindsay Anderson). 17 *Sunday Bloody Sunday.*
18 Robert De Niro. 19 Albert Finney. 20 Elizabeth Taylor. 21 Eva. 22 Yitzhak Rabin.
23 *Home For The Holidays.* 24 Leslie Halliwell. 25 Mr North. 26 Lt Saavik (*Star Trek II*).
27 Linda Blair. 28 *A Prayer for the Dying.* 29 Holly Hunter. 30 Dayan.

ANSWERS

QUIZ 29 POT LUCK 13

Answers - see Quiz 31, page 215

1 Which film director said, "Not only is there no God, try getting a plumber at weekends."?
2 What was the first building in England to be illuminated by incandescent light?
3 How is Japan's Inland Sea known in Japanese?
4 Which name is the Hebrew for trickster or supplanter?
5 What was the name of the first nuclear submarine to circumnavigate the world underwater?
6 Who was the first British monarch to visit China?
7 Which were the last two imperial territories in Africa?
8 In which city was the premiere of Orson Welles first film?
9 In India, which is furthest south, Bombay, Calcutta, or Hyderabad?
10 Who developed the computer language Java?
11 Which magazine did Charles Russell found?
12 London's original Globe Theatre burned down during a performance of which Shakespeare play?
13 What did the middle initial stand for in the name of the author who wrote *Three Men in a Boat*?
14 In the UK what was the first speed limit for cars in the country as opposed to town?
15 Which 1960s Norman Jewison film won five Oscars?
16 What does the Arabic word jihad mean?
17 Which island did Columbus call St Iago?
18 Which 19th century Prime Minister was the subject of a biography written by Baron Jenkins of Hillhead after he left Parliament?
19 What was the name of the world's largest ever schooner?
20 Which Henry James novel was the subject of an opera by Benjamin Britten?
21 Who wrote the TV series *Clocking Off* and *Linda Green*?
22 With which architect did Gertrude Jekyll work?
23 Who originally had the slogan "Power to the People"?
24 Which monarch knighted Sir Winston Churchill?
25 In which US state is the George Rogers Clark National Historical Park?
26 Who reputedly said, "Die my dear doctor. That's the last thing I shall do."?
27 Which Pope excommunicated King John and declared the Magna Carta void?
28 In cars, what was the Procon Ten?
29 What did the island of Hispaniola later become?
30 Among his first five consecutive Tour de France wins, in which year did Miguel Indurain set the record for the fastest average speed?

POT LUCK 14 *See quiz 31, page 215*

1 Vermouth (Wermut). 2 Carolyn Murphy. 3 Rachel Portman. 4 Sacred ibis.
5 Marvin C Stone. 6 Madonna. 7 Pam Warren. 8 Eamonn Holmes.
9 Return of Apollo 11 from the Moon. 10 Herbert Marcuse. 11 Jo Moore. 12 Rome.
13 "Diamonds are a Girl's Best Friend". 14 Kirov. 15 Terry Venables. 16 Scott Walker.
17 Thomas Gresham. 18 Chris Smith. 19 Wasp. 20 "Resolution". 21 Claire Danes.
22 *Over The Moon*. 23 Noel Coward. 24 Cairo. 25 Martin Campbell. 26 Dith Pran.
27 Billy Crystal. 28 Albert Camus & TS Eliot. 29 The Cochran. 30 Jim Davidson.

QUIZ 30 WORLD LEADERS

Answers - see Quiz 32, page 216

1 Who did Major run against to become Tory Party leader and PM?
2 Who was the first man to be General Secretary and President of the USSR?
3 Who was Chairman of the Republican National Committee during the Watergate scandal?
4 What was Hosni Mubarak's profession before entering politics?
5 Jacques Santer became president of the European Commission after Britain's veto of whom?
6 What was the name of the autobiography of the first woman leader of a British political party?
7 Who succeeded Willy Brandt as Chancellor of West Germany?
8 Which US president won the Pulitzer Prize for *Profiles in Courage*?
9 Who was Albania's second Prime Minister in 1997?
10 Who was the first President of a united post WWII Germany?
11 Who became Israel's acting PM after the assassination of Rabin?
12 How many children did British Prime Ministers of the 1990s have between them?
13 Which Conservative Canadian politician served between Pierre Trudeau's two terms of office?
14 Who was the first British President of the EU?
15 Before becoming Pope Karol Jozef Wojtyia was Archbishop of where?
16 At which educational institution did Bill Clinton meet Hillary Rodham?
17 Which then leader won the 1969 Hobart Ocean race?
18 How was Prince Ras Tafari Makonnen better known?
19 Who was the first living ex PM of Australia not to accept the Companion to the Order of Australia after he left politics?
20 Who was President of Chile during the Falklands conflict?
21 How long after becoming German Chancellor did Hitler assume the title of Führer?
22 Who was the longest serving US President of the 1970s?
23 Which Austrian president was a former Secretary General to the UN?
24 Winston Churchill became Chancellor of the Exchequer under which PM?
25 Who succeeded Chairman Mao as Chairman of China's ruling Communist Party?
26 What was Tony Blair's first responsibility in Labour's Shadow Cabinet?
27 Who did Ronald Reagan defeat the second time he became US president?
28 Who was the last King of Greece in the 20th century?
29 Who was the second President of France's Fifth Republic?
30 Who was the first and last Executive President of the USSR?

TV ADVERTS See quiz 32, page 216

1 *1984*. 2 Mir. 3 Labi Siffre. 4 "Fly Away". 5 Michael Jackson. 6 Peter O'Toole.
7 "The Joker". 8 Clairol. 9 Frank Muir. 10 Elgar's "Cello Concerto in E Minor".
11 Halifax. 12 (Auto) Windscreens. 13 Benylin. 14 Meg Smith. 15 Penelope Keith.
16 Benecol. 17 David Ginola. 18 Paul Dukas. 19 Gieseppe Verdi. 20 Peter Sellers.
21 *Four Weddings and a Funeral*. 22 Trevor Eve. 23 Sainsbury's. 24 Lesley Dunlop.
25 Mr Oizo. 26 Neil Morrissey. 27 "Pastoral Symphony". 28 John Gordon Sinclair.
29 Cafe Noir. 30 Gibbs SR.

QUIZ 31 POT LUCK 14

Answers - see Quiz 29, page 213

1 Which wine takes its name from the German for wormwood, an early ingredient?
2 Who replaced Liz Hurley as the face of Estée Lauder?
3 Who won an Oscar for the score of *Emma*?
4 What was *Threskiornis aethiopicus*, treated as holy by the ancient Egyptians?
5 Who patented the paper drinking straw?
6 Which superstar had a Max Factor cosmetics contract for just one year?
7 Which co-winner of the Woman of the Year 2001 was a survivor of the Paddington rail crash?
8 Who is the longest serving presenter on breakfast TV?
9 When did Richard Nixon describe as, "The greatest week in the history of the world since the Creation."?
10 Who wrote *One Dimensional Man*?
11 Who sent an e mail saying it would be a good day to bury bad news the day the World Trade Center was hit?
12 Which was the world's largest city at the end of the first millennium?
13 Which song has the line, "We all lose our charms in the end."?
14 Which ballet company was called the Maryinsky until 1935?
15 Which former England football manager shares a birthday with cricketer Kapil Dev?
16 Which 60s/70 star produced Pulp's "We Love Life"?
17 Who founded what was to become the Stock Exchange?
18 Who did Tessa Jowell replace in Tony Blair's Cabinet after the 2001 election?
19 What is an ichneumon fly?
20 What was the name of the first ship to cross the Antarctic Circle?
21 Who was the voice of Princess Mononoke in the *Studio Ghibli* movie?
22 In which play did a 65+ Joan Collins star in skimpy underwear in 2001?
23 Who said, "Work is much more fun than fun."?
24 Where did the last Shah of Iran die?
25 Who directed Pierce Brosnan's first outing as 007?
26 Who is the central character in *The Killing Fields*?
27 Who produced and co wrote the 2001 movie where Julia Roberts and Catherine Zeta Jones played sisters?
28 Which two winners of a Nobel Prize for Literature both died on 4th January, one in 1960 and one in 1965?
29 What was the name of the first dishwasher?
30 Whose autobiography was called *Close to the Edge*?

POT LUCK 13 See quiz 29, page 213
1 Woody Allen. 2 Gateshead Town Hall. 3 Seto Naikai. 4 Jacob. 5 Triton.
6 Elizabeth II. 7 Mozambique & Angola. 8 New York (*Citizen Kane*). 9 Hyderabad.
10 Sun Microsystems. 11 *The Watchtower*. 12 Henry VIII. 13 Klapka. 14 4 mph.
15 *In the Heat of the Night*. 16 Holy War/Struggle. 17 Jamaica. 18 William Gladstone.
19 "Thomas W Lawson". 20 *The Turn of the Screw*. 21 Paul Abbott. 22 Edwin Lutyens.
23 Black Panthers. 24 Elizabeth II. 25 Indiana. 26 Lord Palmerston. 27 Innocent III.
28 Collapsible steering wheel. 29 Haiti. 30 His second win, 1992.

QUIZ 32 TV ADVERTS

Answers - see Quiz 30, page 214

1 The most expensive TV ad ever was based on which novel?
2 Where was the first TV ad filmed in space actually filmed?
3 Who sang the song for the 2001 ad for the Peugeot 307?
4 In 1999 which song was the first advert No 1 for three years?
5 Who was the first artist to appear in a Pepsi ad?
6 Which veteran actor appeared in the ad for Zurich insurance?
7 Which Steve Miller Band song advertised jeans?
8 Who in had the catchphrase "Does she or doesn't she?"?
9 Which writer advertised Cadbury's Fruit & Nut accompanied by music by Tchaikovsky?
10 Which music used in *Hilary & Jackie* encouraged the drinking of Buxton Spring Water?
11 Which building society fell foul of Equity for using its own employees in an ad?
12 Which part of a car is connected with the "Toreador's Song" from *Carmen*?
13 Which cough mixture was Pavarotti's 'theme song' used to advertise?
14 What was the name of the first woman to appear in a UK TV ad?
15 Which ex *Good Life* cast member became the voice behind Lurpak butter?
16 *Countdown*'s statistician extolled the virtues of which margarine?
17 Which footballer was 'worth it'?
18 Who wrote the "Sorcerer's Apprentice", used in an ad for round tea bags?
19 Whose "Requiem Mass" accompanied the virtues of Irn Bru?
20 Who was the first voice of the PG Tips chimps?
21 In which movie did one of the people who are 'worth it' appear with Hugh Grant?
22 Which actor's wife was in the famous long running Gold Blend coffee ad?
23 Which supermarket chain employs The Naked Chef?
24 Which *Where The Heart Is* star passed around the Kleenex tissues?
25 Who recorded the seventh No 1 hit to be associated with Levi jeans?
26 How was Bob the Builder seen at Homebase?
27 Which Beethoven Symphony advertised Blue Band margarine?
28 Which star of musicals and comedies is the hapless son in law to 'Sybil Fawlty'?
29 Which coffee was advertised by a French international soccer star?
30 Toothpaste was the first product advertised on UK TV – but which brand?

WORLD LEADERS See quiz 30, page 214
1 Michael Heseltine and Douglas Hurd. 2 Leonid Brezhnev. 3 George Bush Sr. 4 Pilot.
5 Jean Luc Dehaene. 6 *Margaret Thatcher:The Downing Street Years*. 7 Helmut Schmidt.
8 JF Kennedy. 9 Bashkim Fino. 10 Richard Von Weizsacker. 11 Shimon Peres.
12 Seven. 13 Joseph Clark. 14 Roy Jenkins. 15 Cracow. 15 Yale Law School.
17 Edward Heath. 18 Haile Selassie. 19 Paul Keating. 20 Augusto Pinochet. 21 A year.
22 Richard Nixon. 23 Kurt Waldheim. 24 Stanley Baldwin. 25 Hua Guofeng. 26 Energy.
27 Walter Mondale. 28 Constantine II. 29 Georges Pompidou. 30 Mikael Gorbachev.

QUIZ 33　POT LUCK 15

Answers - see Quiz 35, page 219

1 At which meeting was the establishing of an International Monetary Fund proposed?
2 How is Iran's Dasht e Kavir also known?
3 Which is farthest north – Kerry, Limerick or Munster?
4 Which famous car did Issigonis design as well as the Mini?
5 WG Grace died on which future England captain's 15th birthday?
6 Where was the first permanent English settlement in the New World?
7 Which cigarettes had the slogan "Blow Some My Way"?
8 Who described Herbert Von Karajan as "a kind of musical Malcolm Sargent."?
9 What does M stand for in HTML?
10 In 1994 Johannesburg was made capital of which region?
11 Which painter, and sister of a famous painter was the model and mistress of Rodin?
12 What is the southernmost city of New Zealand?
13 Who is the heroine of *Fear of Flying*?
14 Who made his debut in *The Wise Little Hen* in 1934?
15 Which classic did Kylie Minogue sing when she starred in the show which opened the Fox Studios in Sydney in 1999?
16 On which Channel is Alaska's capital?
17 Who broke the solo flight record to Cape Town in 1932?
18 What was the speed limit raised to when it no longer required a person with a red flag to walk in front of a motor vehicle?
19 Where did *The Mousetrap* have its first night in the West End?
20 Which newspaper published the first crossword?
21 Where is Yupik or Yuk spoken?
22 How are the Sandwich Islands now known?
23 Which UN Secretary General negotiated peace in the Iran–Iraq War?
24 Who did Helmut Kohl overtake as Germany's longest serving Chancellor in 1995?
25 What was Prince Philip's military rank when he married Princess Elizabeth?
26 How was Angelo Giuseppe Roncalli better known?
27 What is the English title of the play *La Cantatrice Chauve*?
28 What was southern Ireland called before becoming the sovereign state of Eire in 1937?
29 In which city did Tchaikovsky die?
30 In which month did Margaret Thatcher announce her resignation as Prime Minister?

ANSWERS

POT LUCK 16 *See quiz 35, page 219*

1 Prince Charles & Lady Diana Spencer. 2 The Colosseum in Rome. 3 David Scarboro.
4 Wrigley's Chewing Gum. 5 Likeness. 6 Rue Cambon. 7 Jordan. 8 Alexander Korda.
9 Yvonne Ridley. 10 Appendix. 11 Kuwait City. 12 Margarine. 13 P Kropotkin.
14 Under a Blackpool tram. 15 Cramp. 16 Grover Cleveland. 17 1400. 18 Millais.
19 Thomas Jefferson's. 20 *The Catcher in the Rye*. 21 Diane Pretty. 22 Sweden.
23 Steve Penk. 24 2 mph. 25 Idaho. 26 Lambeth. 27 Lanzarote. 28 Pall Mall.
29 Hamburg. 30 John F Kennedy.

QUIZ 34 NATURAL PHENOMENA

Answers - see Quiz 36, page 220

1 What was the name of the first storm to be given a name?
2 Which volcanic rock is named after a mountain range in South America?
3 What is our Solar System's nearest stellar neighbour?
4 Which Asian country has the greatest area of inland water?
5 What is the highest waterfall in Norway?
6 What is the next largest body in the Solar System after Venus?
7 What is the largest lake in the UK after Neagh?
8 In which US state is the Mammoth cave system?
9 What is V4641 Sgr?
10 What was the first asteroid to be discovered?
11 Where was the meteorite Hoba West found?
12 What is the world's highest island after New Guinea?
13 What is the name of the nearest planetary nebula to the Earth?
14 What percentage of the sky does the smallest constellation take up?
15 Which of the following is the brightest – Rigel, Sirius or Vega?
16 What was the second planet to have been visited by a spacecraft?
17 What is the maximum time a rainbow has been visible in the UK?
18 Which state along with Texas and Nebraska is known as Tornado Alley?
19 About how many million years did the longest ice age last?
20 Which planet has the longest day in the solar system?
21 Which element discovered in 1931 is the rarest on Earth?
22 What is the defined visibility of a sea fog?
23 Which nebula is brightest in the night sky?
24 In which constellation is Procyon?
25 In which constellation is the Hyades cluster?
26 At which university is the McDonald Observatory?
27 Where was the meteorite Rowton found?
28 Which Asian Sea is the deepest?
29 From which country was the Andromeda Galaxy first observed?
30 After Pluto which is the next furthest body from the Sun?

QUIZ 35 POT LUCK 16

Answers - see Quiz 33, page 217

1 To whom was Archbishop Runcie speaking when he said, "My advice was delicately poised between the cliche and the indiscretion."?
2 Which famous landmark was called the Flavian Amphitheatre when it opened?
3 Who originally played the Mark Fowler *EastEnders* role which Todd Carty took on?
4 What was the first recorded purchase using a bar code?
5 The word icon comes from a Greek word meaning what?
6 In which street did Coco Chanel found her fashion house?
7 What is pop star Gabrielle's son called?
8 Who founded London Film Productions in 1932?
9 Which Sunday Express reporter was imprisoned by the Taliban in the autumn of 2001?
10 In 1885, Mary Gartside was the first person to have which part of the body successfully removed?
11 The industrial suburb of Shuwaikh is in which city?
12 Which food item was patented by Hippolyte Mege Mouries?
13 Who wrote the political writing *Fields, Factories and Workshops*?
14 In *Coronation Street*, how did Alan Bradley meet his death?
15 What is the result if lactic acid accumulates in the muscles during exercise?
16 Who was the first US President to marry while in office?
17 How many kilometres are there from Great Britain's most south westerly tip to its northernmost one?
18 Who painted the picture which gave Lillie Langtry her nickname of the Jersey Lily?
19 Which President's grand child was the first baby to be born in the White House?
20 Which book was John Lennon's murderer carrying when he killed the rock star?
21 In 2001 which lady faced the High Court in a bid to let her husband help end her life?
22 What was the first European country to issue banknotes?
23 Which DJ famously phoned Tony Blair pretending to be William Hague?
24 In the UK what was the first speed limit for cars in town?
25 What is the USA's Spud State as it produces over a quarter of the country's potato crop?
26 In which London borough is the cricket ground owned by the Duchy of Cornwall?
27 What is the most easterly of the Canary Islands?
28 What was the first street in the world to be lit by gas lamps?
29 The first hour of *Tomorrow Never Dies* is set in which European city?
30 Who, when asked how he became a war hero said, "they sank my boat."?

POT LUCK 15 See quiz 33, page 217

ANSWERS

1 Bretton Woods Conference. 2 Great Salt Desert. 3 Limerick. 4 Morris Minor.
5 Douglas Jardine. 6 Jamestown. 7 Chesterfield. 8 Thomas Beecham. 9 Mark up.
10 Gauteng. 11 Gwen John. 12 Invercargill. 13 Isadora Wing. 14 Donald Duck.
15 "Diamonds are a Girl's Best Friend". 16 Gastineau. 17 Amy Johnson. 18 14 mph.
19 Ambassadors Theatre. 20 *New York World*. 21 Southern Alaska/Siberia. 22 Hawaii.
23 Perez De Cuellar. 24 Konrad Adenauer. 25 Lieutenant. 26 Pope John XXIII.
27 *The Bald Prima Donna*. 28 Irish Free State 29 St Petersburg. 30 November.

QUIZ 36 MUSIC WHO'S WHO?

Answers - see Quiz 34, page 218

1 Which star's husband produced the best selling album in the USA by a female?
2 Which single gave The Spice Girls their ninth No 1?
3 Which non British group has been No 1 in Australia more than any other?
4 On which label did Jamiroquai release their first single?
5 From which city does the performer of CrazySexyCool come from?
6 Who directed the video of Michael Jackson's best selling album?
7 How is Eileen Edwards better known?
8 For which 1980s movie did the oldest woman to have a UK No 1 win an Oscar?
9 How was Chris Hamill better known?
10 Which actress directed the video of Belinda Carlisle's first No 1?
11 Who was the first band to top both the singles and album charts with their debut releases?
12 Who sang "I Don't Like Mondays" with Bob Geldof in a Wembley Stadium concert in 1995?
13 Who produced the John Lennon single voted the BBC's Top Lyric of the Century?
14 Who won the Best New Act Grammy of 1983?
15 How was Hilary Lester known on the single "Save Your Love"?
16 Who was the first British female to top the charts on both sides of the Atlantic with the same single?
17 Which soccer star provided rap contributions to "World In Motion"?
18 Who had the original hit with Bombalurina's biggest 1990 hit?
19 Who sang Bart's lines on The Simpson's first No 1 hit in the UK?
20 Who was the oldest lady Eric Clapton was singing with on his first No 1?
21 Who was the first non-Briton to represent the UK in the Eurovision Song Contest?
22 Which singer's brother was drummer with Billy J Kramer's backing band?
23 Who released the album *Organic* in 1996?
24 Who had a 1990s No 1 from the West End show in which he was starring?
25 Which Eurovision Song Contest winner hosted the radio show *Mother Angella* in the USA?
26 Who made the album *Almost Naked*, with appropriate sleeve, in 1996?
27 Which singer, nephew of band leader Ray Ventura, has appeared on the *Mrs Merton Show* and *Absolutely Fabulous*?
28 Which late singer wrote the musical *Apples* in 1989?
29 The bands Garden Wall and Anon amalgamated to form who?
30 Who collaborated with Elvis Costello on "Painted From Memory"?

Answers - see Quiz 34, page 218

NATURAL PHENOMENA See quiz 34, page 218
1 Carol. 2 Andesite. 3 Proxima centauri. 4 India. 5 Utigard. 6 Mars. 7 Erne. 8 Kentucky. 9 Black hole. 10 Ceres. 11 Namibia. 12 Akutan. 13 Helix. 14 0.16%. 15 Sirius. 16 Venus. 17 Six hours. 18 Iowa. 19 70. 20 Venus. 21 Astatine. 22 1000 yds. 23 Orion. 24 Canis minor. 25 Taurus. 26 Texas. 27 Shropshire. 28 South China. 29 Germany. 30 Neptune.

ANSWERS

QUIZ 37 POT LUCK 17

Answers - see Quiz 39, page 223

1 The first top ten hit for Sash! had a title in which language?
2 In which decade was the Italian Grand Prix first held?
3 How long is the rope at the start of a water-skiing competition?
4 How many red blood cells does an average-sized drop of blood contain?
5 What contained a poleyn and a pauldron?
6 In which country is the city of Cali?
7 Apart from in America, in which country is the city of Salem found?
8 Which Bananarama star went on to join Shakespear's Sister?
9 In which TV series did Johnny Depp play a character named Tom Hanson?
10 How is TV comic Cyril John Mead better known?
11 In which century was Leonardo da Vinci born?
12 In what type of car did James Dean meet his death?
13 How many rivers are there in the United Arab Emirates?
14 In which avenue is The White House situated?
15 How is French Somaliland now known?
16 What was the first Top Ten hit for Nightcrawlers?
17 Where is Hellgate Bridge?
18 Mt Godwin-Austen is also known by which letter and number?
19 Who was Education Secretary, Home Secretary and Chancellor of the Exchequer in the 1990s?
20 How many James Bond films were released during the lifetime of creator Ian Fleming?
21 Which vitamin is also known as biotin?
22 Astraphobia is the fear of what?
23 What common factor links children of Cheryl Baker and children of Mollie Sugden?
24 Who played Ron Jenkins in *Coronation Street*?
25 Which hit got to No 2 simultaneously in November 1995 with two separate groups?
26 Who in Gilbert and Sullivan is 'a dealer in magic and spells'?
27 Which country do the Aleutian Islands belong to?
28 What does the Arabic word intifada mean?
29 In which ocean are the Maldives?
30 In which London borough was the first cash dispenser installed?

CELEBS *See quiz 39, page 223*

1 Catherine Zeta Jones. 2 Anna Kournikova. 3 Nino Cerruti.
4 Richmond upon Thames. 5 Moses & Dylan. 6 Kate Capshaw. 7 Julia Roberts.
8 Lauren. 9 *A Ruling Passion*. 10 Elizabeth Taylor. 11 Victoria. 12 Burt Reynolds.
13 Transplant patient. 14 Ian Hislop 15 Neil Cunningham. 16 Politicians' wives.
17 19. 18 Cheshire. 19 Custard pie. 20 Balloon. 21 Los Angeles Dodgers.
22 Wilnelia. 23 Lawson. 24 Elton John. 25 Renny Harlin. 26 Meg. 27 18 years.
28 Advertiser's logo. 29 1958. 30 Elton John.

QUIZ 38 WORLD TRAVEL

Answers - see Quiz 40, page 224

1 How many bicycles are there in Bejing – 8 million, 10 million or 12 million?
2 Where was the world's largest shopping centre opened in 1985?
3 In 1990, in which country was the world's largest McDonald's?
4 Which Tower in Hong Kong is 100 storeys high?
5 What does Oklahoma mean?
6 What is Ecuador's largest Pacific seaport?
7 Where is the Seacon Square shopping centre?
8 Where is the largest casino in the world?
9 Who designed the most expensive museum in the world?
10 Where was the first state-subsidised theatre in the English-speaking world opened?
11 Which Canal links the Ebrie Lagoon and the Gulf of Guinea?
12 Which of these islands is the largest – Great Britain, Java or Sumatra?
13 What does the Mississippi-Missouri eventually flow into?
14 Which of these deserts is the smallest – Great Basin, Great Sandy or Great Victoria?
15 Why is Amarillo, Texas, so called?
16 On which river is Jordan's capital?
17 The capital of Maryland is on which river?
18 Which of these Seas is the largest – Arabian, Coral or South China
19 The Appalachian mountains end in the centre of which state?
20 On which island does the Otira Rail Tunnel run?
21 Which of the following Australian cities is the most southerly – Melbourne, Perth or Sydney?
22 What is the Great Slave?
23 What was Brazil's first planned city?
24 What is the principal language of Andhra Pradesh?
25 Palmerston, Mangaia and Rarotonga are among which islands?
26 In which sea do the so called ABC islands lie?
27 Which town is closest to the Everest base camp – Kathmandu, Namche or Sagarmatha?
28 In 2000 which was the largest city in the world by population?
29 Where is the "Leap The Dips" roller coaster?
30 The Dogon are inhabitants of where?

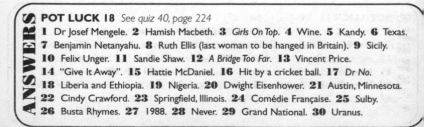

POT LUCK 18 *See quiz 40, page 224*
1 Dr Josef Mengele. 2 Hamish Macbeth. 3 *Girls On Top*. 4 Wine. 5 Kandy. 6 Texas.
7 Benjamin Netanyahu. 8 Ruth Ellis (last woman to be hanged in Britain). 9 Sicily.
10 Felix Unger. 11 Sandie Shaw. 12 *A Bridge Too Far*. 13 Vincent Price.
14 "Give It Away". 15 Hattie McDaniel. 16 Hit by a cricket ball. 17 *Dr No*.
18 Liberia and Ethiopia. 19 Nigeria. 20 Dwight Eisenhower. 21 Austin, Minnesota.
22 Cindy Crawford. 23 Springfield, Illinois. 24 Comédie Française. 25 Sulby.
26 Busta Rhymes. 27 1988. 28 Never. 29 Grand National. 30 Uranus.

ANSWERS

QUIZ 39 CELEBS

Answers - see Quiz 37, page 221

1 Who was the highest placed mother in *Celebrity Bodies* magazine poll of autumn 2001?
2 According to the *Guinness Book of Records*, who is the most searched for sportswoman on the Internet?
3 For which fashion house did Armani first work?
4 The older Attenborough brother is Baron of where?
5 What were the names of Woody Allen's adopted children with Mia Farrow?
6 Who was Mrs Spielberg after Amy Irving?
7 Which actress was the biggest earner of 2000?
8 Which designer's real surname is Lifschitz?
9 Which Joan Collins novel did Random House not publish, despite paying out a $1.2 million advance?
10 Who hosted *Victoria's Secret Fashion Show* in Cannes in 2000 with Elton John?
11 What was Princess Diana's sister in law Countess Spencer called?
12 Who was the first male centrefold in *Playgirl* magazine?
13 In 1997 Baebhen Schuttke became Britain's youngest what?
14 Who said, after losing a libel case, "If this is justice, I'm a banana."?
15 Who designed Ffion Hague's wedding dress?
16 Linda McDougal wrote a book about which group of women?
17 How old was Lady Diana Spencer when she became engaged?
18 Where did Posh and Becks (Victoria Adams and David Beckham) announce their engagement?
19 What was Bill Gates hit in the face with on a trip to Belgium in 1998?
20 Andy Elson attempted to fly round the world in a what?
21 Which baseball team did Rupert Murdoch buy?
22 What is Mrs Bruce Forsyth called?
23 What was Twiggy's surname when she was a presenter of *This Morning*?
24 Who is the famous partner of David Furnish?
25 Who was Geena Davis's third husband?
26 What was the first name of the first Mrs Noel Gallagher?
27 For how many years did Andrew Lloyd Webber's show on roller skates run in the West End?
28 In 1987 Luis Reina became the first matador in the bull ring to wear what?
29 In which year were Michael Jackson, Madonna and Prince all born?
30 Which pop star received a knighthood in the same honours list as Tom Finney?

POT LUCK 17 *See quiz 37, page 221*

ANSWERS
1 French. 2 1920s. 3 23m. 4 100,000,000. 5 A suit of armour. 6 Colombia.
7 India. 8 Siobhan Fahey. 9 *21 Jump Street.* 10 Syd Little. 11 15th. 12 Porsche.
13 None. 14 Pennsylvania Avenue. 15 Djibouti. 16 "Push The Feeling On".
17 New York. 18 K2. 19 Kenneth Clarke. 20 Two. 21 B6. 22 Lightning.
23 Twins. 24 Ben Kingsley. 25 "Wonderwall". 26 John Wellington Wells. 27 Alaska.
28 Uprising. 29 Indian. 30 Enfield.

QUIZ 40 POT LUCK 18

Answers - see Quiz 38, page 222

1 Which real life villain did Gregory Peck play in *The Boys From Brazil*?
2 Which series took place in Lochdubh?
3 In which sitcom was there a magazine called "Spare Cheeks"?
4 What would stum be added to, to give it more strength?
5 How is the sacred city of Senkadagala now known?
6 Odessa is found in Washington and which other US state?
7 Who beat Simon Peres in the Israeli elections of 1996?
8 *Dance With The Stranger* was about whom?
9 Marsala wine is produced on which island?
10 Which character did Jack Lemmon play in *The Odd Couple*?
11 Who was the first British female soloist to have a hat trick of chart No 1 hits?
12 In which war film did the character Major General Roy Urquhart appear?
13 Known for his spooky voice, which actor voices over on Michael Jackson's video *Thriller*?
14 What was the first Top Ten hit for Red Hot Chili Peppers?
15 Who was the first black actress to win an Oscar?
16 In what unusual circumstances did George II's eldest son die?
17 Which Bond movie dealing with world threatening scenarios opened during the Cuban missile crisis?
18 Who were the only independent nations in Africa at the outbreak of WWI?
19 In which country was Lassa fever first identified?
20 Who was the first US President to appear on colour television?
21 Where is there a Spam Museum?
22 Which model lost her Revlon contract in her mid 30s?
23 Which town in which state was the home of Abraham Lincoln?
24 What was the world's first national theatre?
25 What is the longest river of the island which has a Parliament called Tynwald?
26 Trevor Smith became known as which rapper?
27 In which year did the £1 note cease to be legal tender in England?
28 How many times was the great Stirling Moss the Grand Prix world champion?
29 Which Grand event was first broadcast live on BBC television in 1960?
30 Which planet was the first to be discovered by use of a telescope?

WORLD TRAVEL *See quiz 38, page 222*

ANSWERS

1 8 million. 2 Alberta, Canada. 3 Russia. 4 Nina. 5 Red People. 6 Guayaquil.
7 Bangkok. 8 Ledyard Connecticut. 9 Richard Meier. 10 Dublin. 11 Vridi.
12 Sumatra. 13 Gulf of Mexico. 14 Great Sandy. 15 Yellow colour of a creek bank.
16 Zarqa. 17 Severn. 18 Coral. 19 Alabama. 20 South island, New Zealand.
21 Perth. 22 Lake. 23 Aracaju. 24 Telugu. 25 Cook Islands. 26 Caribbean.
27 Namche. 28 Tokyo. 29 Lakemont Park, Pennsylvania. 30 Mali.

QUIZ 41 MUSICAL MOVIES

Answers - see Quiz 43, page 227

1 Who sang the title song of a movie for which Marvin Hamlisch won two 1974 Oscars?
2 Who did Betty Hutton replace in *Annie Get Your Gun*?
3 *Fiddler on the Roof* and which other big musical did Norman Jewison direct in the 1970s?
4 Who was Gene Kelly's co-star in his Hollywood debut?
5 Which character did Debbie Allen play in the movie and TV show about Manhattan's High School for the Performing Arts?
6 For which song from *Lady be Good* did Oscar Hammerstein II win an Oscar?
7 Which novelist, when a Pinkerton detective in real life, investigated the gambling affairs of the man Barbra Streisand married in *Funny Girl*?
8 What was the Hollywood debut of the man born Harold Leek?
9 Who directed the first movie Nicole Kidman starred in after divorcing Tom Cruise?
10 Who did Miss Olsen fall in love with in the movie where she was a lead character?
11 Where does Tony Manero do his day job in a big 1970s musical?
12 In which city is the song "Do Re Mi" sung in a musical?
13 Who wrote the music for the last Best Oscar winning song of the 1990s?
14 Who played the male lead in the musical which included "Let's Hear It For the Boy"?
15 Who said, "I am simple, complex, generous, selfish, unattractive, beautiful, lazy, driven."?
16 In which musical do teenagers tune in to Wolfman Jack's rock 'n' roll show?
17 What does Madonna have most of *Evita*: earrings, hair styles, shoes?
18 Where is the 1983 musical with Jennifer Beals and Michael Nouri set?
19 Which future TV cop plays the angry young intellectual in *Fiddler On The Roof*?
20 Who played Janet in the musical movie with the song "Dammit Janet"?
21 Who directed and choreographed the original production of *West Side Story* on stage before being involved in the movie?
22 In which state is the movie based on the life of Loretta Lynn set?
23 Which was the first Disney musical of the 1990s to win Best Song Oscar?
24 Who sang "Honeysuckle Rose" in *New York New York*?
25 What won the Best Song Oscar in Julie Andrews first Oscar-winning film?
26 For which movie did Howard Ashman win his last Oscar in his own lifetime?
27 Which musical film included an psychopathic agricultural worker called Fry?
28 Who directed *Spiceworld: The Movie*?
29 What was Olivia Newton John's surname in *Grease*?
30 What was Jennifer Beals studying at university while she was making *Flashdance*?

QUIZ 42 POT LUCK 19

Answers - see Quiz 44, page 228

1 Mr Ashwell of Herne Hill patented which famous sign?
2 Which product had the advertising slogan, Desperation, Pacification, Expectation, Acclamation, Realisation?
3 Junta is the Spanish word for what?
4 What was usually the penultimate word in an episode of *The Two Ronnies*?
5 Which world leader was executed on Christmas Day 1989?
6 Which 1960s classic song had the line, "Nobody knows were my Johnny has gone."?
7 Which website address was the drama series *Attachments* famous for?
8 Which favourite sitcom star played Jeremy Parsons QC in *Crown Court*?
9 What did Radovan Karadzic practise before founding the Serbian Democratic Party?
10 Grace Stafford was the voice of which cartoon character?
11 Which father of an ex *Coronation Street* star wrote over 100 episodes of the soap including one of Elsie Tanner's weddings?
12 What was the name of the evacuation operation which created the artificial Lake Kariba?
13 To the nearest 20 degrees centigrade what is the melting point of iron?
14 Which Emperor was responsible for building The Great Wall of China?
15 What in London was originally called Nottingham House?
16 Which Florida port and tourist city used to be known as Cayo Hueso or Bone Island?
17 What was the name of the first kibbutz?
18 In what year did "The Star Spangled Banner" become the US National Anthem?
19 Who wrote the novel on which Quentin Tarantino's follow up to *Pulp Fiction* was based?
20 Which politician, still going strong 50 years later, said in the 1950s, "I am on the right wing of the middle of the road with a strong radical bias."?
21 The phrase 'iron curtain' was first used by Churchill but who is credited with the idea behind it?
22 What is the oldest lead and zinc mining town in Zambia?
23 Elizabeth Taylor's second divorce was from whom?
24 In which game reserve are the Kapachira Falls?
25 What is the Burmese name for the main river of Myanmar?
26 Who wrote a poem about the Tay Bridge Disaster of 1879?
27 What is the 21st-century name of the country where the first known map was found?
28 Where was the first purpose-built music hall built?
29 Which was the last navy to scrap the daily rum ration?
30 Michael Crick was the biographer of which convicted criminal?

21ST CENTURY HEADLINES See quiz 44, page 228

1 Michel Desjoyeaux. 2 Donald Rumsfeld. 3 New York. 4 I Love You. 5 Brooklands.
6 Dennis Tito. 7 Selby. 8 MacPherson. 9 Hinduja. 10 Douro. 11 Australian.
12 Peter Tachell. 13 Poole. 14 Kimberley & Belinda. 15 Mahzer Mahmood.
16 Steven Spielberg. 17 Refused to use metric measures. 18 Vandevelde. 19 NBC.
20 Kursk. 21 Chesterfield. 22 Barak. 23 His TV set. 24 Gerbeau.
25 Alun Michael. 26 Chappaqua. 27 Croatia. 28 Mark Richardson.
29 Freedom Party. 30 110.

QUIZ 43 HORSE RACING

Answers - see Quiz 41, page 225

1 In which county was the first steeplechase held?
2 Which horse won the first post-WWII Grand National?
3 Which jockey rode the 2,000 Guineas-winner four times between 1972 and 1989?
4 Which horse ran the fastest Epsom Derby of the 1990s?
5 Who sponsored the Derby at the turn of the century?
6 Who resigned as the Queen's trainer towards the end of the 1990s?
7 Who was the first jockey in the 1990s to ride 200 winners?
8 Who owned Sagamix when he won the Prix de l'Arc de Triomphe in 1998?
9 The steeplechaser One Man had to be put down after being injured in which race?
10 Which horse finished first in the last Grand National of the millennium to be abandoned?
11 What was the first filly to win the Derby?
12 Which horse won the Derby the year WWI began?
13 What was Frankie Dettori's first 1000 Guineas win of the 1990s?
14 Which horse ran the fastest Grand National of the 1990s?
15 What was Mick Kinane's second 2000 Guineas win of the 1990s?
16 Which horse won the Grand National the year that Nijinsky won the Derby?
17 Which jockey won his third successive Prix de l'Arc de Triomphe in 1998?
18 Which horse won the St Leger the year that Mill Reef won the Derby?
19 Who rode the only Derby winner with Shirley in its name?
20 Which member of the Royal family got married the year Aldaniti won the National?
21 Which horse won the Derby the year after the legendary Shergar?
22 Which horse won the Grand National the year of the first 1990s General Election?
23 What was Lester Piggott's first 1000 Guineas winner in the second half of the 20th century?
24 Rodrigo de Triano was which jockey's thirtieth Classic winner?
25 What was the last year before 1993 that the Grand National was not run?
26 Before Royal Athlete what was the last Grand National winner to have Royal in its name?
27 In which park is Ireland's Clonmel Racecourse?
28 What was the first 1000 Guineas winner of the 1990s to have two words in its name?
29 Which was the fastest of the first four British horses in the 1998 French 2000 Guineas?
30 Which horse ran the fastest Epsom Derby of the 1980s?

QUIZ 44 21ST CENTURY HEADLINES

Answers - see Quiz 42, page 226

1 Who beat Ellen MacArthur in the Vendee Globe race 2000–001?
2 Who was George W Bush's first Defence Secretary?
3 The plane involved in the first supersonic air crash was heading for where?
4 Which computer virus was first detected in Hong Kong in May 2000?
5 From which airfield did Jennifer Murray begin and end her helicopter circumnavigation of the world solo in 2000?
6 Who was the first private individual to make a journey into space?
7 Where in England was there a major rail crash in March 2001?
8 What was the name of the inquiry into the death of Stephen Lawrence?
9 Passports regarding which brothers brought about the demise of Peter Mandelson?
10 Over which river did a bridge collapse in 2001 causing the resignation of that country's minister of public works?
11 At which 2001 Grand Prix was a marshal killed after he was struck by a wheel?
12 Who tried to make a citizen's arrest on Robert Mugabe in Brussels in 2001?
13 Which judge presided over the first Lee Bowyer and Jonathan Woodgate trial?
14 What were the so called Internet adoption twins called?
15 Which reporter set up the 'Sophiegate' scam?
16 Who directed the drama which was the highest amount the BBC had paid?
17 How did Steve Thoburn hit the headlines?
18 What was the name of the Belgian that M & S appointed to turn around the company's ailing fortunes?
19 Which station aired Anne Robinson's ruthless quiz show in the US?
20 Which Russian nuclear submarine sank in 2000?
21 Towards the end of the 2000–01 football season which side was docked three points for financial irregularities?
22 Who did Ariel Sharon replace as Israeli PM in February 2001?
23 Mitch Hallen hit the headlines as he married what?
24 Who succeeded Jennie Page as chief executive of the Millennium Dome?
25 Who did Rhodri Morgan replace as First Secretary of the Welsh Assembly?
26 Where did Hillary Clinton buy a home before announcing she would run for the Senate?
27 Stipe Mesic was elected President of where?
28 In February 2000 which British 400m runner was banned after testing positive for nandrolone?
29 Which political party did Jorg Haider head?
30 How many storeys did the twin towers of the World Trade Center have?

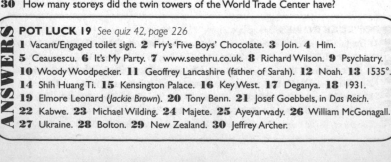

POT LUCK 19 See quiz 42, page 226

ANSWERS

1 Vacant/Engaged toilet sign. 2 Fry's 'Five Boys' Chocolate. 3 Join. 4 Him.
5 Ceausescu. 6 It's My Party. 7 www.seethru.co.uk. 8 Richard Wilson. 9 Psychiatry.
10 Woody Woodpecker. 11 Geoffrey Lancashire (father of Sarah). 12 Noah. 13 1535°.
14 Shih Huang Ti. 15 Kensington Palace. 16 Key West. 17 Deganya. 18 1931.
19 Elmore Leonard (*Jackie Brown*). 20 Tony Benn. 21 Josef Goebbels, in *Das Reich*.
22 Kabwe. 23 Michael Wilding. 24 Majete. 25 Ayeyarwady. 26 William McGonagall.
27 Ukraine. 28 Bolton. 29 New Zealand. 30 Jeffrey Archer.

QUIZ 45 POT LUCK 20

Answers - see Quiz 47, page 231

1 Which French region incorporates the city of Paris?
2 The character Pulcinella, who lived on as Punch in *Punch & Judy*, has a name which means what?
3 Which Betty Marsden character's catchphrase was, "Many many times," in the radio classic *Round the Horne*?
4 What was Kazuo Ishiguro's next novel after *Artist of the Floating World* which won the Booker Prize?
5 Which Beatles song was recorded as *Sie liebt dich* in West Germany?
6 What was the codename of the bomb which was dropped on Nagasaki?
7 Which port is Italy's chief naval station?
8 Who did Robin Givens divorce in 1989?
9 Which DH Lawrence novel was set in Mexico?
10 Who spent more years as Chancellor of the Exchequer in the 1980s than anyone else?
11 On which river is the Yorkshire city which hosts a piano competition every three years?
12 Whose death meant that Boudicca became head of the Iceni tribe?
13 What do the Greeks call Nicosia?
14 In which church is JS Bach buried?
15 Which was the last European power to have imperial territories in Africa?
16 Who was chief photographer of *Rolling Stone* magazine from 1973 to 1983?
17 In which country is the city of Tetouan?
18 Which singer/actress played the character Lola Lovell in *The Delinquents*?
19 What type of wine is described by the term frizzante?
20 Which country did the group Rednex come from?
21 Which movie great had his final TV role as Daniel Reece in *Dynasty*?
22 In which country is the city of Brasov?
23 Kim Basinger lost a multi-million-pound lawsuit after pulling out of which movie?
24 In which decade was the Mexican Grand Prix first held?
25 Who played Sir Arthur Sullivan in *Topsy Turvy*?
26 In which London borough is Sadlers' Wells Theatre?
27 In which key is Schubert's "Unfinished Symphony"?
28 Which leaders signed the SALT II treaty?
29 The Silk Road ran from Shanghai to which Sea?
30 Which actor manager was born Henry Brodribb?

POT LUCK 21 *See quiz 47, page 231*

1 "Stupid Girl". 2 H. 3 *Minder*. 4 Kandahar. 5 1920s. 6 Lemur. 7 David Wasco.
8 *Ben Hur*. 9 Gambia. 10 *Goldeneye*. 11 The Bangles. 12 Mayor Of Casterbridge.
13 Seven. 14 Elizabeth II's Coronation. 15 "Heart-Shaped Box". 16 Gladys Aylward.
17 William IV. 18 Cissy Houston. 19 Argentina. 20 Bond movie. 21 Bolivia.
22 The Flintstones. 23 Sherlock Holmes. 24 Barbara Bach. 25 Venezuela.
26 Bryn Terfel. 27 Ronnie Barker. 28 Tarsiers. 29 Bulgaria. 30 Angell.

QUIZ 46 TV CLASSICS

Answers - see Quiz 48, page 232

1 In which month in 1966 was *Star Trek* first broadcast?
2 Which Briton won an Emmy as Best Supporting Actress in 1971?
3 Who directed the series *7 Up* and its sequels, about the lives and aspirations of a group of children?
4 Which studio was the first *Blue Peter* filmed from?
5 Whose music was used for the series *Light Of Experience*?
6 Who was known as "The Switchboard Girl"?
7 The first TV broadcast of *Alice in Wonderland* was under which banner?
8 What was the name of the very first programme designed for children of school age?
9 Who presented *Cookery Lesson* in the 1950s?
10 In which year was the first General Election results broadcast production?
11 Who was the creator of Mr Pastry?
12 Which town was shown on the first cross-Channel broadcast?
13 Which children's title replaced *Watch With Mother*?
14 Who replaced Eamonn Andrews on *What's My Line*?
15 At what time was the first BBC TV news broadcast put on air?
16 Which Olympics was *Sportsview* the first to cover?
17 Who was the first presenter of *Sunday Night at the London Palladium*?
18 What was the UK version of *Tic Tac Dough*?
19 Which series's spin off was called *Oxbridge 2000*?
20 How long had *Grandstand* been running before a regular Sunday programme was introduced?
21 On which day of the week did *Juke Box Jury* begin?
22 In which series did Chief Supt Lockhart appear?
23 The Ponderosa Ranch was near which City?
24 Which puppet series featured Tex Tucker?
25 Which *Dad's Army* regular appeared in *It's A Square World*?
26 Ian Hendry played which crime-buster alongside Patrick Macnee in *The Avengers*?
27 Which astronomer created *A for Andromeda*?
28 Which Prime Minister appeared with Morecambe & Wise?
29 Who wrote *Brothers in Law*?
30 In what year did *Top of the Pops* celebrate its 2000th show?

SCIENCE *See quiz 48, page 232*

ANSWERS

1 Star sailor. 2 Charles Kowal. 3 Mars. 4 Kentucky. 5 Kodak. 6 Czechoslovakia. 7 Humerus. 8 Calcium hydroxide. 9 Tanzania. 10 Orion. 11 Tibia. 12 Vomiting. 13 Titan. 14 Dialysis machine. 15 Five. 16 90+. 17 Neptune. 18 Therapeutics plc. 19 Lungs. 20 Jupiter. 21 1880s. 22 John Russell Hind. 23 Leicestershire. 24 Carbon. 25 Titan. 26 Benthos. 27 Lakes. 28 13. 29 Triton. 30 Heavy water.

QUIZ 47 POT LUCK 21

Answers - see Quiz 45, page 229

1 What was the first top ten hit for Garbage?
2 On a computer keyboard what letter is below and between Y and U?
3 Which TV series featured a pub called The Winchester?
4 What was the first capital of Afghanistan after it became independent?
5 In which decade was the Monaco Grand Prix first held?
6 Which creature is also known as the aye-aye?
7 Who co wrote the screenplay of *Pulp Fiction* along with Quentin Tarantino?
8 Which 1950s film cost $4million, double the maximum spend of the time?
9 In which country is the city of Banjul?
10 Xenia Onatopp was the villain in which movie?
11 The girl band once known as The Colours made the charts using which name?
12 In fiction, what position did Michael Henchard rise to?
13 How many TV Doctor Who's had there been before Sylvester McCoy?
14 For which occasion did TV cameras first film in Westminster Abbey?
15 What was the last Top Ten hit for Nirvana?
16 Whose story was told in *Inn Of The Sixth Happiness* with Ingrid Bergman?
17 Who was the first British monarch to be born in Buckingham Palace?
18 Who recorded the original "Midnight Train To Georgia" before Gladys Knight had the big international hit?
19 Falabellas are native to which country?
20 Rowan Atkinson made his big screen debut in a movie in which series of films?
21 In which country were Butch Cassidy and Sundance finally tracked down?
22 On TV which family read *The Daily Slate*?
23 Who in London had 221B as part of his address?
24 Which Bond girl married a Beatle?
25 Barcelona is found in Spain and which other country?
26 Who made the albums *Some Enchanted Evening* and *We'll Keep A Welcome*?
27 Gerald Wiley was an assumed name of which TV comedy writer?
28 The term monkey includes all the primates except man, apes and what else?
29 In which country is the city of Varna?
30 What was Zoe's name before her marriage to Alec in May to December?

POT LUCK 20 See quiz 45, page 229

1 Ile de France. 2 Little chicken. 3 Lady Beatrice Counterblast. 4 *The Remains of the Day.*
5 "She Loves You". 6 Fat Man. 7 La Spezia. 8 Mike Tyson. 9 *The Plumed Serpent.*
10 Nigel Lawson. 11 Aire. 12 Prasutagus. 13 Lefkosia. 14 St Thomas's Leipzig.
15 Portugal. 16 Annie Leibovitz. 17 Morocco. 18 Kylie Minogue. 19 Semi sparkling.
20 Sweden. 21 Rock Hudson. 22 Romania. 23 *Boxing Helena.* 24 1960s.
25 Allan Corduner. 26 Islington. 27 B Minor. 28 Jimmy Carter and Leonid Brezhnev.
29 Mediterranean. 30 Henry Irving.

ANSWERS

QUIZ 48 SCIENCE

Answers - see Quiz 46, page 230

1 What did the word astronaut originally mean?
2 Who discovered the mystery object Chiron?
3 What was the third planet to have been visited by a spacecraft?
4 In which US state is the Fisher Ridge cave system?
5 Which company introduced Photo CD?
6 What was the third country to have a man in space?
7 Which is the longest bone in the arm?
8 What is another name for slaked lime?
9 Where was the meteorite Mbosi found?
10 In which constellation is Rigel?
11 Which bone is named after the Italian for flute?
12 What is emetophobia a far of?
13 What is Saturn's biggest moon?
14 Willem Johan Kolff devised which item of equipment, a pioneer in medicine and health?
15 How much faster does the strongest wind blow on Neptune than on Earth?
16 How many miles below the Earth' surface do diamonds form?
17 What is the next largest body in the Solar System after Uranus?
18 Which company created Dolly the Sheep?
19 What is the next largest human organ after the brain?
20 Asteroids usually appear between the orbits of Mars and which other planet?
21 In which decade were contact lenses first devised?
22 Who discovered the asteroid Flora?
23 Where was the largest meteorite in the UK found?
24 What is the most common element in the human body after oxygen?
25 Which satellite has the thickest atmosphere?
26 What name is given to the animal and plant life which lives at the bottom of the sea?
27 What does a limnologist study?
28 How many people were in space on 14th March 1995, a then record?
29 What is Neptune's largest moon?
30 What is D_2O?

TV CLASSICS See quiz 46, page 230
1 September. 2 Jenny Agutter (*The Snow Goose*). 3 Michael Apted. 4 Lime Grove.
5 Gheorge Zamfir. 6 Joan Miller. 7 *Theatre Parade*. 8 *For The Children*. 9 Philip Harben.
10 1940. 11 Richard Hearne. 12 Calais. 13 *See Saw*. 14 David Jacobs. 15 7.30pm.
16 Melbourne (1956). 17 Tommy Trinder. 18 *Criss Cross Quiz*. 19 *Emergency Ward 10*.
20 23 years. 21 Monday. 22 *No Hiding Place*. 23 Virginia City. 24 *Four Feather Falls*.
25 Clive Dunn. 26 Dr Keel. 27 Fred Hoyle. 28 Harold Wilson.
29 Frank Muir and Denis Norden. 30 2001.

QUIZ 49 POT LUCK 22

Answers - see Quiz 51, page 235

1 *Titanic* overtook which movie as the most costly ever made?
2 Which animal is linked with the US state of Minnesota?
3 In which American city sharing its name with a European city were R.E.M. formed?
4 In which month did the Japanese launch the 1941 attack on Pearl Harbor?
5 Who or what is a merlon?
6 The unlikely sounding writing duo Ham and Evans penned which song that made No 1 for two different artists?
7 Which Ms Smith wrote the book on which the cartoon *101 Dalmatians* was based?
8 What goes with *Blue* in the title of Tom Sharpe's novel that featured David Jason when adapted for TV?
9 How long was the run of Arthur Miller's first Broadway play?
10 What was the creature-named publishing company set up by Paul Hamlyn?
11 What was the occupation of Louis Washkansky, the first heart transplant recipient?
12 For how many years was the TV quiz show *Mastermind* broadcast?
13 What was Eternal's first single not to make the Top Ten?
14 Who drew the cartoon caricature sequences at the start of TV's *Yes Minister*?
15 Which character did Jim Davidson play in *Up the Elephant and Round the Castle*?
16 In 1824 William Buckland named the first what?
17 What was the middle name of the first sub-four-minute-miler Roger Bannister?
18 Which creatures were wild in the title of a Jung Chang novel?
19 In which royal residence did Queen Victoria die?
20 What was Mary Decker's married name when her husband was an Olympic thrower?
21 What was the first – and only – Top Ten hit for Silver Convention?
22 Which was the first planet to be discovered in the 20th century?
23 From which play was the movie *Casablanca* adapted?
24 "June is Bustin' Out All Over" features in which musical?
25 Which horse was the first ever winner of The Derby?
26 In which country is the city of Kumasi?
27 What is the postcode of Albert Square, Walford?
28 How many Motown acts recorded "I Heard It Through The Grapevine" before Marvin Gaye?
29 Laennec is credited with inventing which medical aid?
30 What percentage of zebras have exactly the same pattern of stripes?

POT LUCK 23 See quiz 51, page 235
1 Order of discovery. 2 *The Man Without A Face.* 3 Iran. 4 "One By One".
5 Janice Long. 6 Anaemia. 7 Samuels. 8 Carrie Fisher. 9 Influenza. 10 Benson.
11 2000 Guineas. 12 George Clooney. 13 Mariah Carey. 14 Richard III.
15 David Copperfield. 16 Nicholas Lyndhurst. 17 Dulwich College. 18 Peru.
19 Angela Rippon. 20 Snodgrass. 21 Gall bladder. 22 South Africa.
23 Malcolm Bradbury. 24 *The House of Eliot.* 25 JCB. 26 Nigel West.
27 Billy the Kid. 28 1951. 29 Uncle. 30 Alphabetical order.

QUIZ 50 WORDS & MUSIC

Answers - see Quiz 52, page 236

1 On the soundtrack of *Bridget Jones's Diary* who sang the only song with Miss Jones in the title?
2 "Virtual Insanity" originally appeared on which album?
3 Which musical was the most costly in terms of insurance premiums?
4 Which duo was the duo with the best selling single of the 1990s in the UK?
5 Whose No 1 had the line, "You're about as easy as a nuclear war"?
6 In which year was the album *1* the bestseller in over six countries despite only being released in the November?
7 What was the second of Motown's first two consecutive No 1s?
8 Who wrote the Spanish lyrics "Volver A Empezar" to a Cole Porter classic?
9 Survivor were commissioned to write which song for the third *Rocky* film?
10 Which famous writing team wrote Phil Collins' first solo No 1?
11 With which single did Whitney Houston's husband top the chart in the 1980s when part of a band?
12 What was the Freddie Mercury song on *Five Live* EP?
13 Who penned Michael Jackson's "You Are Not Alone"?
14 Who was Guiot, a provider of words and music on Shakespear's Sister's "Stay"?
15 Which single topped the charts in the US after being used in a movie based on a 1970s TV series?
16 What was the first German Eurovision winner to top the UK charts?
17 What was the name of the third single written to raise funds for Comic Relief?
18 Who wrote Take That's first No 1?
19 Which Motown star co wrote Paul Young's first No 1?
20 What was The Jam's last single before disbanding?
21 Who was the first person to write five No 1 singles as sole composer?
22 Who joined Skinner & Baddiel as writer of the Euro 96 anthem?
23 From which album was The Fugees second No single taken?
24 What was the first No 1 of the 21st century to have a boy's name in the title?
25 What was Oasis's first No 1 with Noel Gallagher as writer and lead vocals?
26 How did Bucks Fizz's second No 1 finish?
27 What was the first new song used for a Levi's ad?
28 To which charity were royalties from the last No 1 of 1991 given?
29 The Bluebells 1993 hit was used to advertise what?
30 What was the shortest title on the compilation EP *Abba-esque*?

TRANSPORT *See quiz 52, page 236*

ANSWERS

1 Jahre Viking. 2 Chicago. 3 Farringdon. 4 Volkswagen Beetle. 5 Imperial Airways.
6 General Motors. 7 Little Piece of Coal. 8 Czechoslovakia. 9 District. 10 Maggiore.
11 Helicopter. 12 Easyjet. 13 Jeantaud. 14 Honda. 15 Tractor. 16 Nissan Sunny.
17 Finland. 18 Bugatti. 19 Ice. 20 Wilbur Wright. 21 Charles de Gaulle. 22 Russia.
23 Honda. 24 1948. 25 Jeep. 26 St Petersburg. 27 Buick. 28 Fire engine.
29 Lada Riva. 30 Blackbird.

QUIZ 51 POT LUCK 23

Answers - see Quiz 49, page 233

1 Which order is the system of numbering asteroids?
2 In which 1993 movie did Mel Gibson direct himself?
3 In which country is the city of Qom?
4 What was Cher's last Top Ten hit before the massive No 1 "Believe"?
5 Who was the only female presenter at the Live Aid concert?
6 Which blood disorder is caused by a lack of folic acid?
7 Which surname does Janet Leigh's character use when signing in to The Bates Motel?
8 Who wrote Postcards from the Edge and Delusions of Grandma?
9 John Huxham coined the name for which common illness?
10 What was the surname of Cherie Lunghi's character Gabriella in The Manageress?
11 In 1998 which race did Aiden O'Brien not win – the Ascot Gold Cup, King George VI and Queen Elizabeth Stakes or the 2000 Guineas?
12 Who plays the villain alongside Quentin Tarantino in From Dusk Til Dawn?
13 Who became the first solo female singer to enter the UK charts at No 1?
14 The bones of which king were thrown in the River Soar after his grave was desecrated?
15 In fiction, whose first wife was called Dora Spenlove?
16 Who played Ronnie Barker's son Raymond in Going Straight?
17 PG Wodehouse and Raymond Chandler both went to which English school?
18 In which country is the city of Chiclayo?
19 Who was the first female to present TV's Top Gear?
20 Which Carrie featured in Clint Eastwood's Pale Rider?
21 Which part of his anatomy did Jim Carrey have removed following the making of the movie The Mask?
22 In which country did Harold Macmillan deliver his famous 'Wind of Change' speech?
23 Who dramatised Tom Sharpe's Porterhouse Blue for television?
24 Which TV House was created by Jean Marsh & Eileen Atkins – The House of Eliot, Hector's House or House Of Cards?
25 What were the initials of Mr Bamford who gave his name to a heavy vehicle?
26 Under what name is one time MP Rupert Allason known as an author?
27 Aaron Copland composed the ballet music about which Billy?
28 In what year was the first colour TV programme transmitted in America?
29 In motor racing, what relation was Emerson to Christian Fittipaldi?
30 Earth comes first of the planets in order of what?

POT LUCK 22 See quiz 49, page 233

1 Waterworld. 2 Gopher. 3 Athens. 4 December. 5 Part of a parapet.
6 "Without You". 7 Dodie. 8 Porterhouse. 9 One week. 10 Octopus. 11 Dentist.
12 20. 13 "So Good". 14 Gerald Scarfe. 15 Jim London. 16 Dinosaur. 17 Gilbert.
18 Swans. 19 Osborne House. 20 Slaney. 21 "Get Up And Boogie". 22 Pluto.
23 Everybody Comes To Rick's. 24 Carousel. 25 Diomed. 26 Ghana. 27 E20. 28 Two.
29 Stethoscope. 30 None.

QUIZ 52 TRANSPORT

Answers - see Quiz 50, page 234

1 In 2000 what was the world's largest ship?
2 Where did the first car hire company start, in 1918?
3 The first Underground railway ran from Paddington to which Street?
4 In the 1970s which vehicle became the most constructed car of all time?
5 Which airline served the first cooked meals on a scheduled flight?
6 Which was the largest Internet advertiser in 2000?
7 What was the meaning of the name of the dog Ugolek who was a space traveller in the 1960s?
8 Which was the first country to make seat belts compulsory?
9 What was London's second underground railway line?
10 On which Lake was the first hydrofoil tested?
11 What is a Mil Mi 26?
12 Which airline has the largest percentage of its tickets sold over the Internet?
13 Which car held the first land speed record?
14 Of the following, which make of motor cycle was made first – Honda, Suzuki or Yamaha?
15 What was Henry Ford's Fordson?
16 Which of the following was produced first – Ford Escort, Ford Orion or Nissan Sunny?
17 The cruise ship Explorer of the Seas was built in which country?
18 Which company holds the record for producing the largest car ever?
19 On what surface did Henry Ford set a land speed record in 1904?
20 Who piloted the first flight of over one hour with a passenger?
21 Which is the busiest airport in the world which shares its name with a person?
22 Which country has the most submarines?
23 Which company produced the first zero level emission engine?
24 Which year saw the arrival of the Land Rover and the 2CV?
25 Which vehicle was known as the Bantam, the Gnat and the Peep before its final name stuck?
26 Which Russian city has the most comprehensive tramway system?
27 What was the make of the first car to have front and rear flashing indicators?
28 What type of vehicle is a Hawaiian Eagle?
29 Which of the following was produced last – Lada Riva, Nissan Pulsar or Renault 4?
30 Which reconnaissance aircraft is the world's fastest?

WORDS & MUSIC See quiz 50, page 234

QUIZ 53 VILLAINS

Answers - see Quiz 55, page 239

1 Which right hand man of Slobodan Milosevic was arrested in March 2001?
2 Which country does Osama Bin Laden hail from?
3 In 1998 General Pinochet was arrested in the UK pending extradition to where?
4 What was the job of Anthony Blunt when he was stripped of his knighthood?
5 Michael Barratt was not the last person to be hanged in the UK but why was he a famous 'last'?
6 Where was the murderer of 10 Rillington Place executed?
7 Which villain died on the same date as Freddie Mercury but almost 30 years earlier?
8 How many patients was Harold Shipman originally convicted of killing?
9 Which celebrity surname did Barry George use?
10 Timothy McVeigh was executed for which bombing?
11 On what date did Lord Lucan disappear?
12 Which father of a famous novelist played the villain *Captain Hook* in the first production of Peter Pan?
13 Who married Grant Ferrie while in a Saudi prison in 1997?
14 What was the nickname of Protestant paramilitary leader Billy Wright?
15 Who was the first woman to be executed in Texas in the 20th century?
16 Ta Mok was a successor to which leader?
17 On TV what was the surname of the Weatherfield One?
18 In 1902 Harry Jackson was the first person convicted on the basis of what evidence?
19 How was Illich Ramirez Sanchez better known?
20 Who said, "I would never deliberately hurt a fellow professional" after an opponent was apparently kicked in the face in Newcastle?
21 What was the name of Jack the Ripper's final victim?
22 The book *Cried Unheard* was about which convicted killer?
23 Which movie was about pardoned murderer Derek Bentley?
24 Who did James Earl Ray shoot?
25 Where did Michael Ryan carry out his murders?
26 How did Great Train Robber Charles Wilson meet his death?
27 Which group captured hostages John McCarthy, Brian Keenan and Frank Reed in Lebanon?
28 Which of the three men in the Guinness scandal received an 18-month jail sentence?
29 Who was the first person to be executed by lethal injection in the USA?
30 Which villain was born on the day Princess Elizabeth became engaged?

OLYMPICS *See quiz 55, page 239*

ANSWERS

1 Paris. 2 Donovan Bailey. 3 Sinclair. 4 Spiridon Louis. 5 London. 6 Sergey Belov.
7 1916. 8 Averoff. 9 Upton Park FC. 10 John Boland. 11 Luigi Carrozza. 12 80.
13 1 May 2001. 14 Birgit Fischer (nee Schmidt). 15 Gymnastics (Nikolai Andrianov).
16 Norway. 17 Al Oerter. 18 Italy. 19 Miroslav Mecir. 20 Los Angeles (USA).
21 Ornskoldsvik, Sweden. 22 Equatorial Guinea. 23 Discus. 24 10. 25 1960s.
26 Millie. 27 1500 metres. 28 Steve Redgrave. 29 Montreal. 30 1940/1944.

QUIZ 54 POT LUCK 24

Answers - see Quiz 56, page 240

1 In which decade did Mountain biking become an Olympic event?
2 What was the occupation of the Jack Russell who gave his name to a breed of dog?
3 What was the first Top Ten hit for rapper Warren G?
4 Which was the first country to give women the vote?
5 On average, how many times does an adult heart beat a minute?
6 Which country does former Newcastle Utd favourite Faustino Asprilla play for?
7 Quarter, quell, quote – which of these words is made from letters on the top row of a keyboard?
8 In *Just Good Friends*, what were the first names of Vince Pinner's parents?
9 In which country would you watch Polonia play a home soccer match?
10 In the Bible what is the name of John the Baptist's mother?
11 Which country did Martina Hingis represent when she first won Wimbledon?
12 Who directed Jamie Bell's major debut movie?
13 Collectively, who were Bobby Farrell, Marcia Barrett, Liz Mitchell and Maisie Williams?
14 What does the Archbishop of York signs himself as?
15 Burt Reynolds was born in which American state?
16 How is vichyssoise soup usually served?
17 What type of *Schoolboy* appears in the title of a John Le Carre novel?
18 Delft pottery is usually which colours?
19 Which Hill is the highest point in the Cotswolds?
20 Which song begins, "I see trees of green, Red roses too"?
21 In sport, who was the first world champion on both two and four wheeled vehicles?
22 In which decade of last century was Andy Warhol born?
23 What was held at Mount Tremblant, Mosport and Montreal at different years in the 1970s?
24 What was the name of Steptoe and Son's horse?
25 In which country did the Russian revolutionary Leon Trotsky die?
26 What was the first Top Ten hit for Go West?
27 In 1919 the Curzon Line divided Poland on what basis?
28 What was founded following the Dumbarton Oaks Conference of the 1940s?
29 Which present day county goes with White to name the favourite horse of the monarch Richard III?
30 Who did Cassius Clay beat when he first became world heavyweight champion?

POT LUCK 25 See quiz 56, page 240

ANSWERS

1 Church. 2 10. 3 India. 4 Danish. 5 Glass. 6 The New York Dolls. 7 Basketball.
8 Mary Carillo. 9 Annapurna. 10 British Honduras. 11 28. 12 Harness racing cart.
13 Basketball. 14 "Sorry Seems To Be the Hardest Word". 15 Polio.
16 "When I Need You". 17 Arms and hands. 18 50. 19 Gloucester Cathedral.
20 30. 21 Waterloo Bridge. 22 Switzerland. 23 Charles the Mad. 24 Portugal.
25 Pointed. 26 Santo Domingo. 27 Jimmy Young. 28 Elizabeth. 29 1930s.
30 86 minutes.

QUIZ 55 OLYMPICS

Answers - see Quiz 53, page 237

1 Where did the first man to win five Olympic gold medals in one Games win them?
2 Who lowered Carl Lewis's Olympic 100m record in Atlanta?
3 What was the middle name of the athlete disqualified from the 100m in Seoul?
4 Who won the first Marathon of the Modern Olympics?
5 Of the first three Marathons of the Modern Olympics which had the longest course?
6 Who scored the winning basket in the controversial Olympic basketball final in 1972?
7 Which Olympics were cancelled due to WWI?
8 In which stadium were the first Modern Olympics held?
9 Who represented Britain the first time soccer was included in the Olympics?
10 Who won the first men's singles tennis final of the modern Olympics?
11 In 20th century Olympics, who made the highest batting average in baseball?
12 In the new millennium's first Olympics how many different countries won medals?
13 On which date was the first Briton to win five consecutive gold medals knighted?
14 Which woman won four gold medals in successive games starting in Seoul?
15 Which discipline was practised by the man who won 15 Olympic medals between 1972 and 1980?
16 In the 20th century which country won most medals at the Winter Olympics?
17 Other than Carl Lewis who is the only other Olympian to win four consecutive individual titles in the same event?
18 Who were the silver medallists in basketball the year the US boycotted the Games due to the Soviet invasion of Afghanistan?
19 Who won the first Olympic gold for the men's singles in tennis after it was reinstated after 60 years?
20 Where was the record set for most gold medals in a single Games?
21 Where were the first Winter Paralympics held?
22 From which country does the competitor nicknamed Eric The Eel come from?
23 The oldest female gold medallist won in which event?
24 By winning the dressage in Sydney, Germany made it a total of how many team golds in this event?
25 In which decade were the first Summer Paralympics held?
26 Which creature went with Syd and Olly in the Sydney Olympics?
27 In Sydney, which discipline did Dean Macey compete in last?
28 Which Olympic gold medallist was a member of the team which won the British four man bobsleigh championship in 1989?
29 Where did the first Olympic women's basketball tournament take place?
30 Which Olympics were cancelled due to WWII?

VILLAINS See quiz 53, page 237
1 Markovic. 2 Saudi Arabia. 3 Spain. 4 Surveyor of the Queen's Pictures.
5 Last man to be hanged in public. 6 Pentonville. 7 Lee Harvey Oswald. 8 15.
9 Bulsara. 10 Oklahoma. 11 7 November. 12 Gerald Du Maurier.
13 Lucille McLauchlan. 14 King Rat. 15 Karla Faye Tucker. 16 Pol Pot. 17 Rachid.
18 Fingerprints. 19 Carlos the Jackal. 20 Alan Shearer. 21 Marie Kelly. 22 Mary Bell.
23 *Let Him Have It*. 24 Martin Luther King. 25 Hungerford. 26 Shot in Spain.
27 Hezbollah. 28 Tony Parnes. 29 Charles Brooks. 30 OJ Simpson.

QUIZ 56 POT LUCK 25

Answers - see Quiz 54, page 238

1 In what type of building would a dossal be hung?
2 Shergar won the 1981 Derby by a record how many lengths?
3 In which country is the city of Meerut?
4 What is the nationality of speedway champion Hans Hollen Nielsen?
5 Nelophobia is the fear of what?
6 As a teenager Morrissey ran a fan club for which American band?
7 In which sport does a slam dunk occur?
8 Who was John McEnroe's partner in his first Grand Slam title, a mixed doubles win in the French Open?
9 Maurice Herzog was the first person to conquer which mountain?
10 Belize changed its name from what?
11 How many dominoes are there in a double six set?
12 Who or what is a sulky?
13 In the mid 1970s the NBA and the ABA merged in which sport?
14 What was Elton John's first solo hit on his own Rocket label?
15 The Salk vaccine was developed in the fight against which disease?
16 Which Leo Sayer hit gave the Chrysallis label their first No1?
17 In sepek takrow you can hit the ball with any part of the body except which?
18 How old was James Herriot when he began writing books?
19 In which cathedral was King Henry III crowned?
20 How old was Eric Cantona when he retired from soccer?
21 What was Vivien Leigh's first movie after *Gone With The Wind*?
22 Which national team was managed by Englishman Roy Hodgson?
23 How was Charles II King of Spain unkindly known?
24 Which country joined the European Union in the same year as Spain?
25 What shape is the top of a lancet window?
26 What is the capital of the Dominican Republic?
27 Who had the first UK No 1 with "Unchained Melody"?
28 What is Julie Andrews' middle name?
29 In which decade of last century was the first Archery World Championship held?
30 In minutes, how brief was the movie *Brief Encounter*?

POT LUCK 24 See quiz 54, page 238

ANSWERS

1 1990s. 2 Clergyman. 3 Regulate. 4 New Zealand. 5 60–80. 6 Colombia.
7 Quote. 8 Rita & Les. 9 Poland. 10 Elizabeth. 11 Switzerland. 12 Stephen Daldry.
13 Boney M. 14 Ebor. 15 Georgia. 16 Cold. 17 *Honourable*. 18 Blue and white.
19 Cleeve Hill. 20 "What A Wonderful World". 21 John Surtees. 22 1930s.
23 Canadian Grand Prix. 24 Hercules. 25 Mexico. 26 "We Close Our Eyes".
27 Language. 28 United Nations. 29 White Surrey. 30 Sonny Liston.

QUIZ 57 MOVIE LEGENDS

Answers - see Quiz 59, page 243

1 Who was the male star of the first film to have a Royal Command Performance?
2 Which first name was Harpo Marx born with?
3 What was Woody Allen's first film with Mia Farrow?
4 Which actress wrote an autobiography called *Every Frenchman Has One*?
5 Lauren Bacall was 'discovered' when she appeared on the cover of which magazine?
6 What was Ingrid Bergman's final film for the big screen?
7 On which ship was Humphrey Bogart injured in WWI?
8 On which island was Yul Brynner born?
9 Who was the mother of Cary Grant's only child?
10 Which director fired Bette Davis on her very first professional engagement?
11 Ann Margret's screen debut was as which Hollywood legend's daughter?
12 What did Walt Disney do in WWI?
13 What was Robert Donat's last word on screen in the last film before his death?
14 Who played jazz piano in *In The Line of Fire*?
15 Whose debut movie *Every Sunday* also featured the star born Frances Gumm?
16 How was Mrs Charlie Chaplin, Paulette Goddard billed when she was a Ziegfeld Girl?
17 After making his way to the US alone aged 13 Sam Goldwyn was apprenticed as a maker of what?
18 In which movie did the first Mrs Charlie Chaplin play Dorothy?
19 What was the British title of the movie where Alfred Hitchcock made his first cameo appearance?
20 Who played Judy Holliday's tutor in the 1950 film directed by George Cukor?
21 In which year between 1941 and 1953 was Bob Hope not in the Top Ten Hollywood money making stars?
22 Which Hollywood gossip columnist was born Elda Furry?
23 Who played the title role in the movie about the greatest escapologist of all time?
24 Which movie gave Trevor Howard his first Oscar nomination?
25 What was Rock Hudson's debut movie where he needed 38 takes to say one line?
26 Which Howard Hughes movie launched the career of Jean Harlow?
27 Who in the movie industry was knighted by King Olav V in 1979?
28 Who did Susan Hayward play in the penultimate film for which she was Oscar nominated?
29 Who was introduced to the public in *Orphan's Benefit*?
30 Irving Berlin could only write music in which key?

QUIZ 58 POT LUCK 26

Answers - see Quiz 60, page 244

1 David Bryant became the first world champion in which sport?
2 In which country is the city of Karaj?
3 Which silent movie comic turned director used the pseudonym William Goodrich?
4 In which decade of the last century did women's hockey become an Olympic event?
5 In the 1997 Tory leadership election, who finished third?
6 Who first took Led Zeppelin's "Stairway To Heaven" into the singles charts?
7 Which newspaper was involved in the Jonathan Aitken court case?
8 Which Briton held the record number of Grand Prix victories before Alain Prost set a new record?
9 Which animated film was Walt Disney working on at the time of his death?
10 *GoldenEye* was named after Ian Fleming's home in which country?
11 Who found more success after leaving his band King Crabbs?
12 Which character does James Stewart play in the movie classic *Harvey*?
13 In which country is the port of Lobito?
14 What was the first Top Ten hit for Morrissey?
15 How many bones are there in the human neck?
16 What was the first movie that The Marx Brothers made for MGM?
17 Which English king was nicknamed because of his red face?
18 How many Oscars did composer Tim Rice win during the 1990s?
19 In which movie did the character Kimberly Wells feature?
20 Jim Clark spent all his racing career with which team?
21 Who plays the older detective in TV's *Dalziel and Pascoe*?
22 When did Munch paint his famous picture *The Scream* – 1840s, 1880s or the 1920s
23 Who was the first PM to move to 10 Downing Street?
24 How many chapters are there in the first book of the Old Testament?
25 Which Dickens' novel featured Jerry Cruncher?
26 Which team won the first University Boat Race?
27 Who starred as Isadora Duncan in the movie *Isadora*?
28 A barrico is a type of small what?
29 The 1930s movie classic *It Happened One Night* was originally called what?
30 Which Patty was the first woman to win golf's British and US Opens in the same year?

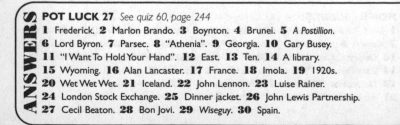

QUIZ 59 CRIME

Answers - see Quiz 57, page 241

1 Guy Trebert was the first person apprehended due to what?
2 In which state were Bonnie & Clyde arrested?
3 In 1960 in which country was Adolf Eichmann apprehended?
4 What does the word guerrilla mean?
5 What was the name of the Internet site used by US anti abortionists which resulted in a massive fine for them?
6 Where is the USA's Ellis II prison unit?
7 In which prison was the electric chair first used?
8 In which county is Schotts prison?
9 Dawn Alford of which newspaper wrote about a cabinet Minister's son selling drugs?
10 In 1998 two schoolboys were tried in which state for shootings at Westside Middle School?
11 Elaine Whitfield Sharp was a chief defence lawyer in whose trial?
12 Linford Christie won a libel case after a John McVicar article in which magazine?
13 In which southern England town was Billie Jo Jenkins murdered by her foster father?
14 Which team was suspended from the Tour De France over drug allegations in 1998?
15 Other than Nairobi where was a US embassy attacked at the end of the 1990s?
16 In which Street was the Omagh bomb detonated?
17 Which British prison was the scene of a major riot in 1990?
18 In which city was Yitzhak Rabin shot?
19 Which Judge in the early 1990s famously imprisoned a teenage shoplifter and her baby?
20 Farzad Bazoft was convicted and executed for spying where?
21 In which country were Karen Smith and Patricia Cahill accused of smuggling heroin in 1990?
22 What type of institution is Glenochil – remand centre, women's prison or young offenders?
23 Ian Gow was MP for where when he was killed by an IRA bomb?
24 Where in Egypt was there a massacre of tourists in 1997?
25 Why was Kevin Yates given a six month suspension by the rugby union in 1998?
26 Jim Sutherland was the first man to be convicted of which crime?
27 Where were incriminating photos found in the Gary Glitter case?
28 In which hospital did Reggie Kray receive his final treatment before his death?
29 Where in America was George Michael arrested in 1998?
30 What is the name of the famous prison in Yorkshire's major city?

QUIZ 60 POT LUCK 27

Answers - see Quiz 58, page 242

1 In *The Pirates Of Penzance* who was born on the 29th of February?
2 Which famous male movie star was born on the same day as Doris Day?
3 What does the B stand for in J.B. Priestley's name?
4 Bandar Seri Begawan is the capital of where?
5 In the title of Dirk Bogarde's autobiography what was *Struck By Lightning*?
6 Who said, "I awoke one morning and found myself famous"?
7 Which unit of measurement equals 3.2616 light years?
8 Which British liner was the first to be sunk by a U-boat on the first day of the Second World War?
9 Which state is Otis Redding's home in the lyrics of "On The Dock Of The Bay"?
10 Who played Buddy in the 1970s movie *The Buddy Holly Story*?
11 What was the Beatles first No 1 in America?
12 Manhattan lies between the Hudson and which river?
13 To the nearest million, what is the population of Portugal?
14 Where do tragic lovers Jenny and Oliver meet for the first time in *Love Story*?
15 In which US state was the first National Park established?
16 Who was Francis Rossi's school mate and long time bass player in Status Quo?
17 Which was the first country in the world to introduce national conscription?
18 At which Grand Prix circuit did Ayrton Senna die in an accident?
19 In which decade was the surgeon Christiaan Barnard born?
20 Who were the first Scottish group to have three No 1 singles?
21 USA's Reagan and Russia's Gorbachev first met in which country?
22 Which prominent figure did Mark Chapman murder?
23 Who was the first winner of consecutive best actress Oscars?
24 In 1973 Susan Shaw became the first woman to work on the floor where?
25 Which item of evening wear for men was created by Griswold Louillard?
26 "Never knowingly undersold" was the slogan of which chain store?
27 Which designer created the Ascot scene costumes for the film *My Fair Lady*?
28 Tico Torres was drummer with which globally successful band?
29 The movie *Goodfellas* was based on which novel?
30 In which country is the city of Murcia?

QUIZ 61 TV SITCOMS

Answers - see Quiz 63, page 247

1 Which star of a classic sitcom is the son of the actor born Alphonso Giuseppe Giovanni Roberto d'Abruzzo?

2 In which show did *Star Wars'* Luke Skywalker make his professional debut?

3 Which series did *The Offer* become?

4 Who played Hamish the restaurant critic in *Absolutely Fabulous*?

5 How many couples were *Coupling*?

6 What make of car was Bo & Luke Hazzard's "General Lee"?

7 In what type of establishment was *Desmonds* set?

8 Who said, "I have been complimented on my gestures by the chief psychiatrist of Broadmoor."?

9 In which month and year was the last episode of *Seinfeld* first broadcast in the US?

10 Which sitcom started life as *The Bishop Rides Again*?

11 Who was married to Ben in *My Family*?

12 Which actress/dancer is the elder sister of *The Cosby Show* regular Phylicia Rashad?

13 What was the last screen work of the actor who played Mainwaring in *Dad's Army*?

14 Which gay German officer in *Allo Allo* spent an episode disguised as a flamenco dancer?

15 Who were initially called Bobby and Billy?

16 For which firm did Samantha's husband work in *Bewitched*?

17 Which writer on *Birds of a Feather* also played Tracey's husband on the show?

18 Which *Blackadder* series covered the Regency period?

19 For which character did Kirstie Alley win an Emmy in 1991?

20 Who did the creator of *Ally McBeal* model his main character on?

21 In *Bread* what was the name of the vicar Aveline married?

22 Who sang the theme song to *Brush Strokes*?

23 What type of coat did Wolfie Smith wear?

24 Which character in *Cheers* was the sister in real life of the show's early producer?

25 What was the address of the Huxtables?

26 Which *Dad's Army* regular had written almost 40 plays?

27 In *The Day Today* who appeared under his own name?

28 Who played the Devil in the 2001 *Absolutely Fabulous*?

29 Where was the US version of *Till Death Us Do Part* set?

30 What is the real name of the actor who played George Constanza in *Seinfeld*?

QUIZ 62 POT LUCK 28

Answers - see Quiz 64, page 248

1 The restaurant chain the Spy House was backed by which actor who has played James Bond?
2 Which TV *Mr* was Richard Hearne?
3 In which country would you watch Boavista play a home soccer match?
4 Which herb goes into a bearnaise sauce along with tarragon?
5 What was the first Top Ten hit for 911?
6 What was the surname of the first Peter to be a presenter on Blue Peter?
7 Which singer with No 1's in his own right wrote the Buddy Holly classic "It Doesn't Matter Anymore?
8 Who was murdered in the first ever episode of *EastEnders*?
9 Which black and white cat was for many years on the cover of the Dandy comic?
10 Who was the longest reigning British King?
11 Mesclun is a type of what?
12 Made back in 1950, what was Marlon Brando's first film?
13 Who was the first Prime Minister to use Chequers?
14 What is a Dorset Blue Vinney?
15 Which chart-topper changed his name to Abdul Rahman in 1998?
16 In which year did Ethan Hawke make his movie debut?
17 How many different Olympic Games did Tessa Sanderson compete in?
18 Who visited Kirrin Island?
19 What does a palmiped possess?
20 Chronos was the Greek god of what?
21 Which original Rolling Stone was eligible for a bus pass in October 2001?
22 What is Ted's middle name in the movie *Bill & Ted's Excellent Adventure*?
23 A natatorium is another name for a what?
24 How is comedian Robert Harper better known?
25 In which city were Haagen-Dazs ice creams first sold?
26 Sue Barker and Penelope Keith both married husbands following which career?
27 What is the collective noun for a flock of larks?
28 What was the first Top Ten hit for 2 Unlimited?
29 In Mexican cookery what is a quesadilla?
30 How old was Prince Charles when he was invested as Prince of Wales?

POT LUCK 29 *See quiz 64, page 248*

1 Dolly Parton. 2 The English Channel. 3 K7. 4 Hayley Mills. 5 £20 note.
6 Fletcher Christian. 7 Egypt. 8 Jack Brabham. 9 Otis Redding. 10 George V.
11 "Release Me". 12 Ice cream. 13 Original. 14 Pakistan. 15 50 pence.
16 Mr Loud. 17 A wind which blows from Morocco to Spain. 18 "Go".
19 Paris. 20 Delia Smith. 21 Italy. 22 Maggie Smith. 23 "The Beagle".
24 *Rio Lobos*. 25 Windsurfing. 26 Liechtenstein. 27 Iggy Pop. 28 Big Jazza.
29 Rob Bowman. 30 Apiphobia.

QUIZ 63 MUSIC LEGENDS

Answers - see Quiz 61, page 245

1 Which single did The Rolling Stones release on the day The Beatles received their MBEs?
2 Michael Jackson's longest music video was the concept of whom?
3 Whose piano was bought by George Michael for £1.45 million in London in 2000?
4 What was the highest UK chart position of My Way?
5 Who released the album *Timeless – Live in Concert* in 2000?
6 Which pianist had the real first names Wladziu Valentino?
7 Who wrote the music for the classic movie *Bridge On The River Kwai*?
8 What is Andrew Lloyd Webber's most successful musical in terms of box office receipts worldwide?
9 Who died in the same crash as Hawkshaw Hawkins and Cowboy Copas?
10 Which 1950s chart topper was born Katherine Starks?
11 Who recorded the English lyrics version of "Torna A Sorrento" in 1961?
12 What was the Everly Brothers' first hit on both sides of the Atlantic?
13 Which Mersey band was the first to top the charts not managed by Brian Epstein?
14 In his singing days, DJ Jimmy Young kept which performer at No 2 with "Unchained Melody"?
15 Which songwriters gave The Overlanders their only hit?
16 Who made a *Diamond Tour* in 1998?
17 Whose autobiography was entitled *Killer*?
18 Who was No 1 when Queen Elizabeth II was crowned?
19 Which trio were the subject of The South Bank Show in March 1997?
20 What was the only No 1 for the girl with 'the giggle in her voice'?
21 Who won a Grammy for For The Ladies?
22 Who sang "Ol' Man River" at Frank Sinatra's 80th birthday party?
23 Who won the Best Song Oscar in 1953, in a movie she starred in?
24 What did Leonard Cohen become when he retired from music?
25 Who recorded "Something Stupid" with the lead singer of Culture Club?
26 Which orchestra leader had a hit from a film with the same title as a 2001 blockbuster?
27 Who celebrated their 30th anniversary in the music business with the album *Don't Stop*?
28 Who sang the theme song about the movie on the Profumo Affair?
29 Which 1954 chart topper was, according to the man himself, a huge influence on Elton John?
30 Which composer of Wet Wet Wet's biggest hit is an expert on crop circles?

TV SITCOMS See quiz 61, page 245
1 Alan Alda. 2 *The Cosby Show*. 3 *Steptoe & Son*. 4 Adrian Edmondson. 5 Three.
6 Dodge Charger. 7 Barbers shop. 8 John Cleese. 9 May 1998. 10 *All Gas and Gaiters*.
11 Susan. 12 Debbie Allen. 13 *AJ Wentworth BA*. 14 Gruber. 15 *Beavis & Butt Head*.
16 McMann & Tate. 17 Alun Lewis. 18 *Blackadder the Third*. 19 Rebecca Howe.
20 Michelle Pfeiffer. 21 Oswald. 22 Dexy's Midnight Runners. 23 Afghan.
24 Carla Tortelli (Rhea Perlman). 25 10 Stigwood Avenue. 26 Arnold Ridley.
27 Christopher Morris. 28 Anita Pallenberg. 29 New York. 30 Jay Scott Greenspan.

QUIZ 64 POT LUCK 29

Answers - see Quiz 62, page 246

1 Which singer/actress was Mrs Carl Dean?
2 Harriet Quimby was the first woman to fly over what?
3 The 1990s hit "Come Baby Come" was the first Top Ten appearance for which act?
4 Which British child star did Walt Disney bring to Hollywood in the late 1950s?
5 Scientist Michael Faraday died in 1867 but where was his face much seen late in the 20th century?
6 Clark Gable, Marlon Brando and Mel Gibson have all played which screen role?
7 In which country is the city of Tanta?
8 Who was the first person to win a Grand Prix in a car that he had designed?
9 Who wrote Aretha Franklin's first UK hit "Respect"?
10 Who became the first British monarch to make a broadcast on Christmas Day?
11 Which 1967 No 1 recorded the longest-ever stay in the UK Top 50?
12 A dessert served 'a la mode' in America would include what?
13 Under what name did Everett Bradley and Walter Taieb make the charts in the 1990s?
14 Who won the first ever World Cup in hockey?
15 What was Britain's first issued decimal coin?
16 Who – aptly enough – patented the first upright piano?
17 What is leveche, and where does it come from?
18 What was the first Top Ten hit for Moby?
19 The world's first speaking clock service started in which city?
20 Who is editor and publisher Michael Wynn-Jones married to?
21 Umberto II was the last king of which country?
22 Who played Susan in *Bed Among the Lentils*, part of Alan Bennett's *Talking Heads* series?
23 What was the animal name of Charles Darwin's survey ship?
24 Which movie was John Wayne making when he won his Oscar for *True Grit*?
25 Stephan van den Berg was the first Olympic gold winner in which water sport?
26 Which country are you in if you visit Vaduz?
27 James Jewel Osterberg became better known under which name?
28 Which role did Robbie Coltrane play in *Tutti Frutti*?
29 Who directed the movie *The X Files*?
30 What is a phobia about bees known as?

POT LUCK 28 See quiz 62, page 246

ANSWERS

QUIZ 65 BOOKS

Answers - see Quiz 67, page 251

1 Which book received the greatest publisher's advance in the 20th century?
2 Whose *Decline and Fall* is described in Evelyn Waugh's first novel?
3 Who won the Booker Prize the year after Paddy Clarke first won in the 1990s?
4 The author of *Trieste* and *The Meaning of Nowhere* was previously known as whom?
5 Which zoo was founded by the author of *The Overloaded Ark*?
6 Who are the two sisters in the novel subtitled *The Sacred and Profane Memories of Captain Charles Ryder*?
7 Where is Michael Ondaatje's *In the Skin of a Lion* set?
8 What was the title of Geoff Hurst's 2001 bestseller?
9 In which village does the hero of George Eliot's first full length novel live?
10 Whose diary opens Bram Stoker's most famous novel?
11 Who wrote the novel about the WWII drama brought to the small screen by Steven Spielberg and Tom Hanks?
12 *One Flew Over the Cuckoo's Nest* is told from whose standpoint?
13 What is Charles Dickens' only other work of historical fiction along with *A Tale of Two Cities*?
14 In *Animal Farm* what is the name of the animal seen as Trotsky?
15 Which painting did Donald Sassoon write about?
16 What is the title of journalist John Simpson's *Tales From A Traveller's Life*?
17 What was the first novel in which PD James' Cordelia Gray appeared?
18 Which poet is the official biographer of Philip Larkin?
19 Which sportsman's autobiography was called *A Season in Paradise*?
20 Which Award did *A Stitch in Time* win?
21 Who was the youngest of the *Little Women*?
22 Who is the subject of *Dear Tom*?
23 Approximately how many books per year did Barbara Cartland write during the last 20 years of her life?
24 From which Shakespeare play does the title of *Brave New World* come?
25 Which novel by *The Snowman*'s author was about a nuclear attack?
26 Which novel did the author of *Akenfield* write in 1960?
27 What is *Barchester Towers* the sequel to?
28 What was the title of the 2001 bestseller by the writer who had achieved 20th century success with *The Day of the Jackal* and *The Odessa File*?
29 What was the first novel in which Hercule Poirot appeared?
30 *Killing Dragons* is about the conquering of what?

FAMOUS NAMES See quiz 67, page 251

ANSWERS
1 Zak Starkey and Stella McCartney. 2 Jack Ryan. 3 Desperate Dan. 4 Alan Shepherd.
5 Jelly Roll Morton. 6 Elzie Sagar. 7 George W Bush & Tony Blair. 8 Mariel Hemingway.
9 Francis Ford Coppola. 10 Stella Rimington. 11 Bill Hudson and Goldie Hawn.
12 Columbia. 13 Patricia Highsmith. 14 Alfred Butts. 15 Ernie Wise. 16 Jackie Coogan.
17 Sam Wanamaker. 18 Harry Secombe and Peter Sellers. 19 Eric Idle. 20 L'Oreal.
21 Swimmer. 22 Kennedy. 23 London Eye. 24 Tiger Woods. 25 Kate Greenaway.
26 Stevens. 27 Medicine. 28 Bernard. 29 Astronomer Royal. 30 Trent.

QUIZ 66 POT LUCK 30

Answers - see Quiz 68, page 252

1   In motor racing, who was the first driver to be sacked twice by Benetton?
2   Who was the first *Coronation Street* actress to be awarded an OBE?
3   A brochette is another name for what type of food?
4   Who adapted *The Cider House Rules* into a movie?
5   In which country is the city of Makeyevka?
6   What does a lapidary deal in?
7   Last century, who was the first child born to a reigning British monarch?
8   Which group had 1970 top ten hits with "Sunny", "Belfast" and "Painter Man"?
9   What did D stand for in Franklin D Roosevelt's name?
10   In which 1980s movie did Mr & Mrs Harvey Keitel star?
11   Victor Emmanuel was the first King of which European country?
12   Leander is the oldest club in the world in which sport?
13   In which year did John Lennon perform his final live concert?
14   What is Sebastian Coe's middle name?
15   Which 1990s English soccer champions have a ground with the Darwen End?
16   Where in the US was the first artificial turf soccer pitch?
17   What was the first Top Ten single for Iron Maiden?
18   Which city hosts the oldest modern day marathon race?
19   Whose wives included Helen Menken and Mary Philips?
20   On TV for many years Michael Miles invited contestants to do what?
21   Paris and which other capital city were the first to be linked by telephone?
22   What was Gary Cooper's job before he became an actor?
23   The Strathcona Cup is competed for in which sport?
24   What was the first Top Ten single for James?
25   What was the name of the board game launched by Terry Venables?
26   Who dropped out of *The Godfather, Part III*, allowing Sofia Coppola to play the role?
27   Michael Fagan made the headlines when he broke into where?
28   In which film did a pilot named Klaatu appear?
29   How does Roger Peterson fit into the history of pop music?
30   Geraldine Rees was the first woman jockey to finish which race?

QUIZ 67 FAMOUS NAMES

Answers - see Quiz 65, page 249

1 Which two Beatles children had the same birthday?
2 Who invented the Barbie doll?
3 Which fictional Dan first put in an appearance in 1937?
4 Who was the first person to hit a golf ball on the Moon?
5 How was Ferdinand Joseph Lamothe better known?
6 Who created Popeye?
7 Which famous names expressed they used the same toothpaste in 2001?
8 Which member of a famous film and writing family owned Sam's Restaurant in Manhattan?
9 Which film director is the son of a former first flute of the New York Symphony Orchestra under Toscanini?
10 Who wrote an autobiography called Open Secret?
11 Who are Kate Hudson's parents?
12 Which university awarded the Prize named after publisher Pulitzer?
13 How is Patricia Plangman better known?
14 Who invented Scrabble?
15 Which late comedian's autobiography was called Still On My Way to Hollywood?
16 Who was the first movie child to earn a million dollars?
17 The rebuilding of the Globe Theatre on the south bank of the Thames was the brainchild of whom?
18 Which two Goons had the same birthday?
19 Which member of the Monty Python team wrote The Rutland Dirty Weekend Book?
20 Liliane Bettencourt is heiress to which company's fortune?
21 What type of sports person tested the first Rolex Oyster watch?
22 Which father of a future President was executive producer on many Gloria Swanson movies?
23 Which London landmark was designed by David Marks and Julia Barfield?
24 According to the Guinness Book of Records, who is the most searched for sportsman on the Internet?
25 Which author has a prize for children's book illustration named after her?
26 Who owned the original yacht after whom The Americas Cup was named?
27 What did Giorgio Armani study at university?
28 What was the first name of 'Mr Laura Ashley'?
29 Which position was held by Sir Martin Rees at the turn of the century?
30 Jesse Boot, of Boots fame, was which Lord when he died in 1931?

BOOKS See quiz 65, page 249

1 *Without Remorse*. 2 Paul Pennyfeather. 3 James Kelman. 4 James Morris. 6 Jersey.
5 Julia and Cordelia. 7 Toronto. 8 *1966 And All That*. 9 Hayslope. 10 Jonathan Harker.
11 Stephen Ambrose. 12 Bromden. 13 *Barnaby Rudge*. 14 Snowball. 15 Mona Lisa.
16 *A Mad World, My Masters*. 17 *An Unsuitable Job For A Woman*. 18 Andrew Motion.
19 Henrik Larsson. 20 Whitbread. 21 Amy. 22 Tom Courtenay. 23 23.
24 *The Tempest*. 25 *When The Wind Blows*. 26 *A Treasonable Growth*. 27 *The Warden*.
28 *The Veteran*. 29 *The Mysterious Affair at Styles*. 30 The Alps.

QUIZ 68 POT LUCK 31

Answers - see Quiz 66, page 250

1 At the 1948 Olympics in which two events did Fanny Blankers Koen choose not to compete despite holding the world record in both?
2 Who was the only British male to feature in the first ever UK album chart
3 In *Mike Bassett: England Manager* who does Bassett manage before coaching England?
4 In 1900, which country had the world's tallest habitable building?
5 Who was Southampton manager for 113 days in 2001?
6 In 2001 which jockey was the fastest to ride 100 winners in a season?
7 Which well known literary figure wrote the screenplay for the movie *Billy Bathgate*?
8 How many women had been a Prime Minister before Indira Gandhi took office?
9 Dodi Fayed was co producer on which Oscar winning film?
10 Susan Brown was the first woman to compete in which race?
11 What was Carl Lewis's third Olympic gold among the four he won in Los Angeles?
12 Who directed the movie The Empire Strikes Back?
13 In which country is the city of Culiacan?
14 Who played the part of Frankenstein in the 1930s classic movie?
15 Before losing to Rocky Marciano who said, "If I can't beat this bum take my name off the record books."?
16 In which country did malmsey wine originate?
17 Which US President patented a type of lifebelt?
18 In London what was built on the site of Newgate prison?
19 In which country were post codes first introduced?
20 How many Die Hard movies were made before Samuel L Jackson was introduced as Bruce Willis's sidekick?
21 Australian prime minister Harold Holt died in what circumstances?
22 Imelda Marcos had hundreds of pairs of what?
23 What was the first Top Ten hit for Prodigy?
24 Lassa Fever was named after who or what?
25 Lord Brabazon was the first Briton to receive which type of licence?
26 In which country was the first HQ of the French Foreign Legion?
27 If Alexander Graham Bell had been a few hours later to claim his patent for the phone, who would have got it?
28 What was Tony Bullimore's craft when he capsized in the 1996 Vendee Globe?
29 Which month of the year was part of the name of a Bond girl?
30 Who did Yannick Noah beat to become the first Frenchman to win the French Open tennis champion for 37 years?

QUIZ 69 CRICKET

Answers - see Quiz 71, page 255

1 Who took 107 international wickets in 1998?
2 Who won the toss when Lancashire lost the NatWest Trophy Final in 1986?
3 Who won the County Championship the year England won the soccer World Cup?
4 By how many wickets did Middlesex win the last Gillette Cup?
5 In the 1970s which NatWest Trophy winner had the shortest name?
6 Which humorous writer said October was a strange month for the real cricket fan as it was then he discovered his wife had left him in May?
7 Which was the most northerly side to share the County Championship in 1977?
8 Who captained the first South African side after the fall of apartheid ?
9 Against which side did Sachin Tendulkar score his 18th one day international century?
10 Who, in 1991, had sponsored what became the AXA Life League in 1992?
11 Who took eight wickets for England in the first ever Test match?
12 Where did Brian Lara score 390 runs in one day in June 1994?
13 Who was man of the match after taking a Test hat-trick against the West Indies in 1995?
14 How was Mansur Ali Khan better known?
15 Who was the first Pakistan cricketer to score 1000 runs and take 100 wickets in a year twice?
16 Which captain won every toss against South Africa in 1960?
17 Who was the first player to score 2000 first-class runs in a season without scoring a century?
18 Who played for Australia between 1982–83 and 1985–86 and for South Africa in 1991?
19 Which then Lancashire soccer club did EH 'Patsy' Hendren play for?
20 Where was the first Oxford and Cambridge match played?
21 Which former England soccer captain became a playing member of the MCC?
22 Who took all 10 wickets against Pakistan in February 1999?
23 Which football club does former England captain Rachael Heyhoe Flint support?
24 Which Englishman overtook the Englishman who overtook Geoff Boycott's record of runs scored in Test cricket?
25 Why was Geoff Boycott banned from Test cricket in 1982?
26 To the nearest 20, how many record breaking Test runs did Isaac Vivian Alexander Richards make in one calendar year in 1976?
27 Which was the first city to have four Test grounds?
28 How many runs did Jim Laker concede in his 19 wicket haul against Australia in 1956?
29 Who won the County Championship for seven consecutive years in the 1950s?
30 Where did Brian Lara score 375 runs against England in April 1994?

ANSWERS

HOLLYWOOD See quiz 71, page 255

1 Mrs Deisda Wilcox. 2 *Ordinary People* (Tim Hutton). 3 *Peggy Sue Got Married*. 4 *Apollo 13*.
5 Fatty Arbuckle. 6 *The Harder They Fall*. 7 *Main Street To Broadway*. 8 Warner Bros.
9 *Wired*. 10 Jason Robards Jr. 11 *He Knows You're Alone*. 12 Cat. 13 *Pentimento*.
14 Cosmopolitan. 15 *Woman of the Year*. 16 *Stardust Memories*. 17 William Holden.
18 *Invitation to the Dance*. 19 Joaquin Phoenix. 20 *Godzilla*. 21 DW Griffith. 22 Elaine May.
23 *Waiting To Exhale*. 24 Elliott Gould. 25 Amy Irving & Priscilla Pointer. 26 Julianne Moore.
27 *The Country Girl*. 28 *Pearl Harbor*. 29 Dr Cameron. 30 M Night Shyamalan.

QUIZ 70 POT LUCK 32

Answers - see Quiz 72, page 256

1 Who played Bill Sikes in the movie when Alec Guinness was Fagin?
2 Which manager signed Matt Jansen at Blackburn Rovers?
3 At which university did Anthony Minghella teach before becoming an Oscar winner?
4 Balti is the Indian word for what?
5 Who won an Oscar for the song "Three Coins In The Fountain"?
6 Frank McCourt's memoirs were set in which Irish county?
7 Which Elvis single made him the first artist to have three consecutive British No 1s?
8 Hanepoot is a type of what?
9 What was named after Buck's Club in London?
10 Which food item comes from the Turkish for rotating?
11 Kummel is a Russian liqueur extracted from what?
12 Which country has a wine growing area called O'Higgins?
13 Which rays did Ernest Rutherford discover?
14 What subject did TV cook Sophie Grigson study at university?
15 What is added to an omelette to make an Omelette Argenteuil?
16 After winning the world title, who was Jack Dempsey's first opponent where the fight went to the full distance?
17 Who did Tottenham Hotspur beat in the final to become FA Cup and League Champions for the first time?
18 Which No 1 single mentions Jackie – Madame – Onassis?
19 Who was the first professional to captain England at cricket?
20 In 1952 at the Chateau de Chambord what type of display was first shown?
21 In which country did the card game canasta originate?
22 What did the Tower Commission investigate in the US in the 1980s?
23 Which band's vocalists have included Blaze Bayley and Bruce Dickinson?
24 On TV, who had a house featuring a dog, cat and a frog?
25 In which city did Kurt Cobain die?
26 How is writer Salvatore Lombino better known?
27 Radium has the atomic number of which bingo call?
28 How is TV comedian Edward McGinnis better known?
29 Cocose is a butter made from what?
30 Which was the first US state to abolish slavery?

POT LUCK 33 *See quiz 72, page 256*

ANSWERS

1 Savage Garden. 2 Gary Oldman. 3 Have a heart transplant. 4 Bertie Mee.
5 "Three Times A Lady". 6 Angling. 7 Texas. 8 Hampton Court maze. 9 Harmonica.
10 "Do They Know It's Christmas?". 11 Lacrosse. 12 Peru. 13 Boxing. 14 House.
15 Rudolph. 16 A Rabbi. 17 Boisterous. 18 Lev. 19 Elizabeth Taylor. 20 Iowa.
21 Kenya. 22 *Gandhi*. 23 Roper. 24 Handkerchief. 25 Wilhelm. 26 Pack horse.
27 Germany. 28 Winston Churchill. 29 Symptoms of disease. 30 Connie Francis.

QUIZ 71 HOLLYWOOD

Answers - see Quiz 69, page 253

1 Who named Hollywood?
2 What was the first film of the actor married to Debra Winger from 1986 to 1990?
3 Helen Hunt's fourth movie shares its name with which later musical?
4 What was music composer James Horner's first Oscar nomination of the 1990s?
5 Who used the pseudonym William Goodrich when Hollywood turned his back on him after a scandal?
6 Humphrey Bogart underwent surgery for cancer of the oesophagus after making which film?
7 In which 1953 film did Oscar Hammerstein II appear as himself?
8 Which studio gave Lauren Bacall her film debut?
9 Which movie was based on the life of John Belushi who died in a Beverly Hills hotel?
10 Who portrayed the author of The Maltese Falcon in Julia?
11 His directorial debut was That Thing You Do, but what was his first movie as an actor?
12 What type of screen animal was Rhubarb?
13 Which Lillian Hellman novel became a movie where she was portrayed by Jane Fonda?
14 Which company did William Randolph Hearst found with the express purpose of making his mistress Marion Davies a star?
15 Which MGM movie did Katharine Hepburn make directly after The Philadelphia Story?
16 What was Woody Allen's last film with United Artists?
17 Which Hollywood star was co owner of the Mount Kenya Safari Club?
18 What was Gene Kelly's solo directing debut?
19 Who played Commodus in Russell Crowe's Oscar winning movie?
20 "Deeper Underground" was written for which Hollywood movie?
21 Which Hollywood legend did Charles Dance play in Good Morning Babylon?
22 Who co wrote Heaven Can Wait with Warren Beatty?
23 What was Whitney Houston's follow up to her on screen debut?
24 Who was the first non Swede to star in an Ingmar Bergman movie?
25 Which mother and daughter appeared in Carrie?
26 Who played opposite Anthony Hopkins in the follow up to Silence of the Lambs?
27 In which movie did the future Grace Kelly win the New York Film Critics Award playing the wife of an alcoholic actor singer?
28 Which movie had the largest pre shooting budget?
29 Which role did the marvellously named Spottiswoode Aitken play in DW Griffiths' Birth of a Nation?
30 Who wrote and directed The Sixth Sense?

ANSWERS

CRICKET See quiz 69, page 253
1 Allan Donald. 2 Sussex. 3 Yorkshire. 4 Seven. 5 Kent. 6 Denis Norden.
7 Middlesex. 8 Kepler Wessels. 9 Zimbabwe. 10 There was no sponsor.
11 Alfred Shaw. 12 Edgbaston. 13 Dominic Cork. 14 The Nawab of Pataudi.
15 Imran Khan. 16 Colin Cowdrey. 18 David Green, Lancashire. 17 Kepler Wessels.
19 Manchester City. 20 Lord's. 21 Gary Lineker. 22 Anil Kumble. 23 Wolves.
24 Graham Gooch passed David Gower. 25 Went on a rebel tour to South Africa.
26 1710. 27 Colombo. 28 90. 29 Surrey. 30 Recreation Ground, St John's Antigua.

QUIZ 72 POT LUCK 33

Answers - see Quiz 70, page 254

1 Daniel Jones and Darren Hayes made the pop charts under what name?
2 To whom was Uma Thurman married before Ethan Hawke?
3 Philip Blaiberg was the second person to do what?
4 Which double winning soccer manager died in October 2001?
5 Which Commodores hit became Motown's best ever UK seller?
6 CIPS is the body which regulates which sport?
7 The gigantic nightclub Gilley's Club is in which US state?
8 London and Wise designed which famous much visited feature?
9 Charles Wheatstone is the creator of what?
10 Which debut single became the first to enter the charts straight at No 1?
11 Baggataway developed into which game?
12 In which country is the city of Callao?
13 What was the first sport screened on ITV?
14 What name is given to the circular target in curling?
15 What is the middle name of former US President Gerald Ford?
16 What was the profession of Harry Houdini's father?
17 What does the musical term strepitoso mean – boisterous, in military style or in strict tempo?
18 What is the unit of currency of Bulgaria?
19 Who has been married to Larry Fortensky, John Warner and Nicky Hilton?
20 Which state in America is known as the Hawkeye State?
21 Princess Elizabeth was visiting which country at the time that she become Queen Elizabeth II?
22 "No man's life can be encompassed in one telling" are the opening words of which epic movie?
23 What was the surname of sitcom marrieds George and Mildred?
24 Richard II is said to have popularised the use of which everyday item?
25 What is Leonardo Di Caprio's middle name?
26 Who or what is a sumpter?
27 In which country is the city of Wuppertal?
28 Whose only novel was called *Savrola*?
29 What is semeiology the study of?
30 Concetta Franconero took old standard songs back into the pop charts under which name?

POT LUCK 32 *See quiz 70, page 254*

QUIZ 73 PLANET EARTH

Answers - see Quiz 75, page 259

1. In which US state is the Jewel cave system?
2. The largest man made excavation in the world mines which element?
3. Which animal weighs the most – grizzly bear, polar bear or a walrus?
4. What is Europe's largest island which is not a country in its own right?
5. Which desert is on the US–Mexico border?
6. What is the most common element in the earth's crust after oxygen?
7. Which planet orbits the Sun fastest?
8. Acid rain results due to a pollution of the atmosphere with oxides of nitrogen and what?
9. What is another name for a tsunami?
10. What colour is apatite?
11. Where was the meteorite High Possil found?
12. Where is the highest waterfall outside South America?
13. What is the world highest island?
14. How many states does Lake Michigan cover?
15. Which planet has the hottest surface?
16. Orogenesis is concerned with the formation of what?
17. Which unit measures distances beyond the solar system?
18. Where was the meteorite Armanty found on Earth?
19. Actinobiology studies the effect of what on living organisms?
20. Cryogenics studies materials under what conditions?
21. Of the five largest glaciers in the world which is the only one not in Antarctica?
22. Which part of planet Earth would a pedologist observe?
23. The Appleton layer plays a role in what – heat control, sifting of toxic gases or radio communication?
24. It isn't a sea, but what is the Afsluidijk Sea?
25. How many countries does the Mekong river flow through?
26. What is the most common element in the universe after hydrogen?
27. Which planet is the lightest?
28. Which scale measures the hardness of substances?
29. How many light years is Alpha Centauri from the Earth?
30. What substance is around 90% of the Earth's core made from?

TV DRAMA *See quiz 75, page 259*

1 *Hearts & Bones.* 2 DCI Tom Barnaby. 3 William Boyd. 4 Ian Rankin. 5 *Mersey Beat.*
6 Sherlock Holmes. 7 Ken Loach. 8 *Band of Brothers.* 9 Arthur Parker. 10 *Holding On.*
11 Victoria & Albert. 12 *Peak Practice.* 13 Hamish Macbeth. 14 James Nesbitt.
15 Sabbach. 16 Chicago. 17 *The Final Cut.* 18 *The Way We Live Now.* 19 Warren Clarke.
20 Hamble. 21 John Sullivan. 22 *Masterpiece Theater.* 23 Anthony Minghella.
24 Colin Bateman. 25 Alan Davies. 26 *Jewel in the Crown.* 27 Chris Kelly.
28 Pharmaceutical. 29 Sir Godber Evans. 30 Telly Savalas (*Kojak*).

QUIZ 74 POT LUCK 34

Answers - see Quiz 76, page 260

1 Which country is directly south of the southern area of Morocco?
2 Which band has had Briana Corrigan and Jacqui Abbot among its vocalists?
3 To the nearest ten, how many minutes did the original *Planet of the Apes* movie last?
4 Which Elton John song mentions a "man who sells potions?
5 Who wrote the screenplay for the phenomenally successful movie *The Bodyguard*?
6 In which country is the city of Chiba?
7 The song "Secret Love" came from which movie?
8 In which country is the city of Constanta?
9 Which Offenbach composition was used to advertise Bailey's Irish Cream?
10 TV's popular sitcom *To The Manor Born* was set in which village?
11 Who is Postman Pat's wife?
12 Pete Townshend's first No 1 as a producer was for which group?
13 Who was the first non African to win the Olympic 5000m after Lasse Viren in Canada?
14 How did James Wight become better known to the reading world?
15 Dao wine comes from which country?
16 Who received an Oscar nomination for the original score for *The Talented Mr Ripley*?
17 *Thirtysomething* was set in which US state?
18 Sibbald's rorqual also known as what?
19 A passata is made from which vegetable?
20 What was the first Top Ten hit for Corona?
21 Who won the Best Director Oscar for the movie *Cavalcade*?
22 Which country borders Argentina, Brazil and Bolivia?
23 Who conducted the Three Tenors in their Italia 90 concert?
24 Which Springsteen song was a hit for Manfred Mann's Earth Band?
25 Who directed the first *Terminator* film?
26 In which country is the city of Campos?
27 Which poet wrote *Sea Fever*?
28 Cartagena is found in Spain and which other country?
29 "Crash" was the only top ten hit for which act?
30 A maxwell unit is a measure of what?

POT LUCK 35 See quiz 76, page 260
1 Mark Little. 2 Spit. 3 Space Shuttle launch. 4 Angus Deayton. 5 "Ticket To Ride".
6 Oenology. 7 Valentino Rossi. 8 Roberta Flack. 9 Jean Terrell. 10 Jürgen Hingsen.
11 Private Godfrey. 12 One. 13 Crescent shaped. 14 Princess. 15 William.
16 Azerbaijan. 17 Bryan Robson. 18 Poles. 19 Daniel Day-Lewis. 20 James Naughtie.
21 Bernard Herrmann. 22 Sandwich. 23 John Travolta & Olivia Newton-John.
24 India. 25 *Twin Peaks*. 26 2061. 27 Three. 28 Maurice Jarre. 29 Betty Stove.
30 *The Phil Silvers Show*.

QUIZ 75 TV DRAMA

Answers - see Quiz 73, page 257

1 In which drama did Rich, Emma, Annie and Sam share a surname?
2 Who is Sgt Gavin Troy's boss?
3 Who wrote the novel on which *Armadillo* was based?
4 Whose novels were used as the basis for the drama series Rebus?
5 In which series did Supt Susan Blake take charge?
6 *Murder Rooms* was a drama series about which detective?
7 Which veteran film maker wrote *Navigators* about the break up of the rail network?
8 Which series was about Easy Company, a unit of paratroopers?
9 What was the name of the songsheet salesman in *Pennies From Heaven*?
10 Which 1990s Tony Marchant series about life in London starred Phil Daniels ?
11 Which famous couple were portrayed by Jonathan Firth and Victoria Hamilton in a 2001 drama?
12 In which series did character Erica Matthews replace Beth Glover?
13 Which detective was played on TV by the star of *The Full Monty* and *Angela's Ashes*?
14 Who played Adam in *Cold Feet*?
15 Where was the German made series *Heimat* based?
16 The outside scenes for *Hill Street Blues* were filmed in which city?
17 What was the last part of the trilogy which began with *House of Cards*?
18 In which series was Auguste Melmotte a central character?
19 Who played Faith's husband in *Down To Earth*?
20 Alongside which river was *Howard's Way* set?
21 Who wrote the David Jason series based on an infamous Dickens character?
22 Under what label was *I Claudius* broadcast in the USA?
23 Which early writer of *Morse* went on to write the movie *Truly Madly Deeply*?
24 Who wrote *Murphy's Law* for James Nesbitt?
25 If Lesley Sharp played Rose, who played Bob in 2001?
26 Which epic won the 1984 International Emmy for Best Drama?
27 Which one time food show presenter produced *Kavanagh QC*?
28 *Swallow* was about which industry?
29 Who did Ian Richardson play in *Porterhouse Blue*?
30 Which actor who played a TV cop won a Purple Heart in Korea in real life?

QUIZ 76 POT LUCK 35

Answers - see Quiz 74, page 258

1 Who was the main co presenter of *The Big Breakfast* at the same time as Zoe Ball?
2 Which dog did Chris Tarrant have to contend with on *TISWAS*?
3 John Young was the commander on which notable flight?
4 Who played Mike Channel in *KYTV*?
5 What was the first No 1 single from the Beatles' film *Help!*?
6 What is the study of wine known us?
7 Which motor cyclist took his 10th win of the 2001 season in the Malaysian Grand Prix?
8 Who sang the title song in *Someone to Watch Over Me* with Sting and Gene Ammons?
9 Who replaced Diana Ross when she left The Supremes?
10 Who was world record holder when Daley Thompson won Olympic gold in 1984?
11 In sitcom, which character had sisters called Dolly & Cissy?
12 On average, how many hours does a giraffe sleep in a 24 hour period?
13 What shape is a roll if it is rugelach?
14 "Say I'm Your Number One" was the only Top Ten hit for which act?
15 What was Clark Gable's real first name?
16 In which country is the city of Baku?
17 Who else hit a hat-trick for England during the time that Gary Lineker was notching his five hat-tricks?
18 What did the initial P stand for in the name of writer LP Hartley?
19 Julia Roberts turned down *Shakespeare In Love* because which actor of her choice did not get to play Shakespeare?
20 Which newsman replaced Richard Baker as the presenter of the Proms on BBC?
21 Who scored the music for *Psycho*'s famous shower scene?
22 Which food item was linked to Colin in the title of a Mel Smith sitcom series?
23 In the pop charts which male/female duo have spent most weeks at No 1?
24 In which country is the city of Guntur?
25 As well as being an ex US President, Harry S Truman was a sheriff in which TV series?
26 When is Halley's Comet predicted to make its next visit in Earth's vicinity?
27 How many books were there in Mervyn Peake's *Gormenghast* series?
28 Who produced the stirring movie music for *Lawrence Of Arabia*?
29 Who won the first set in the last Wimbledon Ladies Singles final to have a British competitor?
30 Which sitcom was first called *You'll Never Get Rich* in the US?

POT LUCK 34 *See quiz 74, page 258*

ANSWERS

QUIZ 77 20TH CENTURY 1951–1999

Answers - see Quiz 79, page 263

1 Which minority tribe did Rwanda's majority tribe tried to wipe out in the 1990s?
2 On which day of the week in 1953 was Everest conquered?
3 Which Apollo mission saw the fastest human speed record?
4 In 1990 who was granted a US patent for an energy saving double filament light bulb?
5 The Clean Air Act was introduced after which year when 4,000 people died in London's worst recorded smog?
6 Where did Francisco Bahamonde rule?
7 Radio Caroline first began broadcasting five miles off which port
8 What was the name of the commander who took the first nuclear submarine under the North Pole?
9 On which day of the week was the Channel Tunnel opened?
10 How many nations allied against Iraq in the Gulf War – was it 24, 28 or 32?
11 Which country was the first to have a postcode made up of letters and numbers?
12 What was the "Queen Elizabeth" being used as when sabotaged in Hong Kong harbour?
13 Which US President during the height of the Cold War, said there would be no Soviet domination of Eastern Europe?
14 In which city was the first Cadillac made?
15 In 1951's general election where was Margaret Roberts (later Thatcher) defeated?
16 For how many years in World War II were the lights in Piccadilly Circus blacked out?
17 Who was the first centre spread in *Playboy*?
18 Jacqueline Cochrane was the first woman to break what?
19 Who was the first cartoon character to appear on a US postage stamp?
20 Who or what were Able and Baker, the first pair of their kind to return from space?
21 Who devised transparent solar panels which can be used as windows and as a means of producing solar power?
22 Che Guevara was killed while training guerrillas against which government?
23 In which hospital was the world's first test tube baby born?
24 Who was the youngest winner of the Nobel Peace Prize when a winner in 1964?
25 Which charity began as a newspaper appeal called "The Forgotten Prisoners"?
26 In what year was the first phone card issued in Japan?
27 Which play was first to win five of the awards named after actress Antoinette Perry?
28 In 1997 which country saw the largest and most numerous forest fires?
29 Which company owned the pesticide plant in Bhopal which saw a tragic chemical leak?
30 In which game did Nintendo's Mario character first appear?

MUSIC SOLO PERFORMERS See quiz 79, page 263
1 Microsoft Network. 2 Marian Anderson. 3 Craig David. 4 "Tears on My Pillow".
5 Anita Harris. 6 Mary Hopkin. 7 Jilted John. 8 Courtney Love. 9 Barry Gibb.
10 "Frozen". 11 Liza Minnelli. 12 Kylie Minogue. 13 Prince. 14 Suzi Quatro.
15 *Greetings From Asbury Park*. 16 Alvin Stardust. 17 Brentford. 18 "Evergreen".
19 Smokey Robinson. 20 Barry Manilow. 21 Apple. 22 Marty Wilde. 23 Paul Simon.
24 58. 25 *Jewel of the Nile*. 26 Peter Asher. 27 Sinead O'Connor. 28 Don McLean.
29 Eartha Kitt. 30 Carole King.

QUIZ 78 POT LUCK 36

Answers - see Quiz 80, page 264

1 Whose world 200m record did Michael Johnson break in June 1996?
2 Capybara is the name of the world's largest what?
3 "Run To You" was the only Top Ten hit for which act?
4 Dzongkha is the official language of which monarchy?
5 Which Spice Girl wrote "Girl Power" by her signature on the cover notes of the album *Spice*?
6 What's the number of HAL the computer in Kubrick's movie 2001?
7 Which capital is furthest north – Addis Ababa, Kampala, Khartoum or Nairobi?
8 Who came between Sebastian Coe and Steve Ovett in the Final of the 1500m at the Moscow Olympics?
9 What was the final Bond film in which Lois Maxwell played Miss Moneypenny?
10 In which country is the city of Las?
11 Nice ads, but which make of car were Papa and Nicole advertising?
12 Who was the first female presenter of TV's Grandstand?
13 Which Rod Stewart No 1 was originally the flip side of "Reason to Believe"?
14 The man who broke Sebastian Coe's 800m world record was running for which country?
15 Who was the first jockey to win the Derby in three consecutive races?
16 Mungo Park, the explorer of the River Niger, came from which country?
17 In sitcom, which vehicle was connected with Stan Butler?
18 Ambergris obtained from which sea creature?
19 "You'll Never Find Another Love Like Mine" was the only Top Ten hit for which singer?
20 Which screen tough guy made his debut as a mugger in Woody Allen's *Bananas*?
21 On a computer keyboard where is the letter B in relation to V?
22 Which group still meeting up for reunions included Peter Tork and Michael Nesmith?
23 In round figures, what was Irving Berlin's output of writing popular songs?
24 In which decade was the Argentinian Grand Prix first held?
25 Who gave Stock/Aitken/Waterman their first No1 hit?
26 What was first held at Philip Island, Victoria in 1928?
27 In fiction which detective married Harriet Vane?
28 Which country can have the letters NO added to its name to name its currency?
29 Which cereal is polenta made from?
30 Which organisation known by its initials did Anthea Turner work for before becoming a TV presenter?

QUIZ 79 MUSIC SOLO PERFORMERS

Answers - see Quiz 77, page 261

1 Which on line company broadcast Madonna's Brixton Academy concert live on the Internet?

2 Who was the first black performer to sing at the New York Metropolitan Opera?

3 Who was the youngest male singer to enter the UK charts at No 1?

4 What was Kylie Minogue's last No 1 produced by Stock, Aitken and Waterman?

5 Which solo performer promoted Slendertone keep fit equipment in 1997?

6 Which solo singer married record producer Tony Visconti?

7 How did Graham Fellows aka John Shuttleworth appear in the UK charts in 1978?

8 Which singer's daughter by a controversial performer was called Frances Bean?

9 Who produced Lulu's album which included the tracks "Every Woman Knows" and "How 'Bout Us"?

10 What did Madonna sing on her first live UK TV show for 15 years in 1998?

11 Which music and musical star deputised for Julie Andrews on Broadway in *Victor/Victoria* in the mid 1990s?

12 Who was about to release an album called *Impossible Princess* in 1997 but changed the title after the death of Princess Diana?

13 Who married Mayte Garcia in 1996?

14 Which singer appeared as Leather Tuscadero in *Happy Days*?

15 What was 'The Boss's' debut album?

16 Which singer has appeared in *Hollyoaks* and was Gaston in *Beauty & The Beast* in the West End?

17 Which club gave a teenage Roderick David Stewart a soccer trial?

18 For what did Barbra Streisand win an Oscar for Best Song?

19 Which singer had children called Berry and Tamla?

20 Whose musical *Harmony* opened on Broadway in 1998?

21 Which company released James Taylor's debut album?

22 Which 1950s star wrote Status Quo's "Ice In the Sun"?

23 Which singer wrote the then biggest musical flop in New York history in 1998?

24 How many albums had Cliff Richard made by his 40th year in show business?

25 From which movie soundtrack was Billy Ocean's biggest hit?

26 Which 1964 chart topper won the Producer of the Year Grammy in 1977?

27 Whose debut album was *The Lion and the Cobra*?

28 Who was the subject of the song "Killing Me Softly"?

29 Which vocalist who recorded with Bronski Beat in the the late 1980s was described by Orson Welles as 'the most exciting woman in the world'?

30 To which singer was the album *Tapestry Revisited* dedicated?

20TH CENTURY 1951–1999 *See quiz 77, page 261*

1 Tutsi. 2 Friday. 3 Apollo 10. 4 Nelson Waterbury. 5 1952. 6 Spain (Gen. Franco).
7 Harwich. 8 Anderson. 9 Friday. 10 28. 11 Great Britain. 12 University.
13 Gerald Ford. 14 Detroit. 15 Dartford. 16 Five. 17 Marilyn Monroe.
18 Sound barrier. 19 Bugs Bunny. 20 Monkeys. 21 Michael Gratzel. 22 Bolivia.
23 Oldham General. 24 Martin Luther King. 25 Amnesty International. 26 1992.
27 *A Man For All Seasons*. 28 Brazil. 29 Union Carbide. 30 Donkey Kong.

QUIZ 80 POT LUCK 37

Answers - see Quiz 78, page 262

1 Who designed the first lightning conductor?
2 The soundtrack of the movie *Philadelphia* featured songs by Bruce Springsteen and who else?
3 Which sitcom introduced viewers to the 1-2-1 Club?
4 The trudgen is a movement in which sport?
5 Where are denticles found on a shark?
6 He made the Top Twenty in 1999, but before that when did Elvis Costello last make the Top Ten?
7 Which country is home to the airline Pluna?
8 Who was the first actor ever to refuse an Oscar?
9 Who lived at Cemetery Ridge?
10 Under which name did Orson Whipple Hungerford III become an actor riding across our screens?
11 Who described himself as "an average guy who could carry a tune"?
12 Who is the smallest Teletubby?
13 What was Jude Law's first film?
14 Which movie great set up the American Foundation for AIDS Research?
15 The Kakadu National Park is located in which country?
16 What could Sean Connery's character change in *The Avengers*?
17 Which docu soap did Emma Boundy find fame?
18 Which TV star is mum to Robert, Ben and Jack Willis?
19 Charles Townes pioneered what?
20 Where in America was Alcoholics Anonymous founded in the 1930s?
21 In the Elvis song, which two words follow "Return to sender"?
22 Kalium is an alternative name for which element?
23 What was the title of Whitney Houston's first album?
24 Which musical work for the stage is set in the town of Titipu?
25 Which Count is the villain in *The Woman in White* by Wilkie Collins?
26 John Potter became the most capped English player in which sport?
27 What is the unique about the flight of a hummingbird?
28 Which mainland European country produced most players for the postponed 2001 Ryder Cup team?
29 Calzone, a folded pizza dough dish, takes its name from what in Italian?
30 What was the first Top Ten hit for Sheryl Crow?

POT LUCK 36 See quiz 78, page 262
1 Pietro Mennea. 2 Rodent. 3 Rage. 4 Bhutan. 5 Geri. 6 9000. 7 Khartoum. 8 Jürgen Straub. 9 *A View To A Kill*. 10 Romania. 11 Renault. 12 Helen Rollason. 13 "Maggie May". 14 Denmark (Wilson Kipketer). 15 Steve Donoghue. 16 Scotland. 17 Bus. 18 Sperm whale. 19 Lou Rawls. 20 Sylvester Stallone. 21 Right. 22 The Monkees. 23 900. 24 1940s. 25 Mel and Kim. 26 Australian Grand Prix. 27 Lord Peter Wimsey. 28 Bolivia. 29 Maize. 30 AA.

QUIZ 81   FOOD AND DRINK

Answers - see Quiz 83, page 267

1   On which food item was a bar code first used?
2   What type of milk was first processed in 1899?
3   In which year did Bird's Eye Fish Fingers first go on sale in the UK?
4   Which drink had the first registered British trademark?
5   Which French city is famous for Cointreau?
6   Which author of *La Bonne Chère* ran the French Pavilion at Disneyworld, Orlando?
7   Which type of pasta lends it name to a type of chocolate decoration?
8   Who created vichysoisse?
9   Who founded the restaurant with Rose Gray where Jamie Oliver was 'discovered'?
10 Which area is the only one not to grow a Muscat which is sweet?
11 The Chardonnay grape is a native of where?
12 Which food or drink was named after American John McAdam?
13 Where did Balti cooking originate?
14 In wine making what is another name for tartrate?
15 What are the most common herbs in a bearnaise sauce?
16 Which herb is used in gremolata?
17 When were pressure cookers invented – 1891, 1905 or1933?
18 Where was Anton Mosimann's first post as chef in the UK?
19 Which size of wine bottle is the equivalent of 12 standard bottles?
20 Which monk was responsible for putting the liqueur Chartreuse on sale?
21 Which nuts are usually used in a pesto sauce?
22 Which food item comes form the Hindi meaning pounded meat?
23 Pyrex was made originally to be used where?
24 What is arborio?
25 Auslese is usually made from which grape?
26 Which food comes from the Tamil word meaning pepper water?
27 Dom Bernardo Vincelli devised which drink?
28 Who opened the Miller Howe restaurant in 1971?
29 Fitou is made from which grape?
30 What is unusual about the harvesting of Spätlese grapes?

ANSWERS

THE OSCARS *See quiz 83, page 267*

1 *The Piano.* 2 *L'Histoire d' Adele H.* 3 Carole Bayer Sager. 4 *This Sporting Life.*
5 *Driving Miss Daisy.* 6 Russell Crowe. 7 Sgt Elias. 8 Gwyneth Paltrow. 9 58.
10 *Places in the Heart.* 11 *Driving Miss Daisy.* 12 Marvin Hamlisch. 13 Best Screenplay.
14 *Cleopatra.* 15 None. 16 Writer. 17 Barbra Streisand. 18 *The People vs Larry Flint.*
19 *With A Song In My Heart.* 20 Gregory Peck. 21 Justin Henry (*Kramer vs Kramer*).
22 17. 23 Bernard Hill. 24 Cary Grant. 25 Bob Hope. 26 *Carnal Knowledge.*
27 *Separate Tables.* 28 *Chariots of Fire* (Ian Holm). 29 Five. 30 *Lenny.*

QUIZ 82 POT LUCK 38

Answers - see Quiz 84, page 268

1 Kubrick's movie *Eyes Wide Shut* used the music of Jazz Suite No 2 by which composer?
2 In which country is the city of Joao Pessoa?
3 On a computer keyboard what letter is below and between G and H?
4 Which English palace was used for the Kenneth Branagh's movie version of Hamlet?
5 What was the first name of owner Mr Maplin in the sitcom *Hi De Hi!*?
6 "Cathy" and "Claudette" appear in No 1's for which artists?
7 What is the opponent's goal called in shinty?
8 Frankie Goes to Hollywood's "Relax" got lots of publicity when which Radio 1 DJ refused to play it?
9 On a computer keyboard what letter is below and between J and K?
10 What was the female name that Lovejoy gave to his Morris Minor?
11 Which warrior ruler had a horse called Bucephalus?
12 Agatha Christie wrote romantic novels using the pen name of which Mary?
13 Eric Oliver was the first world champion in what?
14 What did the second A stand for in ANZAC?
15 What was Cliff Richard's first million seller?
16 Which term indicates the amount of wine by which a container falls short of being full?
17 King Edward VII's father in law was king of which country?
18 In which country is the city of Hermosilla?
19 In the Bond movie what was Goldfinger's first name?
20 When was *The Highway Code* first published?
21 On which horse did Gordon Richards have his only Derby triumph?
22 Which cards were not included in a pack of cards until 1857?
23 Which number followed NCC on the side of the "Starship Enterprise"?
24 What did Harry Brearley invent in 1913 to revolutionise kitchens?
25 In movies, what is the first name of Ralph Fiennes' character in *Schindler's List*?
26 What is Madame Harel credited with creating around 1790?
27 Whose play was turned into the movie *Shadowlands*?
28 Romana Barrack is better known as a TV playwright under which name?
29 What was the first Top Ten hit for Five?
30 The Ishihara Test is a test for what?

QUIZ 83 THE OSCARS

Answers - see Quiz 81, page 265

1 Which Oscar movie shared the Cannes Palme d'Or with *Farewell My Concubine*?
2 What was the French title of the movie giving Isabelle Adjani her first nomination?
3 Who was Burt Bacharach's lyricist on the song which won an Oscar for *Arthur*?
4 For which film made in the same years as JFK's assassination, did Richard Harris receive his first nomination?
5 In which movie did Dan Aykroyd play Jessica Tandy's son?
6 Which future Oscar winner won the Australian Film Institute Award as Best Supporting Actor for *Proof*?
7 Which character did Willem Dafoe play in *Platoon*?
8 Which Oscar winning actress is the daughter of stage actress Blythe Danner?
9 How many years did Robert Donat age in the movie for which he won a 1939 Oscar?
10 Which movie led to Sally Field's "You like me you really like me," acceptance speech?
11 What was Morgan Freeman's second Oscar nomination?
12 Who was the first person to win three Oscars in one night?
13 Which Oscar did Woody Allen win when Michael Caine also won for the same movie?
14 For which movie did Rex Harrison receive a nomination the year before his first win?
15 How many films had Goldie Hawn made before she had her first nomination for Best Supporting Actress?
16 In which category did *The Piano*'s director win an Oscar?
17 Lauren Bacall won her first Oscar nomination playing whose mother?
18 For which movie did *Cheers'* Woody receive his first nomination?
19 Legend Susan Hayward received five nominations; her third was for which movie?
20 Audrey Hepburn won her first nomination for a role opposite whom?
21 Who was the youngest performer ever to be nominated for an Oscar?
22 How many years were there between Julie Andrews' second and third nominations?
23 Who played the husband in the movie for which Pauline Collins was nominated?
24 Who played opposite Joan Fontaine when she won her Oscar for a Hitchcock movie?
25 Who first hosted the Oscar ceremony in 1940?
26 For which Mike Nichols' film was Ann Margret nominated for an Oscar?
27 For which movie did Wendy Hiller win between her nominations for *Pygmalion* and *A Man For All Seasons*?
28 For which film was the husband of Penelope Wilton nominated for an Oscar in 1981?
29 Between 1940 and 1965 how many Special Academy Awards did Bob Hope win?
30 For which film did Dustin Hoffman have his third nomination?

SPORTING WHO'S WHO? See quiz 85, page 269

1 Cincinnati Red Stockings. 2 Malavai Washington. 3 Mia Farrow. 4 Cuba.
5 Unified Team. 6 46. 7 Alex Corretja. 8 Ligier (Alain Prost). 9 Baltimore Bullets.
10 Teresa Edwards. 11 Jonathan Gould. 12 1998 (Snowboarding). 13 Justine Henin.
14 Stuttgart. 15 John Kagwe. 16 Andres Gimeno. 17 John Landy. 18 Tokyo.
19 St Louis Cardinals. 20 West Germany (Boris Becker). 21 Two. 22 Antonio Pinto.
23 South Africa. 24 Annika Sorenstam. 25 35. 26 Christine Arron.
27 Suzuki (Barry Sheene). 28 Lleyton Hewitt. 29 Stefan Edberg. 30 Warriors.

QUIZ 84 POT LUCK 39

Answers - see Quiz 82, page 266

1 To ten years when was the Rotary Club founded?
2 Which horse with a John Wayne link won the first Grand National?
3 What does the second R stand for in the acronym RADAR?
4 Which monarch attended the very first Royal Ascot?
5 Which country was the first to introduce vehicle registration plates?
6 Jo-Raquel Tejad become known as which movie actress?
7 What is the largest castle in England?
8 Who scored the quickest ever FA Cup Final goal?
9 What was George II supposedly sitting on at the time of his death?
10 EOKA was an active terrorist organisation on which island?
11 Who wrote the novel *The Ordeal of Gilbert Pinfold*?
12 A cross between a Scottish draught horse and a Flemish horse produced which breed?
13 Under what name did Paul and Phil Hartnoll have hit records?
14 Who did James Earl Ray murder?
15 How is Denali in Alaska also known?
16 Which place used to form part of The Stranglers name?
17 In which year did Bernhard Langer first play in a Ryder Cup?
18 What is the usual general temperature requirements for serving sake?
19 Who combined with Lieber to write the rock classic *Jailhouse Rock*?
20 Which food additive prevents fat and water separating out?
21 What was the first name of Letitia Dean's character back in her in *Grange Hill* days?
22 What was the only Top Ten hit for US female group First Choice?
23 At which track did Michael Schumacher achieve his record breaking 52nd career win?
24 Dyce Airport serves which city?
25 Who was born first Albert Einstein or Charles Darwin?
26 In "Penny Lane", what is the occupation of the person selling poppies from a tray?
27 Alan Shearer scored his only England hat trick against which team?
28 In which country is the city of Tabris?
29 What was the first Top Ten hit for Nicki French?
30 What was Somerset's margin of victory over Leicestershire in the 2001 C&G Trophy final – 24 runs, 41 runs or 4 wickets?

POT LUCK 38 See quiz 82, page 266

ANSWERS

1 Shostakovich. 2 Brazil. 3 B. 4 Blenheim. 5 Joe. 6 Everly Brothers.
7 Hail. 8 Mike Read. 9 M. 10 Miriam. 11 Alexander the Great.
12 Westmacott. 13 Sidecar. 14 Army. 15 "Living Doll". 16 Ullage.
17 Denmark. 18 Mexico. 19 Auric. 20 1931. 21 Pinza. 22 Jokers.
23 1701. 24 Stainless steel. 25 Amon. 26 Camembert cheese.
27 William Nicholson. 28 Carla Lane. 29 "Slam Dunk". 30 Colour blindness.

QUIZ 85 SPORTING WHO'S WHO?

Answers - see Quiz 83, page 267

1 Who were the first fully professional team of baseball players?
2 Who was runner up when a Dutchman won Wimbledon's Men's Singles in the 1990s?
3 Which actress named her son after baseball pitcher Satchel Paige?
4 Which country won the baseball silver medal at the 2000 Olympic Games?
5 The last time they won Olympic gold in ice hockey in the 20th century the USSR team was known by what name?
6 How old was Jack Nicklaus when he became the oldest player to win the US Masters?
7 Who won the longest match in a Grand Slam in the 1990s?
8 Which motor sport team did the then record holder for Grand Prix victories buy in 1997 before giving it his own name a year later?
9 Who were the second winners of the NBA in the US?
10 Which woman has been in every Olympic gold medal basketball team for the USA?
11 Which English-born footballer was picked to play for Scotland during the time his father played for Wales?
12 When did Karine Ruby's sport become an Olympic event?
13 Who did the older Williams sister beat in her second Wimbledon final?
14 Where did Linford Christie win his fastest 100m?
15 In the 1990s who was the fastest winner of the New York City Marathon?
16 Who was the oldest winner of the singles at the French Open Tennis?
17 Who was the first non European to run a mile in under four minutes?
18 Where did Carl Lewis set his personal best in the long jump?
19 In 1998 which team's player set a new baseball record for most home runs in a season?
20 Which country did the youngest ever Wimbledon Men's Singles winner represent?
21 How many gold medals did Carl Lewis win at his second Olympics?
22 Who won the first London Marathon of the new millennium?
23 Which country was the second to play Test cricket against England after Australia?
24 Who holds the record as the biggest money earner between 1993 and 2001 in women's golf?
25 How many world records did Sergey Bubka break before the end of the millennium?
26 Who, by the end of the millennium, was the fastest European woman in the world?
27 On which make of motor cycle was the fastest world championship of the 1970s raced?
28 Who became the youngest man to end the year as World No 1 in 2001?
29 Who was the European who won most US Open Men's Singles titles in the 1990s?
30 Which name was added in the 1990s to the side which has won the Challenge Cup most times in Rugby League?

ANSWERS

FOOD AND DRINK *See quiz 81, page 265*
1 Wrigley's Chewing Gum. 2 Evaporated milk. 3 1955. 4 Bass Pale Ale. 5 Angers.
6 Paul Bocuse. 7 Vermicelli. 8 Louis Diat. 9 Ruth Rogers. 10 Alsace. 11 Burgundy.
12 Macadamia nuts. 13 Britain. 14 Argol. 15 Tarragon & chervil. 16 Parsley.
17 1905. 18 Dorchester. 19 Salmanazar. 20 Jerome Maubee. 21 Pine nuts.
22 Kofta. 23 Railroad kitchens. 24 Rice. 25 Riesling. 26 Mulligatawny.
27 Benedictine. 28 John Tovey. 29 Carignan. 30 Harvested late.

HOW TO SET UP YOUR OWN
PUB QUIZ

What you will need:

- A good selection of biros (never be tempted to give your own pen up, not even to family members)
- A copy of *The Best Pub Quiz Book Ever! 4*
- A set of answer sheets photocopied from the back of the book
- A good speaking voice and possibly a microphone and an amp
- A pub
- At least one pint inside you
- At least one more on your table
- A table

What to do:

Choose your local to start with, there is no need to get halfway through your first quiz and decide you weren't cut out for all this and then find yourself in the roughest pub in Christendom 30 miles and a long run from home.

Discuss with the landlord whether you will be charging or not, if you don't then there is little chance of a prize for the winners other than a free pint each and this is obviously at the landlord's discretion – if you pack his pub to bursting then five free pints won't worry him, but if it's only you and a two others then he may be less than unwilling.

If you decide on a payment entry keep it reasonable, you don't want to take the fun out of the quiz; some people will be well aware that they have very little hope of winning and will be reluctant to celebrate the fact by mortgaging their house.

Once location and prize are in the bag then advertising the event is paramount, get people's attention, sell sell, sell or, alternatively, stick up a gaudy looking poster on the door of the bogs. Be sure to specify all the details, time, prize and so on – remember you are selling to people whose tiny attention span is being whittled down to nothing by alcohol.

After this it is time for the big night, if you are holding the event in the 'snug' which seats ten or so you can rely on your voice, if not you should get hold of a good microphone and an amplifier so that you can boom out your questions and enunciate the length and breadth of the pub (once again, clear this with the landlord and don't let liquid anywhere near the electrical equipment). Make sure to practice, and get comfortable with the sound of your own voice and relax as much as possible, try not to rely on alcohol too much or "round one" will be followed by "rown' too" which will eventually give way to "runfree". Relax with your voice so that you can handle any queries from the teams, and any venomous abuse from the 'lively' bar area.

When you enter the pub make sure you take everything listed above. Also, make sure you have a set of tie-break questions and that you instruct everybody who is taking part of the rules – and be firm. It will only upset people if you start handing out impromptu solutions and let's face it the wisdom of Solomon is not needed when you are talking pub quiz rules; "no cheating" is a perfectly healthy stance to start with. Banning mobile phones may also be a good idea to stop your contestants being tempted to "phone a friend".

Finally, keep the teams to a maximum of five members, hand out your answer papers and pens and, when everybody is good and settled, start the quiz. It might not be easy and it might not propel you to international stardom or pay for a life of luxury but you will enjoy yourself. No, really.

ANSWERS

ROUND ....

1 _____

2 _____

3 _____

4 _____

5 _____

6 _____

7 _____

8 _____

9 _____

10 _____

11 _____

12 _____

13 _____

14 _____

15 _____

16 _____

17 _____

18 _____

19 _____

20 _____

21 _____

22 _____

23 _____

24 _____

25 _____

26 _____

27 _____

28 _____

29 _____

30 _____